BRISTOL CHANNEL

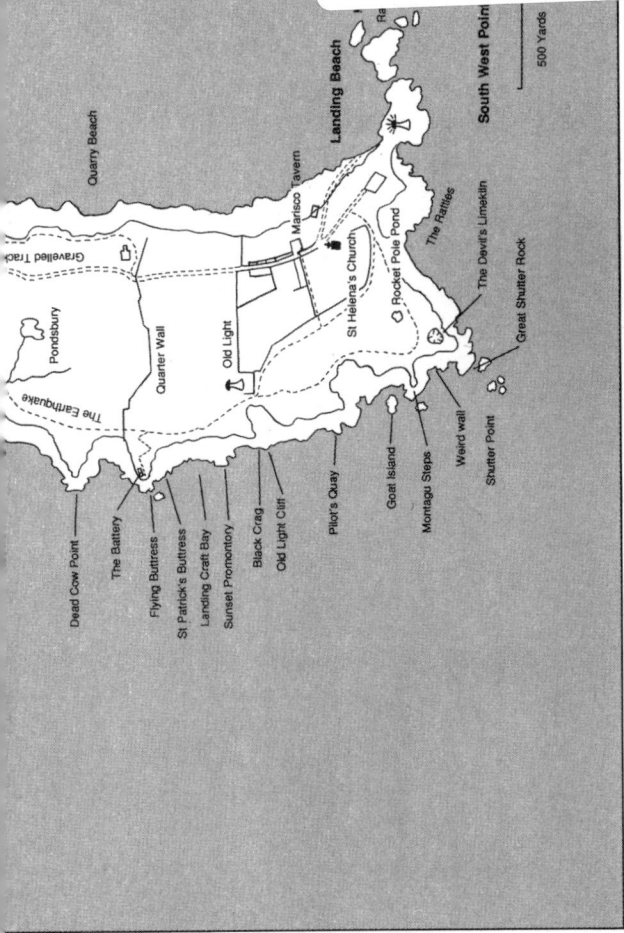

Quarry Beach

Landing Beach

South West Point

500 Yards

Gravelled Track

Pondsbury

The Earthquake

Quarter Wall

Old Light

Marisco Tavern

St Helena's Church

Rocket Pole Pond

The Rattles

The Devil's Limekiln

Great Shutter Rock

Dead Cow Point

The Battery

Flying Buttress

St Patrick's Buttress

Landing Craft Bay

Sunset Promontory

Black Crag

Old Light Cliff

Pilot's Quay

Goat Island

Montagu Steps

Weird wall

Shutter Point

Brinkman's Ship The Flying Buttress
Climber: Steve Boydon   *Photo:* Mike Snell

Tyrolean Traverse on Gannet's Rock 1971   *Photo:* John Cleare

CLIMBERS' CLUB GUIDES
Edited by John Willson

Lundy

by Gary Gibson and Paul Harrison

Maps by Gary Gibson

Photodiagrams by Simon Cardy

Drawings by Hazel Gibson and Dawn Syron-Jones

Cover photographs by Hazel Gibson and Mike Snell

Published by the CLIMBERS' CLUB

Rock Climbing in Devonshire 1966
by R D Moulton

Lundy Rock Climbs 1970
by R D Moulton

Lundy Rock Climbs 1974
by R D Moulton

Lundy Rock Climbs 1980
by R D Moulton

Lundy Rock Climbs 1985
by G Gibson

Lundy 1994
by P Harrison and G Gibson

© The Climbers' Club 1994

Gibson, Gary
Harrison, Paul
    Lundy
    (Climbers' Club Guides)

British Library Cataloguing in Publication Data

A catalogue record for this book is available from the British Library.

769.522

ISBN 0-901-601-55-1

Reprinted 2001

Front Cover:	*Mal de Mer* (first ascent), The Parthenos *Climber:* Matt Ward *Photo:* Hazel Gibson
Back Cover:	*Badlands* (first ascent), Wonderlands Wall *Climber:* Simon Cardy *Photo:* Mike Snell

Prepared for printing by: Parker Typesetting Service, Leicester
Produced by The Ernest Press, 595 Clarkston Road, Glasgow G44 5QD
Distributed by: Cordee, 3a De Montfort Street, Leicester, LE1 7HD

Contents

List of Maps and Diagrams

Guidebook Disclaimer

This guide attempts to provide a definitive record of all existing climbs and is compiled from information from a variety of sources. The inclusion of any route does not imply that it remains in the condition described. Climbs can change unpredictably: rock can deteriorate and the existence and condition of *in-situ* protection can alter. All climbers must rely on their own ability and experience to gauge the difficulty and seriousness of any climb. Climbing is an inherently dangerous activity.

Neither The Climbers' Club nor the authors and editor of this guidebook accept any liability whatsoever for any injury or damage caused to climbers, third parties, or property arising from the use of it. Whilst the content of the guide is believed to be accurate, no responsibility is accepted for any error, omission, or mis-statement. Users must rely on their own judgement and are recommended to insure against injury to person and property and third party risks.

The inclusion in this guidebook of a crag or routes upon it does not mean that any member of the public has a right of access to the crag or the right to climb upon it.

Many cliffs and climbs on Lundy are subject to seasonal restrictions. These restrictions have been imposed to allow for bird-nesting and have been agreed to by the BMC. Full details are given on pages 14 and 15.

Acknowledgements

For the first time, a Lundy rock-climbing guidebook appears in the form of a Climbers' Club publication. Previous guidebooks to the island have all been published by the Royal Navy and Royal Marines Mountaineering Club, and it is therefore necessary and appropriate to acknowledge here the sterling work of that club in laying down the foundations for this guide and future publications.

One person alone has been responsible for documenting the formative years of Lundy rock-climbing and in doing so produced three ground-breaking guidebooks. Bob Moulton's enthusiasm continues unabated and his knowledge and experience have been invaluable as well as having provided a much-needed steadying hand.

Lundy activists past and present have helped fill the gaps in the island's relatively short yet fascinating climbing history. In particular we are very grateful to Frank Cannings, Pat Littlejohn, Ken Wilson, Nick White, and particularly Bob Moulton for use of the early history and his seemingly endless collection of Lundy archives.

A large selection of photo-diagrams have been used, an important part of any guidebook. For these we have been most fortunate to be able to call upon the emerging expertise of Simon Cardy; and we are indebted to Ken Wilson for the loan of a number of his prints. The line drawings of The Diamond and The Constable were the work of Hazel Gibson and Dawn Syron-Jones respectively.

Proof-reading is perhaps one of the most time-consuming and tedious aspects of any guidebook work. We are therefore very thankful for the studious attentions of Chris 'Boris' Gilbert, Doug Kerr, Sue and Martin Wilson, Mike Snell, Neil Harrison, Nick Jowett, Anne Piercy, Roy Thomas, and Ian Wyatt. Special thanks are also due to Pete 'fingers' Long, who contributed a highly informative fauna and flora section.

Finally, the following Lundy 'devotees' have supplied information and opinions regarding routes, grades and quality, photos for consideration, and just plain gossip: Mark Bartley, Steve Boydon, Ian Butterworth, Paul Clarke, Pete Cobb, Dennis Crampton, Paul Dearden, Dave Hillebrandt, Alan James, Mike Lynch, Pete Milner, Ian Smith, Olly Stephenson, Dave Thomas, Tom Valentine, Matt Ward, Martin Whittaker, Ian Wright.

Introduction

Some twenty miles off the north coast of Devon lies a pocket domain of romance and diversity, one of the strangest and least known of the islands of Britain.

Lundy keeps a stern eye on the Bristol Channel, its granite forehead whitened by the spray of Atlantic gales. No island in the world can lay claim to so much within so little space: a hermitage for early Christians, a nest of pirates, a king's retreat, the hiding place of an assassin, a stronghold of royalists, headquarters of English, French, Spanish and even Turkish sea rovers, a convict settlement, a bird sanctuary.
(The Tempestuous Isle, 1950 by Colonel P T Etherton & Vernon Barlow)

Those who have yet to visit the island may be excused for mistaking Lundy for merely an interesting alternative to mainland climbing; however, no one ever leaves it with such delusions.

Rising from the Bristol Channel, on the fringes of the Atlantic Ocean, Lundy is a veritable jewel, remote and inaccessible; its enchantment is due in some part to its harsh and rugged beauty and the overall atmosphere of feat and challenge.

Lundy is twelve miles from the nearest mainland: Hartland Point on the North Devon coast. The island consists of a broad, wind-swept plateau. Three miles long, half a mile across at its widest point, and reaching over 400 feet at its highest, it commands some magnificent views of the surrounding coastlines of North Devon, North Cornwall, and South Wales. To the west, across the vast expanse of the Atlantic, no land intervenes before the coast of Newfoundland 3,000 miles away.

The west coast of Lundy is one of the most impressive climbing coastlines in Britain. Here can be found just about every sea-cliff climbing experience: sun-kissed slabs, lofty granite spires, deep sunless zawns, and huge brooding precipices. Visiting the island is not straightforward; it requires planning and commitment and, despite improved rescue arrangements, it should be stressed that Lundy is a bad place to have a climbing accident. However, far from detracting from, this all contributes to what is one of this country's last great climbing adventures.

HOW AND WHERE TO STAY ON LUNDY

The island is owned by The National Trust and administered and maintained on their behalf by The Landmark Trust. The trust is an independent charity, the purposes of which are to acquire and restore buildings and places of historic and architectural interest, and where possible to make them available for renting as holiday accommodation.

There are at present over 20 different buildings available in which to stay on Lundy. They range from a thirteenth century castle to an old lighthouse or an Admiralty lookout. Popular with large parties of climbers is 'The Barn', a converted threshing house offering hostel-style accommodation. The most economical means of staying on the island is camping. Good facilities are provided although a sturdy tent is strongly recommended. The number of visitors to the island is limited, and to avoid disappointment it is advisable to book all accommodation up to a year in advance or to be flexible with travel arrangements.

Amenities on the island are basic but practical. A well-stocked shop caters for most needs and, of course, The Marisco Tavern, the hub of island life, provides bar meals and liquid refreshment.

Throughout the year the island's ship, the *MS Oldenburg*, carries visitors and supplies to Lundy from the North Devon ports of Bideford or Ilfracombe on a voyage that takes approximately two and a quarter hours. For those lacking sea-legs it is possible to charter a private helicopter from the mainland. The company to contact is Lomas Helicopters in Bideford (*tel.* 0237 421054).

For further information regarding bookings contact: The Landmark Trust, Shottesbrooke, Maidenhead, Berkshire SL6 3SW. (*tel.* 0628 825925).

ROCK TYPES

Formed from an intrusion of igneous rock, the island is principally composed of Tertiary Granite, approximately 52 million years old, with Devonian Metasedimentary rock forming the south-eastern peninsula. There are also several intrusive dykes of igneous basalt rock, distinctive features around the coastline, and often forming large sea-caves where the sea has pounded away at their base.

The granite is very similar to that of Cornwall, and varies from perfection on many of the cliffs, through the crystalline variety on a handful, to the consistency of decaying gravel on the worst.

Apart from the semi-improved grassland of the farmed southern end of the island and the wooded and rhododendron areas along the eastern slopes, the island habitat is predominantly maritime heath, with large areas of *Sphagnum* peat bog.

WEATHER and TIDES

Lundy high, it will be dry, Lundy low, it will be snow,
Lundy plain, it will be rain, Lundy in haze, fine for days.

(Old Devonian weather lore)

Lundy's exposed position puts it at the mercy of the elements; the island can change dramatically from a sheltered sunny haven to a storm-lashed rock. Gale force winds can turn the sea into a foaming cauldron and make just walking difficult and climbing impossible. Lundy also experiences a considerable amount of mist and fog which frequently covers the plateau and can hang around for days. Despite this, the island can often receive more sunshine and less rain than the mainland.

The majority of cliffs have a southerly or westerly outlook, allowing them to dry quickly after rain and enabling the sun to be enjoyed when it is shining.

The Bristol Channel has one of the highest tidal ranges in the world. The information given regarding tidal access to the cliffs is at best approximate since the difference between spring-tides and neap-tides is considerable. Spring-tides rise the highest but also go out the furthest, consequently giving the best access to sea-level cliffs either side of low water. Neap-tides have less of a rise and fall and certain sea-level cliffs can become inaccessible.

Tide-tables are available from some shops in Bideford and Ilfracombe; there is also a tide 'clock' above the bar in the Marisco Tavern.

In certain sea conditions, normal tidal considerations do not apply. A stormy sea or heavy swell can be very deceptive and swamp the base of a cliff in seconds. **Always belay** at the base of the cliff, and **never underestimate** the sea!

FAUNA and FLORA
Its location in the Bristol Channel and resulting isolation add more to the island than just a unique ambience.

Sited on major bird migration routes, from the Mediterranean and Eastern Europe especially, and with the Americas being the next landfall to the west, Lundy receives many rare and interesting visitors. Surrounded by many square miles of open sea, and so often the only suitable landfall during fog or bad weather, it ranks amongst the top few locations in Britain for rare firsts.

Of the many birds that have visited or bred on the island, one of the most famous was a small insignificant-looking black and white individual, an Ancient Murrelet. Its arrival in 1990 and subsequent return the following year prompted several thousand people to visit the island, desperate for a brief glimpse of this tiny Pacific seabird, which it was believed had traversed the North Pole.

Other less notable, though more recognizable species have included Peregrine, Osprey, an occasional Golden Eagle, Quail, Grouse, Curlew, Fly Catchers, Willow Warblers, Storm Petrels, Manx Shearwaters, the Great Auk (now extinct), Fulmar (the cliff-climber's friend), and of course the Puffin, from which the island takes its name: the Icelandic word for Puffin is *Lunde*. Predatory rats and the increasing number of gulls have been cited as reasons for the decline in Puffin numbers since the end of the last century, although changes in the marine ecosystem leading to a reduction in food supplies is the most probable cause.

Although it is important for birds, there is much more to Lundy than merely a 'twitcher's treasure-trove'; the resident fauna and flora are of special importance owing to the island's biogeographical isolation. Put simply, the fauna and flora of islands have fewer species than comparable areas of mainland; and many of the species are subtly or profoundly different from those in such areas. Much of the work that has been carried out into Lundy's fauna and flora has been conducted by the Lundy Field Society, and records are available on the island for reference and new additions.

Of the animals present on the island, the mammals are particularly restricted; records show rabbits, Pygmy Shrews, various bats, and of course the ubiquitous rats so often associated with islands. In addition there are goats, Soay Sheep, and Sika Deer, which have all been introduced. Grey Seals inhabit the caves and coves around the entire circumference of the island, their woeful calls lending a particularly spooky atmosphere to still foggy nights.

The seals spend most of the time enjoying the riches of Britain's first Statutory Marine Nature Reserve, which surrounds the island and are disturbed only by sub-aqua and snorkel enthusiasts. The shallow waters around Lundy boast 216 wrecks and, being washed by the Gulf Stream, contain some of the richest marine life in the British Isles; it is the only place where all five species of British coral have been recorded. Perennial visitors to these waters are Basking Sharks, Turtles, Sunfish, numerous species of Jellyfish, and several species of Dolphin and Porpoise, which often school in large numbers close to the shore.

To return to dry land once more, Lundy is an entomologist's dream, with numerous species of insects, especially beetles and butterflies/moths; there are also 114 recorded species of spider. The invertebrate fauna are not restricted to the terrestrial environment alone; there are several ponds and numerous streams which all contain specialized members of various aquatic families. One reason that some insects occur in large numbers could be the lack of any reptiles on the island; there are no lizards or snakes.

Although existing in an incredibly harsh environment, a diverse wildlife is sustained by the island's variety of habitats. Contributing greatly to this are the trees, shrubs, plants, and grasses found there. The beauty of Lundy owes much to its flora: Sundew, Marsh and Spotted Orchids, the Scarlet Pimpernel, swathes of Sea Campion and Thrift, and the beautiful though invasive Rhododendron. However, Lundy is famous for a plant which grows naturally nowhere else in the world, the Lundy Cabbage – it has to be seen to be believed.

Finally, no introduction to Lundy would be complete without a mention of one of its more notorious inhabitants, the Harvest Mite, better known as the Bracken Bug, although often referred to in ignorance as the Bed Bug. From the end of July to mid September, these ravenous little creatures lurk in the prolific bracken waiting to pounce. Once attached, the mites show no mercy, gorging themselves on the flesh of their unwitting victims. The result is often a series of irritating bites around the waist where clothes are tight, or on ankles, groin, and armpits where the skin is tender. Packing some antiseptic cream is a wise precaution.

BIRD RESTRICTIONS

Lundy is renowned for its breeding seabird populations. It is very important that climbers recognize the restrictions imposed on certain cliffs during the breeding season. **The restrictions run from April 1st to July 31st inclusive** and are subject to continual review. The restricted cliffs may vary slightly from year to year and it is important that climbers contact the resident Warden on arrival or before if planning a trip within this period (*tel.* 0237 431831).

A number of popular climbs have been left open even though they are very near to bird colonies. If these climbs are to remain open, it is important that climbers do not encroach onto nearby restricted climbs or cause disturbance to breeding birds. Care must also be taken to see that access routes do not go through restricted areas.

Unrestricted Cliffs

Atlantic Buttress
Beef Buttress
Black Bottom Buttress
Black Hole, The
Celtic Buttress
Constable, The
Damocles Buttress
Devil's Limekiln, The
Devil's Slide, The
Devil's Slide Approach Cliff, The
Dihedral Zawn
Earthquake, The
First Buttress North
First Buttress South
First Knight Templar
Focal Buttress
Freak Zawn
Grapefruit Buttress
Goat Island
Halfway Buttresses
Kistvaen Buttress
Knight Templar Rock
Leaning Buttress Area
Montagu Buttress
Montagu Wall
Picnic Bay Cliff
Quarries, The
Robbie's Redoubt
Second Buttress North
Second Knight Templar
St Patrick's Buttress
Sunset Wall
Weird Wall

Restricted Cliffs

Alpine Buttress
Arch Zawn
Back of The Slide, The
Banana Buttress
Battery Cliff, The
Benson's Buttress
Beaufort Buttress
Black Jack Zawn
Big Zawn
Black Crag
Bomber Buttress
Box Zawn
Cheeses, The
Christos Bitas Buttress
Cormorant Zawn
Crenellation Buttress
Crunchy Toed Zawn
Cyclops Zawn
Deep Zawn
Devil's Chimney , The
Devil's Chimney Cliff, The
Devil's Tower, The
Diamond, The
Double Headed Zawn
Fighter Buttress
Fluted Face
Flying Buttress Main Cliff
Forgotten Pinnacle
Fortress, The
Funfair Zawn
Gannet's Buttress
Gannet's Rock
Ghostbusters Wall
Grand Falls Zawn
Great Shutter Rock
Heron Zawn

Hidden Slab Area
Hidden Zawn
Immaculate Slabs
Lifeboat Buttress
Long Ruse Ridge
Marisco Walls
Narrow Zawn
Needle Rock
North Light Area
Ocean Promontory
Old Light Cliff, The
Parthenos, The
Pathfinder Slabs
Pilot's Quay
Phantom Zawn
Punchbowl Cliff
Pyramid, The
Rock Pool Buttress
Seal Slab
Short Story Zawn
Small Black Crag
Squires View Cliff
Starship Zawn
Storm Zawn
St James' Stone
St Peter's Stone
Sunset Promontory
Ten Foot Zawn
Threequarter Buttress
Torrey Canyon Cliff
Two Legged Buttress
Two Legged Zawn
Winston's Wall
Wolfman Jack Wall
Wonderlands Wall

GRADES

The cause of many an argument in The Marisco Tavern! The established adjectival system is used, with numerical technical grades for pitches of 4a and above. For the more established climbs a consensus has been obtained from Lundy 'regulars' and the island's log book. Where disagreements occur the higher grade has been chosen.

As in previous guidebooks, the large number of routes only recently established has made it impossible to check every climb. Routes that are not known to have received a second ascent have been marked with a † symbol, and this indicates that the grading should be treated with caution.

When used in conjunction with the year of the first ascent this gives any would-be ascensionist an idea of the likely condition of the route and any *in-situ* gear on it.

STAR RATINGS

Stars have been used to help guide climbers to the best routes. There are so many good routes on Lundy that any rating has to be extremely economical to give credibilty to the system. Thus ★★★ should be exceptional and equal to anything on the mainland, ★★ excellent, and ★ good. A no-star route is not necessarily of poor quality.

EQUIPMENT

A standard rope length of 150 feet (45m) is adequate for the majority of climbs within this guide. A number of the more demanding routes require a minimum of 165 feet (50m) to reach a satisfactory belay; where this is necessary it has been stated in the relevant text. Abseil ropes are essential on some cliffs and optional on others. A spare rope is strongly recommended for emergencies or just to safeguard an awkward descent. If in doubt, **put a rope down it!**

A standard rack of wires, hexes, camming devices, and slings will suffice for the majority of routes. Salt water and sea air may adversely affect ropes and gear after only a short time; it is therefore advisable to wash equipment in warm fresh water after use and lubricate moving metal parts.

PEGS

There are a large number of pegs on the climbs described in this guidebook. It has been impossible to check the condition or exact whereabouts of all the *in-situ* pegs mentioned, some of the routes not having seen a second ascent for over twenty years. The standard warning should therefore be: **do not trust *in-situ* gear**. This includes any jammed wires and slings.

DRILLED PEGS AND BOLTS

Over the past decade, the issue of bolt and drilled-peg protection has raised its head. In 1988 a major campaign was launched against its use with the result that many formerly bolt-protected routes have had their fixed protection eliminated. This is an encouraging trend, though a number of routes in this guidebook still contain drilled gear. Climbers wishing to repeat these routes in their current (1994) state are recommended to consult the island's climbing log-book in The Marisco Tavern. It is requested that any climbers removing such gear should record their actions in the aforementioned log.

GUIDEBOOK LAYOUT

The majority of climbers will find themselves based in accommodation at the southern end of the island. The cliffs are therefore described in the order they are approached, from south to north. In general the climbs have also been described from south to north, or **right to left** as one looks at the cliff. However, on the east coast and in some cases where routes are approached from the north, the climbs are described from left to right; this is clearly stated in the relevant text.

The main mass of the island is in the form of a plateau some 300 to 400 feet above sea-level. This is conveniently divided by three prominent stone walls: Quarter Wall, Halfway Wall, and Threequarter Wall, all useful reference points. An eight-figure grid reference has been included for each cliff to help identification. This is intended for use in conjunction with the Ordnance Survey six-inch-to-one-mile map of the island, which is available from the Lundy shop.

A final word of warning: although every effort has been made to ease the task of cliff and climb location, Lundy does not give up its secrets easily. The best advice for a first-time visitor is to read the next section and take a leisurely stroll around the island.

A COASTAL JOURNEY
For most, the first impressions of Lundy are of a stiff walk up from the Landing Beach to have their thirst quenched by a refreshing drink in the bar of The Marisco Tavern, a convenient point to start an island tour!

Strolling out towards the south-west corner of the island, one can see the prominent Rocket Pole on the high point; below lies the yawning abyss of The Devil's Limekiln, a huge funnel 250 feet across at its top, with sea-level boulders a giddy 350 feet below. Offshore is The Great Shutter Rock which, local legend has it, if turned over, would exactly fit and close The Limekiln. Opposite The Great Shutter Rock and forming the seaward or outside of The Limekiln is Focal Buttress.

A good path now contours north along the plateau's edge. After a short while, a flight of steps, Montagu Steps, can be seen leading down to sea-level. The steps were hewn out of the cliff-side to assist salvage operations on the *HMS Montagu*, a 14,000-ton battleship wrecked on the rocks below in 1906. Continuing north, the coastline becomes generally broken and of little interest to the climber. A prominent landmark is the Old Light, a disused lighthouse standing on Beacon Hill, at 463 feet the highest point of the island. This was the Old Light's downfall: its lofty elevation meant that its light was often obscured to shipping in fog! Immediately below the Old Light lies The Old Light Cliff, which forms the southern end of an unbroken line of steep tidal cliffs. Shortly after a stile in the wall below the Old Light, a shallow valley marks the descent to a large open bay, the popular Landing Craft Bay. To the north again, and 150 yards south of Quarter Wall, a second shallow valley leads down via steps and a walled path to the derelict remains of The Battery.

Beyond Quarter Wall lies a huge open bay, the surrounding cliff-side of which appears to be slowly subsiding into the sea. To its north is a large rocky headland known locally as Dead Cow Point. Beyond the headland and just below plateau-level is The Earthquake, a huge chasm said to be linked, albeit tenuously, to the great Lisbon earthquake of 1755. At the foot of the broken ridge leading down from The Earthquake can be seen the small offshore pinnacle of Needle Rock. A small and often muddy valley, Punchbowl Valley, is now crossed before the whole of the coastline opens up into the superb vista of Jenny's Cove. *The Jenny*, a schooner homeward bound from Africa with a cargo of gold-dust and ivory, was wrecked in the cove that now bears her name; the crew perished and the gold-dust sank to mingle with the silt on the sea-bed. The cove offers some of Lundy's finest climbing, from the magnificent sea-stack of The Devil's Chimney to the huge, medieval-dungeon-like atmosphere of Deep Zawn. On the northern side of Jenny's Cove is The Pyramid, its southern slope once sometimes used to land or take off passengers when strong easterly winds were blowing.

North of Halfway Wall the cliffs lose some of their height, dropping down to Beaufort Buttress at the northern point of Jenny's Cove, before once more reaching almost all the way to plateau-level in the vicinity of Threequarter Wall. Directly below the wall lies a large open zawn with a huge vegetated slab at its base, the aptly named Big Zawn. To the south lies The Parthenos with Grand Falls Zawn immediately south again. Just north the rocky headland of St James' Stone offers a superb view of Lundy's most celebrated rock formation, The Devil's Slide. To the north of The Slide is Squires View Zawn, a large open cove with the rock island of St Peter's Stone in its centre. The brown rock of Squires View Cliff on the north side of the zawn is in marked contrast to that of the gleaming Diamond opposite. Forming the western point of the cove is a steep, grooved cliff, The Fortress.

The coastal cliffs now begin to lose height but are more continuous. The golden hue of Torrey Canyon Cliff is terminated by a large overhang-capped zawn, north of which lie the delightful hidden zawns and walls of Phantom Zawn Area; 150 yards north again is the large cove of Arch Zawn. The path continues along the top of some plateau-level buttresses before descending gradually towards the North West Point of the island. From here a series of steps lead steeply down to the North Light, auto-matic since 1971. To the west of the lighthouse, and on the northern coast, stands an isolated pinnacle some 100 feet above the sea, The Constable.

To the south, the easterly or central path now becomes a track, the Lundy highway. The large silvery buttress on the east coast is Gannet's Buttress, something of a misnomer since the gannets are long gone. Just beyond Gannet's Buttress it is possible to drop down below plateau-level onto a good, sheltered path. This leads beneath Tibbett's, a curiously-shaped Admiralty lookout, and past the Knight Templar Rock, with its uncanny warrior-face profile, to a series of old quarry workings, the remnants of The Lundy Granite Company. The path contours round the South East Point of the island, above the Landing Beach, to the South Light. The energetic may prefer to lengthen the walk by a detour down to the Landing Beach and around Rat Island at the south-east tip of the island. The return journey north leads past The Castle, a thirteenth century fortress built by Henry III to prevent the island from falling into the hands of his enemies. A short stroll past the church of St Helena brings us back to our starting-point.

History

THE EARLY YEARS: THE PINNACLES OF SUCCESS

The complete history of Lundy is peppered with legend and lore of infamous pirates, veritable heroes and villains, ship-wrecks and vivid colour. So, too, can the relatively short period of its rock-climbing history be described. Hero and villain alike have visited these shores for the purposes of adventure, bravado, glory.

The island's first rock-climbing suitor was Tom Longstaff in the late 1890s; and he paid further visits in 1903 and 1927. While records of his successes have never been discovered, it is known that the first routes climbed on the island were on St James' Stone. He also made a boat trip to Gannet's Rock but was unable to accomplish an ascent of The Constable, despite a determined effort.

The first recorded climbing on the island must therefore be attributed to a party in June 1961. After a reconnaissance day-trip by Admiral Keith Lawder and Ted Pyatt in 1960, which included a hurried walk around the island, the pair returned the following year with Jimmy Logan and Robin Shaw. Their initial fears were that the 'bird sanctuary aspect' might constitute an obstacle to climbing, but application to the authorities showed that this was not the case. They crossed on *The Lundy Gannet* with a few other passengers, including the then owner of the island, Albion Harman. As they reached anchorage, a salutary rocket was fired to signal the arrival of what was thought to be the first-ever party intent on climbing on the island. Although they looked closely at a variety of possibilities, they concentrated on the major isolated pinnacles, which in climbing tradition generally were the first objectives, and The Constable, The Devil's Chimney, and Needle Rock were all climbed by various members of the party. The biggest and most important climb, though not the hardest, was the ascent by Lawder and Logan of *The Devil's Slide*, establishing what became the island's first major classic. Pyatt later wrote of the climb: 'We had several times noticed how the goats (unroped) skipped across the top of the slab from right to left below the final vertical wall. When the climbers (roped) reached this they had the utmost difficulty in utilizing the holds on this section, so that everyone acquired a great respect for caprine cragsmanship.'

At Easter 1964, came a young Bob Moulton, son of Major General Jim Moulton RM, who had been Vice President of the RNMC and the original Colonel of *Colonel's Arête* at the Dewerstone in Devon. In later years Bob's enthusiasm never waned, though his general conclusion on this trip was, 'we won't be going back'. In fact, he was to act as 'organizer general' of numerous trips to the island over a number of years as well as proving his dedication by the writing of three excellent guidebooks.

These first recorded activities inevitably set the precedent for the next few years: visits by small parties of climbers whose activities were centred around the more easily-accessible cliffs and most obvious features of the island. Unfortunately, documentation of the activity up to 1965 was thrown into some confusion with the loss of the island's log-book. The most notable route during this period came from Peak and Cornwall pioneer Pete Biven, accompanied by Vivian Stevenson. Their ascent of the left-hand side of The Slide, entitled *Albion* as a gesture to the island's owner, has since become probably Lundy's most popular VS. Otherwise, development came on such cliffs as Knight Templar Rock and Flying Buttress.

In 1965 a well-documented visit was made by a team from the Army Outward Bound School at Towyn. In ignorance of what had gone earlier, they brought order to the confusion that had occurred in the Flying Buttress Area by naming and grading all their routes virtually from scratch. Some of these had undoubtedly been done before but the appearance of *Diamond Solitaire* was particularly worthy of note. It was initially climbed on aid in poor conditions by Frank McBratney and Brian Martindale; but the pair returned the following day for a free ascent in much better conditions.

With one significant exception, development over the next four years was concentrated in the lower grades. Numerous filler-in pitches were done in Knight Templar Rock area, a number of small buttresses were developed, and what later became known as Torrey Canyon Bay was explored. In the last mentioned the discovery and climbing of Seal Slab was of value, as its climbs are amongst the most pleasant of the easier routes on the island.

The one exception resulted from a visit by a strong team from Bradford University in 1967, a forerunner of the mass invasions of later years. They covered a lot of new ground, climbing fourteen new routes in the process, and perhaps their most significant discovery was a new crag north of The Fortress which they christened, rather topically, Torrey Canyon. Amongst all of these routes, *Stingray* remained the hardest climb on the island for quite some time by dint of its strenuous nature and the disintegrating state of its rock. They also added the prominent corner of *Norseman*.

1970 – 1975: THE PROMISED LAND
The initial decade of Lundy climbing ended with the publication of the first guidebook devoted entirely to the island. Having only one HVS and a handful of VSs, it reflected the leisurely pace of development. How quickly things were to change! Within weeks it had been put out of date by South African climber, Paul Fatti. Trapped on the island by adverse weather conditions, he put his time to good use by exploring new rock and creating one great climb, though not without some controversy. *Satan's Slip* took a blank line up the centre of The Devil's Slide and was completely devoid of natural protection on the long crux pitch. Thus it sprouted Lundy's first bolt, an ominous precedent! Fatti, with partner Tom Kerrich, also explored the

large lichen-covered cliffs at the back of The Slide, climbing a one-pitch route that eventually became the first pitch of *Performance*. 'Due to the uninviting nature of the lichen-covered rock above', they traversed off, little realizing that the face was soon to be the scene of heavy gardening activities.

Fatti and Kerrich also opened up Focal Buttress with *Focal Face*; but this avoided the real challenge of the face, one taken up later in the year with the return of Pete Biven accompanied by Ian Howell. Their wandering line of *Ulysses Factor* attacked more centrally but at a surprising grade of VS. The same day, this pair also accounted for the first ascent of, or out of, the awe-inspiring Devil's Limekiln. This last bout of development took place during the first of a series of RNMC Lundy meets, for which the most bizarre forms of transport were used to gain access to the island. On this occasion, a nearby Army depot laid on some DUKWs and a Tank Landing-Craft. The DUKWs took the party from the depot, down the main road, and across the beach to the sea, clearing a way through some surprised bathers. Their wheels changed to propellers, the DUKWs motored out to the waiting Tank Landing-Craft and drove into the bowels of the vessel through its massive bow doors.

The next major visit came in May 1971, courtesy of the RNMC in a euphemistically-named Sea Truck, which looked more like a paint-roller tin. It was on this meet that Pat Littlejohn and Frank Cannings visited Lundy for the first time, and their effect on Lundy's climbing, as it had been on other South-West cliffs, was inevitably immediate. They wasted little time on repeat ascents, each setting to work separately on his own new cliff. Littlejohn took The Old Light Cliff and Cannings Fluted Face. Their climbs were the first seriously gardened routes on the island, and *Magnificat* and *Juggernaut*, the latter named after the beach vehicle that had carried the paint-roller tin to the sea, were Lundy's first routes to be given the Extreme grade. They also notched up two potentially classic HVSs in *Albacore* and *Performance*. Ed Grindley, who was in the same party, was noticeably unimpressed after climbing some 100 feet up the crumbling left wall of the entrance to The Limekiln, his partner giving up climbing and attempting to sell his gear whilst still on the island!

Later in 1971, the island was visited by another strong West Country climber, Keith Darbyshire – famed to his lasting embarrassment by Cleare and Collomb as 'belonging to the first generation of true sea-cliff climbers'. He made his first contribution with the impressively-positioned *Shark* high up on The Devil's Slide.

The season ended dramatically with a visit from a team of varied personalities: Biven, Cannings, Ken Wilson, John Cleare, and Odd Eliassen. Cannings and Wilson, benefiting from their experience on *Performance*, came equipped with large sawn-off brooms specially selected and adapted for Lundy. At the earliest opportunity they set to work, each cleaning lines spied on their previous visit – Wilson a long line at the back of The Slide, and Cannings the then unclimbed Squires View Cliff. His exertions over, Cannings had started the descent of an easy (?) way down that he had previously discovered, when the unthinkable happened: he lost his holds. After an 80-foot fall, half of it free, he was stopped by a ledge-system strewn with jagged boulders.

Luckily, the rest of the party was climbing nearby, and a concerted rescue operation, involving virtually every able-bodied person on the island, took place. This was the first serious climbing accident to occur on Lundy, and it was fortunate indeed that the location was a fairly accessible spot. Cannings, accompanied by his wife Pat, was handed over to the care of the Air/Sea Rescue helicopter, and all was thought to be well. But it was not: the helicopter developed engine trouble well out to sea and the pilot had no option but to ditch. Cannings, in a semi-conscious state, was hurled out of the rapidly sinking helicopter by one of the crew and had to do a Houdini act to escape from the sinking stretcher. His wife, a non-swimmer, fared little better and both ended up clinging to a life-raft while a second helicopter was summoned. Cannings's injuries included a fractured pelvis, a dislocated finger, and severe bruising to the right-hand side of his body.

In the aftermath of the accident, Wilson teamed up with Pete Thexton, who, though not a member of the same party, had helped with the rescue, to climb *Seventh Seal*. Others claimed the first routes on The Fortress, though the challenge of this crag was later taken up by Thexton, who climbed the excellent *Valhalla*, originally graded only Severe.

The 1972 season started early for Lundy, in mid March, with the third of the RNMC meets, the participants this time arriving in a Wessex helicopter. Moulton and Terry Thompson set about opening up yet more cliffs. The first routes on Sunset Promontory, Alpine Buttress, Second Buttress North, and St Patrick's Buttress, with the classic *Shamrock* being particularly noteworthy, were added. A week later, a party spearheaded by Littlejohn and Darbyshire arrived. Such routes as *The Stray* (cleaned by Cannings before his accident), *The Black Hand*, *Destiny*, and *Rampart* fell during the trip; though it was later in the year that Littlejohn firmly established himself as the premier activist on Lundy.

The initial interests of the return trip in September were again in Landing Craft Bay with Littlejohn discovering the aesthetic *Formula One* and Graham Gilbert climbing *Road Runner*. The visit continued with two days in which the first lines were climbed on three of the biggest cliffs on the island. First, Gilbert led *Overlord* on The Devil's Chimney Cliff. Gilbert had a boat to catch and the ascent became a race against time. While Littlejohn completed the gardening on the upper sections, Gilbert and Moulton had started up the imperfectly gardened lower sections. The situation was impressive, with the debris from Littlejohn's feverish work above crashing down into the dark zawn and Gilbert working his way slowly up the walls below. Then, after Gilbert had swiftly completed the climb and rushed off to catch his boat, Littlejohn and Moulton ventured onto Weird Wall for the discovery of *Wodwo*, and on the following day the pair completed *Antiworlds* in Deep Zawn. The latter, of great difficulty and having a strong inescapable line in a serious position, was typical of the best of Littlejohn's creations and was climbed on a grey, overcast day, above the black swirling waters of the incoming tide; the climbers' chilling isolation was completed by the knowledge that they were the only ones on the island.

By now, plans and explorations had reached fever-pitch; and all previous invasions were surpassed when the strongest climbing party yet to have visited the island was assembled by Moulton during Easter week 1973. The weather was fine, and there were five pairs of experienced Lundy climbers all looking for new lines. Conditions were ripe for spectacular developments. The variety and amount of rock on the island were such that there was little overt competition for lines, each team finding a cliff to its liking and working it over. Every night, experiences were compared and the scores hastily totted up. The result at the end of the week was thirty-three new routes, only five of them less than VS. Inevitably Littlejohn was to the fore, continuing where he had left off in Deep Zawn and producing five new lines, of which *The Stone Tape* and *Supernova* were the most impressive. Also to make his mark in Deep Zawn was Darbyshire, who seconded on most of Littlejohn's routes, produced his own *Quatermass*, which has since become one of the most popular routes in the zawn, and opened up Black Crag with *Sambo*. But it was Cannings, now fully recovered from his fall and near-drowning, and John Kingston who emerged as the most prolific team. Reacting against the sweated labour of gardening, they concentrated on two new, small, vegetation-free cliffs: the brutally steep Bomber Buttress with its uncompromisingly strenuous climbs of *Jetset* and *Bender* and the more amenable Arch Zawn with *Stop Press* and *Headline* (these were originally named, somewhat unseriously, The Classic of the South West and The Other Classic of the South West).

Gilbert and Moulton teamed up for a tally of six new routes. On Fluted Face, their additions included the cliff's most popular route in *Magic Flute*, and then a move over to Squire's View Cliff and The Fortress produced *Good Vibrations* and *Prospero*. Another notable addition on The Devil's Chimney Cliff by 'Mac' Macfarlane and Ian Duckworth was the originally underrated *The Fifth Appendage*, though this cliff had to wait another year for its true potential to be realized. The remainder of the year was quieter, but Thexton reappeared to add *The Green Light* on Punchbowl Cliff and *The Vice* on Beef Buttress, and J Lister and M Putnam tamed *Moby Dick* on Alpine Buttress, each of these opening up a further cliff.

Easter 1974 saw another spate of development, most of which centred on the cliffs in Jenny's Cove. Although the number of new routes decreased to fifteen, the quality fully matched that of the previous year, perhaps even surpassed it. The Devil's Chimney Cliff attracted the main attention.

Littlejohn and Darbyshire again spearheaded the attack, peppering the cliff with a network of high-standard challenges: *The Promised Land* and *Spacewalk* stood out as being amongst the best hard routes the island had to offer. The former, a route that amazed its originators by not requiring any aid on its impressive first pitch, bears witness to Littlejohn's pioneering vision.

More than the year before, Littlejohn did manage to tear himself away from the cove, coming up with *Blue Jaunt* on Black Crag and *Wild Country* on Focal Buttress, both cliffs with large areas of virgin rock. The latter was climbed on the same day as *The Promised Land*; two high-standard challenges at opposite ends of the island – an amazing achievement. Thexton also made very worthwhile contributions of more importance than his of the previous year. He created the superb *Wolfman Jack*, albeit with two points of aid after two attempts, as well as the classic *Immaculate Slab*. Later the same year, Darbyshire returned and stimulated interest on Montagu Wall, which he described as heaving with semi-detached bungalows. He made the first route on the wall, *Montagu Python*; and a strong party from North Wales, including Ray Evans and Cliff Phillips, accounted for another four.

At the end of 1974 the now RN&RMMC published a new guidebook to the island under the careful authorship of Bob Moulton. It marked the end of a magnificent era in the history of Lundy rock-climbing, one that had seen major advances in the development of its cliffs on a par with, or perhaps at an even higher level than, the halcyon days of Gogarth. And the way lay open for yet more plundering of the island's almost limitless supply of virgin rock.

1975 – 1977: NEW AND OLD COMBINE

Surprisingly though, interest in 1975 decreased somewhat and, owing partly to snowfall during the annual Easter meet, a rare Lundy occurrence indeed, only a handful of new routes were climbed. The visiting party on this occasion was significantly smaller but, once again, Littlejohn was on hand to add a small batch. In *American Beauty*, he found one of the truly superb, atmospheric slab-climbs for which the island was becoming famous. Nick Allen and Bob Moulton also added a dramatic HVS on Weird Wall, the isolated *Apsara*.

Without Littlejohn's presence in 1976, it was clear that a new driving force would be needed. Easter week saw the return of Frank Cannings, this time accompanied by Bristol-based Arnis Strapcans, who was making a name for himself with a number of first ascents on his local cliffs. With Cannings's knowledge of the island and Strapcans's enthusiasm for new lines it was inevitable that the pair would have an immediate impact. Initially their interest centred on The Old Light Area, where they uncovered *Eclipse* on Sunset Promontory. Then they ventured onto the rarely visited Weird Wall for a line up the overlapping slabs right of *Umbgozi*. With its first pitch, originally aided by Rustie Baillie and John Cunningham, going free, the on-sight ascent of *Mirage Oasis* gave some memorable moments. However, their main contribution of the week was in The Devil's Limekiln. The superb, blank-looking south wall yielded with the lonely and atmospheric line of *The Exorcist*. After several ground-up attempts, Strapcans later wrote: 'There is a strong line connecting the Kiln floor to the route we climbed. The excessive loose nature of the rock repulsed all attempts however, even after trundling sessions'. In August of the same year the pair returned and began where they had left off in The Old Light Area. *Sexcrime* and the superb *Bleed for Speed* were added to Two Legged Buttress. Unfortunately, on reaching the top of the latter climb, Strapcans had to leave the island because of a family tragedy.

1977 was an important year for climbing on Lundy as it saw the return of Littlejohn in very impressive form. Strapcans and Cannings were, however, first to return at Easter for more routes in The Old Light Area. *Scorched Earth* was a fine achievement, but on the South West Point a crack splitting the right wall of the entrance to The Limekiln gave the best pitch of its type on the island at that time: *The Great Divide*. Unfortunately, as the line had not been gardened beforehand, two rest-points had to be used in the crack for the removal of some loose holds as well as the three points of aid required for the start. In August, intent on making up for the previous year's absence, Littlejohn was back with another strong supporting cast, notably Chris King and Cannings. As much as new routes, the free-climbing of some partially aided routes was also on his agenda, in line with trends elsewhere in the South-West. These included *The Great Divide* (three points remained), *Wolfman Jack* (one point remained), *Bender*, *Jetset*, and his own *Time Bomb*. As industrious as ever, he created four new routes. *Captain Cat* on Alpine Buttress and *Astral Traveller* on Weird wall could perhaps be described as minor fare in comparison to his efforts on Focal Buttress. Here, the striking line of *Golden Gate* and the audacious *Olympica*, the first E5 in the South-West, were magnificent achievements. The latter remained one of the most intimidating routes on the island for some considerable time and was to be his last for twelve years.

1978 – 1980: A TIME FOR CONSOLIDATION
1978 signalled the end of an era in Lundy rock-climbing history. Littlejohn was switching his focus of attention to other areas, and without the driving forces of Cannings, Thexton, or Strapcans, the impetus was lost: development drifted into a period of consolidation. Many climbers came to sample the adventurous delights of Lundy but none had the pioneering drive displayed by those that had gone before. New routes came in fits and starts.

In the August of 1978 Roger 'Strappo' Hughes returned to the island having been impressed the previous year putting up *Dark Power* and *Redspeed*. At the time these additions were not seen to be outstanding achievements but they have since joined the itinerary of 'hidden Lundy gems'. Ken Wilkinson and George Hounsome also ventured away from their usual Swanage haunts to add *Genesis* and *American Graffiti*.

By 1979, with the incentive of a new guidebook already in progress, routes were being scattered more liberally around the island. For a short period, Grand Falls Zawn drew the attention, Dennis Carr setting the ball rolling with *A Separate Reality*, soon to be accompanied by a route on either side by Rowland Edwards – *Grand Falls Road* and *The China Syndrome*. Surprisingly, along with the much-awaited free ascent of *Wolfman Jack*, these are Edwards's only contributions to Lundy climbing and did not match the calibre of his routes on his adopted Cornish cliffs. During the same August period, which owing to seasonal bird restrictions has become the most productive month for new-route activity, many other routes were to be added. Brian Wilkinson and Chris Nicholson, working separately, added a handful of routes in 1979, though these did not become popular. Mike Hunt added *Starship Trooper* to the St James' Stone area and it was also interesting to see the cliffs at the northern end of the island opened up with Bruce Goodwin's *Out of the Blue*, perhaps a pointer for future development.

As a whole, 1980 was the best year for quite some time, the development being notable more for its quality than its quantity. The new guidebook became available and proved the catalyst for an increase in interest. The route of the year fell to a youthful Steve Keeling, who set about the wall to the right of *Wolfman Jack*. In the competitive, though friendly, company of his partners, and after three attempts, *Venus Flytrap* was produced; it proved to be in a class similar to its highly-acclaimed neighbour. The two accompanying members of the team went on to add their own routes: Derek Beetlestone, the first free ascent of *Rampart*; and Gary Gibson, *Ice* and *Holiday in Cambodia*. A short while later Chris Nicholson and Andy Gallagher had a productive week venturing into Starship Zawn for the intrepid *Space Bandit*, which still requires its original two points of aid, alongside the more amenable *Mars Bar*. Further north they added the fine *Bulletin* to Arch Zawn and the aptly-named *Thug* to The Constable. To round off the season, M Meysner contributed a trio of routes on Beef Buttress including *Spare Rib* and *Brisket*; the latter, originally graded E2, has been nudged up to E4 and thus provided the hardest climbing since Littlejohn's *Olympica* in 1977.

1981 – 1984: NEW ACTIVIST, NEW IDEAS

With the advent of the 1981 season, Lundy had found itself a new protagonist in Gary Gibson, who was to bring new ideas and a new direction to the development of climbing on the island, to say nothing of a hint of controversy. A good view of the island's potential from the previous year was coupled with a determined drive for fame and fortune. A major supporting role was played by Derek Beetlestone, who produced a competitive edge to matters for a very fruitful two-week visit. With a spell of excellent weather in July, the two set about a number of impressive lines very much in the mould of their illustrious predecessors. Pride of place went to the first breach of the huge, diamond-shaped wall nestling in the back of Squires View Zawn. The ascent of *A Widespread Ocean of Fear* brought Gibson to the fore in Lundy development and created a latter-day classic. But matters did not rest at that. *Second Coming, Slip Tide, Silent Storm*, and *Shotgun Rider*, the latter led by Beetlestone after Gibson's failure, were added to the more easily accessible cliffs. From this, the pair broadened their horizons to seek battle with an impressive crack on Torrey Canyon Cliff. After losing the toss, Gibson had to take up the role of belayer but was subsequently handed the lead after an unproductive attempt by Beetlestone. A suspect block was removed on abseil, and Gibson managed by the skin of his teeth, as well as his hands, to land the plum line of *Controlled Burning*.

The final route of the fortnight was a line on the right-hand side of The Diamond. With little thought of the consequences, Gibson placed a bolt runner and a bolt belay to climb the nevertheless bold, and magnificent, *Smear or Disappear*. Thus a trend was set that was to have serious repercussions over the ensuing years.

The following few weeks continued to produce numerous new routes from activists old and new. One to renew his acquaintance with the island, but sadly to add his last new route before his untimely death on Broad Peak in 1983, was Pete Thexton. Famous for his tireless gardening sessions, Thexton unearthed and then climbed *Friends in High Places* on The Back of the Slide. This was a typical effort and, while not being his best route, remains a fine example of his achievements on the island. Around the same time Goodwin, now a Lundy devotee, reappeared to add a companion route to *Out of the Blue* with *Blues in Sea*; and then, combining forces with John Warburton and Ray Fifield, he began development of the cliffs further to the north. At the same time, Keith Marsden added a trio of routes on Torrey Canyon Cliff and Roger Brookes created *The Brick Wall* on The Old Light Cliff.

As the season drew to a close there remained no lack of enthusiasm for further future development of the Lundy cliffs. In an article to publicize his own *South West Climbs*, Pat Littlejohn had written that Lundy had plenty more potential, and his prophecy was so far proving true. Unfortunately, the expectation did not bear fruit in 1982, which was noticeable for its dearth of new routes; there were only two major ones. True enough, the island was alive with climbers during the unrestricted season but many were sampling Lundy for the first time and had not the energy or the knowledge for new routes. During August only five were added, of which none but *McVitie Man* by Steve Boydon and *Pelmets of Delirium* by Simon Harry were of any significance.

In September, a team from Leeds University arrived on the island with Duncan Drake and Tony Walker at the helm. After a concerted effort they managed to climb a line to the right of *Olympica* which they awarded a plethora of stars in The Marisco Tavern log-book. *Wimp's Wall* was to be straightened out later by Matt Carr but it was still an impressive effort at the time. Perhaps more importantly, the same pair went on to make the second ascent of *A Widespread Ocean of Fear*, to which they conceded 'only' two stars, with the rider that it required 'steel toes and plenty of small wires'. To round off the year, in the latter part of October Matt Priestman made the first true venture onto Black Crag with *Black and Blue*. This was a significant achievement by any standards and pointed the way to the future for bold face routes, of which Lundy had many to offer. Whether these would be tackled in a fashion similar to Priestman's effort remained to be seen.

1983 fared little better. The impact of the 1980 guidebook was spent and the island was quiet by the hectic standards of earlier years. Only two new routes were added during a summer of excellent warm sunshine, both by Gibson: *Treasure Island* and *Pawsher*, the latter after an abortive attempt when the tide was completely misjudged. Ian Cheshire, the unfortunate second man, vowed not to return to the line after a thorough drenching whilst trying simultaneously to belay and tread water!

With the added incentive of the authorship of a new guidebook to the island, Gibson returned in 1984 with a radically greater sense of purpose, and he had with him a trio of reliable seconds in the form of Adam Hudson, Matt Ward, and Simon Whalley. Hours were spent gardening, whether it was early morning or dusk, to achieve success, and the results were impressive: *Matt Black*, *The Indy 500*, *Play Genetics*, and *Immaculate Misconception* were all climbed utilizing Gibson's meticulous analysis of the island's potential. At the end of the week, he surpassed his previous achievements with the first route to pierce the impressive leaning walls of The Parthenos. *Cithaeron*, named after a Greek mountain on which 'imperfect' Spartan babies were lain to fight for themselves, was the result. His partners were no less industrious: Ward unearthed *Leprachauner*, Hudson discovered *Ocean Rain*, and Whalley pieced together the brilliant *Double Diamond*, which had been climbed in parts before, and squeezed *Fear of Faust* onto The Slide.

Gibson added two further routes on impressive areas of rock, first plugging a major gap on The Diamond with *Smear? No Fear* and following it up with an ascent of the striking right arête of Flying Buttress to provide *The Cullinan*. These two routes epitomized the Gibson drive for new routes; however, by the use of one bolt runner on each pitch, they also undermined the traditionalist ethics of Lundy climbing. Although at the time the implications were not fully evident, it was becoming apparent that Gibson was prepared to take such steps to achieve success.

The ensuing week was no less important in terms of new routes and free ascents, as a new team of climbers emerged to rival Gibson's activities. Boydon and Paul Harrison also had become enamoured of the place, and signalled an intention to stamp their own personalities on the island. Boydon aimed his sights high: after climbing the technical *Peanut Power* on Flying Buttress as well as making a superb on-sight ascent of *Eye of the Needle*, he set about a completely free ascent of *Supernova* in Deep Zawn. After a courageous on-sight attempt unfortunately necessitating one point of aid, he returned the following day to complete a superb ascent. Harrison, his partner on all of these, added *Kyalami Caper* to First Buttress South, and during the same week Doug Kerr added *The Ride and the View* on Immaculate Slabs to complete another excellent week.

After such an impressive fortnight it was inevitable that development would slow, but there was one further important event: the visit of the extremely talented Simon Nadin, a young Peak District climber who was later to make a name for himself with his incredible ascents both at home and abroad as well becoming the first World Competition Champion. He added an impressive route up the centre of First Buttress North with *I Scream* and made the first completely free and on-sight ascent of *Supernova*. No one could now be in any doubt about the potential the island offered. It remained to be seen what the new guidebook, which was well on its way to production, would stimulate.

1985: THE GREAT DIAMOND ROBBERY
Gibson's enthusiasm for new routes together with the imminent publication of the guidebook in the middle of 1985 heralded a new era in Lundy development. The previous year had shown that unclimbed lines and completely new cliffs were available for those with the willingness and endeavour to tackle them. It was apparent that Gibson was prepared to take on many of the challenges, and he was about to find a very capable rival in the form of Boydon.

Whilst the book was still at the printers, Boydon and Harrison, along with a number of friends, made an Easter sortie. Unfortunately, in high winds and generally poor weather, little was done. The Fortress was the only venue where any impact could be made, owing to its southerly aspect and shelter from the wind, and only *Stormy Waters* and *Ceaseless Tide* were added. Boydon also made a valiant attempt at the first free ascent of *Vibration*, an old aid route below the arch of Flying Buttress, but failed when he and Harrison were almost drowned in mountainous seas. Doug Kerr almost fell foul of the sea in a similar incident when a high wave washed him off the platform below Immaculate Slabs – only a quick-thinking second dragged him to safety. From that point he kept to plateau-level and climbed the innocuous-looking *Three Mile Island*, a pitch which has since stopped a number of leaders. And so, with the publication of the guidebook in June 1985, the scene was set for an onslaught similar to that of twelve years previously.

At the end of the seasonal bird restrictions, the two teams were ready for action, and it was inevitable that impressive routes would result. Gibson spent three days developing St Patrick's Buttress and gathered in an excellent quartet of routes: *Matt Blanc* (with a bolt) and *Mammoth-Sandwich Island* fell to very determined efforts, whilst *Russian Giant* (solo) and *Tomorrow* were seen off after reassessment of the *Destiny* wall. Partner in most of these events, Matt Ward also discovered *Harbinger*, a companion to *Tomorrow*. At the same time, and after a traumatic crossing when their vessel cut out in stormy seas and the pair had to be rescued by lifeboat, Boydon and Harrison were no less active. In Black Jack Zawn, *Buried Gold* and *Hidden Treasures* were climbed after the removal of a 'car-size block' represented one of the biggest trundles yet seen on Lundy. *Surf City* and *Technicolour Cruise* (with a bolt on the latter) on the lower half of Fluted Face were named after their infamous trip.

These were important events by any standards, but directly upon landing both teams had had one main aim: the challenge represented by the left-hand side of The Diamond. Gibson was lucky enough to be first on the scene and, along with Ward and Simon Whalley, had scurried up the island to clean the lines. For most of the week, a strong north-westerly wind blew straight up the face of the cliff, but as it died Gibson and Ward finally overcame the magnificent central line, later named *Watching the Ocean*, with three bolt runners. Their decision to leave the remaining lines until the following day was unfortunate, as the high winds returned. Gibson had to say farewell with a bold solo ascent of *Egyptian Reggae* on Immaculate Slabs. His chance had passed.

Boydon made the most of the situation. He had begun exploration on this section of the face at Easter and, after finishing the brushing, climbed three outstanding lines. *Diamond Life* and *Ace of Diamonds* plundered the cracklines on the left-hand side of the face and were its first one-pitch routes. Pride of place though went to *Wild Heart*, a suitable companion to, and running alongside, Gibson's addition of five days earlier. He expanded his growing list of impressive achievements with the second ascent of *Watching the Ocean*. To finish matters Harrison, Boydon's partner throughout, added the superb traverse-line, appropriately named *Coast to Coast*.

And so, in a single week, The Diamond had been brought to the forefront of British rock-climbing with a string of unsurpassed face routes on impeccable granite. Much has been written since, but Harrison's appraisal of the cliff from this period as 'having the best concentration of hard, three-star routes in the South-West' was certainly no understatement.

The following weeks were relatively quiet although Kerr opened up Punchbowl Cliff with the excellent *Promises*, and Tony Sawbridge and Nick Halliday added a quintet of routes to the previously overlooked Freak Zawn.

In the Lundy climbing calendar, September is usually a quiet month but Gibson had vowed to return, and towards the end of the month he was back with wife Hazel. On a similar return visit were Kerr and Chris 'Boris' Gilbert and, with a week of excellent weather, more new routes were made and challenges met. Kerr's and Gilbert's main areas of activity revolved around two cliffs, The Fortress and Threequarter Buttress, although they managed to squeeze in *Naughty but Nice* on First Buttress North beforehand. Best of the bunch was Kerr's *Nonexpectus Jugsimisius*, a splendid arête, while his other additions, *The Gold Run* and *Hot Spot*, ran it a close second and third respectively. Meanwhile, Gibson continued from where he had left off in August. St Patrick's Buttress was still attracting significant attention with such routes as *Too Salsify*, *Crampant*, and *Boris Karloff*, the latter being the first route to pierce the formidable Wall of Grooves. He also accounted for *Charles Mattless* with a bolt runner but made an impressive solo ascent immediately after. Then he visited Black Crag for the audacious *Death-Watch Beetle-Drive*, Wolfman Jack Wall for *The Midnight Hour*, and Box Zawn for the esoteric *Box of Frogs*. Finally he tackled the crack below the arch on Flying Buttress where Boydon had failed previously and produced the awesome *Brinkman's Ship*, named tongue firmly in cheek. It was a fitting finale to an industrious year of activity by all concerned.

1986 – 1988: GIBSON – BOLT AND BELIEVE IT

Gibson was to remain heavily involved in the new-route scene for the next three years. His approach, exemplified initially by a 'minimalist' use of the bolt, was also to flourish, though this was not to go unnoticed by the majority of activists, past or present. Whether these ethics were to be challenged remained to be seen, but Gibson was prepared to do battle with any line. Although by no means every route suffered this way, if Gibson felt he needed a bolt, then he would probably bolt.

In 1986 he began his long association with Black Crag, a face that, over the next few years, would be exemplified in both directions of change. Enlisting considerable help from Ward, who did not at this stage partake in the bolting, he soon added six new routes. After almost receiving a fatal injury when a block was dislodged from above, Gibson quickly accounted for *Doctor's Orders* on the fringe of the crag. Two days later the pair were back, and the routes to fall were rather more significant. *My Life in My Hands* (two bolts), the brilliant crackline of *Emergency Ward Ten* (two bolts), and the incredible central line of *Mayan Skies* (six bolts) pointed clearly towards Gibson's adoption of the 'sport climbing' ethic. Ward accompanied these with the milder *Pastiche*, on the fringe of the main face.

Strong winds having delayed their return journey and given them an extra day, Ward and Gibson made the most of the situation, setting their eyes on the sheltered Punchbowl Cliff. Here, Ward was to the fore with superb leads of *The Golden Handshake* and *Look Daggers* on very damp rock. Gibson, not to be outdone, replied with the majestic *Atlantic Mocean* (one bolt) an appropriate name for a route on such a wild day.

These inroads had certainly opened Gibson's eyes even further; and the following year saw him taking two weeks on the island. The routes created were no less impressive, though the lines tackled were on cliffs

Lundy Pioneers: Pete Thexton, Pat Littlejohn, Keith Darbyshire   *Photo:* Ken Wilson

Alternative Transport: 'The Paint-Roller Tin'   *Photo:* Ken Wilson

Stalingrad (first Ascent) The Devil's Chimney Cliff
Climber: Pat Littlejohn   *Photo:* Ken Wilson

spread round the island. Hazel was sole companion during the first week and, with weather of unmatched quality, routes came thick and fast. On First Buttress South he took the line *The Italian Job* had avoided with the impressive *Le Mans*, the only big route of the week without a bolt. On The Diamond he plugged an obvious gap with *Chase the Ace* (two bolts) as well as returning to Black Crag for the technical *Intensive Care* (three bolts). To conclude the week he took a step beyond even his achievement of the previous year with *Mayan Skies*: *Mexico Speaks* (six bolts) scythed straight up the centre of the crag, giving the island its first route in the E7 grade.

For the second week, Gibson was joined by the ever faithful Ward. On The Parthenos both came up with classics after backing a hunch that lines existed on their respective sections of rock. *Too Precious* by Gibson and *Mal de Mer* by Ward both received fame, thanks to impressive photographs in *High* magazine. Gibson continued to press home his advantage of knowledge: *Alpless* and *Who Can Wait?* (one bolt) on Alpine Buttress, *Head-Strong* and *Arm-Strong* on The Devil's Chimney Cliff, *Zorba the Greek* (one bolt) on The Parthenos, and *Vincent Price* on St Patrick's Buttress. Ward retaliated on Gibson's rest day with the immaculate *Sea of Tranquility* on Needle Rock.

Gibson, though, had saved himself for one last purge, that of the diagonal break across Black Crag. After an evening in The Marisco Tavern, Ward was persuaded to second the route the following day. Having completed the first pitch, he became enmeshed in the difficulties of an awkward sequence. He insisted that he did not want to follow and promised to abseil to retrieve any remaining gear; but, after Ward had unclipped a *Friend*, Gibson reminded him of his duties, the rope was quickly taken in, and he completed *The Colour of Life* amidst much distress. That evening the pair returned to the tavern to reflect on a very successful week's activity.

1988 was the year that was to prove the turning-point in the bolting issue. This time Gibson came armed with a rotary hammer-drill and was prepared to do battle with the aid of technology. Bolts were easier to place and so routes were quicker to prepare. Previous exploits on Black Crag were matched with the awesome *Hey Gringo* (six bolts) to provide one of the island's most arduous pitches and this was complemented with *Out Come the Freaks Again* (one bolt) in The Black Hole, *That Semi-Detached Feeling* (one bolt) on Alpine Buttress, *The Pyramid of Success* (three bolts) on The Pyramid, and *Roy of the Rovers* (four bolts) on Pathfinder Slabs. These were not isolated events by any means but they were clearly indicative of Gibson's attitudes to the issue. He summed up the week both in name and in deed with the first breach of the back wall of Heron Zawn: *The Demons of Hilti*, with its three bolts and two drilled pegs, was the acme of difficulty, yet symbolized all that was good and bad about the ethical debate ready to unfold.

Gibson's seconds on these routes were slightly less industrious. Roy Thomas, who had mistakenly cleaned *Roy of the Rovers*, created its inevitable companion. *On the Beach*, with its two drilled peg runners, had something of a mixed reception but has subsequently become a classic of its type. Ward also contributed significantly to the activity, as well as to the island's collection of crag ironmongery. *Blood Poison* in Dihedral Zawn sprouted six stainless steel peg runners and had Gibson, in a reversal of roles, treading water whilst the pitch was completed: a fair return, perhaps, for the traumas that Ward had suffered in previous years. He also added two excellent pitches to The Old Light Cliff in the form of *Saffron* and *Asafoetida*, with a joint bolt belay. The latter has since become the most popular route on the slab.

1986 – 1988: A COMPETITIVE EDGE

The spirit of 1985 and the renewed fervour shown by a number of activists heralded a new age in the history of Lundy development. The domination by Gibson's activities through the early 80s along with the increased publicity brought a period of refreshing development from a variety of people prepared to sample the delights of Lundy.

Almost inevitably, Boydon was back in 1986 to sustain the competitive spirit, though his form did not enable him to match successes of the previous year. He doubled the number of routes on the Wall of Grooves with *Bertie's Route* but unfortunately had to use a rest-point on *Half Man, Half Biscuit* to the left of *Controlled Burning*. The name of the route perhaps sums up the nature of the rock and no one has returned for a free ascent. Kerr and Gilbert were also members of the team and set about climbing a number of new routes, *A Pack of Lies* in Short Story Zawn and *Wishful Thinking* on Punchbowl Cliff being two. However, their greatest achievement was tackling the immense gardening session required to clean the huge slab of rock below Threequarter Wall, affectionately known as 'The Ocean' by many Lundy devotees. After a thoroughly gargantuan effort involving at least two or three hours of earth-moving on each of nine consecutive days, the line was eventually climbed, with Sandy Wilkie drafted in to lead the lower pitches. It has since become the island's longest climb. When viewed from the sea the gleaming white streak can be seen from quite some distance, and the name of *The Ocean* was indeed appropriate. Harrison and Wilkie were also a productive pairing, taking the powerful corner-line of *Carol Anne Butler Corner* on The Fortress and making the exciting on-sight ascent of *Poltergeist* on The Devil's Chimney, so named because of the large amount of moving rock on the pitch.

Whilst all this was going on, Lyndsay Foulkes and Mick Learoyd had picked an opportune moment to pay a first visit to the island. Their adventurous nature plunged them into The Black Hole, their name for the back one-third of Freak Zawn, for one line each, both routes giving classic climbs of their type. First, Foulkes applied the finishing touches to a long, diagonal line of cracks to give the unusual and very atmospheric

Milky Way. Learoyd then took over and, after a very protracted effort, which included a third man's passing down extra runners, *Andromeda* was created. In typical Lundy fashion it was climbed on the day of departure and the route was only just finished in time for the return ferry to Bideford.

If 1986 brought an increase in activity, then 1987 saw an avalanche. For two weeks the island was full of climbers, including the talented pair of Dave Pegg and Dave Thomas, who were intent on repeat ascents of some of its hardest climbs as well as treading new ground: they must have thought it was birthday-time! Starting off with Thomas's *Bite Size* in Crunchy Toed Zawn and Pegg's *Space Oddity* in Freak Zawn, they went on, with Pegg in the lead, to tackle the superb wall right of *Genesis* in Deep Zawn, coming up with the fine *Gracelands*, as well as accounting for the second ascent of *Mayan Skies*. Their major addition of the week, however, was to climb the first new route in Two Legged Zawn since the heyday of Strapcans in the mid 70s. Their ascent of *Voyage of the Acolyte* was a magnificent achievement with its roots planted firmly in the traditional era of times past. Pegg later wrote of the ascent: 'Thomas was heard to sell his soul as he pulled off a hold and penduled into the stratosphere'. To finish things off, the pair changed leads for Thomas to grab his *Dirty Lundies* on Punchbowl Cliff before returning home, for a bath presumably.

Other climbers were no less resourceful. Harrison and Simon Cardy, both true Lundy devotees, were now casting an eye over new rock. They used their extensive knowledge to develop the Arch Zawn Area with six routes including the excellent *Today* (which had repulsed Gibson four years previously after a tidal misjudgement and a thorough soaking), *Letters to the Editor*, and *Archie Gemmill*. They also accounted for the remaining lines on the north wall of Freak Zawn with four new pitches, two to each climber, as well as the pleasant *Atlantic Grey* in the Phantom Zawn Area. Matt Carr was also on the island and, after a significant gardening effort, climbed the imposing wall right of *The Exorcist* in The Devil's Limekiln: six peg runners, much bold climbing, and a satanic setting provided the appropriately christened *The Antichrist*.

As the relatively short season came to a conclusion, Nick Steen forced the thin crack-system left of *Immaculate Slab* with a point of aid to create *Tutenkhamun*, leaving a line awaiting the jackals.

1988 continued apace with early-season activity in the form of Steen's return for a free ascent of his own route, and Damien Carroll's excellent *Lightspeed* on The Back of the Slide. Dave Thomas also returned, a little earlier in the season than normal, evidently attempting to steal a march on other activists, and he brought along Nick White, a Devon climber of no little talent and vision. The outcome should have been impressive but some very unseasonal weather and strong winds limited their success. Thomas had clearly learned from the previous year and accounted for three very bold routes in the Phantom Zawn Area: *Things That Go Bump in the Night, Something in the Shadows*, and the challenging *On a Wing and a Prayer*, a very worrying arête. Not content with the latter, he soloed an even bolder variation finish. Pressing home his advantage, he moved round the corner to Torrey Canyon Cliff and climbed the impressive *Wall of Attrition* to the right of *Norseman*, which he later likened to *Lord of the Flies* on Dinas Cromlech. The final addition of his stay, *Ark of the Covenant*, was to take another of the groove-lines in Two Legged Zawn, a cliff that he was to make his own over the next couple of years.

The following week saw the annual visit from the Harrison-Cardy-Boydon team and they continued where Thomas had left off in the Phantom Zawn Area, but this time they gave the place a thorough going over and left no piece of rock untouched. Harrison climbed the unfashionable *Flares Are In*, the delightful *Howling* with its *Banshee Finish*, and the poignant *Bed Bugs Bite My Bollocks*, a fallacy to which many Lundy climbers have mistakenly subscribed. Boydon flexed his muscles on *Seal of Approval*, later to be followed by the desperate *Friction Impossible*. Cardy was also *Clinging to the Wreckage* with *An Audience of Seals* that went *Woooooo!*. Other members of the team joined in the spree: Mark Bartley had an *Achilles' Seal* before capturing *Nous Sommes de Soleil*, and Mike Snell evidently liked *Ghostbusters* so much that he went and sprained his ankle playing football the next day and was relieved of duty.

Between all these rich pickings in the one area, Boydon and Harrison ventured further afield. On The Devil's Chimney Cliff, *The Reluctant Teamaker* had been crying out for a free ascent. After doing the honours, they accompanied it with *The Beguiled* and then climbed the centre of the face to the left. *The Satan Bug* required a point of aid to start: three broom sticks were borrowed from Tibbett's, tied together, and used to clip the peg: a free ascent is awaited with interest! In Heron Zawn, Boydon and Cardy climbed the impressive crackline on the left-hand side of the back wall with *Bosch Street Kids* to give an arduous pitch. Harrison had the final word with *Supercharged* on The Battery Cliff just before their departure.

Other climbers duly joined in the action. Julian Chapman and Carr were responsible for three superb routes in the aptly-named Hidden Zawn. Chapman climbed *The Demons Within* and *The Stone Gollum*, while Carr captured *The Lost Banshee* to complete three routes that should be on any climber's 'esoterica list'. Howard Darwin also popped up to create *Wonderlands* on the obvious wall at the back of Seal Slab, thus opening up yet another area. Finally, Mike Owen weighed in with important second and third ascents of *Emergency Ward Ten* and *Mayan Skies* respectively, proving that not all the climbers on the island were intent only on first ascents.

1989: A RETURN TO TRADITIONAL VALUES

1989 was the beginning of a transitional period in the history of Lundy climbing. For the previous eight years, and more specifically from 1985 to

1988, Gibson had been forcing the bolt issue. Without doubt, *The Demons of Hilti*, both in name and in deed, had taken the matter one step too far. The time had come for action.

May saw the timely return of Pat Littlejohn after an interval of twelve years, ably assisted by Nick White. His intentions were made perfectly clear in notes he had written in the island's climbing log-book: 'The spread of bolting on the island is wretched. Unless action is taken, the future of climbing on Lundy will be dictated by the cordless drill'. Without further ado, and with a drive reminiscent of that of the mid 70s, he embarked on a series of impressive bolt-free ascents. *Charles Mattless* was first (though this had been soloed by Gibson after the first ascent), followed by *The Cullinan*. The latter had its line varied slightly and the new name of *Flying the Colours* was offered. He then switched to The Diamond and captured perhaps his finest achievement of the week with a bolt-free ascent of *Watching the Ocean*, a grade of E7 being suggested into the bargain. As a final gesture, Littlejohn climbed the impressive groove system in the centre of the Wall of Grooves to produce *The Price of Admission*, commenting: 'Climbed on sight, which was just as well because if we'd inspected it first we may never have gone near it!'. Nesting restrictions limited him, but his actions, as well as some heated letters written in the magazines of the day, were to have the desired effect.

With an excellent spell of weather, June also saw the return of Boydon to add a few more routes to the island's growing repertoire. *Ticket to Ride* was the highlight of the week and took an impressive line up The Devil's Slide's retaining wall. Preceding this came *Powerplus* and *Ever Ready*, two more routes on The Battery Cliff, as well as a bolt-free ascent of his own *Technicolour Cruise*. The issue was clearly hitting home, though there was still Gibson's attitude to change.

As the seasonal restrictions ended, Gibson returned in late July with the intention of righting a few wrongs. His first port of call was The Diamond, and in a single day he eliminated the remainder of the bolts on the face with leads of *Chase the Ace*, *Smear? No Fear* and *Smear or Disappear*, the latter route name becoming particularly pertinent to all three routes. He then returned to *Watching the Ocean* and, after learning that Littlejohn had not actually removed the bolts until after his ascent, made an undeniably bolt-free ascent.

As the week progressed he switched areas. On Punchbowl Cliff he made a daring solo of *Atlantic Mocean* along with a hideous direct start. Moving over to Black Crag, in another notable day he grabbed bolt-free leads of *Emergency Ward Ten*, *My Life in My Hands* and *Mayan Skies*. The latter proved to be the island's most serious lead for quite some time and confirmed the strength of his determination to be once again in the vanguard of a new turn of events.

And, with faithful support from Ward and Roy Thomas, he was no less industrious in the finding of more new routes. Having considered six bolts the previous year, he exemplified his new-found boldness with *Bathfinder* on Pathfinder Slabs, and followed it with *Silver Smile* over on Punchbowl Cliff, the latter due mainly to Ward's excavations on his own route *Dweebland* a few hours earlier. Thomas was responsible for *Douglas Bather* on Pathfinder Slabs, named in deference to the route's original gardener.

These events were by no means the most important of the first two weeks in August. Dave Thomas and White were resident on the island with the intention of plundering more first ascents. In the company of Simon Berry and Tim Gallagher, Thomas made a girdle-traverse of Two Legged Zawn: *The Grail Trail*. *The Last Crusade*, a tit-bit on the fringes of the face, was to follow, with *The Quest*, right of *Voyage of the Acolyte*, providing the Zawn's hardest route to date. During this period, Thomas made valiant efforts upon the last groove-line in the wall, but without success: the ascent of this was to wait a few more years.

Thomas, though, was not resident on the one crag. Having accounted for the second ascent of *Too Precious* in 1987, he also had designs on the crackline to its right. Inevitably, *Ex-Cathedra* was to prove an extremely strenuous pitch but it was also extremely well protected. He then switched cliffs again for the *direttissima* line of *Waves of Emotion*, claimed to be 'the best route on The Diamond' at that time. (Though aren't they all?)

White was no less involved in the activities, though somewhat surprisingly it was taking him longer to get going. In May he had been attempting the stunning north wall of The Flying Buttress, but it was not until August that his efforts came to fruition. After a handful of attempts and some monster falls, *The Flying Dutchman* was completed and provided one of the toughest leads on the island. White also had his say on The Parthenos with an ascent of the huge hanging groove that dominates the face. *The Earthsea Trilogy: Part Two* was the second in a trio of awesome routes, parts one and three being on mainland Devon. He then plucked the fine *Shardik* from Seal Slab, and rounded off with impressive solo ascents of *Gale Force* and *Stormbound* on Gannet's Buttress.

Harrison and Cardy were increasingly developing a stranglehold on the cliffs at the northern end of the island, and in 1989 each increased his tally of new routes. Harrison weighed in with *Pathetic Sharks* in Arch Zawn, which was becoming an attractive venue, and later opened up Grapefruit Buttress still further with *Mussel-Up* and the evocatively named *Serious Lobster Juggling*. The Constable yielded *The Chief Constable*, after a bit of top-roping, before he labelled a line on Beef Buttress after his favourite football player, *Steve Bull*. Bartley and Harrison also accounted for *Crack Climbing for Beginners* in the claustrophobic Narrow Zawn. Cardy continued with *Beach and Surf Check* in Cyclops Zawn, *The Buoy Prophet* and *The Great White* in the newly-christened Cormorant Zawn, and *The Bottom Inspectors* on Black Bottom Buttress, a memorable route-name!

As the customary 'two-week season' drew to a close, Carr made the long-awaited first free ascent of *Antiworlds* as well as second ascents of *Ark of the Covenant* and *Space Oddity* before retiring injured to Barnstable Casualty with a dislocated shoulder. Pete Cobb dug out and then ascended the groove right of *Play Genetics* in Deep Zawn for *A Friction Romance*. Perhaps the final word, though, went to Owen who, as well as making a series of other notable repeat ascents, went one step further than most by leading and then reversing *The Colour of Life* and making the second ascent of *Mexico Speaks*.

That would normally have been the end of the season, but this was by no means a typical one. Carr and Cobb had some unfinished business to attend to and their return visit in October, blessed with some superb weather, resulted in a string of further successes. Carr set the ball rolling with *Atlas* on Focal Buttress a route that straightened out Duncan Drake's earlier *Wimp's Wall*. He followed up with a micro-gem of no less importance on The Pyramid. *A Wild Trip on Jugs* was an apt name for a superb route. Cobb retorted *If I Should Fall from Grace with God*, a line essentially straightening out the upper pitches of *The Stone Tape* with a few harder variations, and a diagonal crossing of the upper section of The Diamond entitled *Mocean in the Ocean*. Carr, though, was not to be outdone. On a wild and stormy day and in one final draining effort he managed to climb the awesome crackline in the overhanging wall opposite Seal Slab. *The Tempest* was a fitting finale to their efforts, though, somewhat mysteriously, a bolt-hole was found *en-route*.

At even a cursory glance it is quite clear that 1989 was a watershed in the history of Lundy climbing. For a few years, the traditional ethics of the 60s and 70s had been challenged, but public pressure and the deeds of a handful of climbers had put the issue to right. Littlejohn and others had firmly rejected Gibson's use of the bolt, and Gibson accepted the strongly expressed wishes of the majority of climbers. Lundy could now look to the continuation of the traditionalist approach for its future development.

1990: INTO THE FUTURE
After the frenzy of 1989 it was inevitable that activity would slow somewhat. Gibson was absent and other individuals could take the limelight. But in 1990 Harrison, Cardy, Bartley, and Snell were back for their annual visit and found a barrage of routes in hidden zawns and cliffs towards the north end of the island. Cardy produced the micro *Like it or Limpet* above Torrey Canyon Cliff, an imaginative name stolen from Harrison. Bartley chipped in with *Neptune Rising* on a wall on St James' Stone as well as the strangely-named *Ain't No Weinie Roast* on Grapefruit Buttress. The latter had become a long-term project for Bartley but it succumbed only after top-rope inspection. Meanwhile Harrison and Snell accounted for *Naked Gun* and *Caught in the Act* on The Constable, the latter with Snell in the lead.

White had by now become well and truly hooked, and it showed in his handful of superb climbs during the next two years. *Wolfsbane*, on the back wall of Crunchy Toed Zawn, was a significant achievement by any standards and proved that White's eye for a line, as well as his climbing ability, could match the best; a subsequent ascent by Steve Mayers confirmed the achievement. The following year the groove-line in Two Legged Zawn, attempted so tenaciously by Thomas previously, was dry enough for an ascent. It was climbed in the company of Neil Foster to give *The Dog's Bollocks*. He also opened up the huge, undercut wall in Starship Zawn with *Araucaria*, the first pitch taking an incredibly suspended 'beam' of rock by an almighty hand-traverse. Just looking at this makes the heart flutter. In addition, he climbed *Zorba the Greek* on The Parthenos without the bolt.

These events were difficult to compete with and, significantly, only one route came close. The stunning crack at the back of The Devil's Chimney had been admired by many, past and present, but no one so far had plucked up the courage to attempt it: certainly bravado and skill were needed. In September 1990, Crispin Waddy, a climber fitting the mould perfectly, tackled the line on-sight and had the sensational *Uncontrolled Gurning* as his prize. Other sporadic efforts came from Steve Findlay, the only remaining member of the 'Clean Hand Gang', with *Sea of Dreams* on Needle Rock and from Martin Corbett with *The Last Rubber* – the last line on The Diamond? Finally, to surpass all previous bold achievements, Dave Thomas grabbed a series of impressive on-sight solos, of which *Olympica* was outstanding.

1991 saw a fleeting visit by Dave Lyon and Norman Clacher who turned their attentions to the back wall of Arch Zawn, an area that catches the early evening sun only; hence the After Six Wall. On consecutive days they accounted for three worthwhile routes with *Smoke on the Water*, *Woman in Chains*, and *Rigging in the Frigging Arête*.

However, Harrison and Cardy, with varying support from Snell and Bartley, must receive credit as the most prolific activists. Their knowledge of and liking for the northern end of the island had already been demonstrated and, while in 1990 their interests had been taken up with a number of esoteric zawns and faces, the following year the routes proved more important. Cardy spent a long time on *Badlands* on Wonderlands Wall, so much that the round-island boat trip passed by on three occasions! Then Bartley grabbed the nearby *Dreamlands*, a bold undertaking, before Harrison wrestled with the mighty *Sumo*, a huge hidden groove on Seal Slab. Harrison and Cardy continued their interest in hidden new faces and opened up Benson's Buttress with one route each. Harrison settled a score with *Bastard Wet Crack* in Arch Zawn and as a final gesture improved on the already excellent *Redspeed* with a superb direct start.

The climbing season in 1992 was controlled more by the elements than by any other issue, though during breaks between some foul weather Harrison opened up The Marisco Walls with *The Islander*, *Marisco Striptease*, named after a particularly wild night in the Marisco Tavern, and *Taxiarchis*. Cardy free-climbed *The Vice* on Beef Buttress by a variation start before uncharacteristically venturing south for *Salvaged* on Montagu Buttress. Bartley set up *Elan* just as the sun dipped below the horizon, ensuring a late shift for his seconds, Harrison and Cardy.

1993 saw first the return of Gibson, and later the inevitable visit from Harrison with team ('the boys from the black country'), both for guidebook field-work. Gibson started off on St Patrick's Buttress with an impressive top pitch for and complete lead of *Vincent Price*, the first having been originally climbed in 1987, and followed up with a very bold solo of *Matt Blanc* to eliminate the bolt. The previously bolted *Jack 'O' Bite* on Wolfman Jack Wall was annulled by *An American Werewolf on Lundy*, an imposing route direct up the wall, and the bolts on *That Semi-Detached Feeling* and *Who Can Wait* on the adjacent Alpine Buttress also went. Small Black Crag gained two more pitches in the form of the excellent *Metamorphosis* and the brutal *Chameleon Kiss*.

Moving northwards to cliffs of which he had become previously enamoured he boldly tackled *The Hanmer House of Horror*, possibly the last line of Needle Rock, while *Right Between the Eyes*, *Specific Nocean*, and *Innocent Moves* took further challenges on Punchbowl Cliff. Similarly, The Pyramid was peppered with five routes, the best being *A Geometric Study*, the eponymous *Sphinx Crack*, which bears no resemblance to its American counterpart, and *Carnage in Carthage*. A wandering line on Pathfinder Slabs, in the company of Martin Wilson, was named after two passing nude swimmers: *Bathing Beauties*.

Gibson's two final offerings, perhaps his most important of the fortnight, were in the company of Roy Thomas and both were on his favourite cliffs. The Diamond's final gap was well and truly plugged by the audacious *Blood, Sweat and Smears*, and the inevitable diagonal crossing from left to right of Black Crag succumbed after much cursing to produce the impressive *Chitzen Itza*. Thomas, though, had the last word. After spending many hours gardening during his week-long stay, he eventually climbed the final line of Pathfinder Slabs on his day of departure for the appropriately named *Bath out of Hell*.

During the following fortnight Paul and Neil Harrison along with Cardy continued where Gibson had left off. *Song to the Siren* on the *Date with the Dawn* wall became Paul Harrison's one hundredth first ascent on the island, and was later to be accompanied by *The Abyss*. Cardy entered what was possibly the last unclimbed zawn on the island and emerged with *Herbert Bronski's Back*. Not to be outdone, the Harrisons continued to plunder a clutch of middle-grade routes in the North Light Area before Paul Harrison and Cardy captured *Mary Patricia Rosalea*, proving that quality at that standard could still be found.

The Harrison brothers chose to move south for further new additions. On

Torrey Canyon Cliff, *Mono Man* was a fine, short, fingery pitch, while the nearby Marisco Walls yielded to *Friday I'm in Love* and *Harrison Crusoe*. Their final and perhaps best route of the fortnight, was on The Devil's Chimney Cliff. *Psylocybin* gives an excellent 'trip' up the left arête of *The Fifth Appendage* slab and proved a fitting conclusion to Paul's involvement to date with the island over the past eleven years.

The activities of 1993 made a strong and encouraging conclusion to this relatively short period of Lundy's rock-climbing history. Over a mere thirty years a number of highly talented and motivated individuals have tested their abilities and adventurous spirit on the island's superb coastline. One major issue was tested to the full, but its subsequent rejection has allowed a resurgence of the earlier adventurous style. Long may it remain so, and long may Lundy remain an isolated haven of such tradition: the place for which dreams were made!

The South Coast

The south coast provides a myriad of small, nondescript cliffs of no interest to the climber. In fact, from South East Point to a distance some 300 yards east of South West Point the rock is a form of culm akin to that of the nearby North Devon Coast.

Three hundred yards east of South West Point, and more noticeably at the dramatic Devil's Limekiln, the rock changes type to provide the true start to the granite cliffs for which the island has become famous. Many small and insignificant buttresses remain uncharted and are probably best left as such, though a couple have a handful of climbs deserving limited merit. The one advantage is their south-facing aspect, which gives some form of protection from the strong westerly winds that sometimes batter the island.

DAMOCLES BUTTRESS   OS Ref 1360 4342

Two hundred yards east of The Devil's Limekiln, a lichenous rock ridge leads down to the cliffs. Eighty yards east of this ridge a small rounded promontory on the west side of a long grassy gully forms this buttress. It is also recognizable by a spiked summit with a small, 6-foot pinnacle nicknamed The Sword just below. Access is by abseil from The Sword down to the high water-level.

Wright-Hand Rib (80 feet Severe † 10.10.92) takes the ramp and right-hand arête of the buttress via three overhangs. **Anna's Arête** (80 feet Difficult 10.10.92) winds its way up the right-hand side of the front face. **The Sickle** (80 feet Very Severe † 10.10.92) climbs an obvious steepening ramp in the west side and passes through some overhangs to a rightward exit.

KISTVAEN BUTTRESS   OS Ref 1352 4339

This small cliff of excellent rock and pleasant aspect is clearly visible from the approach to The Great Shutter Rock and provides enjoyable climbing of a go-anywhere nature. The approach is by scrambling directly down the ridge 200 yards east of The Limekiln, between it and The Rocket Pole. This ridge leads down to a headland with the buttress lying to the west.

The first small zawn to the east of the main buttress provides one route in the form of **The Washing Machine** (80 feet Very Difficult 9.10.92) via a rightward line across its west wall. This is gained by a traverse from Kistvaen Buttress 100 feet above sea-level.

The main buttress is up to 100 feet in height and the climber can wander more or less at will. **First Blood** (60 feet Severe 7.87) takes a line up the wall at the foot of the descent. Starting at a lower level there are four climbs on the slabby face left of the easy way down: **Justine** (100 feet

Very Difficult 6.67) takes some corners immediately left of the way down to finish up the tower above; **Mount Olive** (100 feet Very Difficult 6.67) starts up the obvious curving groove in the centre of the face, moving left after 40 feet; **Clea** (80 feet Hard Severe 6.67), after starting up *Mount Olive*, takes the overlapping slabs between it and *Justine*; the slab left of *Mount Olive* gives **Bitter Lemons** (110 feet Severe 6.67), which takes a line up and to the left.

The face further to the left is approached via **The Dark Labyrinth** (90 feet Severe 6.67). After a 30-foot traverse left below the previous climbs, a move up is made to below an overhang, which leads to a stance on a steep slab. **Balthazar** (100 feet Very Difficult 6.67) goes up this slab for 10 feet, then left to a line of slabs leading to the top. **The Girdle Traverse** (Hard Very Severe) traverses right above the overlaps from the east side of Hidden Zawn to an obvious fault. It finishes up a groove on the right of the crag.

Another face further left can be gained by scrambling down the ridge over loose ground, keeping to the left (facing out) to large boulders at the foot of some slabs. Low tide is essential.

The Mermaid (90 feet Hard Very Severe 5a) takes the first wall direct, then the centre of an alcove and slabs above. **Putrid Puffin** (90 feet Very Severe 4b) continues from the start of *The Mermaid* up the centre of the middle slab to finish via a ramp on the headwall. **Awkward Arête** (95 feet Very Severe 4b) starts slightly lower and climbs a series of arêtes in a fine position to finish up the golden-coloured slabs on the left.

From the base of the last three routes, scramble directly down to a black groove. **Sliding Devil** (70 feet Hard Very Severe 5a) climbs the left-facing wall to finish easily over some blocks above. **Seagull Symphony** (70 feet Very Severe 4b) starts 70 feet to the left again via a groove and takes a series of overhangs in the same line to the top.

South West Point

The main landmark on the south-west tip of the island, beyond The Rocket Pole, is The Devil's Limekiln, an incredible 300-foot blowhole close to the coastline. Just seaward of this, forming the very tip of the headland, is a huge triangular blade of rock known as The Great Shutter Rock. Between the two stands an area of cliffs, one of which, Focal Buttress, is amongst the most impressive on the island. Further esoteric gems are scattered about the headland amongst other zawns and buttresses: Hidden Zawn, for example, a huge tunnel and chasm which branches off from the very foot of the Limekiln.

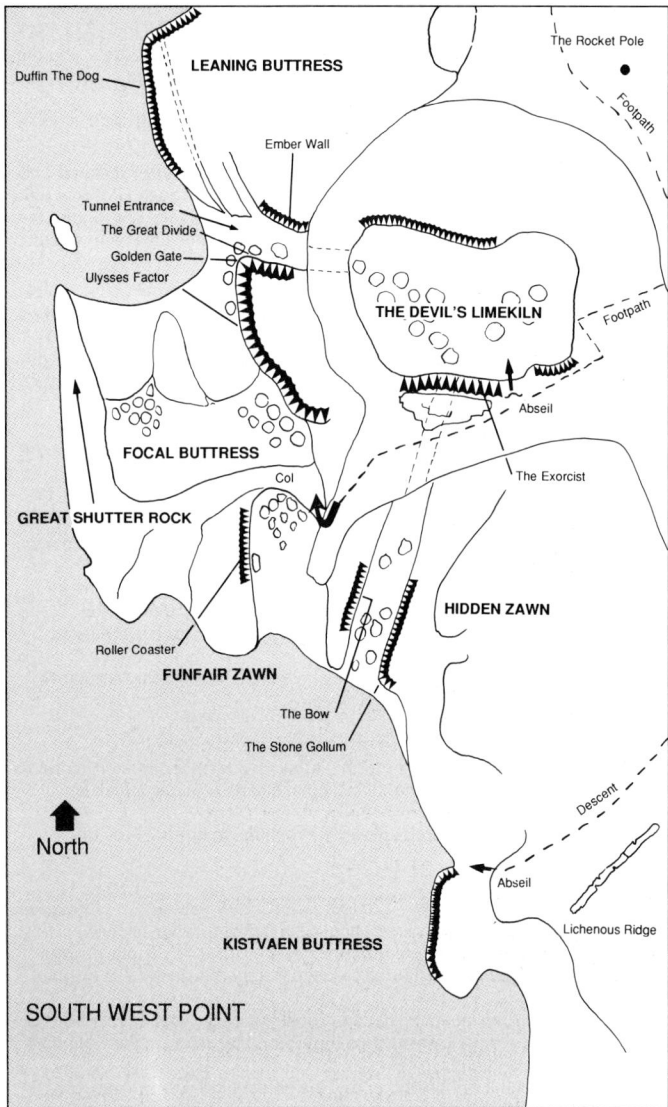

The Rocket Pole

Footpath

LEANING BUTTRESS

Duffin The Dog

Ember Wall

Tunnel Entrance
The Great Divide
Golden Gate
Ulysses Factor

THE DEVIL'S LIMEKILN

Footpath

Abseil

FOCAL BUTTRESS

The Exorcist

Col

GREAT SHUTTER ROCK

HIDDEN ZAWN

Roller Coaster

FUNFAIR ZAWN

The Bow

The Stone Gollum

Descent

North

Abseil

Lichenous Ridge

KISTVAEN BUTTRESS

SOUTH WEST POINT

THE DEVIL'S LIMEKILN   OS Ref 1338 4349
'Frank thought I was necky, but I was just committed. All around you the Kiln grotts out and towers up, hideously unsettling. Frank's pitch was absolute angel's delight.'

Arnis Strapcans, 1976

Two of the routes that emerge from this amazing feature, the first two described, start from its floor. The most common approach is at low tide via the large cleft bounding Focal Buttress to its north; see under the approaches to that buttress. The remaining routes are unique in access, which is described in context.

The character of The Limekiln is that of some sort of a lost world, cloaked in vegetation, with large areas of decaying ground. For this reason, it is well worth an exploratory visit if only to sample its unique and inhospitable atmosphere. The climbs are all character-building experiences, each having its own qualities.

The Kiln   340 feet   Hard Very Severe   (TD)   (29.8.70)
It is questionable whether the atmosphere and unusual setting for this climb compensates adequately for some of the awful climbing and rock that it incorporates. And a recent rockfall has rendered the climb even more testing. Helmets and some Alpine gear may prove useful, hence the qualifying grade. Serious with dirty rock and a wet start. It is advisable to preplace a rope to the edge from boulders well back. Enter The Limekiln at low tide, via the approach from Focal Buttress, and grovel up the muddy slope at the back to the far end of the Limekiln; take a sheltered stance!
1 90 feet 4a. Struggle up the chimney in the left, north, wall; then move right and continue up a gully to a peg belay.
2 75 feet. 'Climb' the chimney above to a detached flake. Traverse left across mixed ground to the base of an obvious slab and belay.
3 100 feet 4a. Continue up the slab, initially by its right corner, and then trend leftwards via a flake-line. Climb up to a grassy bulge, which is passed to a belay in a corner.
4 75 feet 4c. Trend leftwards along the faultline to finish. Belay to preplaced rope.

Flashing into the Dark   220 feet   Hard Very Severe   (4.8.77)
A peculiar route suitable for the connoisseur of hole-in-the-ground climbing. It takes the impressive chimney in The Limekiln's south-eastern corner and though previously well cleaned is now returning to its original state.
1 150 feet 5a. Grovel up the chimney past two peg runners (very hard to find) to a grass field. Belay here on a thread and large nut to the right; this may also be hard to find.
2 70 feet. From the right-hand end of the field, climb suspect rock for 10 feet; then bear left to the top.

★★**The Exorcist** 180 feet E3 (24.4.76)

A supernatural experience up the left-hand side of the blank-looking wall on the south side of The Limekiln. The wall is undercut for one-third of its height, giving the route a feeling of great commitment and isolation. While the climbing is never really hard it is always intricate, extremely bold, and very atmospheric. Start by abseiling 130 feet down the basalt chimney on the left-hand side of the wall from a huge earth bridge. Belay to the abseil rope on a small ledge alongside a decaying bong and slanting crack on the right wall.

1 70 feet 5b. Move carefully out to the slanting crack and from its end gain an overlap (peg runner). Make a short traverse left and pull over its left-hand side to reach a stance below a crescent-shaped overhang. Large nut and peg belay.

2 110 feet 5a. A pitch requiring faith in what lies above. Step left before following a series of holds into a smooth scoop (peg runner). Continue via a faint rib on the right to a horizontal break (peg runner); then step left and follow a shallow depression to a small ledge. Move up and leftwards for 15 feet, and step right to a small overlap. Climb this and the wall above to the top.

★★**The Antichrist** 200 feet E6 (7.8.87)

A big, serious outing up the right-hand side of the expansive wall containing *The Exorcist*. The bold and sustained nature of the climbing coupled with the satanic setting makes this an intimidating proposition. Remember, there are no atheists on a sinking ship! Start as for *The Exorcist*.

1 70 feet 5b. *The Exorcist* pitch 1; or abseil to the stance and belay to the abseil rope.

2 130 feet 6a. Move down from the belay and traverse rightwards to a small ledge (peg runner). Continue across the blank-looking wall (peg runner) to gain a groove on the right (peg runner). Climb the groove (two peg runners) to reach an undercut hold (two peg runners) and continue via a large flat hold to some flakes. Traverse left to a large flake (*Friends 1* and *3*) and finish more easily up the wall above. Stake belay.

Note: many of the pegs on this pitch are hand-made and have very small eyes, thus requiring small karabiners.

The Shutter Point Area

The approach to the cliffs in this area – Funfair Zawn, Focal Buttress, the base of The Devil's Limekiln, and Hidden Zawn – is by descending a steep grassy spur south of The Limekiln until about 150 feet above sea-level. From here, scramble down and across a steep, well-trodden slope to the north. This rough path leads down over mixed ground to a col of rubble running out to The Great Shutter Rock. Funfair Zawn is immediately obvious to the south. Focal Buttress and the entrance to The Limekiln are approached at low tide. In the case of the latter, scramble down the slightly unstable bouldery scree-slope to the north of the col, though the track is difficult to locate. *Ulysses Factor* and the climbs to its right are unaffected by the tide, but the remainder of the routes on Focal Buttress and The Limekiln are tidal. The entrance to The Limekiln bounds this face immediately to the north.

FUNFAIR ZAWN   OS Ref 1346 4343
This is the zawn on the left-hand side (facing out) of the col. Careful scrambling down the bouldery slope leads to the zawn bed. Its west wall (right facing out) contains a hanging corner low down and a large cracked overhang towards its top.

Roller Coaster   220 feet   E2   (9.8.80)
An interesting route but with a degree of vegetation on the easier sections. It takes the hanging corner and overhang gained via the interconnecting slabs. Start to the right of a large boulder.
1 150 feet 5b. Make an awkward traverse left onto the wall and climb it to gain the top of the corner. Swing out left onto the slab and pick the easiest and cleanest line up this to a good nut belay at the left-hand end of the overhang.
2 70 feet 4c. Traverse rightwards under the overhang, and continue over some unsound blocks to finish.

Takes the Biscuit   140 feet   E2 †   (19.8.89)
'A route to take home with you' (Pete Bull). The slabs to the left of *Roller Coaster*. Start a few feet left of that route, on the huge boulder at the bottom of the zawn.
1 90 feet 5a. Step off the boulder onto a square ledge and follow a ramp-line leftwards until below the end of a strip roof. Pull awkwardly over this and then climb more easily, but boldly, up the slab slightly rightwards to reach an earthy ramp. This leads leftwards to a nut and spike belay on the edge of the buttress.
2 50 feet. Scramble easily up the slope above.

The next route can be found in the final major zawn to the west, gained by continuing along the path from the col overlooking Funfair Zawn. Follow this to The Great Shutter Rock, and scramble up grassy slopes on the left to gain the ridge above the path. The long ridge running down to a prominent rock island can then be descended until a low-tide traverse leads into the back of the zawn to the east of the ridge. The zawn bites deep into the hillside and at its back lies a large jammed boulder.

The Minatour   220 feet   Hard Very Severe †   (27.8.77)
This route climbs the slab on the left to reach the overhang and then traverses above its lip in a good position.
1 30 feet. Follow a rightward-trending series of holds to gain the top of the jammed boulder at the back of the zawn.
2 90 feet 4c. Traverse left across the slab for 40 feet; then climb its

centre to reach the overhang. Continue up to a good stance.
3 50 feet 5a. Step down and right to cross the slab before moving up into an overhung groove. Swing right out of this and move up to a belay.
4 50 feet. Climb a chimney to the top and belay well back.

THE GREAT SHUTTER ROCK   OS Ref 1332 4333
When viewed from the vicinity of The Limekiln, The Great Shutter Rock presents a lichenous triangular face connected to the mainland by an earthy rib, part of which is used on the approach to The Minatour. The whole face is very unstable and appears to be in a state of continuous collapse, so much so that a route up its right-hand side has completely disappeared. Another route is reported to have been climbed but this has no noteworthy qualities, and for ecological reasons, including bird restrictions, it is best left undescribed.

FOCAL BUTTRESS   OS Ref 1338 4343
This is the large, conical buttress that stands proudly guarding the main entrance to The Devil's Limekiln and lies directly opposite to The Great Shutter Rock. The right-hand section of the buttress, clearly visible from the col above Funfair Zawn, is rather broken. It rises above the huge bouldery scree-slope used as part of the descent to the foot of the routes. Apart from the final tower, taken by *Ulysses Factor* and *Messin' With the Kid*, this section of cliff is broken in appearance. In stark contrast to this, the lower left-hand section of the buttress is a magnificent golden wall of unblemished granite, a 150-foot face equal to the best that the island, or indeed the South-West, can offer.

The dominating feature of the lower section of the buttress is the striking left arête taken by *Golden Gate*, which is accessible only at mid to low tide. The rock on the right-hand part of the cliff, while being more broken, is much better than first appearances might suggest. Upon closer inspection, the worst rock proves to be on the ledges; whereas that in between is relatively solid, though still rather lichenous in places.

Messin' With The Kid   180 feet   E3   (31.3.75)
This route climbs the thin crack in the right-hand side of the summit tower and is gained by a scruffy first pitch. The main pitch is now returning to its previously vegetated state and gardening may be necessary. Take some small wires. Start 20 feet down the scree slope below the face, where broken turf ledges lead out onto it.
1 90 feet 4c. Traverse left across the ledges to below a groove. Climb this before moving up a ramp for 10 feet and belaying.
2 90 feet 5b. Sustained. Move up to gain the thin crack in the wall above and follow it, passing a small spike at 60 feet with care. Good holds on the right lead to the top.

Focal Face   260 feet   Very Severe   (31.3.70)
The main focus of attention on this route is the depression in the left side of the main summit tower, taken also by *Ulysses Factor*. This makes the

access pitches rather pointless in view of the superior quality of that route. Start below a short vertical step roughly 100 feet up from the foot of the scree-slope.

1 130 feet 4a. Trend leftwards to gain a shallow groove just left of some black streaks. Climb the groove and easier rock above, keeping left of an obvious crackline. Continue up to a ledge which slopes up and to the left, and move up again to a prominent niche and nut belays.

2 40 feet. Climb up to the right out of the niche, and continue over broken rock to the left to good belays below the depression.

3 90 feet 4b. Climb up to reach the depression and follow it, exiting left at its top to finish.

Lucifer 300 feet Very Severe   (8.4.71)
A wandering line of little virtue up the broken rock to the left. Start 30 feet down the slope, roughly 70 feet from the bottom, and level with a prominent white ledge on the face to the left.

1 30 feet 4c. Make an intimidating traverse up and left via a series of flakes to gain the ledge and peg belay, as for *Ulysses Factor*.

2 70 feet. From the right-hand end of the ledge, climb the centre of the face above on sound rock before moving right to a ledge and belay.

3 30 feet. Move left from the corner; then climb diagonally left across the face to an obvious horizontal fault (peg belay).

4 70 feet. Traverse right along the fault, crossing *Focal Face*, to gain a white slab. Climb this to a horizontal break and peg belay.

5 100 feet. Climb the obvious rake for 50 feet; then continue up the face to a stance in a small corner. Finish by scrambling to belays well back.

★Ulysses Factor 340 feet Very Severe   (29.8.70)
An interesting and very enjoyable expedition giving a climb of mountaineering stature in fine surroundings. Well balanced throughout. Start as for *Lucifer*.

1 30 feet 4c. Make an intimidating traverse up and left along a line of flakes to a ledge and peg belay.

2 120 feet 4b. Climb up and right from the right end of the ledge to reach a traverse-line, and follow this leftwards to gain a crack. Climb this to reach a black groove and follow it until a move left gains some wide ledges and a peg belay.

3 50 feet. Continue on the right via a jagged crack, and climb over easy ground to a belay below a wall.

4 50 feet 4b. Move down rightwards for 10 feet, and then climb back up a yellow wall, trending right, to some ledges below the summit tower. Move right to good nut belays below a depression.

6 90 feet 4b. Excellent climbing leads up right to and through the depression to an exit left at the top.

The sheer golden wall forming the lower part of the buttress provides five climbs of impeccable quality. Unfortunately, the upper walls give climbing of little merit, which is somewhat out of context with that below. For this reason no specific upper pitches have been described.

★★Atlas 300 feet E5 (13.9.82/14.10.89)

An excellent route with bold technical climbing up the right-hand side of the wall. This incorporates *Wimp's Wall*, which avoided the direct challenge by coming in from the right. Start 30 feet right of the arête of the wall, on a flat boulder below a slight arch of black rock.

1 140 feet 6b. Climb direct through the arch to reach a good handhold at 25 feet. Attain a standing-position on this using holds up and to the right. Continue directly to a good ledge to the left of the large ledge of *Ulysses Factor* (good wires up and left). From the right-hand end of the ledge, climb up and rightwards to a thin break. Stand in the break and continue via a thin crack to good holds at the foot of the obvious leftward-trending ramp-line. Follow this, and at its end climb direct up the final wall on good holds to ledges and an old peg belay.

2 160 feet 5a. Pick the easiest line up the broken walls to the top.

★★★Olympica 300 feet E5 (28.8.77)

For many years the hardest route on the island, taking a harrowing line towards the left-hand side of the wall. As standards have risen over recent years, this route has become much sought after, whilst maintaining its bold and daunting status. Now a classic. Start as for *Atlas*.

1 140 feet 6a. Pull through the left side of the arch and move up to gain better holds and a break after 30 feet. Trend diagonally leftwards towards the arête and achieve a position below and 15 feet right of a thin flake, that of *Wild Country*. Now trend back slightly rightwards via a series of vague breaks, generally on good holds, and after 25 feet ascend more directly to reach the sanctuary of ledges at the top of the face (old peg belays).

2 160 feet 5a. Continue up more friendly walls to the top.

The starts of the final trio of routes are based on the lower, water-washed section of the striking arête. These were all originally started on aid from pegs and small wires but the placements are now worn out. A novel and quite commonly used approach is by the use of a 'nailed plank' to reach a thread at 15 feet (not *in situ*, 1993), after which free-climbing can begin. Other interesting ideas such as a human pyramid may spring to mind, though the source of manpower may border on collapse. To make matters worse, the thread itself usually needs replacing at the beginning of every climbing season owing to the effect of high seas.

★★Wild Country 330 feet E4 (2 pts aid) (16.4.74)

A high-class route taking the face right of the arête via an enticing flake high up. Excellent. The described start is rather worn out, so using the aforementioned tactics and then moving right from the thread may be in order. Start 12 feet right of the arête, on a huge boulder.

1 150 feet 5c. Using the shoulder of a strong friend, place a poor peg and use this for aid to place another poor aid peg. Move up and then leftwards to gain a good small ledge on the arête (belay possible should the tide threaten). Continue rightwards to a series of good holds leading up the impending wall to below the flake. Move up and climb the flake to

gain easier ground. Continue slightly left to a slabby rib and follow this to
a belay on a cracked slab.
2 180 feet 5a. Continue by taking two pitches over easier ground to the
top.

★★★**Golden Gate** 320 feet E3 (1 pt aid)   (27.8.77)
Thoroughly absorbing and majestic climbing up the striking arête.
Superb. Start at the foot of the arête.
1 150 feet 6a. Gain the thread by aid, a human pyramid, or the plank;
then step right onto the face and move up to good holds after 15 feet.
Continue direct to a good ledge and optional belay. Now climb the thin
crack almost on the arête, tricky to start, to reach much easier climbing up
the slabby rib. This leads to a nut belay on a cracked slab below a small
overhang.
2 100 feet 5b. Make a rising traverse leftwards to reach a block-filled
corner. Go up this until level with a tall pointed block at about 15 feet, and
then move onto the wall on the left. Continue diagonally left and, just
before the wall's edge, climb direct to a stance and nut belay.
3 70 feet 5b. Climb easily up a ramp for 15 feet, and enter the
overhanging groove above. Climb this to easier ground and belay well
back.

★★★**The Great Divide** 320 feet E3 (1 pt aid)   (13.4.77)
A magnificent pitch up the aesthetically pleasing, gently overhanging
crack in the left wall of the huge arête. Sustained, with positive climbing,
but the route can suffer from a little dampness due to its enclosed nature.
Late afternoon provides the best conditions but only if it is sunny! Start as
for *Golden Gate*.
1 150 feet 5b. Gain the thread of *Golden Gate*; then move left into the
crack and reach good holds above a thin section. Follow the crack with
improving jams until it relents over onto the slab.
2 170 feet 5a. Move up and rightwards and climb up over easier walls
in two pitches to the top.

The huge chasm formed by the wall containing *The Great Divide* leads to
the main tunnel entrance at the base of The Devil's Limekiln.

HIDDEN ZAWN   OS Ref 1346 4344
If you walk through the tunnel entrance into The Limekiln, after 50 yards or
so a narrow, boulder-blocked tunnel will be seen running off to the right.
Struggle down into this and walk carefully through it until it opens out into
a remote and impressive zawn. A more straightforward, but less adventurous approach is by making a scrambling descent of the rib bounding
the zawn to the south of The Limekiln. The rib leads to ledges on its west
side, the boulders at the foot of the rib being accessible only at low tide.
The zawn harbours some excellent routes, which are described **from left
to right.**

THE EAST WALL
The Bow   140 feet   Hard Very Severe   (1 pt aid) †   (1.8.70)
A rightward-slanting line up the wall on the east side of the zawn. Start at
the foot of a steep, black wall, left of a huge block overhang just outside
the tunnel exit.
1 100 feet. Climb the wall, very slippery, and continue leftwards into a
corner. Where the angle steepens higher up, follow a curving line back to
the right on sloping holds beneath overhanging rock. Using a peg for aid
(not in place), step around the arête to a small stance and nut belay.
2 40 feet. Step down for 5 feet and traverse round the arête. Continue
round the next arête and then go easily up to the top.

The following routes take the fine, golden wall to the right, composed of a
series of grooves and cracklines. A black, blocky arête at its foot provides
the starting-point for all the routes.

The belay at the top of these routes is on a large cracked platform. To
regain plateau-level it is best to traverse right across mixed ground and a
small gully to easy boulder-slopes. The direct approach is significantly
steeper and less stable.

⋆⋆**The Lost Banshee**   130 feet   E3 6a   (25.8.88)
Excellent climbing with a technical, yet well-protected crux. From the top
of the black arête, move left to climb up and slightly rightwards to the
base of some thin cracks. Follow these to their end, and then move right
into a rightward-leaning groove. Continue up this until an awkward step
up can be made to gain holds at its top. Finish leftwards via good holds.

⋆⋆⋆**The Demons Within**   135 feet   E4 5c   (25.8.88)
A superb, varied route with excellent exposure. Climb the arête and
continue up the left-most groove to where it becomes stepped. Stride right
onto a sloping ledge and continue past a short crack to gain a shallow
groove. Follow the groove rightwards until a layback move into space
gains good finishing holds.

⋆⋆**The Stone Gollum**   135 feet   E3 5c   (25.8.88)
A fine complement to the neighbouring routes. From the top of the arête,
traverse right along the hanging slab of the lower groove until forced to
make a long reach into an obvious groove. Continue right along the
prominent diagonal, rightward-trending crack to an easier finishing
groove. Alternatively, take the upper hanging slab and continue
rightwards to meet the original route at the diagonal crack (E1 5b).

THE WEST WALL
Labyrinth   220 feet   Very Severe   (23.4.76)
This route follows the diagonal ramp that splits the wall on the west side of
the zawn. Start from the largest boulder in the zawn bed.
1 20 feet 4b. Climb flakes on the left to a ledge and belay.
2 80 feet 4c. From the right end of the ledge, follow the ramp rightwards

until it is possible to step left to a ledge and belay.

3 120 feet 4b. Continue rightwards up a second ramp to an overlap, which is passed to reach the slab above. Climb this via another overlap to the top. Scramble up to block belays on the path.

LEANING BUTTRESS AREA
In the section of cliff north of Focal Buttress and the chasm leading into The Devil's Limekiln there are a series of prominent diagonal faults bounded to the north by a huge leaning buttress. This is in turn separated from the mainland by a gully with a jammed boulder near the top.

Ember Wall   250 feet   Very Severe   (3.6.66)
The steep wall right of the gully with the jammed boulder, on the south side of the buttress. The top pitch is loose. Start at the foot of the rib leading up to the wall from the right.
1 60 feet. Gain the rib from 10 feet up the chimney on the right and follow it until it steepens.
2 40 feet. Move round the arête on the left and climb up to a flake belay on a ledge 15 feet right of the jammed boulder.
3 150 feet. Various lines are possible. Climb the steep wall above; near to the top, traverse either right or left to get off the face. The right exit allows a stance to be taken after 100 feet.

The next three climbs lie immediately to the north of the leaning buttress and are just south of Weird Wall. They can be approached at low tide by wading and climbing through the cave/tunnel beneath the gully separating the leaning buttress from the mainland. This approach adds to the adventure of the routes. They could (possibly) be gained rather wetly by another tunnel 30 feet inland which leads off due north from the main entrance to The Limekiln.

Muffin the Mule   280 feet   Severe †   (8.4.77)
An interesting expedition up the northern face of the huge leaning buttress. Reach the front of the face by a lasso and tyrolean onto low ledges on the other side of the cleft.
1 70 feet. Climb the extreme right-hand edge of the slab to a poor stance but with good belays beneath the large overhang.
2 80 feet 4a. Traverse left to a crack leading up from the left edge of the overhang. Climb this to a recess in the slab above and traverse horizontally into the cleft. Belay on a large boulder.
3 130 feet. Continue up the gully to the gap and go over grassy walls finishing diagonally left to easy ground.

Duffin the Dog   270 feet   Severe †   (30.9.81)
Start at a groove beneath a hanging slab. This is to the right of the nearest slab on the landward side of the cave/tunnel.
1 140 feet. Climb a short groove onto the slab, which is followed to a move right into a chimney. Climb up this and go behind the chockstone to belay on the large boulder as for *Muffin the Mule*.
2 130 feet. *Muffin the Mule* pitch 3.

Pony and Trap   160 feet   Severe †   (8.4.71)
As the name implies in rhyming slang, a climb of dubious quality, though
the dramatic surroundings may be some compensation. Start below the
nearest slab on the landward side of the cave/tunnel.
1 80 feet. Climb the slab to a ledge. Continue up behind the jammed
boulder at the top of the gully to a point where the buttress makes contact
with the mainland.
2 80 feet. Traverse diagonally left on dubious rock to the skyline. Belay
some 30 feet above.

Weird Wall Area

In the bay north of The Shutter Point Area lies a peculiar cliff composed of
a series of rightward-slanting slabs with steep retaining walls below
grassy slopes – Weird Wall. The southern part of this bay is formed by the
headland containing the leaning buttress of *Pony and Trap* et al.

The prominent headland forming the northern part of the bay has a
well-trodden path followed by a flight of steps running down to sea-level.
These were once used to salvage cargo and munitions from the *HMS
Montagu* in 1906, hence the name of Montagu Steps. This headland
contains two buttresses; Montagu Buttress lies just to the south of the foot
of the steps, and Montagu Wall on the south side of the peninsular facing
in a southerly direction.

WEIRD WALL   OS Ref 1328 4352
A strange cliff. The climbing here and on Montagu Wall is of the adventurous type with routes that are rarely repeated. Their atmosphere is enhanced by the complicated and at times mildly desperate approach. The
routes are described from north to south, i.e. **left to right.**

The path leading down to Montagu Steps begins from a small, plateau-
level outcrop, 100 yards north of The Devil's Limekiln. To locate the
descent to Weird Wall, scramble down the grassy slopes below the mid
point of this path to locate a trio of stacked boulders 50 feet below. From
threads on these boulders, abseil down for 60 feet over loose terrain and
a series of small rock spurs onto the top of a large, grassy ramp. Scramble
down the slope formed by this and then across a basalt dyke onto the
summit of a small, south-facing tower. From here the approach involves
some Hard Severe climbing on which the use of a rope may be preferred.
Reverse down the south-facing tower for 20 feet or so; then traverse back
south towards the main cliff, recrossing the dyke to an amorphous juggy
wall. From here the descent depends upon which climb is chosen.

The first two climbs are approached by working up and right, after
recrossing the dyke, to a square, jutting ledge at the left-hand side of the

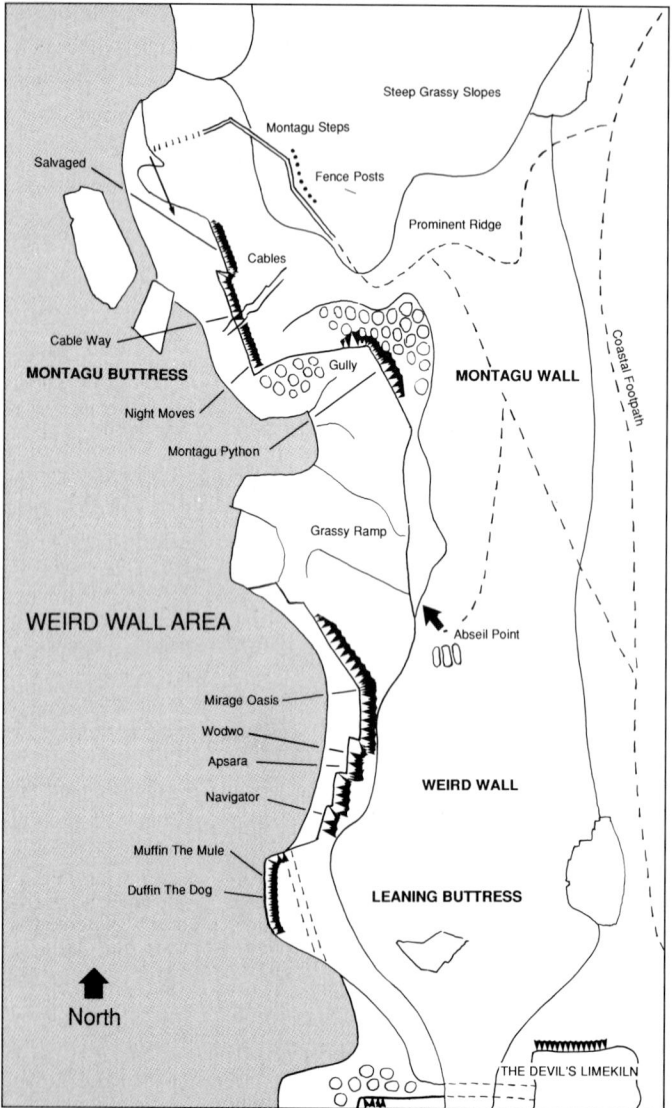

Steep Grassy Slopes

Montagu Steps

Fence Posts

Salvaged

Prominent Ridge

Cables

Cable Way

Coastal Footpath

MONTAGU BUTTRESS

Gully

MONTAGU WALL

Night Moves

Montagu Python

Grassy Ramp

WEIRD WALL AREA

Abseil Point

Mirage Oasis

Wodwo

Apsara

Navigator

WEIRD WALL

Muffin The Mule

Duffin The Dog

LEANING BUTTRESS

North

THE DEVIL'S LIMEKILN

steep slab above a large sea-cave. Belay here on pegs and/or nuts. *Wodwo* and the climbs to its right are gained by picking a route down to the right of the amorphous juggy wall. Continue the approach at low tide by jumping across a gap to slabby rock beneath the big wall. *Astral Traveller* and *Navigator* are then gained by a further 150-foot traverse along the base of the cliff (some Hard Severe climbing) to a black, crack-seamed slab. This point can also be reached, albeit rather wetly, by wading through one of the tunnels north of The Shutter Point Area at low tide.

As an alternative to gaining the summit of the south-facing tower, it is also possible to traverse round from the foot of Montagu Steps underneath Montagu Buttress and so around to the foot of the large grassy ramp. This approach requires low tide but proves far less traumatic for all involved.

Umbgozi   260 feet   E3   (7.75)
Some spectacular climbing on the slabs above the cave is spoiled only by some very loose rock near the top.
1 120 feet 5a. Traverse right across the slab to its right edge and a peg runner. Swing awkwardly round the overhanging arête on the right (some loose rock) to the bottom of a second slab. Climb this to where it vanishes, and then cross the steep wall onto the continuation slab. Move up to a grassy ledge and nut belay.
2 100 feet 5a. Move up the slab for 15 feet, and climb a crack in the left wall. Continue up the face above this to a high, steep slab and climb its corner until close to the top.
3 40 feet 5a. Climb the slab and finish up an unstable final wall.

Mirage Oasis   300 feet   E3   (19.4.76)
The impressive white slab up and to the right of *Umbgozi*, gained via that route's initial pitch. The better of the two routes.
1 120 feet 5a. *Umbgozi* pitch 1.
2 80 feet 4a. Continue pleasantly up the corner of the slab to a nut belay below the final headwall.
3 100 feet 5b. Climb the groove above onto a narrow rightward-leaning ramp. Follow this to a steep exposed groove which leads, with some friable holds, to the top. Scramble up to belays.

★Wodwo   270 feet   E1   (10.9.72)
The main feature of the central wall is a black, slabby groove above an obvious white slab. This route takes these features and offers climbing of an unusual nature with sustained quality but short difficulties. Start below a short, jutting groove, 30 feet right of the gap that is jumped.
1 130 feet 4b. Climb the awkward groove onto the white slab and continue up its left corner to easier ground. This leads to a stance and belay below a steep flake crack and a black, slabby groove.
2 140 feet 5b. Enter the flake crack with difficulty from the right (or directly with even greater difficulty) and follow it to the first slab. Continue past an impressive rock tooth to gain a steep layback-crack leading to the

long, final slab. Climb the slab; then break out left across its left retaining wall to a grassy ledge. Peg belays. Move left and scramble up to the top.

Apsara   280 feet   Hard Very Severe   (13.4.75)
This route follows the long, broad slab taken by the first pitch of *Wodwo* in its entirety. A good route with a big feel to it. Start as for *Wodwo*.
1 140 feet 4a. Traverse right from the ledges into a wide crack leading up and left onto the long slab. Climb this easily to a peg belay at a detached flake half-way up the pasture.
2 140 feet 4c. Continue up the slab to the top, mainly by its right edge. At the finish take care with loose rock and vegetation. Good thread belays well back.

Astral Traveller   200 feet   E3 †   (22.7.77)
A fine and direct route with sustained climbing on the top pitch up the wall left of *Wodwo*. Start at a belay 10 feet left of the black, crack-seamed slab.
1 80 feet 5b. Climb up to gain a sloping ledge beneath a short corner. Move up this, and then follow a thin crack diagonally right to reach good holds on the wall above. Move left, then up to the main slab of *Wodwo*. Continue up this to the belay of that climb.
2 120 feet 5c. Follow *Wodwo* for 6 feet; then move left and climb the obvious flake crack, stepping left at its top into a groove. Move up to the overhang above, and then trend rightwards across the pocketed wall and pull over an overhang to gain a shallow groove. This leads to a spike on *Mirage Oasis*. Traverse right for 6 feet; then climb direct up the wall on widely-spaced holds to reach the exposed finishing groove of *Mirage Oasis*. Climb it with care and belay well back.

★Navigator   200 feet   E1   (18.4.73)
An excellent and varied route centred on the wide impending crack rising from the cave at the right-hand side of the wall. Start near to the top of the black, crack-seamed slab.
1 90 feet 5b. Make a rising traverse up into the crack and follow it to a small stance where the crack gives over onto the slab. Peg belays.
2 50 feet 5b. Continue up the wall above the stance to a large slab, which is climbed to an overhang (peg runner). Using the overhang, traverse right to the arête and climb up to a stance on the big final slab (peg belay).
3 60 feet 4b. Climb a bulge and the slab above to the top. Scramble back to belays.

MONTAGU WALL   OS Ref 1324 4359
'A big yellow wall which on first sight appears to be heaving with semi-detached bungalows. The rock is in fact quite solid once gardened.'
(Keith Darbyshire, 1974)

The buttress is distinguished by the roof-crack of *Montagu Python* at the top of the face. The base of the cliff has a large basalt dyke in its centre.

Access to the foot of the cliff is via the descent to Weird Wall, down the grassy ramp and across the basalt dyke. Alternatively, it is possible to avoid the potential dangers of this more direct approach by traversing round at low tide from the foot of Montagu Buttress. Owing to the unstable nature of parts of the cliff a direct abseil descent is not recommended.

Sunblest   120 feet   Very Severe †   (16.10.74)
The obvious depression on the right-hand side of the face. Climb a corner and good slabs, and then enter a groove from the left. Climb it to a large ledge (belay possible). Regain the groove and follow it to the top.

The most prominent feature at the foot of the face, beside the black dyke, is a steepening gully with a rocky base.

Hooka   140 feet   Hard Very Severe †   (16.10.74)
Start on a pillar 10 feet right of a shallow groove at the foot of the gully.
1 70 feet 4c. Climb up to a rightward-slanting slab and traverse awkwardly right across this. At the end of the traverse, continue straight up a groove, and climb over loose blocks to a ledge and block belay.
2 70 feet 4c. Make a short traverse across the steep wall on the right to a groove. This leads over dubious blocks to a good spike. Traverse right along the obvious line for 10 feet; finish straight up.

The Good Ship Lollipop   190 feet   E1 †   (16.10.74)
Start at the obvious small groove.
1 130 feet 5a. Climb the initial groove and continue straight up to the left of a slab. Gain this and traverse right for 10 feet until below a bulge at the foot of a groove. Climb it direct until a stance can be taken 10 feet to the right of a prominent overhang.
2 60 feet 5a. Climb the steep groove above until a slab beneath the overhang is reached. Traverse left and swing round the arête to a groove leading to the top. Belay well back.

Montagu Python   190 feet   E1   (10.74)
The best route on the face, which gave rise to the 'semi-detached bungalows' quotation. It takes a direct line to finish via the obvious roof-crack. Start as for *The Good Ship Lollipop*.
1 130 feet 5a. Climb the groove to a possible stance at 20 feet. Traverse left for 15 feet to a flake, and then climb a groove to a stance under the prominent overhang.
2 60 feet 5a. Tackle the overhang via the crack to easy but loose ground. Poor belay on a small boulder.

The Queen's Gambit   205 feet   E1 †   (16.10.74)
This climb is centred on the large basalt dyke in the centre of the face, 70 feet to the left of *Montagu Python*. Start 30 feet right of the dyke.
1 35 feet 4b. Climb a steep slab to a ledge and nut belays below a large overhang.
2 50 feet 5b. Traverse left and step across the dyke. Climb up beside it

for 20 feet to a slabby scoop (peg runner). Make a hard move across the steep wall on the right to regain the dyke. Peg belays in the chimney.
3 80 feet 4c. Continue up the dyke until the angle relents and it is possible to gain the steep slab on the right. Climb this and trend right, almost to *Montagu Python*. Move up and left to belay at the foot of a short overhanging groove.
4 40 feet 4b. Climb the groove and loose rock above to the top. Belay well back.

Verdict   230 feet   E1 †   (3.4.75)
Steep climbing with fine positions, though the rock is friable in places. Start at a narrow dyke 50 feet left of the wide basalt dyke taken by *The Queen's Gambit*.
1 100 feet 5a. Follow the dyke over several overhangs until beneath a large roof split by a wide crack (peg runner). Move into the crack above the overhang from the right and climb it to easier ground. Above is a small stance and peg belays.
2 80 feet 4b. Take the obvious line rightwards to a groove on the very edge of the buttress. Continue up it and move left when possible into another groove. Climb this to a large sloping ledge and peg belays.
3 50 feet 4b. Climb the buttress above on good holds to a groove leading to the boulder-slope above.

MONTAGU BUTTRESS   OS Ref 1316 4360
'It must be a million to one shot that the HMS Montagu should run aground at Montagu Steps!'
                                                        (1987 log book)

This small compact cliff offers good climbs, the only misfortune being that those on the left-hand side of the face are crossed by a wide ramp. However, the cliff is of a very pleasant aspect and worth a visit.

The buttress faces west, is about 120 feet high, and is triangular in appearance, the left edge of the triangle being formed by the lower portion of the steps. The apex of the buttress is clearly marked by a group of rusty posts, from which old cables hang down the face. There are two wide rakes slanting up the buttress from left to right. One rake is just below the left edge of the buttress; the other cuts across the centre of the face, some 30 feet left of the right edge of the buttress. Cable Way takes the easiest line up the steep rock below the central rake and finishes close to these cables. The routes are described **from left to right.**

A couple of routes have been climbed on the small subsidiary buttress at the foot of the steps, before the traverse south onto the buttress front is made. Slanting up beneath the buttress is an easy-angled slab.

Built to Destroy   50 feet   Hard Very Severe 4c †   (8.4.87)
From the toe of the buttress, traverse right to gain a large shelf. Follow a slanting break to an overhang, which is passed on its left to gain the slab above.

Salvaged 90 feet E2 5c † (3.8.92)

At the foot of the steps is a steep slab beneath a large, open-book corner of newly-exposed rock. This route climbs the west-facing wall. From well down the slab, follow the wall to a horizontal break and climb this to reach a peg runner. Step back left and continue to the top. Alternatively, finish direct from the peg. Belay to some posts well back.

From the foot of the steps, continue the traverse south across seaweed-covered rock to reach the base of the buttress front. This is possible only at low tide. A slightly higher traverse can be made to the same point but with some climbing of Very Difficult standard involved. Otherwise, an abseil from the iron posts at the top of the cliff will have to be made, in which case it is advisable to use an extra rope to reach back to the posts.

Cable and Wireless 120 feet Hard Very Severe (30.8.70)

A contrived line but with some worthwhile climbing. Start below a small overhang beneath the mid point of the central rake, 10 feet left of the foot of a prominent, slanting crack.

1 50 feet. Climb the wall to belay on the rake.

2 70 feet 5a. Wander up the rake to reach the cables and climb up just to the left of these for 20 feet. Traverse horizontally left with difficulty to reach a vegetated layback-flake leading to the top.

★Cable Way 110 feet Very Difficult (30.9.69)

A good and well-situated route with very enjoyable climbing. Start below a prominent rightward-slanting crack.

1 60 feet. Climb the crack for 20 feet; steeper climbing on good holds leads to a recess. Move right and up to a ledge. Continue direct, or move right and then back left, to reach a broken corner. Climb this to belay on the highest point of the central rake.

2 50 feet. Climb steep broken rock above, just left of the cables, to the top. Take care with some unsound rock on this pitch.

Variations

1a 60 feet 4b. From the start, move across at a lower level until below the end of the obvious break. Climb steeply on spaced holds to finish up cracks on the right to the stance.

1b 60 feet 4b. After the original start has moved right then up, continue rightwards for 30 feet in the diagonal faultline. Climb round two corners, almost to the cables, and then continue up flaky corners beside these to a pinnacle above an earthy ledge.

Below the right edge of the buttress is a slab above the seaweed level. This marks the start of *Sundance; Night Moves* starts at the left-hand side of this slab.

Night Moves 105 feet Hard Severe 4b (2.9.87)

Climb the slab diagonally rightwards for 30 feet to a steep broken wall. Move up this on large spaced holds and trend rightwards to pull onto the large sloping block beneath a small black roof. Move up and pull out right around this; then climb steep broken rock above. Finish left onto a large ledge above.

Sundance   120 feet   Severe   (25.8.71)
A pleasant climb over steep rock and with good holds. Climb up to the top of the slab and move up to an overhang. Traverse right under this to a crack and follow it for 20 feet. Traverse right across a black wall, past a dubious block, to a groove in the right edge of the buttress. Climb the groove to an overhang, which is passed on its right to a leftwards finish.

Montagu Steps to the Old Light

The section of coastline between Montagu Steps and the Old Light is of little interest to the climber, with scrappy cliffs and poor routes. So much so that many have not been repeated for twenty years! Climbers seeking complete esoterica without the prying eyes of others will find queuing totally unnecessary but a yard brush and excavator essential!

GOAT ISLAND   OS Ref 1310 4370
In the bay north of Montagu Steps is an obvious large island connected to the mainland by boulders on its eastern side. An easy grassy gully gives the descent to the island. One route has been recorded: **Black Beard** (90 feet Very Severe 4c 26.8.89) climbs a corner and rightward-slanting crack above a high-tide ledge and gives a pleasant outing.

South of Goat Island lie three sea stacks, Les Aiguilles du Montagu, the eastern two providing a trio of routes: **Flash Dance** (80 feet Very Severe 5a 8.4.88) takes the central crack on the south-west face of the eastern stack, while **Flight of the Valkyrie** (60 feet Very Severe 5a 8.4.88) passes an overhang and takes a crack on the south-west face to the apex of the central stack; **Gollum's Revenge** (60 feet Very Severe 4c 8.4.88) follows a corner 10 feet to its left.

ROBBIE'S REDOUBT   OS Ref 1317 4378
The bay containing Goat Island is formed to the north by a headland. On its southern side is a small, steep cliff gained via a difficult descent of the headland, followed by a traverse in. **Strider** (150 feet Severe 25.3.74) takes a line right of an obvious faultline in three pitches via a series of cracks and grooves.

CELTIC BUTTRESS   OS Ref 1313 4380
This buttress lies to the north of the headland and is gained via a northwards traverse after the same initial descent as for Robbie's Redoubt. **Celtic Shield** (250 feet Very Severe 4c 5a 4c 7.7.73) climbs a

groove to below an impressive retaining wall, makes a long traverse right via a crack to avoid it, and escapes via a corner and slabs.

ATLANTIC BUTTRESS
OS Ref 1302 4389

Two hundred yards north of the headland containing the last two cliffs, a broken path leads down just north of a dammed stream to a flight of steps, Pilot's Quay. A hundred yards south of this lies Atlantic Buttress, which can be gained by descending the rocky rib leading down to a small headland. A traverse is then made to the south until a very-far-from-obvious 20-foot abseil goes down an overhanging groove. The traverse is then continued until a faultline slanting up and to the right is reached. **Atlantic Reject** (160 feet Very Severe 4c 5a 7.7.73) follows this faultline in two pitches before making a third, exit pitch over easier terrain. **Irish Roulette** (100 feet Severe 20.3.74) takes two pitches to climb an easier line 20 feet to the left via a half-height belay on a pile of boulders.

PILOT'S QUAY
OS Ref 1299 4396

The broken path and flight of steps previously mentioned lead down to a small buttress. This buttress is detached from the mainland in a fashion similar to Flying Buttress, though it is much smaller and less fine.

A short route is given by the north face of the buttress: **Quay Hole Corner** (70 feet Very Difficult 7.7.73), which starts by a downward traverse to a small ledge on the edge of the arch and follows the left arête of the slabs pleasantly to the top. The broken right arête of the front of the buttress gives a rather artificial route when followed closely: **Pacific Portal** (100 feet Very Difficult 7.7.73) has some pleasant exposure if the easy rock to one side is avoided and the line followed closely.

Old Light Area

From the Old Light northwards, and for quite some distance, the cliffs regain their grandeur and provide a series of imposing faces, zawns, and promontories with a wealth of superb and varied climbing. Originally climbed on in the early 70s, these faces have been more recently developed to give some of the hardest and most arduous routes on the island to date.

Directly beneath the Old Light lies a huge gully with a fence overlooking its northern rim. This fence runs down to the top of a prominent buttress, outlined by a large slabby arête: The Old Light Cliff. Immediately to the north lies the imposing Black Crag, its once lichen-covered face now gardened to give some impressive routes. This face is bounded by a huge zawn, Two Legged Zawn, the scene of many newly-climbed groove-lines. Two Legged Buttress is the final cliff of the area, proudly guarding the entrance to its neighbouring zawn and giving a handful of pleasant routes.

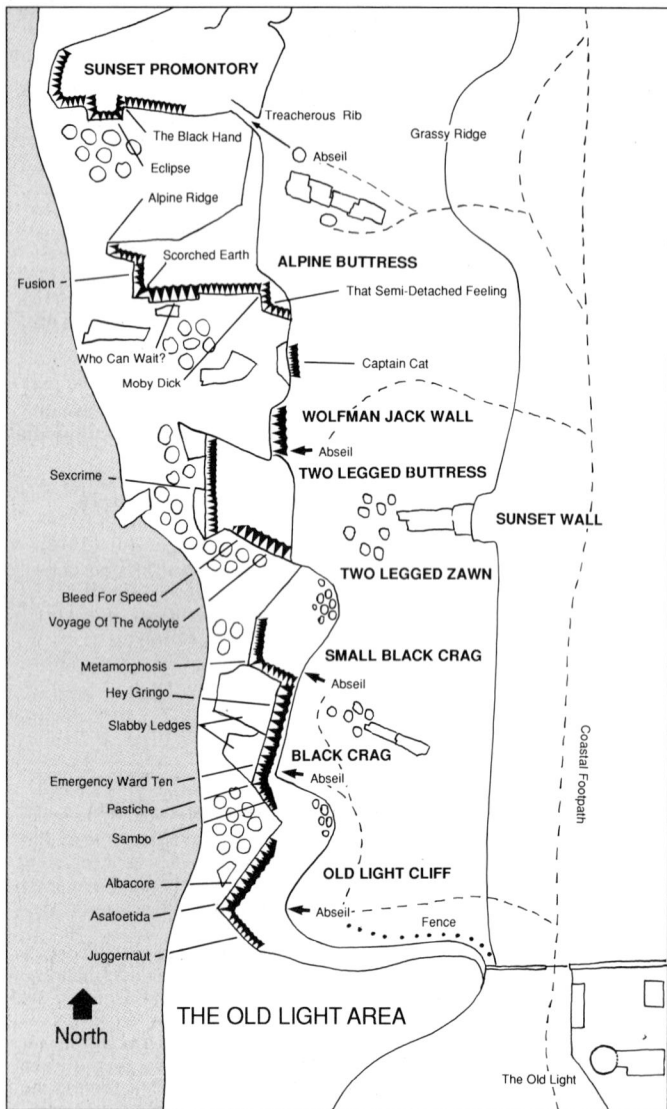

SUNSET PROMONTORY

Treacherous Rib

Grassy Ridge

Abseil

The Black Hand

Eclipse

Alpine Ridge

Scorched Earth

ALPINE BUTTRESS

Fusion

That Semi-Detached Feeling

Who Can Wait?

Captain Cat

Moby Dick

WOLFMAN JACK WALL

Abseil

TWO LEGGED BUTTRESS

Sexcrime

SUNSET WALL

TWO LEGGED ZAWN

Bleed For Speed

Voyage Of The Acolyte

Metamorphosis

SMALL BLACK CRAG

Hey Gringo

Abseil

Slabby Ledges

BLACK CRAG

Emergency Ward Ten

Abseil

Pastiche

Sambo

Albacore

OLD LIGHT CLIFF

Asafoetida

Abseil

Fence

Juggernaut

Coastal Footpath

THE OLD LIGHT AREA

North

The Old Light

Diamond Solitaire The Flying Buttress
Climber: Bob Moulton   *Photo:* Tom Valentine

Emergency Ward Ten Black Crag
Climber: Mike Owen   *Photo:* Gary Gibson

THE OLD LIGHT CLIFF   OS Ref 1295 4428
The huge, slabby arête dominating the cliff is flanked to the north by a
large, predominantly lichenous face. The gardened streaks up this repre-
sent excellent climbs in the form of *Albacore* and *Asafoetida*. To the right
of the arête the cliff is less friendly and split by the large slanting crack of
Juggernaut. The top of this section of buttress, especially in the region of
Time Bomb, is potentially dangerous ground owing to an earthquake-like
ravine that has opened up, separating it from the mainland.

The most popular mode of descent to the boulder-beach at the foot of the
cliff, for which low tide is required, is a 200-foot abseil down the slabby
north face from good block belays. This approach also gives a good
anchor should the dangerous boulder-slope at the top have to be
renegotiated; and it enables the starts to be omitted if the tide is too high.
Otherwise, one can approach via steep and unstable ground to the south
– one of the most harrowing descents on the island. The grassy slopes on
the south side of the large gully lead down until about 150 feet above
sea-level, where a northwards descent over treacherous ground gains the
boulder-beach. Low tide is then required to gain the routes in the vicinity
of *Albacore*, though routes to the south may be reached via a traverse at a
higher level. The cliff can also be approached from the north by one of
many descents to other cliffs followed by a traverse south across the
boulder-field.

The Brick Wall   200 feet   E2 †   (30.8.81)
The crack-seamed wall to the right of the prominent slanting cracks in the
south face. A good route marred by an appallingly loose finish. Start on
some ledges at 20 feet.
1 120 feet 5b. Climb the initial slanting cracks to a ledge; continue up a
groove and further cracks to below an overhang. Turn this on its left; then
step right to a groove leading to a second overhang. Move right to a
sloping ledge to belay.
2 80 feet 5c. Follow a slanting groove on the left to a ledge and move
left to a corner. Climb up for 10 feet; then traverse left to finish up some
thin cracks in the right-hand side of the arête. Belays lie well back.

Juggernaut   200 feet   E1   (9.5.71)
A bold and strenuous route requiring a forceful approach. It takes the
prominent slanting crackline right of the central arête.
1 70 feet 5a. Climb the crack to a pedestal stance.
2 80 feet 5a. Follow the crack for 20 feet to where the rock becomes
loose; then trend right across the wall on good flakes. Move up to a
horizontal crack, and step back left to continue up the wide crack to a
stance.
3 50 feet 4c. The corner above. Exit left at the top to a loose finish.

Time Bomb   210 feet   E3   (29.5.72/8.77)
Intimidating and strenuous. The cracked, orange wall between
Juggernaut and the arête. Not for the faint-hearted.

1 120 feet 4b. Follow some cracks just right of a groove in the arête, via pleasant climbing, to a terrace below the upper wall.
2 90 feet 5c. Climb the obvious crack to its end and continue via a second crack on the right for a few moves. Cross the wall to the right to gain an overhanging groove. This gives an invigorating finale.

For the next three routes, it is advisable to prefix a rope on the top, earthy slope to safeguard the finishes.

★Saffron   200 feet   E2   (5.8.88)

The first of a number of less harrowing routes takes the faint groove in the right-hand side of the arête. Enjoyable climbing with reliable protection when needed. Start on some rounded boulders at the foot of the arête.
1 50 feet 4c. Climb the arête and an obvious V-groove in its right-hand side to reach some ledges. Nut belays in a diagonal crack to the left.
2 100 feet 5c. Move right and up to gain the groove, where pleasant climbing (small wires) leads to a peg runner in the left wall. Make a stiff pull onto the right side of the arête, where further difficult moves (peg runner) gain a small ledge up and left. Two-bolt belay.
3 50 feet 4c. Traverse left to gain the wide crack of *Albacore*, and finish up it and the earthy slope. Prefixed rope strongly advised – see note above.

★★Asafoetida   200 feet   E1   (5.8.88)

Since its discovery, this has proved to be the most popular route on the slab, taking its right-hand and cleanest side. Amenable, with good protection. Start as for *Saffron*.
1 50 feet 4c. Follow the arête before stepping left and continuing up a thin crack-system to gain a small ledge and nut belay.
2 100 feet 5b. Move leftwards to gain the continuation crack and follow it, passing an easier central section, until awkward moves gain a small ledge on the arête. Two-bolt belay.
3 50 feet 4c. Traverse left to gain the wide crack of *Albacore*. Finish up it and the earth slope. Prefixed rope strongly advised – see note above.

★Albacore   200 feet   Hard Very Severe   (8.5.71)

A good route taking the thin crack-system 20 feet left of the arête. Sustained, and with a finish that will test the nerve of most leaders. Start on a huge boulder 30 feet left of the arête.
1 140 feet 5a. Stride left onto the slab and then take a rightward-rising line to gain the crackline. Climb this past an overhang where the crack strikes left to a stance with a poor belay. Alternatively, better belays but a less comfortable stance are available below the overhang. The latter is safer for the second man in view of the nature of the second pitch. (If this is not used, extreme care is needed on the next pitch to avoid dislodging stones onto the rest of the party.)
2 60 feet 4c. Take the crack above, which gradually opens out onto an unstable earth slope. Fifty feet of scrambling remains: prefixed rope strongly advised – see note above.

The left-hand side of the slab is becoming increasingly overgrown and covered in sea-grass. Two routes once traced cleaned lines up this area of rock but they are slowly becoming difficult to identify. Should anyone feel eager enough to reclean these, they may find the following descriptions and a large brush useful.

The Lantern Man   270 feet   Very Severe   (5.10.78)
Start just left of the boulder at the foot of *Albacore*.
1 120 feet 4b. Climb up to a terrace at 25 feet; then go up a thin jagged crack to the right until a rising traverse can be made to the left of a recess. Move a few feet further left and climb up, trending right, to a stance and good nut belays.
2 150 feet 4c. Traverse left; then move up and back right to the foot of a crack. Climb this until a step left can be made to a small corner and continue to the top. Scramble to block belays.

Lady in White   265 feet   Hard Very Severe   (9.10.78)
Start 20 feet left of *The Lantern Man* below some obvious cracks.
1 140 feet 5a. Climb the cracks to the left end of a terrace at 25 feet. Continue up the same crackline to ledges. Move up and rightwards for a few feet, in common with *The Lantern Man*, and then take a line up to the left. After 25 feet, step left to a point beneath a bulging, shield-like feature. Climb steeply up to gain small ledges (nut belay to the left). The initial cracks can be avoided if they are wet or inaccessible owing to the tide by climbing the first 25 feet of *The Lantern Man* and walking along the terrace.
2 125 feet 5a. Climb the cracks above the stance and move right where they peter out. Move up and left with difficulty to good finishing holds. Scramble steeply to boulder belays.

The original route in this area, **Hunky Dory** (210 feet Very Severe 21.7.73), took the line of *Lady in White* for 80 feet and then followed *The Lantern Man* to its stance. After this a rightward traverse into *Albacore* was made.

BLACK CRAG   OS Ref 1294 4436
For many years this magnificent face lay virgin whilst others were peppered with routes. As standards increased and attitudes changed, it was inevitable that this face should draw its own suitors. After an early and bold undertaking by Matt Priestman, sound *in-situ* protection and hard routes became the order of the day in 1986/7. Since those bastardized origins, enormous pressure was exerted and the bolts have begun to be whittled away. Now the face is one of the best of its type on the island. Here, technical and sustained wall-climbing can be coupled with good or bad protection according to taste.

The wall is supported by two slabby legs with a slippery V-channel between them. The best access to the legs is by abseil from thread and block belays on the cliff-top, themselves difficult to locate. They are best gained by traversing the bracken slope to the north of the fence at the top of The Old Light Cliff for 50 yards past a small boulder-strewn depression at the top of the cliff to gain a vague grassy spur. A 150-foot abseil from the spur leads down to the apex of the right-hand leg. To gain the left-hand leg it is possible to cross the V-channel at low tide or to boulder-hop from other cliffs to the north or south. This, however, can be slow and arduous, so a 170-foot abseil, from blocks 20 yards further north of the grassy spur, leads down the centre of the face to the slabs below.

Sambo   240 feet   Hard Very Severe   (19.4.73)

Pleasant and open climbing after a dank start. It takes a line up the walls to the right of the main black face and at right-angles to the *Albacore* slab. Start on a rounded boulder in the back of the small zawn to the left of the *Albacore* slab.

1 80 feet 4b. Enter a small sea-cave and climb up the back of it until it is possible to move out left into the obvious crackline.
2 40 feet 4c. Continue up the wall above to a prominent black layback-groove, which is followed to a ledge.
3 30 feet 5a. Climb a diagonal crack round the edge to a small stance.
4 90 feet 4c. The overgrown slabby wall above (peg runner) leads to the top. Thread belay.
Variation
3a 50 feet 5b. Step right into a groove, which leads to the final wall. Sustained.

The remaining routes lie on the main black face, which can be reached by climbing a 5a pitch up a leftward-slanting crack and pleasant slabs in the left wall of the zawn containing *Sambo* or, more appropriately, via one of the aforementioned abseils.

★Pastiche   120 feet   E3 5c   (31.7.86)

The clean brown groove and right arête of the face. A good route, providing a more direct version of *Blue Jaunt*. From the apex of the right-hand leg, move up the faultline and continue up the arête to gain the main groove. Climb this to the roof and turn it on the right to gain the face right of the arête. Cross immediately back to the left to the arête and follow this to easier ground and the top.

Blue Jaunt   120 feet   E3 5c   (14.4.74)

A little overgrown in its upper reaches and somewhat superseded by adjacent routes. Follow *Pastiche* to the roof in the groove, and then move left onto the lichenous arête. Climb a series of dirty cracks to gain a flat-topped spike; then traverse left to a junction with *Doctor's Orders*. Move left and finish up a groove.

★Doctor's Orders   120 feet   E4 6a   (27.7.86)

Worthwhile, though overshadowed by adjacent routes. Start 10 feet left of *Pastiche*. Pull up to and over a bulge to gain some thin cracks. These lead to a sloping ledge, from where the cracks continue up a cleaned streak in the face to a prominent jug on the left. Move left into and finish up a short corner.

★★Black and Blue   120 feet   E5 6a   (10.10.82)
The first route to venture onto this magnificent face. The lack of trustworthy protection and the hollow nature of some of the holds make it a demanding lead. Start as for *Doctor's Orders*. Break out diagonally left across the face to gain a small groove and sloping ledge below a vague, continuous crackline. Follow this by delicate climbing and a peg runner at 70 feet, a scary clip. Once gained, a short bottomless groove leads to the top.

★★My Life in My Hands   120 feet   E6 6a   (29.7.86/5.8.89)
A very fine and sustained pitch up the compact wall to the left. Limited small-wire protection makes this a bold and quite frightening proposition. Start at a short wide crack, 15 feet down the face from the top of the leg. Pull out left onto the face (*Friend 4* useful) and go straight up to a sloping ledge. Move up to a second ledge; then step tentatively left and up to a welcome jug. Stand up rather awkwardly and continue up to and through an overlap, to finish rightwards.

★★The Colour of Life   190 feet   E6   (6.8.87)
Unusual and intimidating climbing across the face via a prominent diagonal break. An invigorating lead and unsuitable for a timid second, unless of course you are prepared to reverse the pitch.
1 120 feet 6b. Pull out left onto the face (*Friend 4* useful) and go straight up to a sloping shelf, as for *My Life in My Hands*. Then go left and descend slightly, hands on the obvious ramp, by precarious moves to gain the break. Swing left into the thin crack of *Emergency Ward Ten* and so gain a good shelf and respite. Move left along the shelf; then swing down and finger-traverse left to reach better holds on a vague rugosity rib on *Mayan Skies*. Move back up to the break (peg runner) and prepare for the final crux sprint. Two peg runners provide protection before moves up lead to a sloping shelf. *Friend 1½*, *Rock 6*, and peg belays.
2 70 feet 5c. Your second's pitch! Climb straight up above the stance, via a series of rightward-slanting flakes, to pass a small overhang to the left. Move up for a further 10 feet, and then go right to gain belays on a ledge. Scrambling remains.

★★Emergency Ward Ten   130 feet   E6 6b   (31.7.86/5.8.89)
The straight thin crack splitting the right-hand side of the wall. A magnificent pitch incorporating immaculate, sustained climbing on a very strong natural line. A modern classic. Start 30 feet down from the apex of the right-hand leg. A scary start up a short, hanging corner leads onto the wall and a welcome peg runner. Technical moves up and then a long reach right lead to the base of the crack. Follow this with continuous difficulties until they ease at the small overlap. Pull over this and saunter up the headwall to the top.

★★Intensive Care 140 feet E6 6b   (26.7.87/5.8.89)
Another highly commendable climb, more technical than its neighbouring
routes but with better resting-places. As for *Emergency Ward Ten*, a scary
start up a short, hanging corner leads onto the wall (peg runner). Now
tackle the difficult wall above to gain a sloping shelf. The next section of the
wall proves even more taxing, via small face holds (bolt and peg runner) to
the right-hand side of a large ledge. Step right and climb the wall through
an overlap to a grassy ledge. *Friend 3* and thread belay well back.

★★★Mexico Speaks 155 feet E7 6c   (31.7.87)
The first of a group of stunning routes up the centre of the sheer black face.
Technically desperate climbing at a couple of points. A classic in the
modern idiom. Start at the right-hand side of the left-hand leg (no belay).
Move up and rightwards to gain a diagonal break and undercut hold.
Stand up (bolt runner, hanger removed) and then make hard, blind moves
right and then up to gain a thin overlap. Undercut right along this and pull
over from a good sidehold (bolt runner) onto the wall. Continue boldly for
20 feet to a good edge (bolt runner) and then step right and scratch
frantically up to a break for wires. Stand up in a shallow groove (peg
runner) and pull onto a ledge (low peg runner). From the left-hand end of
this, make a couple of decisive pulls (micro wires) to reach an overlap and
thread runner. Pull over and finish straight up. *Friend 3* and thread belays
well back.

★★★Mayan Skies 160 feet E7 6b †   (31.7.86/5.8.89)
Since the removal of its four bolt runners, this route must lay claim to being
the most serious route on the island; a fall from hard moves at 80 feet will
leave you on the ground. An abseil inspection is strongly recommended.
Inspirational. Start as for *Mexico Speaks*. Move up just left of *Mexico
Speaks* to gain a bulge and hidden peg runner, and pull awkwardly
through onto a hanging slab and another peg runner. Continue slightly
rightwards onto the foot of a faint rugosity rib, where sustained, technical
climbing, demanding the ultimate in confidence, gains a break (peg
runner). Make a particularly trying move rightwards to gain a ledge (low
peg runner) and sanity. From the right-hand end of this, climb directly on
good holds to an overlap. Pull through and move left to finish at a grassy
platform. *Friend 3* and thread belays well back.

★★★Hey Gringo 155 feet E7 6b †   (6.8.88)
Superlative wall-climbing requiring finesse, stamina, and technical know-
how. Super-sustained. Start 10 feet left of *Mayan Skies*. Pull over an overlap
(bolt runner) to gain a short, hanging groove leading to a slab (bolt runner).
Pull up onto the wall; then, with a concentrated effort, trend slightly
rightwards past two bolt runners to gain a diagonal break crossing the wall
(peg runner). Step left and balance desperately up the smooth wall (bolt
runner) to gain a standing-position on a small black block. Step right and
move up past some sloping breaks (bolt runner) until bold moves gain a
niche and the end of the difficulties.   Finish up a cleaned groove on the
right.

★★★**Chitzen Itza**   165 feet   E6 6c †   (13.8.93)
A sensational left-to-right diagonal crossing of the face. A mixture of hard
and bold moves which, fortunately, are never combined. Start up *Hey
Gringo*. From the second bolt runner, traverse right across the slab to a
thin break (peg runner). Move up for 10 feet before traversing right again
to a good edge on *Mexico Speaks* (bolt runner). Gain the diagonal ledge
out to the right by hard moves; tip-toe down and then up into the thin crack
of *Emergency Ward Ten*. Move up for a few feet and step right to a line of
jugs leading boldly rightwards, as for *My Life in My Hands*, and then into
the thin crackline of *Black and Blue*. Finish up this via a hanging groove. A
preplaced rope is advisable at the top.

SMALL BLACK CRAG   OS Ref 1293 4437

This subsidiary buttress stands forward of the main black face. While its
left-hand side degenerates into a long, grassy ramp forming the south
side of Two Legged Zawn, its right-hand side provides a very compact
face of immaculate black granite.

It is possible to gain the face by either of two means. The best approach is
by making a direct abseil on joined ropes (200 feet) from blocks in the
bracken slopes; these are situated just south of the bouldery, earth cornice
overlooking Two Legged Zawn. Initially this leads down a large grassy
slope to the cliff summit, from where it is best to abseil down its left side
(facing out) to easy slabs below. This method helps procure a safe belay
as well as an escape from the top of the routes. Alternatively, it can be
gained from the left-hand leg of Black Crag but the subsequent escape to
the summit then proves more arduous without the attendant abseil rope.

On all the routes the abseil rope, if in place, provides the belay. Otherwise an *in-situ* peg on the back wall will have to be used.

★★**Chameleon Kiss**   80 feet   E5 6b †   (2.8.93)
Brutal climbing up the brown, south wall via a series of discontinuous
cracks. Start by taking a belay close to the wall. A technical and bold start
gains the cracks, which are followed to their conclusion. Where they fade,
hard moves left gain better holds and the top.

★★**Metamorphosis**   80 feet   E5 6b †   (2.8.93)
A splendid pitch up the arête of the buttress. Technically absorbing with
good protection. From a belay on the slabs, move easily up and left
across a small dyke to a point just left of the foot of the arête. Climb a thin
crack to a block, and then step right. Continue delicately up the arête to
the right-hand end of a sloping shelf (peg runner) and swing precariously
left to a jug. Climb the shallow groove above (peg runner) to gain a thin
break on the headwall (peg runner) and exit right.

★★**Death-Watch Beetle-Drive**   85 feet   E6 6b   (25.9.85)
An esoteric gem up the right-hand side of the face. Sustained difficulties
with just sufficient protection demand a positive approach. Move up the

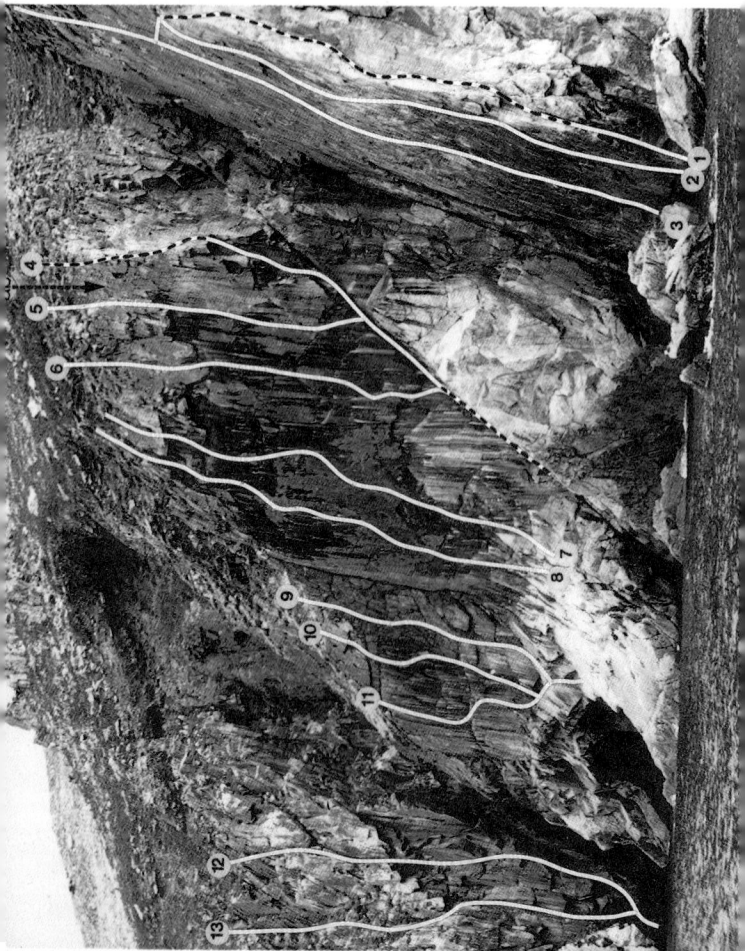

THE OLD LIGHT CLIFF AND BLACK CRAG

slabs and traverse left to a thin crack 12 feet left of the arête. Climb this and a short wall to gain a small groove. Swing out left at the top of this to gain a diagonal crack (small wires) and overcome the crux wall above to gain a wide break. Move leftwards to finish.

Grizzled Skipper 90 feet E5 6a   (25.9.85)
Enigmatic in character, and bold. Follow *Death-Watch Beetle-Drive* up the thin crack to a ledge-system. Traverse left along this for 12 feet; then climb straight up to a good rest before the last, and crux, move.

SUNSET WALL   OS Ref 1299 4442
At plateau-level, 150 yards north of the Old Light, is a large outcrop of rock, the most distinctive hereabouts, with a narrow summit ridge. The seaward face of this provides **Sunset Wall** (50 feet E2 6a 1.8.85), a slight route taking the overhang and slender pillar direct. This outcrop also provides a convenient landmark for access to the top of the next two cliffs.

TWO LEGGED ZAWN   OS Ref 1295 4438
This imposing zawn hosts a congregation of outstanding climbs, mostly created in the mid 80s. On entrance, the most notable features of the north wall are a trio of imposing grooves soaring skywards from a little way above the zawn bed. These provide the meat of the routes. The south wall is slabby and vegetated, and gives no routes. Inevitably, the north wall receives sunshine until about 4 p.m. and is subject to mid-tide access. The face also suffers from seepage after a prolonged wet spell – a few days of good weather with a pleasant coastal breeze usually dries things off.

The top of the zawn is easily gained via the bouldery slopes below Sunset Wall. Reaching the zawn bed is more of a problem. A direct 200-foot abseil down either of the walls leads to the foot of the cliff. Should joined ropes have to be used, on the north wall jumars will be essential to pass the knots; the slabby nature of the south wall makes things less problematic. Easier approaches, by crossing the boulder-field from the north or south, are obvious, most notably from Wolfman Jack Wall. However, as the tide cuts off any form of retreat relatively quickly, this adds further to the seriousness and atmosphere. The route are described **from left to right.**

*★***The Last Crusade** 210 feet E5 †   (1.8.89)
Short, sharp, and worthwhile. Start below the first main groove-line in the left-hand side of the zawn.
1 80 feet 6b. Climb the obvious easy groove to reach an overhanging niche. Pull through and continue up the left-hand side of the wall to easy ground. Move left to a thread and nut belay.
2 130 feet. Finish by following the right-hand side of the arête above, via a small corner, flakes, and cracks.

★★**Bleed for Speed** 260 feet E2   (31.8.76)
The first and left-hand of the three grooves seen when entering the zawn.
Fine technical climbing on excellent rock, which deteriorates only towards
the top of the second pitch.
1 120 feet 5c. Climb strenuously through the guarding overhang at 15
feet, and step left just above into the smooth V-groove. Climb this and make
a steep pull through a small overhang. Continue up the groove to a hanging
belay beneath the large capping overhang.
2 140 feet. Move left; then go up easier corners and very unstable ground
to the top. Block belays well back.

★★★**Ark of the Covenant** 250 feet E5   (1.8.88)
Superb, direct climbing with excellent protection and positions. A good
sampler to the harder routes in the zawn and the quickest line on the wall to
dry.
1 150 feet 6b. As for *Bleed for Speed*, climb through the guarding
overhang at 15 feet and so reach an obvious roof at 30 feet. Then move
awkwardly right to gain a huge flake, above which lies a vertical, left-
facing edge. A few technical moves up this (crux) lead to the base of the
upper groove (peg runner). Follow the groove to some good flakes on the
left wall, just below a small overhang on the right, and layback round to
reach a small, slabby nose and downward-pointing spike on the
right.   Swing right and up via unhelpful cracks to a niche and overhang. Exit
right under a fang of rock to gain a groove leading to a nest belay.
2 100 feet 4b. Go more easily off rightwards, then back left to the
boulder-slope. Belay well back.

★★★**Voyage of the Acolyte** 260 feet E6   (12.8.87)
An awesome route, one of Lundy's finest, up the main central groove-line.
Varied and intimidating, thus placing large demands on the leader. Spaced
protection.
1 90 feet 6b. Climb 15 feet to the guarding overhang of *Bleed for Speed*,
and traverse right below an overhang to a small ledge. Move boldly up to
the foot of an overhanging corner, often damp; then bridge up (peg runner)
and move left onto the wall and up to a break. Gain the overhanging corner
above and stretch for a good hold at its top – cut loose! Continue straight up
(peg runner) and scrabble frantically into the open groove above (crux).
Take a hanging belay in this (*Rock 5, Friends*, and peg).
2 70 feet 6b. Climb up left to the foot of a smooth groove and traverse left
to the arête – hard. Layback up and then climb direct up rounded cracks to
a resting-place in a niche below the capping roof. Exit right below a fang of
rock to a groove and belay above as for *Ark of the Covenant*.
3 100 feet 4b. *Ark of the Covenant* pitch 2.

★★**The Quest** 265 feet E6 †   (6.8.89)
The hardest route in the zawn, using the crux pitch of *Voyage of the Acolyte*
as an entry pitch to gain the wildly-positioned hanging groove to the right.
Very forceful climbing.
1 90 feet 6b. *Voyage of the Acolyte* pitch 1.

TWO LEGGED ZAWN

1 The Dog's Bollocks   E6

2 Voyage of the Acolyte   E6
3 The Quest   E6
4 Ark of the Covenant   E5
5 Bleed for Speed   E2
6 The Last Crusade   E5

2 75 feet 6c. Entry to the base of the right-hand groove proves frustrating and desperate (peg runner). If you find the key, continue past a spike before pulling up through the bulge to the left, rocking up into the base of the overhanging niche. Exit rightwards, with a bit of a squeeze, to finish. *Friend* and peg belay on the ledge.

3 100 feet. 5a. Gain ledges and cracks above the belay. From these, a short traverse left leads to a finishing scramble.

★★★**The Dog's Bollocks** 270 feet E6 †   (3.9.91)

A much sought-after line up the right-hand and final slim groove in the wall. Technical and sustained throughout its length, where dry conditions are essential.

1 50 feet 6a. Climb 15 feet to the guarding overhang of *Bleed for Speed*, and traverse right below an overhang to a small ledge. Move boldly up to the foot of an overhanging corner, often damp, and bridge up to beneath a peg runner; then traverse right to a peg and *Friend 1* belay.

2 120 feet 6b. Step right and climb the slim groove via sustained moves through a series of small overlaps (four peg runners). Where the groove opens out, continue to a good ledge with a *Friend* and peg belay.

3 100 feet 5a. *The Quest* pitch 3.

★★**The Grail Trail** 200 feet E4 †   (30.7.89)

A fine expedition providing a good view of the zawn's routes. Start on a large ledge on the arête of the right-hand leg of Two Legged Buttress. This can be gained by abseil or from *Pinstripe*.

1 100 feet 6a. Climb across rightwards to the corner and pull onto the wall at a short, thin horizontal crack. Hard moves down and right gain a narrow ledge on *Bleed for Speed*. Ascend the groove for a few moves; then move right into *Ark of the Covenant*, which is followed to its final roof. After swinging right, move right again into a hidden niche. A struggle through its top gains a large ledge on the right and a *Friend* and peg belay, as for *The Quest*.

2 100 feet 5a. *The Quest* pitch 3.

TWO LEGGED BUTTRESS   OS Ref 1293 4440

The bounding edge of Two Legged Zawn is formed by an A-shaped buttress with two slabby legs supporting its upper reaches. Above this lies a short earthy bank giving access to the grassy slopes below plateau-level. This face has achieved little popularity though it is of a pleasant sunny aspect and the rock is excellent.

Two Legged Buttress does not have a direct access of its own. The best approach is across the boulder-beach from the north, the descent to Wolfman Jack Wall being the easiest. Similar approaches are also possible from the cliffs to the south but low tide is essential in all cases. It is also useful to have a preplaced rope down the earth bank above the routes to provide a less harrowing exit.

Pinstripe   160 feet   Severe   (3.9.76)
Start at low tide on some green boulders in the zawn bed right of the
right-hand leg.
1 80 feet 4a. A crack on the left and then a slab, crossed leftwards, lead
to a belay on the arête.
2 80 feet. Climb the right-hand side of the arête and then a corner for 10
feet. Move left to a flake and finish up some twin cracks to a block belay.
Scrambling remains.

Chair Ladder   190 feet   Hard Very Severe   (19.4.73)
Pleasantly sustained. Start below a vague crack on the left edge of the
right-hand leg.
1 60 feet 5a. Climb a rounded groove to reach the crack. Follow it to a
ledge on the right.
2 70 feet 5a. Traverse left for 10 feet to gain a crack, and climb it
awkwardly past some chockstones to a grassy ledge on the right.
3 60 feet 4c. Climb the crack and groove above the stance, and finish up
a diagonal crack.

Sexcrime   200 feet   Hard Very Severe   (30.8.76)
A stimulating route up the hanging crack and corner between the two legs.
1 50 feet 4a. Climb the left edge of the right-hand leg but move around
the arête just before it steepens to gain a nut belay below a steep crack. The
fissure directly below this stance can also be climbed direct at a more
difficult 5b.
2 25 feet 4c. Continue up the crack to a good ledge.
3 125 feet 4c. Climb the corner above, and at the overhang move left to
the ridge to belay. Finish by scrambling up to the top or back down to the
zawn bed via the rake beneath Wolfman Jack Wall.

★Winkle Picker   140 feet   E1 5b   (18.4.76)
Pleasant climbing on excellent rock. Climb easily up the centre of the slab
formed by the left-hand leg, and then move left just below the wall to gain a
recess. Follow a ramp on the right to gain a wall split by a crack. Follow this
to belay on the ridge overlooking Wolfman Jack Wall. Finish either by
scrambling up the ridge or, better, via one of the routes on Wolfman Jack
Wall.

Alpine Buttress Area

Alpine Buttress is the first of two small promontories immediately to the
north of Two Legged Zawn and its accompanying buttress. The climbing on
the buttress lies on its two most rugged faces, the relatively slender seaward
wall and the fine south face. Set in the back of the bay formed between the
buttress and the left-hand leg of Two Legged Buttress is a superb, wedge-
shaped wall:

WOLFMAN JACK WALL   OS Ref 1289 4442

This very compact wall has over recent years become a most attractive venue and its original route, the central crackline, still proves most popular. The face now gives a plethora of excellent wall climbs in the Extreme category, all in a non-tidal environment. It receives any sunshine in the afternoon.

To reach the face, scramble down a vague grassy ridge 50 yards north of Sunset Wall and locate a blocky ridge running out to the cliff edge. Thirty yards south of this, the blocky summit ridge of Alpine Buttress is clearly visible, with Wolfman Jack Wall hemmed in to the recess formed to the south. A good view of the wall can be gained from the top of Alpine Buttress

Access is simple. First locate the face, and make a 120-foot abseil from a platform at the top right-hand side of the face onto the grassy ramp and zawn forming the southerly side of the wall (also used as an approach to Two Legged Buttress and Zawn). Alternatively, a sea-level approach can be made from the north or south; low to mid tide essential.

The first three routes start half-way up the grassy ramp, where a series of ledges run out onto the face to the left. They can also be gained by climbing the first pitch of *Wolfman Jack* and moving right to their respective starts.

★★★**Venus Flytrap**   120 feet   E2 5c   (18.8.80)
A magnificent, varied pitch up the right-hand side of the wall. Fingery at the crux and sustained throughout. Move left and climb the short wall to gain a small, shattered flake. Pull up and follow a ramp rightwards to a long slim ledge. From its right end, balance up the wall to gain the long overlap and follow it leftwards to a prominent rock finger. Climb up onto the wall above and gain holds on the lip of the next overlap. Follow these rightwards until a long stretch gains a steep finishing crack.
Variation   80 feet   E1 5c   (27.8.86)
Start from a grassy ledge, 10 feet below where the overlap crossing the wall meets the grassy ramp, as for *Doctor Fever*. Gain the overlap and follow a steep crack to join the original route for its final 20 feet.

★**Silent Storm**   120 feet   E5 6b   (20.7.81)
A tough route with excellent climbing on the lower wall leading to an arduous, bold finale. Direct and to the point. As for *Venus Flytrap*, move left and climb the short wall to gain a small, shattered flake. Step up and right to a black groove. From the top of this, exit left before moving right into a hidden crack. Blind moves reach the prominent rock finger of *Venus Flytrap* and a pull through the overlap gains a standing-position on the headwall. With the comfort of protection far below, make hard moves up and left to thin cracks and the top.

★★**The Midnight Hour**   110 feet   E4   6a   (25.9.85)

An eliminate line squeezed onto the wall left of *Silent Storm*. Superb wall-climbing with good rock and protection. Traverse out left at the lowest possible level until just before the stance on *Wolfman Jack*. Move up to a very thin crack and follow it to a ledge and spike. Climb the wall above via a tiny orange ramp to gain a thin diagonal crack (small wires). Continue direct, past a flake and jug, to a roofed-in recess. Step right and make a difficult pull through onto the headwall (peg runner) and so reach the top.

★★★**Wolfman Jack**   150 feet   E3   (13.4.74/8.79)

The central line of the wall provides a brilliant second pitch with escalating difficulties to the crux right at the top. Well protected but strenuous. Start a short way up the grassy ramp below a prominent wide crack.
1 50 feet 5b. Climb up and step left onto a small arête; then move left and go through the break in the overhang to gain the crack. Battle up this (*Friend 4* useful) to a good stance on the left.
2 100 feet 5c. Move back right into the crack and follow it to a good ledge a short way above. The continuation of the crack now begins to increase in difficulty until a long stretch gains a hanging corner below the final roof. Tackle this direct (peg runner); a decisive approach will pay dividends.

American Graffiti   160 feet   E2   (8.78)

The least inspiring route on the wall; for connoisseurs only.
1 50 feet 5b. *Wolfman Jack* pitch 1.
2 110 feet 5b. Move back right and up as for *Wolfman Jack* and, from its ledge, traverse left to below a hanging groove. Tackle the short wall to gain this, where easier climbing leads to the top.

★★**An American Werewolf on Lundy**   150 feet   E6   6b   †
                                                       (25.9.85/1.8.93)

An impressive pitch taking the black wall left of *Wolfman Jack* in one big pitch. Technical and bold, especially in its lower half. Climb the slab and short flake crack just left of *Wolfman Jack* to a niche below the overhang. Precarious moves left (peg runner) gain the wall, where a straight thin crack eventually leads to the respite of a good ledge. Move left and up onto a shelf and so gain the next ledge-system above, the point where *American Graffiti* crosses. Continue direct up the compact wall (thread runner) to reach a small hanging corner and pull out left onto the wall above. Climb this, via a thin crack, until moves right at the bulge gain a small finishing groove.

Doctor Fever   130 feet   E2   (25.7.81)

An unusual diagonal crossing of the upper part of the face. Best contemplated on a quiet day. Start 10 feet below where an overlap meets the grassy ramp on the right-hand side of the wall.
1 90 feet 5b. From a grassy ledge on the left, move up a shattered crack

WOLFMAN JACK WALL

1 Doctor Fever E2
2 The Midnight Hour E4
3 Silent Storm E5
4 Venus Flytrap E2
5 Wolfman Jack E3
6 American Graffiti E2
7 An American Werewolf on Lundy E6

to the overlap. Pleasant climbing along the line of this leads to a strenuous move to a hanging stance in *Wolfman Jack*.
2 40 feet 5c. Having untangled the enmeshed ropes, step up and move leftwards into a groove, which provides a hasty exit. A nervous second can be belayed from directly above.

ALPINE BUTTRESS   OS Ref 1289 4445

A very worthwhile cliff, providing a host of routes in the extreme category, with a variety of styles and mostly on the highest quality granite. It is an ideal spot for the first climb of the day as the main, south, face gets the morning sunshine.

Access is relatively straightforward. Abseiling from any of a variety of anchors on the summit ridge leads in 150 feet to the zawn bed, from where all the routes can be gained; mid to low tide essential. This point can be reached also via the abseil down Wolfman Jack Wall. If the tide is high, all of the first pitches can be omitted by choice of the appropriate abseil line.

For those with a more adventurous spirit, a slippery boulder-hop from the south or the north, most notably from Landing Craft Bay and Sunset Promontory, can also be made and is perhaps most desirable for *Alpine Ridge*, the cliff's original route. Low tide is essential to pass Sunset Promontory.

Captain Cat   210 feet   E4   (26.8.77)
This route takes the slim face between the dyke forming the left-hand side of Wolfman Jack Wall and the main corner of the bay. A sustained and technical exercise on rock that is, against the trend, not wholly beyond suspicion. Start beneath a small buttress left of the dyke.
1 100 feet 5a. Climb a crack via a tricky bulge to a pedestal stance below the upper face.
2 110 feet 6a. Tackle the thin cracks in the face above strenuously to reach a smooth groove of better rock. Climb the groove (good small-wire protection) and exit easily onto the wall. Continue up this to some sloping ledges and finish up a groove around to the left.

The Day It Rained Forever   200 feet   E5   (1 pt aid) †   (30.7.88)
The thin crackline in the left, south-facing wall of the main corner. The route lacks balance as the main difficulties are concentrated in the last 30 feet. Start on a huge flake at right-angles to *Captain Cat*.
1 80 feet 5a. Climb the easy slab before moving rightwards to belay on ledges below a small corner at the start of the crack.
2 120 feet 6c. Follow the easier lower half of the crack to a good ledge (belay possible); this point can be gained also by abseil. The upper crack provides a mauling effort (rest-point taken on first ascent) until moves right gain a ledge. Squirm leftwards to exit.

Moby Dick   220 feet   E2   (23.7.73)
The slabby, left-hand groove-line forming the angle of the walls between
Captain Cat and the main promontory of Alpine Buttress. A strong line but
the climbing, spoiled (or soiled?) by a lot of vegetation, is poor. A
miniature expedition. Start at low tide, 20 feet right of a narrow black
cave.
1 100 feet 4c. Climb easily over white rock to reach an overhang at 40
feet. Climb awkwardly over this to good holds above. Continue up the
groove to a sloping stance and poor peg belay below the large roof.
2 70 feet 5b. Cross the slab on the right and climb a groove to a good
ledge. Make some awkward moves into the main groove (peg runner)
and climb this to a stance and peg belay on the left wall.
3 50 feet 4c. Climb delicately across the slab on the left (peg runner) to
belay on a col in the summit ridge of the buttress.

The next three routes, though essentially variations on the upper section of
Moby Dick, are described separately. They are usually gained by abseil
from thread belays to a stance at the foot of the main, upper groove. The
belay can become rather uncomfortable.

★★That Semi-Detached Feeling   90 feet   E6 6b †   (4.8.88/2.8.93)
An aptly named route taking the arête of the house-sized block forming
the upper part of the groove. Exhilarating climbing with bold moves and
plenty of fresh air to contemplate. Move right to the slabby arête, and
climb this and a slim groove to reach a large flake (good wires above).
Step left and go up to some good holds before executing a difficult
sequence through an overhang (hidden *Rock 5* slot) to stand on a sloping
ledge. The exciting arête lies above, though protection does not.

The Lesser Spotted Finish   90 feet   E3 5c   (26.7.88)
The thin crack in the right wall of the corner. Climb the corner to reach the
crack, which proves steep but well protected. After a bulge, the angle
relents to an awkward finish. A good pitch.

Terrace Warfare   90 feet   E5 6b   (4.8.88)
Intricate and technical climbing up the slabbier left wall. From the belay,
step immediately left onto the slab and instant difficulties leading to better
holds – falling off before these leaves you on your belayer's head!
Continue direct up the slab via a faint thin crack to gain an overlap.
Stretch up right to clip a peg runner before pulling direct through the
overlap onto an easier-angled slab. Move up this to a niche and exit
leftwards on cleaned holds.

THE SOUTH FACE
★Alpless   145 feet   E6 †   (1.8.87/2.8.93)
A good route with a particularly satisfying and unusual first pitch. It takes
the centre of the main, south-facing wall of the promontory. Start from a
pinnacle/boulder that almost abuts the foot of the wall. The second should
take a stance a little lower.

1 55 feet 6a. Make a novel entry by bridging/falling across the gap onto the face. Hand-traverse right; then pull up the overhanging arête to a prominent sloping hold. Pull up boldly and then right to enter a small scoop by a tricky manoeuvre. Exit directly and continue to a good ledge.
2 70 feet 6a. From the right-hand end of the ledge, follow a thin crack to the next ledge, and then move 10 feet left to a hanging groove. Climb this past a peg runner to a stance on the obvious hanging block.
3 20 feet 5c. Climb the stepped, right-hand crack above the block.
Variation
Alpine Disaster 120 feet E1 5b   (27.9.85)
Essentially, this omits the first pitch and the hard climbing of the second pitch by a detour to the right. Pleasant. Abseil in to the ledge forming the first stance. Swing right into a crack and climb it over a series of ledges to a ledge-system splitting the whole face. Move up onto the next ledge and gain the top via the obvious ramp.

★★★**Who Can Wait?** 150 feet E6 †   (1.8.87/2.8.93)
An alluring route combining three pitches of high merit on flawless granite. Superb climbing. Start as for *Alpless*.
1 60 feet 6a. Climb pitch 1 of *Alpless* to its belay, arrange protection, and then walk left to the end of the ledge. Peg and nut belay.
2 70 feet 6b. Move up the crack above the stance to a ramp 10 feet higher. Pull out right along the obvious thin crack (peg runner) to gain a shallow hanging groove in the centre of the face. Climb this, and exit with difficulty to a fine stance.
3 20 feet 5c. The steep, left-hand crack behind the stance.

★★★**Scorched Earth** 150 feet E2   (11.4.77)
Another excellent, technical pitch on perfect rock. It takes the attractive, golden corner on the southern arête of the buttress. Well protected. Start at a sloping ledge at the foot of the corner.
1 130 feet 5c. Climb the corner, passing the first overhang, to a niche below the second. Move out to the right to reach a small ledge on the arête below a sentry box. Move up to the final roof and make a strenuous swing over it to a good ledge. A short wall leads to a belay on good ledges below a steep crack.
2 20 feet 4c. The crack above.
Variation
Digby 140 feet E4 †   (13.8.89)
A good alternative. Sustained but well protected.
1a 140 feet 5c. Follow *Scorched Earth* to the second overhang and pull over strenuously to gain twin cracks in the headwall. Climb these, and escape rightwards to join the parent route.

Fusion 150 feet E1   (10.4.77)
The crack high in the wall of the seaward face. Start on the ledges below the crack.
1 70 feet 5b. Climb up leftwards via a slab towards a corner, that of *Solomon Grundy*. Traverse right and make a steep move up to the foot of

a crack, which leads to a block belay on the ridge.
2 80 feet. Finish easily up the ridge.

Splitting the Mighty Atom   150 feet   E3 †   (1.8.93)
The steep, twin cracks to the left of *Fusion*.
1 70 feet 5c. Gain the cracks direct via a short wall and climb them to
reach the ridge. Belay a little higher.
2 80 feet. Finish easily up the ridge.

Solomon Grundy   150 feet   Very Severe   (8.8.79)
The corner between the crack of *Fusion* and the ridge.
1 70 feet 4b. Climb over ledges to the crack in the corner. Climb this,
keeping right of the ridge until forced onto it; then follow the ridge for a few
feet to a block belay.
2 80 feet. Finish easily up the ridge.

Alpine Ridge   150 feet   Very Difficult   (19.3.72)
The original route, up the rugged seaward face. Slightly unsound, though
pleasant and with good positions, especially when combined with the
lengthy approach from Landing Craft Bay. Start at the foot of the seaward
arête of the buttress.
1 70 feet Follow the slabby face of the arête; then climb blocks on its
left-hand side to a flat section. Traverse along this to belay below the next
steep section in the arête.
2 50 feet. Climb the left wall of the arête to belay below the final small
tower.
3 30 feet. Climb the short groove above to the top.

Sunset Promontory   OS Ref 1287 4449

The large promontory 50 yards north of Alpine Buttress is the most easily
identifiable landmark from plateau-level on this section of coastline. The
South Face gives a few excellent climbs in the lower grades and is
dominated by the roofed-corner of *The Black Hand* and the elegant arête
of *Eclipse*. A few harder routes adorn the nearby walls. The seaward and
northern faces are less interesting, the latter being very grassy and broken.

The landward section of the promontory is connected to the mainland by a
treacherous earth rib, which makes access to the summit particularly
worrying. The best approach is to descend this rib by the use of an *in-situ*
rope and then to abseil from a cluster of summit boulders down the
seaward (south) face to the tidal zawn bed. Such an approach enables the
mainland to be reached after the chosen route is finished by use of the fixed
rope. One further problem, however, can arise: it is advisable to fix both
ends of the descent rope to prevent it from becoming unattainable in a
strong breeze.

Other approaches are also possible should the prospect of the afore-mentioned problems touch a sensitive spot. The boulder-beach below the face can be crossed from the approach to Alpine Buttress to the south or from Landing Craft Bay to the north at low tide. Alternatively, it is possible to abseil into the small zawn down the north face of Alpine Buttress. This, however, leaves the problem of the treacherous earth rib to be negoti-ated, although it is possible to retreat via a descent down the northern slopes of the promontory into Landing Craft Bay.

THE SOUTH FACE
This is dominated by an obvious large groove-line with triple overhangs taken by *The Black Hand*. To the right of this the face is split by a series of smaller grooves and walls and a prominent diagonal line full of vegeta-tion, below which is a triangular wall.

Tame Zone   130 feet   E1 †   (25.7.84)
A good first pitch is spoilt by poor rock above. The thin crack in the wall is quite clear. Start 10 feet to the right of the crack.
1 80 feet 5b. Move up the wall and swing left into the crack. Follow this with sustained interest to a ledge and poor belay. It may be advisable to continue.
2 50 feet 4a. Take a direct line to the top, exercising care with a few tottering blocks and hence your belayer's head.

The prominent diagonal line is taken by **Garden Rake** (130 feet Hard Severe 19.3.72), a poor route with some decaying rock high up. The route can be split at an obvious pinnacle.

The next four routes lie in the vicinity of the main, central groove, the lower pitch of which can be avoided at high tide by abseiling down the line.

Fished Fingers   150 feet   E3   (23.9.85)
Worthwhile.
1 60 feet. *The Black Hand* pitch 1.
2 90 feet 6a. Move right to the knife-edge arête and climb it with delicate moves over a slight bulge to reach good ledges. Climb up to a niche below an overlap and pull through on good holds. Finish more easily.

★**Shotgun Rider**   140 feet   E4   (23.7.81)
The sharp, V-shaped groove between *Fished Fingers* and the main groove provides a single hard move with poor protection.
1 60 feet. *The Black Hand* pitch 1.
2 80 feet 6a. Climb the slab right of the main groove, trending left into a shallow groove at a flake. Pull up and right to a ledge on the right arête before re-entering the constricting groove by a wild bridge or powerful layback. Muscle up the groove to the top.

★★The Black Hand   135 feet   Very Severe   (31.3.72)
An excellent climb up an impressive feature. The triple overhangs appear
somewhat problematic from a distance but on closer inspection prove far
less intimidating. Start below a chimney and crack leading up to the central
groove.
1 60 feet.   Climb the chimney and crack to the large ledge below the
corner.
2 75 feet   4c.   Take the obvious line of the corner and climb it with
conviction. High in its grade.

Beam Up   140 feet   E1   (18.4.76/23.8.77)
The cracks in the left arête of the corner are combined with a groove-line to
the left, taken from *Eclipse*. Some dubious rock high up. Start below the
obvious diagonal line to the left of *The Black Hand*. Low tide.
1 70 feet   5a.   Climb the groove-line and crack leading onto the left wall of
the main groove. Arrange protection, and then move down to the ledge.
2 70 feet   5a.   Ascend back diagonally left to a spike and continue up the
wall, bearing slightly right to join the arête at the very top.

★★★Eclipse   130 feet   Very Severe   (8.77)
A masterpiece of route-finding giving spectacular and surprisingly
amenable climbing up the broad flat arête to the left of *Beam Up*. Start at
the foot of the cleft to the left of the big arête in the left-hand side of the south
face at low tide.
1 60 feet   4a.   Struggle up the cleft to an overhang and swing out right to
reach a crack in the arête. Amble up this to a good ledge.
2 70 feet   4b.   Trend rightwards to a large spike on the right-hand side of
the arête above. Leave this by a tricky manoeuvre and continue up the
superbly-positioned slab to the top.
Variation
Sunset Rip-Off   E4   (23.9.85)
The left-hand side of the broad arête.
2a 70 feet   5c.   Make a move up the left side of the arête; then step right
and layback up to some good ledges. Continue just right of the arête,
keeping left of *Eclipse*, past small broken flakes to easy ground.

Occidental Groove   120 feet   Hard Severe   (19.3.72)
A short climb, the second pitch of which gives interesting climbing up the
open-book corner left of *Eclipse* and just south of the nose of the
promontory. Start at low tide to the left of the south face of the promontory.
1 60 feet   4a.   Climb seaweed-covered rock and a short steep wall by its
right edge to a large flat ledge. Cross the ledge to belay beneath the corner.
2 60 feet   4b.   Make a difficult move up a small groove just right of the
main corner, and then follow the corner to a flake belay at the top.

THE WEST FACE
This relatively short, slender face is dominated by a central, overhanging
crack.

Second Summer 80 feet E1 5b (24.7.85)
Climb up a corner right of the overhanging crack; then move left and over
easy-angled rock. Continue up and right past a curious flake and
mantelshelf onto a prow. Repeat the same manoeuvre before finishing up
the overhanging wall left of a perched block.

Accidental Crack 80 feet Hard Very Severe 5b (20.7.81)
The overhanging crack, past two sloping ledges.

Flintstone 65 feet Very Difficult (2.9.87)
Start at the left-hand side of the seaward face at the base of some slabs.
Climb the slabs for 25 feet, and then pull up to more slabs above.
Continue up these via a leaning corner on the right. Belay over to the right
on a broad ledge.

The northern face of the promontory is devoid of interest except as a
descent, with grassy slopes above sea-level boulders.

Landing Craft Bay

*An islander's name, the result of a landing craft being wrecked there. The
wreckage is probably under Second Buttress North now!*

(Bob Moulton)

Beyond Sunset Promontory lies a large boulder-strewn bay bounded to
the north by a small headland containing Flying Buttress and The Battery,
complete with cannon and derelict buildings. This bay is close to most of
the accommodation on the island, and it provides a high concentration of
quality climbs throughout the grade spectrum and with ease of access.

The usual approach to the cliffs in the southern end of the bay is by
descending the valley with a small stream running down it, some 300
yards north of the Old Light. Two hundred feet above sea-level, the valley
steepens and widens into an area of broken rock and grass. Descent is
then by the steep, broad gully on the northern side of the spur, which is
overlooked by First Buttress North, characterized by a clean, white sheet
of rock. It is best to follow the spur to a point just above its end and then to
break down and right (facing out) into the gully. An abseil descent of the
gully may also be desirable, since it is starting to show signs of erosion.

Other approaches to Landing Craft Bay are also possible. The sea-level
boulders at the northern end of the bay can be reached by a 70-foot abseil
from the easy way down to Flying Buttress but the subsequent traverse
back south is relatively unpleasant. Direct abseil approach is another
option.

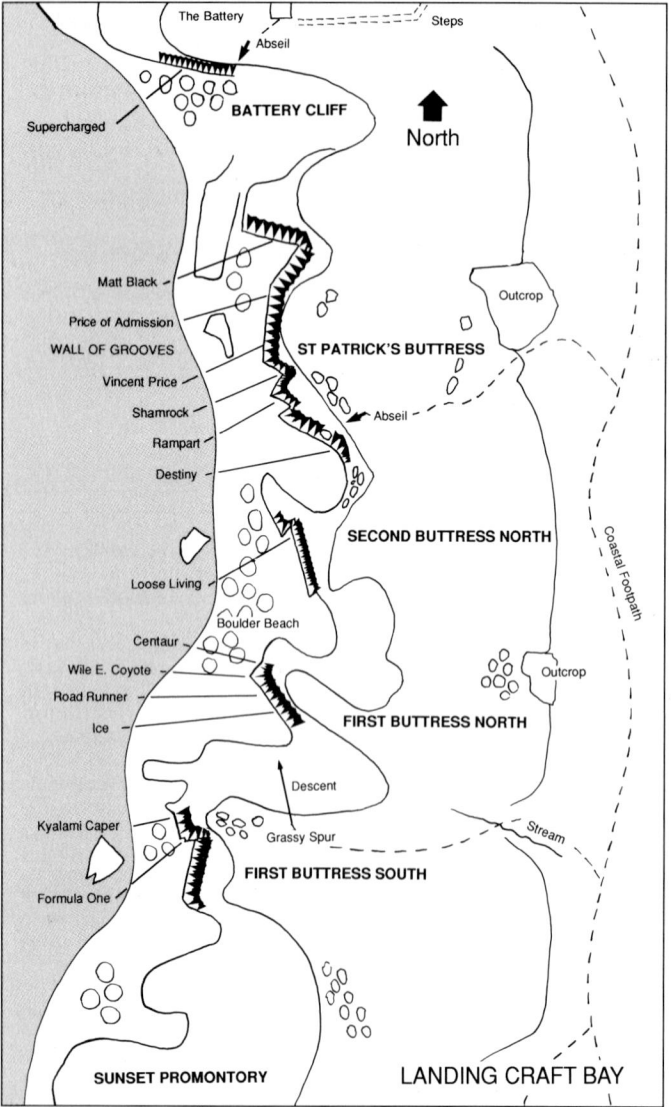

The Battery

Abseil

Steps

Supercharged

BATTERY CLIFF

North

Matt Black

Price of Admission

WALL OF GROOVES

Vincent Price

Shamrock

Rampart

Destiny

ST PATRICK'S BUTTRESS

Abseil

Outcrop

Coastal Footpath

SECOND BUTTRESS NORTH

Loose Living

Boulder Beach

Centaur

Wile E. Coyote

Road Runner

Ice

FIRST BUTTRESS NORTH

Outcrop

Descent

Kyalami Caper

Grassy Spur

Formula One

FIRST BUTTRESS SOUTH

Stream

SUNSET PROMONTORY

LANDING CRAFT BAY

The smaller buttresses in the bay, the first three described, are named in relation to the usual way down. To the south there is first a blocky ridge with First Buttress South to its south. Next is an area of broken rock and grass, with Sunset Promontory to the south again. Overlooking the descent gully is First Buttress North, which is followed by a gully and grassy flank. On the edge of this is a large orange buttress, the remnants of Second Buttress North, then a gully immediately overshadowed by the blackened south face of St Patrick's Buttress. This swings round to the north to be terminated by a huge chaotic gully, with The Battery on the ridge overlooking it at the limit of the bay.

FIRST BUTTRESS SOUTH   OS Ref 1298 4458

This non-tidal buttress is separated from the main descent gully by a small rocky ridge and presents a slender protruding face with a brown groove in its right flank. Right again is a much larger and more heavily vegetated corner with a big slab forming its right-hand side. The rock here is excellent throughout and the climbing is generally of the technical variety. All the routes are blessed with a sunny aspect.

Gulf Stream   150 feet   Hard Very Severe   (9.4.77)

The centre of the big vegetated slab provides a reasonable climb, the lower pitch having most value. Start 20 feet right of the corner.
1 90 feet 4c. Climb up over broken rock for 25 feet, and continue up the slab to a horizontal break. Now climb diagonally leftwards to easier ground and a stance on the right (poor belays). A bold pitch.
2 60 feet 4a. Step up and right, and then move onto the slab above by a short leftwards traverse (direct is 4c). Climb the crack in the slab above and move left to finish.

Hot Rod   135 feet   Very Severe   (11.4.77)

The large corner culminating in a fine crack in its left wall. The approach pitch is rather disappointing.
1 80 feet. Climb the white slab right of the main corner; move left into the corner after 30 feet and continue up to a belay below the crack.
2 55 feet 4c. The crack is taken direct and proves worthwhile.

★★★The Indy 500   135 feet   E1   (22.7.84)

A vintage crack-climb taking the clean, slanting crack in the left wall of the large corner. Sustained, with a tricky start and finish but with more than adequate protection. Not to be missed.
1 45 feet. Climb the large corner to a belay at the point where the crack veers off to the left.
2 90 feet 5b. Gain the crack via a ledge 8 feet above the belay, and follow it, steeply at first but with good face holds, to a ledge. Continue up the crack, which has now become more useful, along with face holds on the right to gain the final headwall. This, though much steeper, provides positive holds and a fitting finale.

★★★Formula One   130 feet   Hard Very Severe   5a   (6.9.72)
An exceptional route providing one of the most coveted pitches of its grade on the island. The slim, brown groove in the arête gives climbing akin to many a gritstone delight, suited to those well-versed in bridging, laybacking, and jamming techniques. High in its grade. Follow a crack to a ledge at the foot of the groove and climb it past a small overlap to a much larger overlap 15 feet above. Move right to climb a slanting crack and then gain a layback flake on the left. Sprint up this and a short finishing corner.

Nigel Mansell   130 feet   E4 6a   (27.7.87)
Contrived but bold. As for *Formula One*, follow a crack to a ledge at the foot of a groove; and then step around the right arête and layback up this side to another ledge. Continue on the right-hand side of the arête past a ledge where the climbing eases before *Formula One* is regained at the flake. Sprint up this and a short finishing corner.

The Wacky Races   130 feet   E4 5c †   (21.6.89)
A route based on the grooves and crack high above where *Formula One* moves out to the right. Airy towards the top. As for *Formula One*, follow a crack to a ledge at the foot of the groove and climb it past a small overlap to a much larger overlap 15 feet above. Move left around this; go up the groove and then back rightwards to rejoin *Formula One* briefly. Step up and leftwards into a bottomless corner. Go up this, exit out left onto the wall and a ledge, and finish carefully.

Two routes take the narrow wall left of *Formula One*.

The Italian Job   130 feet   E3 5c   (24.7.84)
A worthwhile route wandering up the wall. Improbable and fingery in places, where a long reach will help. As for *Formula One*, follow a crack to a ledge at the foot of a groove and climb it to a small overlap. Then swing left and up to a notch on the arête. Stand up in a thin break, and trend rightwards up the face using a thin crack (peg runner) to an obvious fang of rock. Traverse left across the face to the arête and finish intricately and boldly up a shallow groove.

★★Le Mans   125 feet   E5 6b   (27.7.87)
The true direct assault on the arête. Unblemished, technical climbing with good protection and superb exposure. Low in the grade. As for *Formula One*, follow a crack to a ledge at the foot of a groove; then follow a thin crack in the left wall to a good flake. Step right and climb the right-hand side of the arête to the obvious notch. Make hard moves up left onto the arête and make further difficult moves up it (peg runner) to reach the slim groove and intricate finish of the *Italian Job*.

Kyalami Caper   130 feet   E3   (31.7.84)
A series of cracks and a slabby groove in the left extremity of the buttress give a pleasant route. Start below broken rock 30 feet left of *Formula One*.

1 40 feet. Climb up over easy slabs to belay on ledges below the prominent twin cracks.
2 90 feet 5c. Climb the cracks and pull out left onto a ledge below an overhanging finger-flake. Climb this to a jug, standing on which provides the crux. Continue up the slabby, overlapped groove to the top.
Variation
Don Cossack E4 † (25.8.85)
2a 80 feet 6a. Some relatively scruffy climbing though not wholly without merit. Climb the twin cracks of *Kyalami Caper*, and then move diagonally rightwards onto the face. Move up into a slim groove, which is followed to the top.

FIRST BUTTRESS NORTH OS Ref 1292 4462

The main feature of this buttress is its central arête, to the right of which lies a gleaming, white crystalline face, the scene of the cliff's best routes. Once again, the cliff is of great merit and there are no tidal restrictions.

Scrabble 170 feet Hard Very Severe (2.4.72)
A meandering route up the right-hand side of the buttress with some worthwhile climbing. Start below a thin crack splitting the right-hand side of the white face.
1 70 feet 4c. Trend rightwards over easy slabs and ramps to a streaked wall. Avoid this on the right in favour of a slight groove leading to a ledge.
2 35 feet 4c. Stride down and left to a corner and follow this to a multitude of pegs in the back of a large recess.
3 65 feet 5b. Climb the groove above and step right into a second. Now bicycle frantically right along a break to a small ledge, and then go up and slightly left to a recess. Traverse right and finish up grassy slabs left of a long vegetated corner.
Variation 80 feet Hard Very Severe (8.85)
2a 80 feet 5b. Move right to a crack and follow it to a ledge. Go over this onto a sloping shelf beneath a small chimney and then layback up to good holds above. Finish more easily.

The following four routes are often climbed only as far as the peg belays in the large recess at half height. At the time of writing (1994) these can be assumed to be at best in a very poor state and should be approached with caution.

Naughty But Nice 90 feet E3 5c (22.9.85)
Pleasant climbing slotted in to the right of the prominent thin crack in the white face. Climb the faint crack right of the main crack to its end. Step right and move up through a notch onto the slab above. Continue up the corner to the peg belays in the recess. Abseil off.

★★Ice 140 feet E3 (13.8.80)
An intricate first pitch up the tantalizing thin crack in the face. The second pitch provides more of a strenuous struggle and can be omitted by an abseil descent or by finishing up adjacent routes, reducing the grade to E2.

1 90 feet 5c. Gain and then climb the thin crack with escalating difficulties (good small-wire protection) to a slab. Climb the left edge of this to the peg belays. A superb pitch, technically harder for the short.
2 50 feet 5c. The off-putting, overhanging groove above provides a difficult entry. After a step left above, the summit ridge beckons.

I Scream   90 feet   E6 6b   (17.8.84)
Not Ice Cream. A hard, contrived pitch up the centre of the clean, white sheet left of *Ice*, where protection is not overly abundant. A serious proposition. Climb the crack of *Ice* for a few feet before stepping left to a flat block. Climb a desperate thin crack and, from a good hold, continue direct to the final thin break (poor small wires). Summon courage and enough technical know-how before tackling the headwall to reach the peg belays in the recess. Abseil off and award yourself just desserts!

★★Road Runner   140 feet   Hard Very Severe   (1 pt aid)   (9.9.72/89)
The first pitch takes the crack forming the left-hand side of the white face and gives a very enjoyable pitch which can be done on its own at Very Severe. The second pitch turns the overhangs above to their left. Start on a jumbled pile of boulders.
1 90 feet 4c. Gain the crack and follow it on good holds and jams to the peg belays in the recess below the overhangs. It is possible to abseil off from here.
2 50 feet 5b. Use the peg in the left wall for aid (or do it clean – E3 6b and a fine problem) to gain a good hidden hold up and to the left. Swing out left above the void to easier ground and finish up the obvious flake to gain the summit ridge.

Wile E. Coyote   130 feet   E3 5c   (25.7.84)
The arête: a disappointing route for the line of the buttress. Climb the crack of *Road Runner* for 12 feet. Step down and traverse intricately left across the blade of rock to reach a crack. Follow this to its end and then step right onto the arête. Climb it on its right-hand side via some cracks. From the top of these, make strenuous, blind moves up left onto the easier flake-line of *Centaur*. This leads onto the summit ridge and a belay.

To the left of the arête the face is brown, divided by a series of overhangs, and pierced by the chimney/groove-line of:

★★Centaur   160 feet   Hard Very Severe   (30.5.72)
An interesting route on good rock with a short, well-protected crux. Start by scrambling over easy ground on the north face and take a belay where the angle steepens.
1 60 feet 4a. Trend rightwards over slabby rock to nut belays at the foot of the chimney/groove-line.
2 100 feet 5b. Struggle up the chimney to a roof and move right to a ledge. Continue up to the large overhang above, turn it to its right, and move around the arête to a small ledge (peg runner). Climb the groove

above; then go easily up a ramp to where it steepens. Tricky moves here gain a wide flake and easier ground leading to the summit ridge.

SECOND BUTTRESS NORTH   OS Ref 1292 4468

The face of this buttress is easily identified by an enormous yellow scar bounded to the left by a stepped ramp-line and a smaller subsidiary buttress. Two routes once took this buttress: **Zig Zag Zig** and **Mistral** now lie in a jumbled jigsaw at the foot of the cliff.

Access is by a strenuous boulder-hop from First Buttress North. Should you really be keen enough to want to climb here, you will find the cliff non-tidal.

The stepped ramp-line gives a poor route, **Loose Living** (180 feet Very Severe 4b 4b 11.10.81), which proves to be aptly named! A peg belay is available at the second 'step' should the route be undertaken.

Wall Street Shuffle   110 feet   Hard Very Severe   4c   (11.8.81)
A route up the buttress left of *Loose Living*. Start below a corner-crack. Climb the crack to the first sloping ledge. From the right-hand end of this, follow some thin cracks up the slab to belay on the slope above. Desperate scrambling remains, or an abseil off. Alternatively, from the ledge, step back left and climb a flake to a higher ledge (5a).

ST PATRICK'S BUTTRESS   OS Ref 1283 4478

This superb and quite complex cliff lies at the northern end of Landing Craft Bay. There are two main faces divided centrally by a long, open-book corner, the line of *Leprechauner* and the start of the excellent *Shamrock*. To the north of this, with the exception of a black, diamond-shaped wall, the cliff leans rather alarmingly and yields a number of fierce, overhanging cracks and groove-lines. These are clearly visible from The Battery to the north. South of the main corner, the face is somewhat smoother and generally slabby, brown in hue, and giving a wealth of solid technical climbing.

There are two means of approach. Over recent years, a direct abseil has become increasingly common. This enables the cliff to be gained more quickly, and more routes are accessible. For this, the cliff-top is reached by a scramble down the fern-covered slopes below a large plateau-level outcrop some 550 yards north of the Old Light. A small group of boulders lining the rim of the cliff provides a reliable target to aim for. Alternatively, a rather laborious boulder-hop can be made from First Buttress North.

The cliff is tidal in the vicinity of *Shamrock*, but routes on its flanks are usually unaffected if the appropriate abseil-point is chosen and the first pitches are omitted. The whole cliff becomes accessible below mid tide.

THE SOUTH FACE
Towards its right-hand side, the south face is split by the striking diagonal crackline of *Destiny*. An extremely poor route, **Escape Route** (200 feet

Very Severe 7.77), takes the extreme right-hand side of the lower slabs, then an unobvious faultline to join the final few feet of *Destiny*.

Cow Pie   180 feet   Hard Severe   (3.4.72)
A pleasant climb wandering across the south face amongst impressive scenery. Appropriate as an escape route should the need arise. Start below a weakness in the right-hand side of the lower wall and to the right of a shallow groove.
1 80 feet. Climb up and to the left to gain a glacis and continue leftwards along this before moving up to gain a belay on an obvious pedestal.
2 100 feet 4a. Climb the wall above, always trending leftwards, to finish up a short, awkward groove. Scramble carefully – the crux! – to large blocks.

The upper pitches of the next three routes share a common first pitch.

★Harbinger   200 feet   Hard Very Severe   (23.7.85)
Good climbing up the right extremity of the wall and just right of the crack of *Destiny*. Start at a shallow groove in the lower wall, directly below the left-hand end of the diagonal crack.
1 110 feet 4b. Climb the groove to easier ground and continue direct to the foot of the diagonal crack. Traverse right for 10 feet and belay at an unsound block and oblique crack.
2 90 feet 5b. Move up a thin crack for a few feet before stepping right to some slanting flakes. Follow these, awkwardly at first, before improving holds lead to a good ledge. Shuffle right along this; then follow a short chimney to the final obstacle, a short left-facing corner.

★★Tomorrow   200 feet   E4   (24.7.85)
An exciting direct line through *Destiny* giving a technical lower half and a sustained upper. Well protected.
1 110 feet 4b. *Harbinger* pitch 1.
2 90 feet 6b. Climb the difficult thin crack to join the diagonal crack of Destiny. Move up this for 8 feet before swinging left along an edge for 6 feet. From here, continue direct to a short sharp flake; then reach up and left to gain a ledge. Thread belay.

★★Destiny   200 feet   E2   (2.4.72)
The compelling slanting crackline gives a superb pitch, reminiscent of *Bow Wall* at Bosigran. Sustained throughout with plentiful protection but it is a notorious swallower of camming devices; you have been warned!
1 100 feet 4b. Climb *Harbinger* pitch 1, but take a comfortable belay below the start of the crack.
2 100 feet 5b. Attack the smooth crack to reach a good undercut hold. Continue up a slight groove, which finally eases at a sloping shelf. Move right and exit via a short corner. High in its grade.

★Mammoth-Sandwich Island   160 feet   E5 †   (23.7.85)
A mean top pitch with a plethora of difficulties up the left-hand side of the

overlapped wall containing *Destiny*. Start below the twin cracks in the right wall of a shallow groove left of *Destiny*.

1 50 feet 5c. Climb the steep and surprisingly tricky cracks to an easing in angle. Belay down and to the right of an obvious pedestal.

2 110 feet 6c. Follow a very faint crack running up the wall, left of a diagonal line of grass, over a bulge to arrive at a ledge below the headwall (small wires). Step left; then go direct to meet the roof and the horrendous pull-over you have been waiting for! Pump up the twin cracks above to the top. Alternatively, defeat administered, step left below the roof and pull over to join and finish as for Meninirons: **Forgotten Sun** (E4 6a 26.7.90).

★★**Meninirons** 180 feet E1 (19.7.81)

An enjoyable route featuring good but bold climbing up the left-hand side of the headwall. At the upper limit of its grade. Start at the foot of the shallow groove to the left of *Mammoth-Sandwich Island*.

1 60 feet 4b. Follow the groove to easy ground, and then move right and back left to a pedestal 20 feet above.

2 120 feet 5b. Leave the right-hand side of the ledge via a vague, thin flake. Where it fades, step left and continue direct on small positive holds to the left-hand end of the overlap (peg runner). Surmount this on large, hollow holds and finish right and then back left.

Udderwise 160 feet E1 † (23.9.85)

An eliminate line based on the rock left of *Meninirons*.

1 40 feet. Climb the slabby rib left of *Meninirons*, or the obvious wide crack to its left, to a good ledge.

2 120 feet 5c. Take the banana-shaped crack above to the pedestal of *Cow Pie* and *Meninirons*. Continue up a thin leftward-slanting crack through a rock scar to yet another ledge. Above is a thin crack in the leaning headwall. Gain and climb it in an exciting fashion.

To the left is an attractive ramp in the right-hand arête of the large central corner, the line of *Rampart*. The right retaining wall of this forms an overlap, above which lies the straight, thin crack of:

★★**Second Coming** 160 feet E3 (19.7.81)

Excellent climbing up the enticing crack. A neat crux with sound protection and fine positions.

1 40 feet. Climb the wide crack left of *Udderwise* to the obvious ledge.

2 120 feet 6a. Stride left to a large ledge. Step up left again before pulling awkwardly through the overlap to the base of the crack; this point can also be gained by tip-toeing boldly left across the lip of the overlap (E4 6a). Technical moves up the crack lead to easy ground. Wander up to the finishing corner of *Cow Pie*, taking care with the final rubble slope.

★★**Slip Tide** 165 feet E2 (26.7.81)

The hanging slab left of the crack of *Second Coming* provides an absorbing pitch on impeccable rock. Pleasantly sustained but quite bold.

1 40 feet. *Second Coming* pitch 1.
2 125 feet 5b. Continuing as for *Second Coming*, move left to a large ledge, step up left again, and pull out awkwardly through the overlap to the base of a thin crack. Move left along the lip of the roof for 10 feet, and then pull over a tiny overlap onto the upper slab. Pick a line up this keeping left of the corner.

★★**Rampart**   150 feet   E2   (3.4.72/11.8.80)
The immaculate ramp-line gives an exhilarating route with an intimidating crux.
1 40 feet. *Second Coming* pitch 1.
2 110 feet 5c. Stride left to the large ledge and follow the ramp with increasing difficulty as it steepens. Where the ramp fades completely, swing right to gain a welcome but hidden jug. Pull up into a slabby crack and follow it to finish over easier ground.

★★**Crampant**   150 feet   E5 6a †   (8.84/26.9.85)
A good route aiming for the right wall of the large central corner. Strenuous in its upper reaches. Start as for *Rampart*. Climb the initial wide crack for a few feet before transferring left into an obvious flake to the right of the prominent roof. Improvise up this to a good ledge (belay possible). Continue up the ramp on the left, as for *Rampart*, to its end; then swing round left and go up a short wide crack. (Out of sight is out of mind?) Swing left again and move up to gain a thin crack leading to a niche. Scrambling remains.

Leprechauner   150 feet   E1   (23.7.84)
The main central corner.
1 60 feet 4c. *Shamrock* pitch 1.
2 90 feet 5b. The upper corner has a short difficult start and a bold finish. Exit right at the top.

★★★**Shamrock**   160 feet   Very Severe   (17.3.72/74)
A classic encounter with the initial part of the main central corner, then a series of cracks and grooves to its left. A must at the grade.
1 60 feet 4c. Climb the corner, awkwardly at first. Belay at the back left corner of the platform.
2 40 feet 4a. Follow the obvious jagged flake to a second sloping ledge. Walk left to belay at the base of the first corner-line.
3 60 feet 4c. Ascend the crack in the corner and exit onto slightly unstable terrain. Tread carefully up this to large block belays.

★★**Holiday in Cambodia**   150 feet   Hard Very Severe   (11.8.80)
A very fine slab route. Protection is rather spartan throughout and the top pitch could offer some worrying moments for a nervous leader.
1 60 feet 5a. From just left of the main corner, step up onto a sloping shelf. Go straight up the slab above, keeping out of the corner, to the platform. Belay at its back left corner.
2 90 feet 4c. From the belay, tread daintily but boldly up the left edge of

Eclipse Sunset Promontory
Climbers unknown

Photo: Gary Gibson

Le Mans (first ascent) First Buttress South
Climber: Gary Gibson

Photo: Hazel Gibson

the broad slab to reach the left-hand end of a tongue of grass. Traverse left to a crack almost on the arête, and finish direct.

★**Russian Giant** 195 feet E5 †   (24.7.85)
Though a circuitous eliminate, this route gives two worthwhile pitches. Start below the centre of the face left of *Holiday in Cambodia*.
1 60 feet 6a. Attack the centre of the face via an A-shaped weakness in the overlap and a hard, bold pull to gain the platform.
2 60 feet 4a. Follow the jagged flake and, at a sloping ledge, move left past the upper corner of *Shamrock* to the next bay.
3 75 feet 5b. Climb the slight groove in the left wall of the bay, as for *Evictor*, and pull over a bulge. Move left and climb up the cleaned strip, with excellent exposure, to a step left into a groove. Finish direct and more easily.

★**Too Salsify** 130 feet E5 †   (22.9.85)
A worthwhile, though bizarre first pitch is followed by a contrived second pitch. Start below the arête.
1 70 feet 6b. Climb the slab and, at the bulge, undercut left round the corner to a thin crack. Step up, and then move left onto the hanging arête and a novel resting-place. Make a series of baffling moves into a niche above. Move right and then back left onto the sloping ledge below the upper corner of *Shamrock*.
2 60 feet 5c. Climb the left arête of the corner, which becomes rather close towards the top.

THE WALL OF GROOVES
Around the corner to the left lies a forbidding, overhanging wall. This gives some unique and outrageous routes on rock that can become quite slippery after salt spray. A sunny evening and/or a cooling north-westerly breeze should provide ideal climbing conditions.

Evictor 140 feet E1   (1.4.72/74)
A strenuous and aptly-named first pitch leads to an open and far more hospitable second. Start below the large cleft 20 feet from the right edge of the wall.
1 70 feet 5a. Thrash frantically up the awkward, repellent chimney to the upper of two overhangs. Swing out left onto a glacis and climb it to belay in the obvious bay.
2 70 feet 5b. Climb the corner of the bay, gaining it via a slight groove and crack in the left wall. The corner can be approached more directly (short, sharp, and E2 5c).

★★★**Vincent Price** 150 feet E6 †   (31.7.93)
A sensational route with pitches of highly contrasting merit. Start just right of a prominent V-shaped groove 15 feet left of *Evictor*.
1 75 feet 6b. A short wide crack and a difficult wall lead to a sloping ledge (peg runner). Stand up on the ledge by an elegant manoeuvre and climb the leaning wall (peg runner) to follow a flake and chimney to the

shelf. Belay at its back corner.
2 75 feet 6c. Pull up the slab on the left and traverse left to gain a thin crack. From the top of this, make a series of desperate moves up the disappearing ramp (two peg runners) to gain a jug in an incredible position. Pull straight up and finish via a short groove and easy rib.

★★**The Price of Admission**   140 feet   E6 †   (5.5.89)
The formidable set of overhanging grooves to the left. A highly acrobatic climb on superb rock and with perfect protection. Strenuous.
1 70 feet 6b. Climb the groove to a roof at 45 feet. Step left to gain a parallel groove and follow this with interest to reach gratefully the sloping ledge which crosses the buttress.
2 70 feet 6a. Above are two cracks. The left looks reasonable, the right looks wild. Climb the right-hand crack; it is! The left-hand crack is 5c and has been christened **Bella Lugosi** (31.7.93).

★**Boris Karloff**   140 feet   E5 †   (28.9.85)
Strenuous and tiring bridging on the first pitch. A real horror show. Start on the slab below the right side of the funnel/chimney in the left-hand side of the wall.
1 70 feet 6a. Straddle up into the chimney and pull up into its right side. Battle up this, groin permitting, to a small rattling block. Swing blindly right onto a slab, and then move boldly up to a ledge above (peg belay).
2 70 feet 5c. Gain the obvious clean-cut groove and follow it until a thin crack leads out left onto the arête. Move carefully up this; then go rightwards to an unstable finish.

★**Bertie's Route**   150 feet   E4   (12.8.86)
An interesting route up the leaning walls and scoops to the left of *Boris Karloff*.
1 70 feet 5c. Exit from the awful squeeze chimney just left of Boris Karloff to reach a flaky corner. Follow this leftwards to a peg belay in a recess.
2 80 feet 6a. Enter the groove above (peg runner) and then move straight out left onto a slab. Cross under an overlap to reach a groove above (peg runner) and finish up this. Belay well back on some large blocks.

★**Oshun Coming Big**   265 feet   E4 †   (6.87)
A girdle traverse of the overhanging Wall of Grooves giving some good climbing and exposed positions.
1 70 feet 5a. *Evictor* pitch 1.
2 80 feet 5b. Move up the wall on the left and traverse left to its edge. Reverse down the groove just to the left to gain the obvious slabby ledge dividing the face. Follow this to the edge of a large chimney; then move up onto the next ledge (peg belay).
3 35 feet 5b. Traverse delicately left above the chimney, past a protruding rib, to gain a stance in a recess. Peg belay as for *Bertie's Route*.

BUTTRESS

2 Leprechauner	E1	
3 Shamrock	VS	
4 Evictor	E1	
5 Vincent Price	E6	

	Admission	E6
7 Boris Karloff	E5	
8 Bertie's Route	E4	
9 Matt Black	E3	

4 80 feet 6a. *Bertie's Route* pitch 2.

At the left-hand end of the overhanging face is a large, diamond-shaped face flanked to the right by a glacis and rotting corner. The finishing slope to all of its routes is slightly unstable and a prefixed belay rope may feel warranted by some.

★Charles Mattless   120 feet   E6 6a   (22.9.85)
A very bold and technical excursion up the right-hand side of the face. Start 10 feet right of a shallow groove. Climb easily to the highest of a series of ledges. Proceed carefully for 10 feet to a small shelf and tiny wires. Continue, still tentatively, bearing slightly left past a small bulge to the base of a ramp. Follow this to exit via a small corner as for *Matt Black*.

★★Matt Black   130 feet   E3 5c   (21.3.84)
Delightful climbing, with pleasantly sustained technicalities. Apart from a bold start, good wire protection abounds. Gain the obvious shallow groove and follow it to a ledge. Press on directly up the slab to meet a thin crack leading to a break. Swing right; then continue direct to reach a ramp and short finishing corner.

★Matt Blanc   135 feet   E7 6b †   (22.7.85/31.7.93)
A very serious proposition up the blank slab to the left. Appropriately named – with reference to substantial holds and protection? Climb a tiny groove just left of *Matt Black*; then smear out left onto the slab proper. Continuous intricacies lie ahead in reaching the ledge. Keeping left out of *Matt Black*, continue straight up the slab above (small-wire protection) to gain a thin crack and small ledge. Climb a good flake slightly to the right to finish up the corner of *Matt Black*.

Ocean Rain   135 feet   E2 5c   (23.7.84)
The easiest and most mediocre of the routes on the slab but not without interest even so. Start just right of a short chimney at the left-hand edge of the slabby wall. Follow a jagged crack to a ledge, and then step right onto the slab proper. Move up and left to some sloping ledges and continue up to a crack. Climb this and the groove above to a ledge, and finish up the flaky crack above. Take care with the finishing-rock.

To the left lies the large chaotic gully. The right side of this can be ascended as an escape route, but only in desperation!

The Flying Buttress Area

The Flying Buttress is a superb piece of rock architecture and one of Lundy's outstanding coastal features: a huge monolith leaning against the mainland, forming a giant natural arch. The routes here and on the cliffs

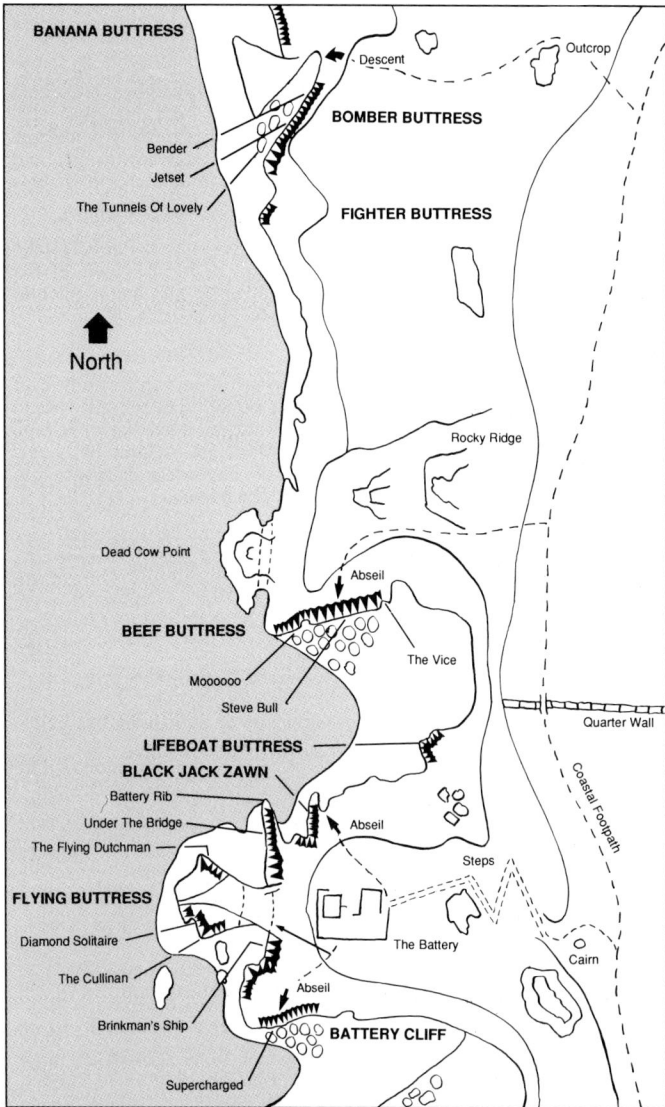

BANANA BUTTRESS

Descent

BOMBER BUTTRESS

Bender

Jetset

The Tunnels Of Lovely

FIGHTER BUTTRESS

Outcrop

↑ North

Rocky Ridge

Dead Cow Point

Abseil

BEEF BUTTRESS

The Vice

Moooooo

Steve Bull

Quarter Wall

LIFEBOAT BUTTRESS

BLACK JACK ZAWN

Battery Rib

Under The Bridge

The Flying Dutchman

Abseil

Steps

FLYING BUTTRESS

Diamond Solitaire

The Battery

The Cullinan

Brinkman's Ship

Abseil

Cairn

Coastal Footpath

BATTERY CLIFF

Supercharged

either side give a large selection of fine, short pitches with easy access and on generally excellent rock.

The approach lies down the small shallow valley, marked by a prominent cairn, 200 yards south of Quarter Wall. A walled path zigzags steeply down to The Battery and its ruined keepers' cottages. This nineteenth century gun emplacement was used as a warning-station to shipping when fog obscured the Old Lighthouse. Today, its firing platform remains complete with the two eighteen-pounder cannon.

THE BATTERY CLIFF   OS Ref 1273 4484
This short, south-facing wall lies directly below and to the south of The Battery, and on the northern side of the large, open gully that terminates Landing Craft Bay. The wall is steep and clean, the majority of the routes following powerful crack and groove-lines.

From The Battery, descend in a south-westerly direction, initially over steep, broken ground and then, at Moderate standard, over better rock to a point some 70 feet above the sea. A short abseil down the steep wall leads to boulders at the base of the cliff, which are exposed two hours either side of low tide. An alternative, but more hazardous approach is to descend the large, open gully to the south of The Battery.

At the far right-hand side of the wall, the gully bears the remnants of a climb known as **Ramrod** which collapsed during the winter of 1979. The first route described lies to the left of the rockfall and 30 feet right of a large basalt dyke.

Duracell   120 feet   Very Severe   (3.8.82)
Not destined for a long life! Start at a V-shaped chimney 30 feet right of the basalt dyke.
1 60 feet 4c. Climb the left wall of the chimney on good holds to a belay ledge.
2 60 feet 4b. Dubious rock. From a large spike on the ledge, follow the rightward-slanting cracks until the rock deteriorates. Climb directly and carefully up the wall above to the top.

Incantations   120 feet   Very Severe †   (29.8.79)
Start at high-tide level, immediately right of the basalt dyke.
1 60 feet 4c. Climb up to an overhang and traverse right above a dubious flake. Swing round the corner on the right to gain a good ledge and belay.
2 60 feet 4b. Step up and left onto a hanging slab and climb it. Continue up the steep wall above on big holds, but poor rock, to the top.

Soho Sue   100 feet   Very Severe 4b †   (8.92)
Steep climbing on dubious rock. Start at the high-water mark atop a large boulder. This is beneath an arête, which is prominent when viewed from the left. Climb the right wall of the arête and move left into a niche. Gain a

sloping ledge above; then move out right onto the wall and climb it to a ledge and flake belay.

★★Supercharged   90 feet   E4 6a †   (6.8.88)
Power-packed. Sustained and technical climbing up the slim groove in the wall left of the basalt dyke. Infinitely protectable with small wires. Start just left of the dyke. Climb a short wall to a ledge; then swing up and left onto a shelf (peg runner). Enter the groove above and follow it directly to good block belays.

★Power Plus   90 feet   E3 6a †   (21.6.89)
Energetic climbing based on the steep crack and groove 15 feet left of *Supercharged*. Climb the crack for 20 feet; then hand-traverse rightwards along a ledge into *Supercharged* (peg runner). Step down, and then move up and left into a crack that splits the bulge above. Climb the crack with difficulty to a groove, which is followed to the top.

★Ever Ready   90 feet   E3 5c †   (18.6.89)
A good, rewarding crack-climb, strenuous but well protected. Start as for *Power Plus*. Climb the initial crack and charge up its direct continuation to the top. Batteries not included!

FLYING BUTTRESS MAIN CLIFF   OS Ref 1271 4489
There are a number of possible approaches, choice depending upon the climb chosen and the state of the tide.
1. *The Flying Buttress* provides a useful approach for the competent to routes in the Diamond Solitaire area. From The Battery, descend north-west over jumbled blocks until a ridge is reached: the top of the route. A straightforward descent of this leads to the seaward tip of the cliff. This descent is possible in all but the highest tides, although great care should be exercised when a big sea is running as the seaward tip of the buttress is particularly exposed.
2. The 'easy way down': the best approach for climbs on the landward cliff is to descend the broken slope south-west of The Battery. Steep scrambling over Moderate standard rock leads down to a narrow sea-channel. A short traverse north (right facing out) then leads to the first climbs described. At low to half tide the channel can be crossed to the base of *The Flying Buttress*. For the routes north of this, continue the traverse beneath the arch at low to mid tide.
3. An alternative high-tide approach to the northern end of the landward cliff is possible but demands care and some prior knowledge of the cliff. Cross the grassy slope to the north of The Battery for some 30 yards and climb carefully down an easy rib at the northern extremity of the cliff. This is immediately south of a large black sea-cave.

Just north of the easy way down is a short steep wall.

The Exorcist (65 feet Very Severe 5a 22.3.74) climbs the obvious leftward-slanting crack in the wall to finish up parallel cracks to the left.

Solitaire View (65 feet Hard Severe 4c 30.3.67) climbs the short corner and crackline immediately to the left.

Diamond Crack   90 feet   Very Severe   5a   (24.10.78)
The corner-crack left of *Solitaire View*: a good little pitch. Climb the crack utilizing the slabby left wall; the difficulties are concentrated into the first 30 feet.

Alouette   100 feet   Severe   (4.63)
At one time the hardest 'Diff' in the South-West! Left of *Diamond Crack* is a large open depression of steep rock. Climb the right-hand corner of the depression and continue up broken rock to a large ledge (belay possible). Climb the steep corner above and exit right at its top to a block belay.

Cappucino   120 feet   Very Severe   (4.63)
A wandering line up the left-hand side of the depression. Slight, but with some good positions.
1 70 feet. Follow the broken left-hand corner of the depression to a good stance.
2 50 feet 4c. Surmount the small bulge above on the left; then take a diagonal line up to the left, beneath an overhang. Move left again and finish easily over broken rock.
Direct Finish   Hard Very Severe   (1975/28.7.84)
A superior finish in an exciting position.
2a 60 feet 5a. Climb the bulge as for *Cappucino* but move right to a large ledge. Follow the thin cracks on the left to a smaller ledge beneath an overhang and pull over this to finish up easier rock above.

★★Brinkman's Ship   125 feet   E6 6a †   (11.7.73/26.9.85)
The left-hand side of the depression is formed by a large impending wall. This striking, previously aided crack in the centre of the wall gives an incredibly strenuous route demanding a Herculean effort. The sloping shelf beneath the crack is gained awkwardly from the left. Difficult moves up the crack, past the remains of two peg runners, lead to a good fist-jam where the crack curves to the right. Haul powerfully over onto the slab above and scramble easily up the slope to The Battery and a solid belay. A preplaced belay rope to the edge of the cliff may be preferred.

Puffins' Parade   220 feet   Very Severe   (5.5.65)
An interesting girdle of the face south of and including Flying Buttress. Non-tidal and with nicely exposed climbing. Start half-way down 'the easy way down'. Substituting *Diamond Crack* for the first pitch gets the route off to a better start.
1 70 feet. Scramble leftwards over broken rock and swing left to a belay in *Alouette*.
2 50 feet 4c. An intimidating pitch. Traverse left with escalating difficulty and exposure on good holds above the impending wall to a flake belay.
3 70 feet 4c. Move left into the corner formed by Flying Buttress. A long stride left leads out onto the buttress front. Move left again, onto an area

The Flying Buttress Area   105

of black-streaked rock, and make a descending traverse to a belay on the shoulder.
4 30 feet. Follow the ridge easily to the top.

★**The Cullinan/Flying the Colours**   140 feet   E5   6a   (26.7.84/6.5.89)
The elegant right arête of Flying Buttress. An outstanding pitch, bold and at the upper limit of its grade. Start by climbing up into a cave-like recess beneath the slab. Pull over the overhang above and make a traverse right, rising slightly, to a line of flakes 6 feet left of the arête. Follow these to a prominent hollow-sounding flake and runners. *The Cullinan* now goes directly over the overlap, before moving rightwards to the arête and following it to a sloping ledge. For *Flying the Colours*, move right below the overlap, where an exposed move around the arête gains a good incut hold and a *Rock 3* placement. Pull back leftwards around the arête and climb to the sloping ledge. Step left onto the slab and continue directly to the top.

★**Double Diamond**   140 feet   Hard Very Severe   5b   (23.7.84)
Exhilarating open climbing up the thin crackline splitting the centre of the slab. Priceless. Start by climbing up into the cave-like recess beneath the slab. Pull rightwards over the overhang above and move up to gain the base of the thin crack just right of the corner of *Diamond Solitaire*. Climb the crack until it is possible to step right into another crack, and continue up the centre of the slab and the headwall above to a steep finish on good holds.

★**Diamond Solitaire**   160 feet   Very Severe   (5.5.65)
One of Lundy's middle-grade classics and deservedly popular. The left-hand corner of the slab. Start at the foot of the slab beneath the cave-like recess
1 80 feet   4c. Move steeply up into the recess (belay possible). Step out right onto the slab and move up and left into the corner as soon as possible. Climb the corner to a good belay on the half-way shoulder.
2 80 feet   4b. Traverse right into the centre of the slab; then climb directly up its centre, trending right where it steepens near the top. Good block belays.
Variation
Riding High   Hard Very Severe †   (9.82)
The evil, off-width crack rising from the cave belay of *Diamond Solitaire*.
1a 70 feet   5a. Gain the crack and struggle up it to the half-way shoulder and a choice of finishes.

★**Horseman's Route**   160 feet   Hard Severe   (10.64)
A wandering but highly enjoyable climb. Pleasantly exposed. Start beneath the short slab on the seaward tip of the buttress.
1 80 feet   4a. Climb direct up the centre of the slab and continue to a belay on the half-way shoulder.
2 80 feet   4a. Step down to the right onto the large slab of *Diamond Solitaire* and make an ascending traverse right to gain a small ledge.

Climb up and left onto an area of black-streaked rock and continue over lichen-covered blocks to the top.

Direct Start   Very Severe   (7.83)
1a 70 feet   5a.   The right arête of the slab is gained via a thin crack just right of its base.

★**The Flying Buttress**   160 feet   Moderate   (8.62)
The ridge of the buttress gives an exhilarating climb at the grade. Take a line up the left edge of the buttress to a more broken section at half height. From here there are numerous variations up the steeper top section.

★★★**The Flying Dutchman**   160 feet   E7   †   (8.89)
A phenomenal pitch of the utmost difficulty and quality; one of the most exacting leads on the island. The route links a series of cracks in the left arête of the north face of Flying Buttress. Start beneath a leftward-leaning finger-crack in the arête.
1 85 feet   6b.   Climb the crack to a niche at 30 feet; then step right and move up to beneath a small overlap (peg runner). Move left to a hidden crack in the arête and climb it and the short wall above to a broad ledge. Small *Friends* and nut belay.
2 75 feet   6c.   Follow an easy ramp leftwards (peg runner); then traverse left to the hanging arête and climb it boldly (peg runner). Continue directly to an overlap in a groove (peg runner above), and gain the slab; then step left to a large spike. Move up and rightwards onto the arête and follow it past some large hanging flakes to the top.

The remaining climbs are on the mainland cliff. Belays at the top of this section are difficult to find and a preplaced belay rope is useful. Ideally this is placed from the small buttress adjacent to the ruined keepers' cottages.

★**The Shadeseekers**   100 feet   E2 5c   (20.6.89)
Fine climbing up the left edge of the steep slab in the shadow of the arch. Start 20 feet left of the large basalt dyke, just north of Flying Buttress. Pull steeply through the initial bulges onto the slab and step left to a good ledge (poor peg runner). Bold moves up the slab lead to a short groove, which is climbed to an awkward exit right. Step up to the short, bottomless groove in the overlap above (peg runner) and pull sharply through onto the slab above. Finish leftwards.

★**McVitie Man**   90 feet   E2 5b   (21.8.82)
A popular route, low in its grade and on excellent rock. Care should be taken to avoid rope drag. Start beneath a steep flake leading to a diamond-shaped niche, 15 feet left of *The Shadeseekers*. Layback convincingly into the niche and climb the slim corner above to a long, thin ledge. Traverse right for 12 feet and continue up the steep rib, just left of the dyke, on good but well-spaced holds to the slab above. Step left and finish diagonally leftwards.

★Peanut Power 85 feet E4 6b (28.7.84)
Although something of a hybrid, this has some extremely thin and technical climbing on perfect rock. Start as for *McVitie Man*. Layback into the niche and follow the slim corner to the thin ledge. Place a good runner in the overlap above; then step down and traverse left to gain a hairline crack. Climb up on very small holds to gain the bottomless groove in the overlap above. Pull over and finish easily up cracks in the slab above.

The next four routes lie in the vicinity of a large cave, 100 feet north of Flying Buttress.

Duelin Mk 1 75 feet Very Severe 4c † (15.10.81)
A line up the large sloping steps 15 feet right of the cave. Start beneath an obvious layback crack. Climb the crack for 30 feet and traverse left to a ledge on the edge of the cave. Regain the original line by a slanting slab and finish direct up the centre of the steep face on good holds.

★Under the Bridge 75 feet E2 5b (23.7.84)
The wedge-shaped buttress just left of the cave. A delightful climb on perfect rock, perhaps a touch under protected for some tastes. Climb up onto the first sloping ledge and gain the second by a decisive mantelshelf. Spaced holds lead up and left to the base of a flake crack; finish up this or, better, step right and continue direct up the face to the top.

Vallum 90 feet Severe (25.9.73)
An interesting climb up the prominent V-chimney just left of *Under the Bridge*. Gain the chimney, either direct or from the right, and follow it onto the rib above (stance possible). Step right and climb the cracked wall to the top.

Step We Gaily 90 feet Hard Very Severe 5a (13.9.92)
Climb the arête just left of *Vallum* to a ledge, step right, and continue up to an overhang. Turn this on its right-hand side and follow the crack above until a traverse right on undercuts gains some hanging blocks in the right-hand corner. Pull over the blocks and finish up the rib above.

★★Battery Rib 95 feet Very Difficult (2.5.65)
Delightful climbing on perfect rock; a mini sea-cliff classic. Start beneath the prominent rib at the northern end of the cliff, just right of a subsidiary rib, the aforementioned descent route. Move up into a recess and traverse right onto the rib proper. Climb its steep left wall on enormous holds and step onto the edge of the rib. Continue up this to the top. Several variations are possible in the upper section.

BLACK JACK ZAWN OS Ref 1277 4495
Immediately north of The Flying Buttress Area is a large black sea-cave, Black Jack Zawn. The black wall to the left of the cave is split by a thin

crack, *Treasure Island*. To its north is a much steeper wall with the big
groove of *Buried Gold* standing out. A slabby rib, the line of the abseil
descent, marks the northern perimeter of the cliff.

From the ruined keepers' cottages, walk 50 yards to the north across a
grassy slope. An abseil from block belays well back (spare rope required
to the cliff edge) leads down the slabby rib immediately north of the zawn.
The large platform at the base of the rib is accessible in all but the highest
seas. A short traverse right around the rib leads into the zawn.

★**Treasure Island**   100 feet   E1 5b   (26.7.83)
A splendid pitch up the enticing thin crack in the black wall, marred only
by some crumbly rock near the top. Start at low tide in a small, often damp
gully, at the foot of the wall. Move up and right into the crack and climb it
to where the angle relents (sustained but well protected). Follow a small
slab up and left before moving back right to finish via a small rotten
groove. Nut belays in a cracked block well back.

★**Hidden Treasures**   95 feet   E5 6a †   (23.7.85)
A strength-sapping proposition up the right-hand line in the east wall of
the zawn. Good protection if you can hang around to place it. Start
beneath a short groove, just left of the corner of the zawn. Climb the
groove, passing a small dubious flake, and move slightly left to a second
groove. Difficult climbing up the groove (peg runner) gains a temporary
respite in the shape of a narrow ledge. Hard moves up and left gain a
crackline, which in turn leads to a good ledge; traverse right onto a large
flake and finish direct up a thin crack.

★**Buried Gold**   90 feet   E2 5c   (22.7.85)
The more amenable left-hand line. An excellent pitch, sustained but with
good small-wire protection. Start beneath a small corner in the centre of
the wall. Climb the corner and the arête above to a narrow ledge. Move
up into the main groove and follow it to a good ledge at its top. Step left
onto the edge of the slab and follow it to the top. Good block belays.

Pieces of Eight   95 feet   Very Severe 4c   (26.7.83)
The corner and slab of the abseil descent. Start beneath a wide crack in
the slabby, eastern arête of the zawn. Climb the stubborn crack to a ledge
and continue up the corner above to another ledge. Finish up the
prominent crackline in the slab above.

LIFEBOAT BUTTRESS   OS Ref 1279 4497
Terminating the southern side of the large boulder-bay directly below
Quarter Wall is a series of broken buttresses. Lifeboat Buttress is the
largest of these and can be identified by a large undercut slab in its
right-hand side. The buttress is divided from Black Jack Zawn by a narrow
sea-channel.

Walk across the grassy slopes to the north of the ruined keepers' cottages for 100 yards. An abseil from good block belays 60 feet back from the cliff-top (spare rope required) gains the large slabby ledges beneath the buttress. No tidal problems.

Marianne   180 feet   Hard Very Severe †   (16.8.86)
An adventurous left-to-right crossing of the large undercut slab. Start beneath a V-groove in the left-hand edge of the slab.
1   100 feet   5a.   Quit the awkward V-groove after 20 feet for the obvious rightward traverse-line across the slab. Continue across a basalt dyke and take a belay on the easy-angled slab below a steep corner-crack.
2   80 feet   4c.   Move up to the corner and climb it to a small ledge. Continue up the groove above to a large nut and spike belay just below the top. Scramble carefully rightwards to finish.
Variation
The 5a Chimney Pitch †   (16.8.86)
For the climber who has done everything else.
2a   90 feet   5a.   From the stance, step down and traverse right to the short chimney/slot in the arête. Once firmly wedged, follow it to block belays just below the top. Scramble to finish.

Man Overboard   100 feet   E2 5c   (30.8.85)
An exciting pitch up the discontinuous groove-line at the left-hand edge of the large slab. Start as for *Marianne*. Climb the V-groove to its top, and step up and right into the continuation groove. Move immediately back left into a prominent V-shaped notch in the arête and continue directly for 30 feet to an overhang. Surmount this by means of a crack, and continue more easily to the top.

All Hands Lost   100 feet   E1 5c   (25.7.85)
The slabby, overlapped groove at the left-hand side of the buttress. A good pitch with a short difficult section that can be well protected. Approach the groove from the left via a delicate slab, and follow it to a large sloping ledge. Gain the larger continuation groove by a perplexing move and climb it with relative ease to the top.

Beef Buttress   OS Ref 1284 4512

Directly beneath Quarter Wall is a large boulder bay, the northern side of which is formed by a large headland known as Dead Cow Point. Beef Buttress is the steep, south-facing cliff on the southern side of the headland and facing The Battery. An obvious feature of the cliff is a large cave right of centre, which is formed by two almost vertical basalt dykes from which *The Vice* exits. To the left is a fine, crack-seamed wall with the straight twin cracks of *Spare Rib* standing out.

There are two possible approaches. The quicker and safer descent is to abseil down the centre of the cliff from good block belays just below the cliff-top. A spare rope is useful to negotiate the earthy slope down to the blocks. The large, slippery boulders below are exposed from low to half tide. The alternative approach is a death-defying scramble down the disintegrating slope below Quarter Wall.

Spanner   120 feet   Hard Very Severe 4c   (17.9.79)
The large slabby corner-line 60 feet right of the cave of *The Vice*. Some poor rock. The corner proves sparsely protected and leads to an awkward mantelshelf at 50 feet. Climb the broken groove just left of the upper arête, and scramble carefully back to a block and nut belay.

★**The Vice**   130 feet   E1   (5.10.73/2.8.92)
Committing climbing on a strong natural line: a bit of a gripper! Start on top of a large flake in the left wall of the cave.
1 80 feet 5a. Gain the obvious line of holds and pull quickly up and leftwards to a small ledge on the arête. (The original start reaches this point via a faint crack and slim groove round to the left with two pegs for aid.) Move up and rightwards to the large downward-pointing fang under the roof of the cave and, using this, make a difficult move up and left to good holds above. Squeeze into the narrow slot in the large overhang and go up to a stance beneath a corner-crack.
2 50 feet. Climb the corner above and scramble back to good block belays.

The next five routes all start from the slim, brown ledge-system that runs beneath the crack-seamed wall 20 feet above the boulder-beach. Access is by abseil and is possible at all states of the tide. The ledge-system can be gained also from the boulder-beach by a short black corner at a rather greasy Hard Very Severe 5a.

★**Steve Bull**   110 feet   E2 5c †   (8.8.89)
Good approach-work and a powerful finish! Start at the right-hand end of the brown ledge-system. Step round the arête and traverse right into a groove. Climb it and move left into a second groove. Continue up this (peg runner) and exit left at its top by a brisk hand-traverse to the base of a thin crack in the headwall. Climb the crack strenuously and finish easily over large blocks.

★**Spare Rib**   85 feet   E1 5b   (20.9.80)
The twin cracks. Excellent, sustained climbing with good protection. Start beneath an overhang guarding access to the cracks. A difficult start over the overhang gains the cracks, which are followed to the top without deviation.

★**Brisket**   85 feet   E4 6a   (20.9.80)
A technically demanding pitch with a bold crux section. Start as for *Spare Rib*. Step left and climb some thin cracks leftwards to beneath an overhanging, blind flake in the steep wall. Committing moves up the flake

lead to a step right at its top and a small crescent-shaped groove. Climb the groove to an overlap, where a long stride left brings good holds into reach on the slab above. Continue more easily to the top.

Jumpers   75 feet   Hard Severe 4a   (20.9.80)
The large leaning corner at the left-hand end of the ledge-system. Steep but with some big holds. Climb the corner with help from the crack in its left-hand side, and finish slightly left.

★**Oxtail Soup**   75 feet   Very Severe 4c   (27.7.84)
Steep climbing on good holds up the prominent wide crack left of the leaning corner of *Jumpers*. Start at the left-hand end of the ledge-system. A traverse left across the gap gains the crack. A stubborn wide section gives way to easier climbing on satisfying holds that lead directly to the top.

★**Moooooo**   90 feet   E2 5b   (23.7.85)
An enjoyable pitch up the slim buttress left of *Oxtail Soup*, with an exhilarating finale up the square headwall. Start from the boulder-beach at a point 10 feet left of where the crack of *Oxtail Soup* begins. Dead low tide required. Climb up to a large sloping shelf and pull leftwards through the bulges above to a large ledge where the angle eases. Traverse right beneath the headwall, and climb directly up its centre to the top.

Two routes climb the small, south-facing wall at the extreme left end of Beef Buttress. The approach lies down the easy rock steps beyond the abseil point to the main cliff. **Beef Curtains** (30 feet Very Severe 4b † 5.4.87) climbs the left-hand crack in the wall, finishing up the slab above. **The Crinkly End** (50 feet Very Severe 4c † 5.4.87) traverses right along the lowest break in the wall to finish up the right arête. To the north a **Shattered Experience** (55 feet Very Difficult † 5.4.87) can be had up the large broken corner right of the huge overhang. Finally **Mad Cow Disease** (20 feet Hard Very Severe 5c 2.8.92) climbs the thin crack in the south-facing wall at the seaward tip of Dead Cow Point.

Bomber Buttress Area

North of Dead Cow Point, the coastline takes on a more broken appearance with few definable features before the offshore pinnacle of Needle Rock. There are three cliffs in this area, of which Bomber Buttress is the most important.

At plateau-level 200 yards south of Needle Rock is an obvious jutting outcrop with a face-like profile. Beneath lie the scattered remains of a German World War II bomber which crashed into the slopes just below the plateau in 1941.

The descent lies directly below the outcrop: scramble down grassy slopes to the top of a wide grassy rake, indistinct at first and descending to the south (left facing out) towards a boulder-bridge which joins a flat-topped rock pinnacle to the mainland. At the base of the rake lie the Tunnels of Lovely, a curiously romantic name for sea-level tunnels formed by huge chaotic boulders. Bomber Buttress is the steep north-facing cliff towering over the foot of the rake. Beneath the foot of the rake, and directly opposite the flat-topped rock pinnacle, is the less distinct Banana Buttress. The third cliff in the area is Fighter Buttress, which is 150 feet south of Bomber Buttress.

FIGHTER BUTTRESS   OS Ref 1284 4532
Although like Bomber Buttress, this buttress faces north and slants up to the left, the similarities end there. Unstable rock in its upper half makes its two routes potentially dangerous undertakings. Approach by a sea-level traverse south from Bomber Buttress. An alternative, but more exhausting approach is to traverse north from below Dead Cow Point.

In the right-hand side of the cliff is a steep wall with a crackline on either side. **Flak** (95 feet Very Severe 4c † 7.9.73) climbs the right-hand crack and corner above, before moving 15 feet left to finish up the centre of the face. **Tracer** (95 feet Very Severe 4c † 7.9.73) climbs the crack left of the steep wall to ledges on the left, before moving back right to follow the crack to the top. For both routes, belay at a good thread 45 feet back from the centre of the cliff. Owing to the looseness of the terrain, this is best approached by making a detour to the right.

BOMBER BUTTRESS   OS Ref 1290 4537
In the centre of the cliff lies a steep, broken corner that divides the buttress into two sections. The left-hand buttress slants up to the left and is dominated by the curving crackline of *Bender*, with the vertical crack of *Jetset* to its right. The remainder of the routes start down to the right, beneath the Tunnels of Lovely, close to the right extremity of the wall.

The first climb described lies on an isolated buttress between Fighter and Bomber Buttresses.

Biggles   120 feet   Very Difficult   (24.4.76)
A slight but pleasant climb up the undulating buttress. Climb the lower slab to a ledge beneath a groove, move up just right of this, and continue direct to the top.

Beamsplitter   110 feet   Hard Very Severe   (16.4.73)
The crack-system in the right-hand side of Bomber Buttress. Start at the foot of the Tunnels of Lovely beneath a short chimney.
1 60 feet 4a. Climb the chimney and then a crack to a small stance on the right.
2 50 feet 5b. Traverse right across a slab to a thin crack, and climb it and its wider continuation to a ledge. Finish up the short corner above.

Flashback   110 feet   E3   (15.4.73/9.8.82)
A tough, technical problem with two sharply contrasting pitches. Start beneath the short chimney at the foot of the Tunnels of Lovely.
1 70 feet   4b. Climb the short chimney and the corner above to a small overhang. Step up and left into a wide crack and follow it to a stance beneath an overhanging prow.
2 40 feet   6b. With the security of two peg runners, battle up the overhanging prow to a niche. Continue up the easier crack on the right to the top. This pitch can be climbed using the two pegs for aid at 5a, giving a pleasant climb of Hard Very Severe standard.

Direct Start   E1   (9.8.82)
1a 50 feet   5a. More in keeping with the top pitch is the jagged crack in the overhanging wall below *Jetset*.

Quandary   210 feet   Very Severe   (17.4.73)
A right-to-left diagonal, skirting beneath the left-hand buttress to give some enjoyable climbing. Start on the boulders at the foot of the Tunnels of Lovely.
1 60 feet   4b. Follow a rightward-slanting ramp into a corner and pull steeply up into a niche. Step right and move up behind a large flake. At its top, traverse 10 feet left to a spacious boulder-stance beneath the vertical crack of *Jetset*.
2 75 feet   4c. Climb the slab above for 15 feet and go up a ramp to where it steepens; continue strenuously to a good stance.
3 75 feet   4a. Move up and right to a smooth groove, and climb the layback flake on the right wall to its top. Hand-traverse left and move up into a gully. Continue up it to the top.

★★**Jetset**   100 feet   E2 5c   (16.4.73/8.77)
A striking line. The uncompromising vertical crack splitting the left-hand buttress. A sustained and strenuous proposition. Start on the large boulder beneath the crack. Step into the crack above the first overhang, or gain it direct. Continue straight up past three more overhangs to an awkward exit at the top.

★★**Bender**   120 feet   E3 5c   (17.4.73/8.77)
A tremendous route up the huge arching crackline in the left-hand side of the wall. Powerful climbing requiring good crack technique. Start on some large boulders beneath a thin crack in the smooth wall. Climb the crack for 10 feet, where a difficult and committing swing right gains a good hold and the wider crack above. Move up to the overhang and turn it on its right-hand side by a good crack. A short ramp leads to a good resting-place a little higher. Step up and left into a deep crack and climb it past a wide section to a point where the crack bends to the left. Traverse left past a useful chockstone to a ramp and climb it to an overhang. The crack above gives a steep finish.

BANANA BUTTRESS   OS Ref 1290 4537
Although slight in appearance, this gives some pleasant climbing in

secluded surroundings. In the right-hand side of the buttress is a corner bounding the right edge of a slab, **Goodnight Dallas** (90 feet Hard Severe 4a † 9.93). The obvious central line of the slab is **Mellow Yellow** (90 feet Difficult 29.3.67): this starts 60 feet left of a jammed boulder at the right-hand end of the face and trends right to a large ledge at 25 feet; the prominent crackline in the left edge of the slab is then followed to the top. **Banana Crack** (90 feet Very Severe 4b 28.3.67) climbs the big curving crack to the right of *Mellow Yellow*; while **Banana Split** (90 feet Hard Severe 30.3.67) follows an indistinct line to the left of *Mellow Yellow*. The large ledge can also be gained from the right to provide a harder start to all the climbs.

North of Banana Buttress is a large basalt dyke. **Lemon Pie** (100 feet Hard Very Severe 5a 11.4.77) climbs the right edge of the triangular slab, 30 feet north of the dyke, to a ledge. It then continues up a groove above, moving right at its top to finish up a slab.

North of Bomber Buttress, the coastline degenerates into fern-covered slopes intermingled with large boulders and small rock faces of little interest to the climber. However, 200 yards further north two noteworthy features can be seen. At sea-level lies the innocuous-looking Needle Rock, a small, almost non-tidal sea-stack of perfect rock, while at plateau-level lurks:

THE EARTHQUAKE   OS Ref 1305 4546
This unusual feature runs from north to south across the top of the ridge leading down to Needle Rock 200 yards north of the descent to Bomber Buttress. The most westerly cleft is about 6 feet in width, its deepest section being the southerly half. The northerly section is much shallower. An earthy scramble can be made through the base of the cleft, though on its perimeters lie two rather more worthwhile pitches on a huge leaning block.

The Dar-Zim Axis   65 feet   E2 5b   (30.7.86)
The striking left-hand arête at the entrance to the cleft gives a good but bold attraction. Alternatively, move right at 20 feet to gain a shallow left-facing groove: **Half Man, Half Hob-Nob** (70 feet Hard Very Severe 4c 16.8.89).

San Francisco   70 feet   E4 6b †   (31.7.86)
Another interesting pitch taking the centre of the face left of *The Dar-Zim Axis*, past a small overlap and peg runner.

A number of climbs, mostly on friable crystalline rock, can be made at Very Difficult to Severe standard up the cracks in the side walls of the cleft. **Epicentre** (60 feet Hard Severe 20.4.73) takes the crack in the left wall on entrance from the lowest point of the floor while **Livin' Outa Tins** (65 feet E2 5b 31.7.86) follows the obvious crack above the boulder-bridge on the opposite wall. An interesting, though somewhat dramatic start to the descent is to jump across the top of the cleft.

Below the cleft, the prominent pinnacle on the arête leading down to Needle Rock, and the spur beneath it provide a number of short pitches.

Needle Rock Area

Beyond the ridge below The Earthquake stretches the impressive open expanse of Jenny's Cove. Numerous cliffs line the back of the bay varying in height from smaller, easily accessible cliffs in the northern section to the huge brooding masses of The Devil's Chimney Cliff, Deep Zawn, and The Egyptian Slabs forming its back. The sea-stacks of Needle Rock at the tip of the ridge, along with the towering Devil's Chimney tucked into the lower half of the cove, add further variety to a section of the island so steeped in climbing history.

NEEDLE ROCK   OS Ref 1292 4557
This superb sea-stack, a miniature version of The Devil's Chimney, marks the southern limit of Jenny's Cove. It is rather difficult of access but once attained gives some fine climbing in a delightfully atmospheric environment. The boulders that lead out to the rock can be crossed at mid tide and below, but there are times, during calm seas and neap-tides, when they are always accessible at high tide. Descent to these boulders is left to the individual. The direct approach via slopes just south of the ridge leading down to the rock is very steep for scrambling. Further south the descent to Bomber Buttress and that to the north as for Punchbowl Cliff are better, but the subsequent traverses to the stack are rather time-consuming. Dry weather conditions are also most certainly needed as the boulders can become extremely slippery.

Descent from the summit of the pinnacle is by a series of steps on the north face to a ledge with a convenient flake on the north-west arête. From this, a short abseil leads to the starting platform. Alternatively, retreat slings provide a direct abseil facility from the summit. *The Ordinary Route* can also be reversed, only the lower section proving difficult.

The routes are described in a clockwise direction starting with the landward face.

★**The Obverse Route**   80 feet   Very Severe   (5.65)
  1 45 feet 4b. Climb up to the groove running from left to right and follow it to a large ledge round to the right on the north face.
  2 35 feet. Climb via two short walls to the top.

★★**The Hanmer House of Horror**   75 feet   E6 6b †   (3.8.93)
Impressive and bold climbing up the face just left of the south-eastern arête. High in its grade. Climb the wall just left of the arête to gain a break (peg runner). Pull over a bulge and make thin moves straight up to gain

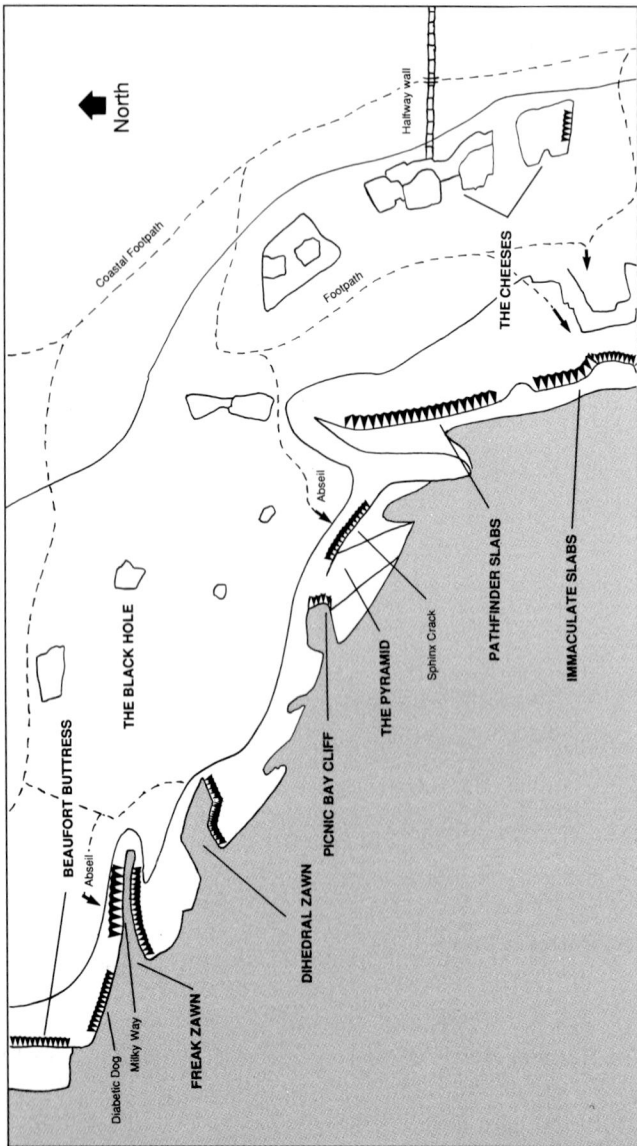

North

Halfway wall

Coastal Footpath

Footpath

THE CHEESES

Abseil

THE BLACK HOLE

PATHFINDER SLABS

IMMACULATE SLABS

BEAUFORT BUTTRESS

Abseil

Sphinx Crack

Diabetic Dog

Milky Way

FREAK ZAWN

DIHEDRAL ZAWN

PICNIC BAY CLIFF

THE PYRAMID

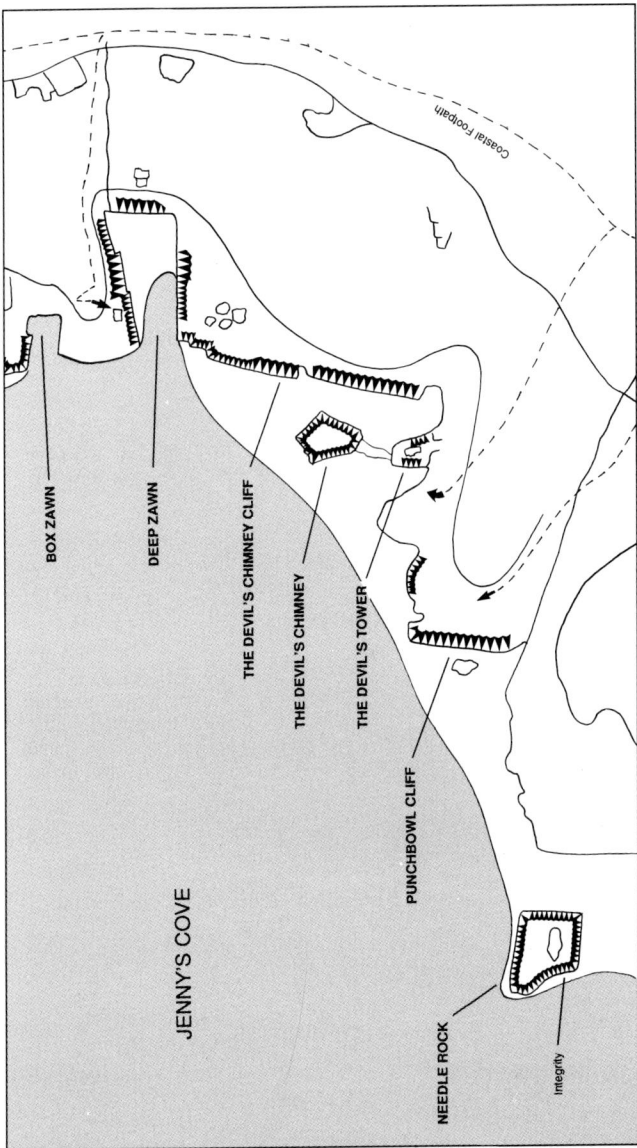

JENNY'S COVE

BOX ZAWN

DEEP ZAWN

THE DEVIL'S CHIMNEY CLIFF

THE DEVIL'S CHIMNEY

THE DEVIL'S TOWER

PUNCHBOWL CLIFF

NEEDLE ROCK

Integrity

Coastal Footpath

the comfort of good incut holds. Continue direct, with an easing in difficulty, to finish just right of a prominent flake.

★★Sea of Tranquility   75 feet   E4 6a   (4.8.87)
A superb little pitch taking the centre of the golden, south face. Small-wire protection provides a modicum of comfort. Enter the prominent slim groove and follow it to its end. Exit onto the wall above (*Friend 3* useful), where difficult moves up a faint crack give way to easier climbing. Continue up the centre of the face, left of the crack, to a large finishing flake.

★Sea of Dreams   75 feet   E3 6a   (9.8.90)
A suitable companion route up the left-hand side of the south face. Follow vague twin cracks to a point where they curve off to the right. Continue directly up the featureless wall via a series of breaks to reach the arête at a clean white fin. Finish up this.

★Invincible   75 feet   Very Severe 4c   (4.8.87)
The fine south-west arête of the pinnacle gives a very pleasant, airy pitch. Absorbing climbing leads directly to a slightly more amenable finish left of *Integrity*.

The seaward face of the rock is relatively steep, yet surprisingly covered in a profusion of good holds. Numerous lines are possible in the lower grades and can be varied at will. One particular line, however, proves of individual merit.

★★★Integrity   80 feet   Severe   (29.3.67)
A brilliant route, the approaches to and atmosphere of the pinnacle making a memorable outing. From the foot of *Invincible*, move round left onto the seaward face and climb a crack 10 feet left of the arête for 30 feet. Move right towards the arête and gain a sharp spur on it; then move up and out right onto the southern face. A large flake on this leads to the top.

★★The Ordinary Route   65 feet   Difficult   (6.61)
Yet another delightful climb. Start from the seaward end of the large platform below the north face.
1 40 feet. An awkward step up and right leads onto the seaward face. Continue diagonally rightwards to a large ledge.
2 25 feet. Move back right onto the face and climb direct to the top. A pitch which can be easily avoided around to the left.

A further short pitch is given by the short steep layback-crack in the north-western aspect of the rock: **Thread** (40 feet Severe 4.63).

PUNCHBOWL CLIFF   OS Ref 1308 4564
Looking along the coastline from Needle Rock one can see the first, and smallest, of a number of cliffs defining the back of Jenny's Cove. An

inconspicuous green arête divides two contrasting faces. The cliff-top is most easily gained by following the stream running down the Punchbowl Valley 200 yards north of The Earthquake from plateau-level, and then breaking out to the right (facing out).

The main, west-facing wall of the cliff is bounded on the right by the stream emanating from the Punchbowl Valley. For the most part, this face's upper quarter is lichen-covered except where extensive gardening has created viable exits.

Access is a little awkward, since there are no substantial anchors lining the rim of the cliff. Belays are well back on a large block and an extra rope is required from this to reach the cliff-top. This enables a 120-foot abseil from here to the boulder-beach below. Otherwise, a lengthy boulder-hop from The Devil's Chimney Cliff has to be made at low tide. It is then also necessary to pull a climbing rope through to reach back to the belay points.

THE WEST FACE
This secluded face gives excellent open climbing and catches the sunshine in the afternoon. The climbs towards the left-hand side of the wall are mid-tide affected.

Immediately left of the stream, the streaked face is split by two diagonal cracks.

★Right Between the Eyes   100 feet   E2 5b †   (3.8.93)
A good route with plentiful protection. Start 15 feet left of the stream. Climb a series of cracks moving leftwards to reach the main, right-hand crack. This gives sustained climbing, through an overlap, to less prominent cracks in the headwall. Follow these to the top.

★Look Daggers   100 feet   E3 6a   (2.8.86)
The left-hand crackline gives some very good climbing. Start at a shallow groove just to the left of the foot of *Right Between the Eyes*. Climb the difficult groove and bulge to a small ledge; then move rightwards to reach the crack and follow it, using a series of face holds, to gain an overlap. With this at chest height, swing out left onto the clean strip in the upper slab. Pick the easiest line, taking care at the top.

★★Atlantic Mocean   95 feet   E6 6a   (2.8.86/1.8.89)
Technical, bold, and intimidating climbing almost devoid of protection where it counts. Move up the groove as for *Look Daggers* and once on the face step left (good small-wire placement up and to the right). Confident edging up the centre of the face on rugosities gains a thin crack and a sigh of relief. Move up to the overlap and pull through onto the cleaned upper face. Saunter up this to finish.
The Direct Start   E7 6b   (1.8.89)
An intense sequence of hard moves up the face left of the original from the

obvious trough in the boulders. A landing-team may be of some use, or a mattress!

In the centre of the face are two wide converging cracks, the most obvious feature hereabouts.

★**Specific Nocean**   105 feet   E3 5c †   (12.8.93)
Pleasantly sustained and on excellent rock. Climb the right-hand crack for 20 feet and then transfer into the thin crack on the right. Climb this, using face holds on the left, to reach an overlap (junction with *Atlantic Mocean*). Pull left onto the upper face and finish up a cleaned thin crack.

★★**Innocent Moves**   110 feet   E4 6a †   (3.8.93)
Fine climbing throughout. Climb the left-hand crack via a steep start and follow a shallow groove to a small ledge above a bulge. Pull out left above the overhang and continue straight up (peg runner) to a small ledge. Step up on the right before moving left to climb some thin cracks to a niche. Exit carefully left from the top of this to a good ledge. Finish up a thin crack.

★★**The Golden Handshake**   100 feet   E4 5c   (2.8.86)
An excellent, varied route up the face left of the obvious wide converging cracks. Good, though spaced protection; and well endowed with positive holds. Start on a block 15 feet left of the left-hand crack, just below a square-cut ledge. A short crack gains the face, from where moves rightwards across the wall lead to an obvious left-facing groove. Move up this for a few feet before exiting right onto the upper face. Traverse delicately back left above the lip of the overlaps for 10 feet to reach a thin crack splitting the upper wall. This gives the finish.

★**Silver Smile**   100 feet   E5 6b †   (3.8.89)
Good climbing with a powerful, then technical crux sequence. Intricate face-work up the thin crack above the start of *The Golden Handshake* leads to the overlap. Difficult moves using a flake (peg runner) and then face holds lead leftwards to good holds. Step left to gain and follow a series of disjointed cracks to a sound exit.

★**Dweebland**   90 feet   E3 6a   (3.8.89)
Direct and worthwhile climbing but with an out-of-character crux. Climb the crack 10 feet left of *Silver Smile* and continue up the face to a niche in the roof. Using a series of undercut holds, muscle through this and exit via technical moves over the lip (peg runner) to ledges. Step left and follow disjointed cracks to finish.

★★**Promises**   125 feet   E1   (1.8.85)
A very enjoyable outing on good rock and with excellent protection.
1 75 feet   5b. Follow the initial crack of *Dweebland*, but branch off to the left to reach the overlap (peg runner). Surmount this and continue steeply rightwards up the crack to a ledge-system. Traverse left to a belay beneath a thin crack.

2 50 feet 5b. Climb the crack to where it curves right, and then move left across the wall to a second crack. Follow this and the wall above to the top.
Variation
★**Wishful Thinking** E3   (4.8.86)
A direct version of *Promises*.
1a 70 feet 5c. Climb the initial crack of Promises but move immediately left and follow a shallow groove to the overlap. Overcome this leftwards past a grey scar to a ledge on the left. Continue up the left side of a short groove to the belay of *Promises*.

★**The Green Light** 90 feet Hard Very Severe 5a   (4.10.73)
The large tapering chimney-line in the left-hand side of the face.
Interesting and varied climbing. Move up the chimney, exiting right onto a short slab. Move back left across the top of the chimney to some ledges and then continue above to more ledges beneath a leftward-slanting crackline. Climb the crack to the top.

Pretender 90 feet Very Severe 4c   (5.8.86)
The cracked wall to the left of *The Green Light*. Follow a leftward-trending crack past a bulge to a ledge. Continue up to an overlap at a square cutaway and balance up and over it. Follow thin cracks to a final step left onto a good ledge on the arête, and belay. Scrambling remains.

Punchbowl Arête 90 feet Very Difficult   (8.69)
The arête terminating the west-facing wall. A pleasant route but with some loose rock. The main difficulties are provided by a short smooth groove at half height, entered from the left.

THE NORTH FACE
The continuation of the cliff is more broken by ledges but provides two routes. A prominent landmark is a large projecting finger of rock, around which the first route is based. The best access to this face is by traversing across the boulder-field from the foot of the descent to The Devil's Chimney Cliff.

Round the Horn 150 feet Hard Very Severe   (14.4.74)
Some loose rock. Start at a groove 20 feet right of a crack leading to the rock finger.
1 90 feet 4c. Climb the groove until it steepens into some loose blocks. Traverse left to the rock finger and belay on it.
2 60 feet 4b. Step left into a groove and climb it to the top.

The final route on this particular cliff is based on a slim wall up and to the left of the rock finger. This lies to the west of the obvious blocky spur descending from the cliff-top, the descent to The Devil's Chimney Cliff.

★**Dirty Lundies** 80 feet E2 5c   (14.8.87)
An enjoyable and accessible pitch up the centre of the slim wall. Start on a

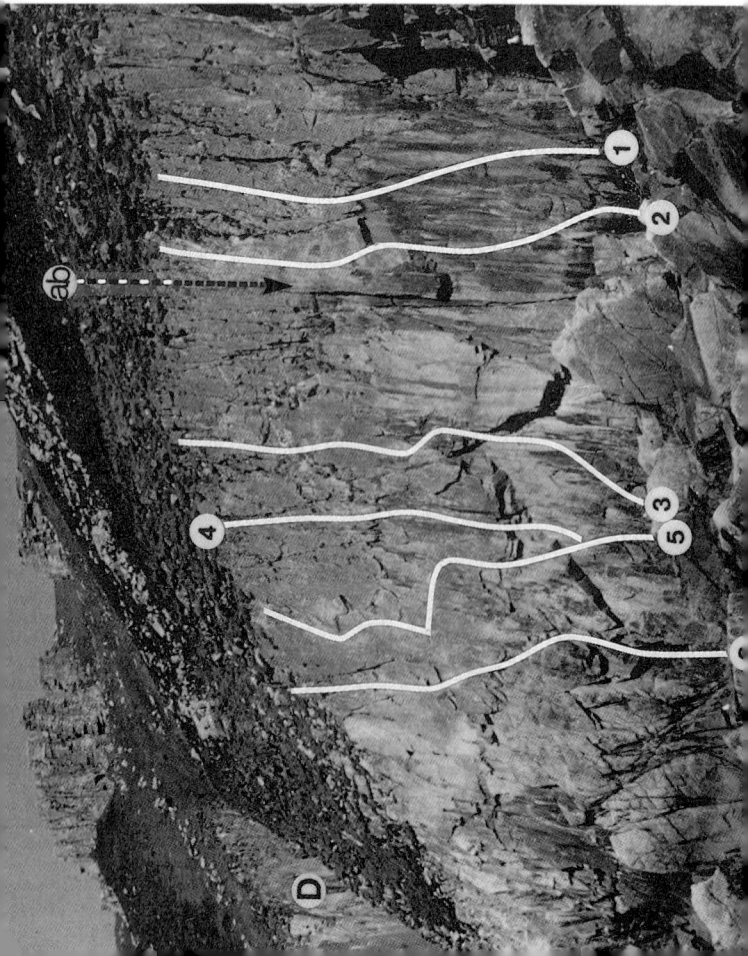

PUNCHBOWL CLIFF

1 Right Between the
  Eyes   E2
2 Atlantic Mocean   E6
3 The Golden Handshake   E4
4 Dweebland   E3
5 Promises   E1
6 The Green Light   HVS

D Deep Zawn

good ledge 30 feet above the sea-level boulders, gained by abseil from a block 30 feet back from the edge, or by traversing left (facing out) from the descent to The Devil's Chimney Cliff. Climb diagonally rightwards to reach a thin crack just left of the arête of the wall, and follow this to a break (peg runner). Make a tricky move up to the next break; then storm the leaning headwall via a thin crack and a profusion of holds.

The Devil's Chimney Area

The Devil's Chimney is the spectacular offshore pinnacle in the southern corner of Jenny's Cove. To its south, barely independent of the mainland, is an impressive pillar of rock, The Devil's Tower. Dominating the cove, however, is the huge, brooding mass of The Devil's Chimney Cliff.

Within this wild and dramatic arena can be found some of the island's longest and most intimidating climbs. The emphasis here is very much on adventure and commitment; particular attention should always be paid to tidal and weather conditions.

The approach to The Devil's Chimney Area is not straightforward and demands care, particularly on first acquaintance. Descend the large grassy slope that forms the southern side of Jenny's Cove: this is just north of the stream in Punchbowl Valley. A small but well-trodden path dips down below the cliff-top onto the top of the large spur south-west of The Devil's Chimney itself. A large detached flake at the top of the spur provides a convenient belay point for a fixed rope. Descend the spur over large jumbled blocks to the floor of the cove; or abseil.

THE DEVIL'S TOWER   OS Ref 1316 4563
This is the narrow buttress of rock passed under on the descent spur. Its west face is split by a prominent straight crack, *Hob's Lane*, the foot of which can be reached from the perilously loose gully beneath the face. A far safer alternative is to abseil either from the top of the tower or from the descent spur.

★Hob's Lane   90 feet   E2 5b   (17.4.74)
A compelling line. After a shaky start the crack gives excellent, steep jamming with good protection. Climb the crack, indistinct at first, directly to the summit. Block and thread belay. Scramble carefully back to the mainland.

Fissure Fergus   220 feet   E2   (3.8.87)
The north face of the tower. The route has plenty of character but some of the rock requires careful handling. Start from the floor of the cove beneath a slabby rib leading up to the tower.
1 90 feet 4c. Climb up to the base of a vegetated groove and follow it to

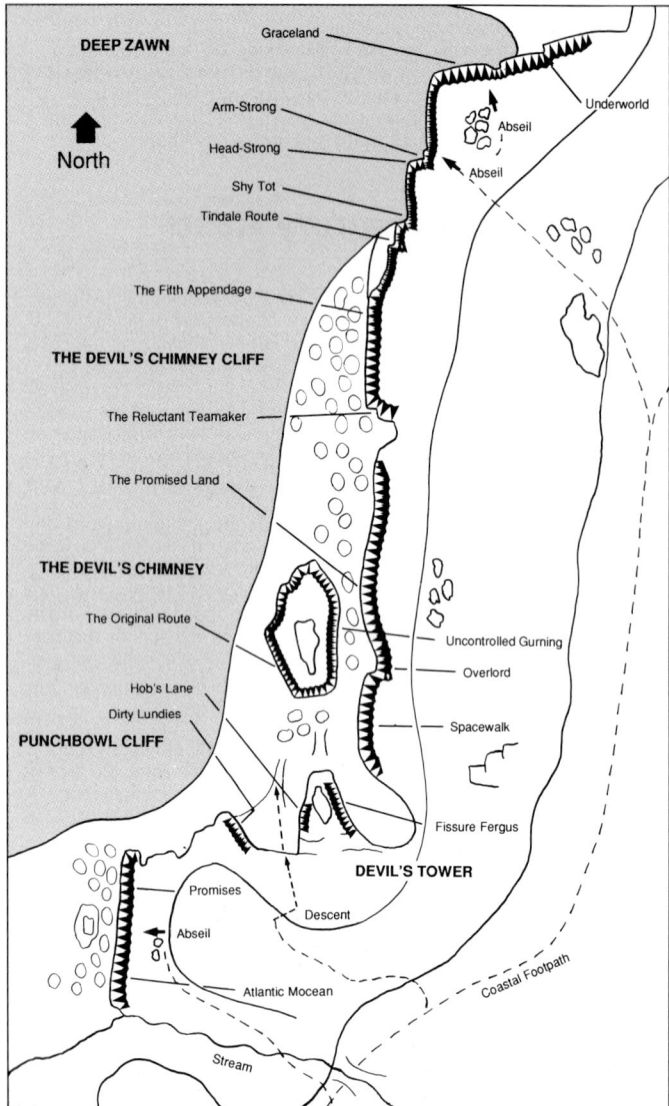

DEEP ZAWN

Graceland

Underworld

North

Arm-Strong

Abseil

Head-Strong

Abseil

Shy Tot

Tindale Route

The Fifth Appendage

THE DEVIL'S CHIMNEY CLIFF

The Reluctant Teamaker

The Promised Land

THE DEVIL'S CHIMNEY

The Original Route

Uncontrolled Gurning

Overlord

Hob's Lane

Dirty Lundies

PUNCHBOWL CLIFF

Spacewalk

Fissure Fergus

DEVIL'S TOWER

Promises

Descent

Abseil

Atlantic Mocean

Coastal Footpath

Stream

a stance where the angle steepens. Good nut belays.
2 130 feet 5b. Move steeply up and right for 20 feet, step right taking care with loose blocks, and follow the rightward-slanting slabs to below a hanging corner. Climb the corner past a hanging flake to a resting-place on its top. Continue up the flakes above to a final corner and the top. A coffin-shaped block provides an appropriate belay. Scramble back carefully to the mainland.

THE DEVIL'S CHIMNEY   OS Ref 1319 4570
This is the largest sea-pinnacle on Lundy, and sports a number of exciting lines to its summit; a must for any aspiring sea-stack climber. Access is from low to mid tide; careful judgement is essential as the return to the mainland is quickly cut off by an incoming tide. Descent from the summit is by abseil from some large blocks; it may be wise to carry some spare pieces of tape to leave *in situ*.
The climbs are described in an **anti-clockwise** direction, starting from the southerly face.

★★The Devil's Chimney 105 feet Very Severe   (6.61/8.69)
A good climb in dramatic surroundings. Start opposite the descent rib, on a large platform at the foot of twin leftward-slanting cracks.
1 35 feet 4a. Climb the right-hand crack; then traverse easily left to a large boulder-strewn ledge.
2 70 feet 4c. Climb the centre of the steep slab above by a thin crack to a small overhang. Surmount this and climb the steep wall above, trending left to the arête, which is followed to the summit.
The Original Finish   Very Severe
2a 70 feet 4b. Climb the steep groove formed by a small pinnacle at the extreme left-hand edge of the boulder-strewn ledge and continue up the arête to the top. Loose and not as pleasant.

★Poltergeist 140 feet Hard Very Severe   (11.8.86)
The south-east arête of the pinnacle has tremendous exposure for the grade. Start at sea-level on the east side of the pinnacle, beneath a shallow groove in a black, often greasy wall.
1 45 feet 5a. Gain the groove in the wall and climb it to the large ledge beneath the twin cracks of *The Devil's Chimney*.
2 95 feet 5a. Climb the right-hand crack for 12 feet before moving right to a thinner crack which leads onto the arête. Go up the arête via a wide, diagonal crack to reach a small ledge. A short wall leads to a larger ledge, from where the slabby left-hand arête is followed to the summit.

The Johnny Weed 90 feet E3 5c †   (23.8.90)
Start on the large platform as for *The Devil's Chimney*. Follow pitch 2 of *Poltergeist* out onto the arête but continue traversing along a line of holds, across the overhanging east face, to a crack on the far side. Climb this directly to the top.

★★**Uncontrolled Gurning**   140 feet   E5 †   (25.9.90)
Outrageous climbing centred on the soaring thin crack in the overhanging east face. This sees little sunlight and is rarely dry. Start at the foot of the face beneath a seaweed-covered ramp, accessible only at low tide.
1 80 feet 6a. Follow the ramp to some small ledges at 20 feet. From their right-hand end, climb boldly up a groove to a vague niche (small-wire protection). Move up and right past a thin crack and climb the smooth wall above to some flakes in the roof. Pull straight over via a solid jammed flake onto the slab above to reach a belay. The ledge at the top of the ramp can also be gained by climbing more easily down flakes from the large platform of *The Devil's Chimney*.
2 60 feet 6a. Step back down and swing round into the diagonal crack. Climb it, initially on good finger-locks, to a large niche. Finish up the slabby arête on the left.

★**White Riot**   130 feet   Very Severe   (1.9.79)
The west face of the pinnacle. A good route with a pleasant, open aspect. Start at sea-level, beneath twin cracks.
1 60 feet 4c. Climb the smaller, right-hand crack to an overhang. Step right and continue up more cracks in the wall above to the large belay ledge on *The Devil's Chimney*.
2 70 feet 4c. Step onto the slab above the left-hand end of the ledge, and move left again onto the face. Go awkwardly up to a flat-topped spike; then move right to finish via some cracked blocks on the right.
Left Hand Start   Very Severe   (4.8.81)
1a 60 feet 4c. Climb the wider, left-hand crack until a swing right leads onto the arête. The cracked wall above leads to a small V-groove. Follow this to some ledges; then move right and up to the large belay ledge.

★★**Eye of the Needle**   140 feet   E3   (1.8.84)
A sensational route, climbing through the very heart of the 'needle' to finish up the hanging slab on the north face of the pinnacle. Start from the large platform on the south face, just left of the twin cracks of *The Devil's Chimney*.
1 80 feet 6a. Bridge through the 'eye' to gain a ledge on the right arête (facing out). Climb a thin crack just right of the arête until a difficult, committing move leads up and left to good holds around the arête. Continue more easily to small ledges at the base of the slab.
2 60 feet 4c. Move left and follow the superbly positioned, snaking crack up the slab, through two overlaps, to a perched block on the arête. Climb the arête on the right to the summit.

THE DEVIL'S CHIMNEY CLIFF   OS Ref 1320 4568
The Devil's Chimney Cliff attracted the main attention: the mornings reverberated to the crashes of loose rock being trundled into the zawn, while the afternoons rang with yells of delight as yet another cherished plum fell to its ambitious pioneers.
                                                            Mountain 37 1974

This impressive cliff plays host to some of the most serious undertakings on Lundy. The cliff is bounded to the right by an immense, dank gully, and in its right-hand side a large leftward-leaning depression indicates the line of the circuitous *Overlord*. Its impending right wall is climbed by *Spacewalk* and *Diablo*. The awesome undercut wall to the left is breached by the formidable *Stalingrad* and *The Promised Land*, the latter one of the island's outstanding climbs. To the north, the cliff gradually diminishes in height taking on a silvery appearance before turning sharply into the mainland in the form of the dungeon-like recess of Deep Zawn.

All the climbs here are tidal. Low tide is required to reach the base of the routes left of *The Reluctant Teamaker*. Access to *The Promised Land* and *Spacewalk* is possible two hours either side of low tide, ideally when any afternoon sunshine helps to dry out the usually damp starts.

★★**Spacewalk**   280 feet   E2   (18.4.74)

A great route giving consistently good climbing in increasingly exposed positions. A good introduction to the cliff. It follows the right-hand edge of the huge impending fault via a series of ribs and spectacular grooves. Start beneath the rib, to the right of the large fault.

1 130 feet 5b. Climb the rib on its right-hand side to a ledge. Continue up the steep groove above and then delicately up the arête to a good stance. Peg and nut belay.
2 80 feet 5a. Follow the groove just left of the stance for 15 feet and move left to good holds on the rib. Climb up to enter the groove above, and follow it for 10 feet until able to stand on a big flake on the right wall. Traverse across the left wall on flat handholds to gain a larger, bottomless groove. Climb this for 10 feet to gain a small stance and nut belays.
3 70 feet 5b. Climb the groove; then move left to an obvious line of holds on the exposed, upper wall. Continue directly to a small ledge before trending slightly left to the top.

Diablo   280 feet   E3   (13.4.74)

A rather sombre undertaking up the right-hand side of the fault. Technical difficulty is not high but some of the holds are suspect and the line is intimidating. Start 30 feet left of the base of the faultline below the wide crack of *Overlord*.

1 130 feet 5a. Climb the crack to a ledge; then move right across the faultline to gain a greenish slab in the spur on the right. Cross the foot of the slab and climb a shallow groove to a ledge. Continue up the spur, trending slightly left to a stance beneath a steep groove.
2 80 feet 5b. Move up and swing cautiously right using an apparently solid but in fact detached column of rock into the first groove of *Spacewalk*. Climb the groove until a sharp flake on the left wall is reached. Move right and up to a poor stance (high nut belay).
3 70 feet 4c. Go up and left and climb the vegetated slab to the top.

Overlord   360 feet   E1   (10.9.72)

Adventure with a capital 'A'. The original route of the cliff, taking a line based on the huge depressed fault. The route begins by climbing up to the right of the fault before a crucial leftward traverse gains the upper slabs. Exposed and serious with some loose and vegetated rock. It is advisable to carry pegs and a hammer as the *in-situ* pegs are in a very poor state. Start 30 feet left of the faultline below a wide crack. Dry conditions recommended.

1 30 feet. Climb the crack to a ledge.
2 100 feet 5a. Climb up to the right, crossing the faultline to gain a greenish slab in the spur to the right. Move across the foot of the slab into a shallow groove and climb it to a ledge. Continue up the spur on suspect rock, trending slightly left, to a stance at its top.
3 80 feet 4c. Step left into the faultline, now a gully, and descend until moves left gain the obvious traverse-line (peg runner). Step up and traverse left along the upper line of flakes to a large pointed block (peg runner). Climb a short steep wall and follow another line of flakes to a stance on the edge of the large slab. Peg belays.
4 150 feet 4b. Move up and left and climb the crackline in the slab to holds which lead rightwards to some short cracks. Ascend these, and then move left to the base of the obvious wide crack, which leads to the top of the cliff. Scramble back to a block belay and 'thank god its Overlord!'

★★**Stalingrad** 270 feet E3   (14.4.74)
A formidable combination of delicate and strenuous climbing gives access to the large, vegetated crack-system in the left-hand side of the upper wall. Start 90 feet left of *Overlord* at a line of holds beneath a corner at 25 feet, often greasy.
1 100 feet 5c. Climb awkwardly up, bearing right, before pulling back left to the base of the corner. Climb this to the left edge of a small slab sandwiched between the overhangs. Traverse thinly right across the slab and move up into a steep crack. Continue strenuously rightwards to a large spike, and then follow a basalt dyke to a small stance (nut belays).
2 50 feet 4a. Climb the crack above. Move left and up a series of steps in the slab to a stance beneath a large crack.
3 120 feet 5a. Climb steeply up the crack and continue directly to the top.

★★★**The Promised Land** 280 feet E3   (16.4.74)
An amazing route weaving an audacious passage through the great barrier of overhangs. One of the great sea-cliff experiences. The climbing is reasonable though highly improbable, and there is generally good protection. Some of the pegs, however, are not wearing too well. Start as for *Stalingrad*.
1 100 feet 5c. Follow a line of awkward, greasy holds for 10 feet; then step left and climb the black slab into a system of grooves leading up to the big roof. Traverse left for 20 feet (often wet but on good holds), to below a bottomless chimney on the left-hand side of the huge block on the lip of the roof. Pull up to get established in the chimney, where outrageous 'back and footing' brings a crack on the right within reach. A wild hand-traverse along this leads to a small stance and peg belays above the lip of the roof.

Out Come the Freaks Again (first ascent) The Black Hole
Climber: Gary Gibson

Photo: Hazel Gibson

Brisket Beef Buttress
Climber: Paul Harrison

Photo: Simon Cardy

2 50 feet 6a. Climb the groove above the belay until the holds run out! A thin sequence right past a peg runner leads to easier climbing trending right to a small stance shared with *Stalingrad*. Using the peg for aid reduces the grade to 5b.

3 130 feet 5b. Climb the crack above the stance to a big spike on the right, and move diagonally right to a juggy ledge. Climb a groove above for 20 feet to a cluster of spikes and then directly to the top. Originally the route traversed right from the spikes to another, now vegetated groove, which led to the top.

Bounding the left-hand side of the undercut wall is a huge, unclimbed corner running the full height of the cliff. A smaller corner to the left is climbed by *The Reluctant Teamaker*. Left again is a large, undercut slab taken by *The Satan Bug* and *The Fifth Appendage*. Beyond the left arête of the slab is a series of grooves and arêtes with a large area of slabby ledges beneath. This is just before the cliff swings sharply round into Deep Zawn. The finishes to all the climbs in this area involve careful scrambling up the steep grassy slopes above the cliff-top.

★★The Reluctant Teamaker 170 feet E3 (17.4.73/2.8.88)
The clean open-book corner gives fine technical climbing, well protected by small wires. Start beneath the corner. Be careful not to knock all the limpets off – some of them prove useful!

1 60 feet 6a. The entry into the corner is difficult and often damp. Once established, continue direct to a small ledge and nut belay.

2 40 feet 5c. Proceed up and rightwards to the top of a large, friable ledge-system (*Friend* runners). Swing boldly left across the steep wall to a good hold on the arête and a ledge a little higher. Continue up the arête to the foot of a long diagonal ramp.

3 70 feet. Follow the ramp leftwards to a block belay. Scrambling remains.

★★The Beguiled 170 feet E4 (2.8.88)
A captivating pitch starting up *The Reluctant Teamaker* before following the right arête of the large slab. Start as for that route.

1 100 feet 6a. Climb the corner to a small overlap and place some small wires above. Hand-or-foot-traverse up this ledge on the left wall to reach a shallow groove in the arête. Climb this and the overlap above by a thin crack and continue more easily to a junction with *The Reluctant Teamaker*. Belay at the foot of the large ramp.

2 70 feet. Continue easily leftwards up the ramp to the top.

★The Satan Bug 180 feet E4 (1 pt aid) † (2.8.88)
A perplexing start gives access to some stylish face climbing up the centre of the steep slab. The peg should be tested (and replaced if necessary) beforehand. Start midway between *The Reluctant Teamaker* and the left-hand arête of the slab on a huge boulder, beneath a thin weakness beginning at 20 feet.

1 110 feet 6a. With the aid of a long stick, clip the peg at 20 feet and

jumar up to it. Difficult free-climbing via a faint crackline leads over a series of overlaps to better holds. Continue straight up the slab before trending rightwards to a large ledge and belay.
2 70 feet. Move up to the ramp and follow it leftwards to good block belays. Scrambling remains.

★★The Fifth Appendage   180 feet   E1   (18.4.73)
A superb open climb up the left-hand side of the large slab. Start at the right-hand end of the large slabby ledges at the left-hand end of the cliff, 20 feet above the boulder-bed and just left of the base of a brown corner.
1 70 feet 5b. Traverse right across slabs beneath an overhang to the base of a rightward-facing groove. Pull into this and climb it for 12 feet until it is possible to traverse delicately right to a small ledge. Move right again for 5 feet, and then trend up and left to a small stance. Poor Belay.
2 110 feet 5a. Climb the slab directly above the belay to the first of two overhangs. Pull over it and turn the second overhang on its right-hand side. Continue up to a good flake, and follow the crack on the right to a good block belay.

Direct Start   E2
1a 70 feet 5c. The rightward-facing groove can be reached direct from the boulder-bed by a difficult, often greasy crack.

The Mexican Connection   475 feet   E2   (3 pts aid)   (17.4.74)
A long expedition with its fair share of loose rock and good positions. It girdles the cliff from left to right starting up *The Fifth Appendage* and finishing up *Overlord*.
1 70 feet 5b. *The Fifth Appendage* pitch 1.
2 85 feet 4b. From the stance, take a rising traverse-line on good holds to a ledge in a corner. Continue in the same line to a stance on the edge of the large gully.
3 80 feet 5a. Move up the grooves and ledges above the stance until it is possible to traverse right into the gully. Move out onto a rib on the other side of the gully and step up to a ledge (peg runner). Traverse right for 10 feet and make a difficult move into a scoop. Climb the wall above with three pegs for aid; then move right to a ledge and belay.
4 55 feet 4a. Traverse right to a stance on *Stalingrad* and descend this route for 25 feet, via the stepped slab, to a small stance.
5 35 feet 4c. Move across the crackline and make a series of delicate moves to reach another crack on the right. Follow this for a few feet until a long step right gains the ledge below the final pitch of *Overlord*.
6 150 feet 4b. *Overlord* pitch 4.

★★Psylocybin   160 feet   E2 5c   (18.8.93)
The elegant, left arête of *The Fifth Appendage* slab leads to an exciting finish up the headwall above. Careful ropework required. Start as for *The Fifth Appendage*. Move up into the groove of *The Fifth Appendage* and pull out left almost immediately to a good hold on the slab. Taking a line just right of the arête, climb straight up the slab with a bold section to reach a small ledge (belay possible). Continue up to the base of the

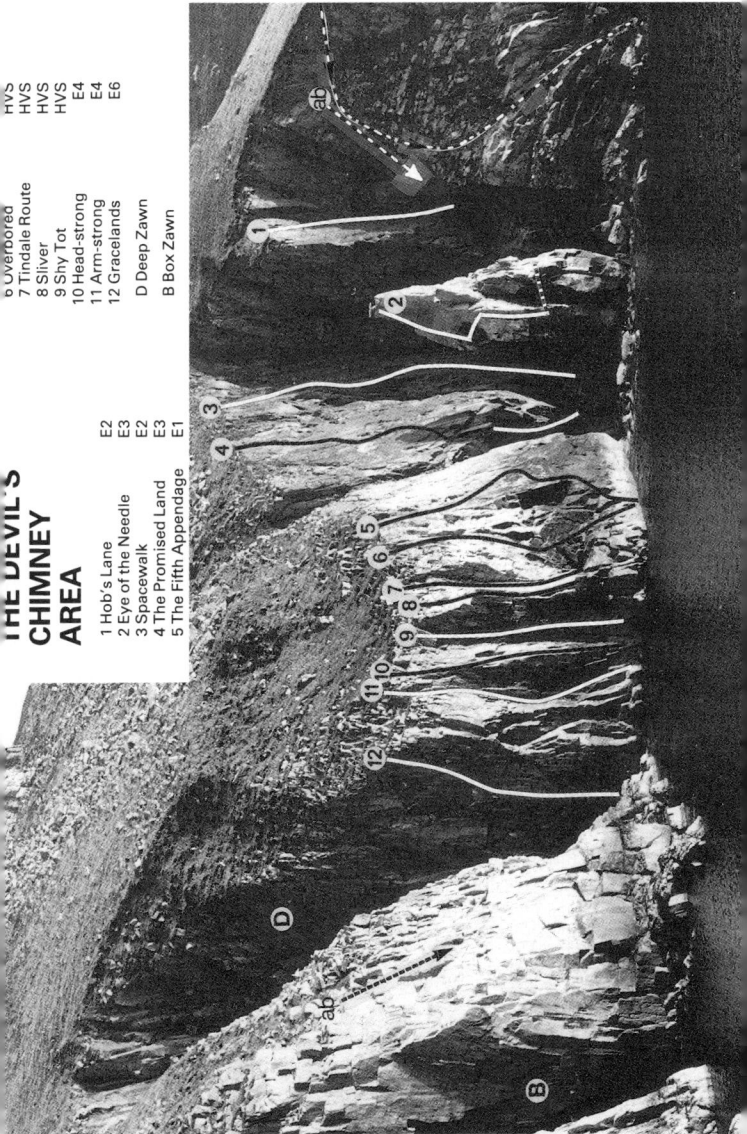

THE DEVIL'S CHIMNEY AREA

1 Hob's Lane	E2
2 Eye of the Needle	E3
3 Spacewalk	E2
4 The Promised Land	E3
5 The Fifth Appendage	E1

6 Overbored	HVS
7 Tindale Route	HVS
8 Sliver	HVS
9 Shy Tot	HVS
10 Head-strong	E4
11 Arm-strong	E4
12 Gracelands	E6
D Deep Zawn	
B Box Zawn	

DEVIL'S CHIMNEY CLIFF – OVERLORD AREA

1 Overlord	E1
2 Stalingrad	E3
3 The Promised Land	E3

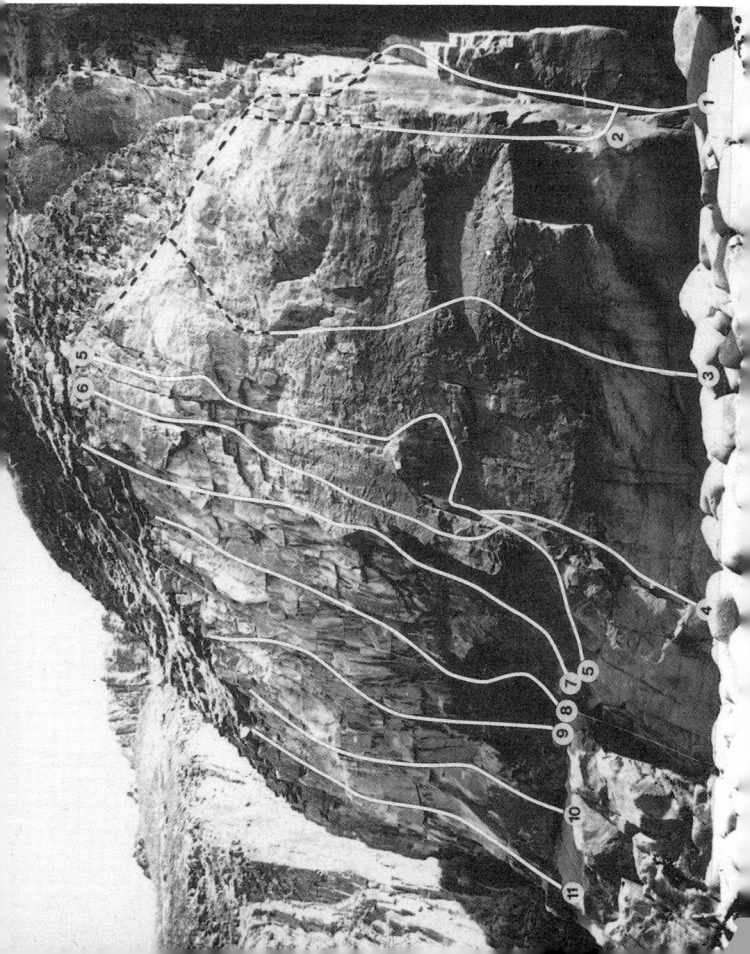

THE DEVIL'S
CHIMNEY
CLIFF – THE
FIFTH
APPENDAGE
AREA

1 The Reluctant Teamaker	E3
2 The Beguiled	E4
3 Satan Bug	E4
4 The Fifth Appendage Direct Start	E2
5 The Fifth Appendage	E1
6 Psylocybin	E2
7 Peyote	E2
8 Overbored	HVS
9 Jezebel	E1
10 Tindale Route	HVS
11 Silver	HVS

headwall, where a line of rightward-trending flakes are followed to the foot of a steep groove. Climb this with difficulty, finishing up an easy crack in the face above.

★Peyote   130 feet   E2   5b   (12.4.74/20.8.86)
The series of grooves in the left arête of the slab give a fine and well-positioned climb. Start as for *The Fifth Appendage*, beneath the large brown corner capped by an overhang. Climb the corner and move right along a line of holds leading onto the arête. Go up a shallow open corner to a small overhang and continue up the slab above to better holds. Trend up and left into a long, slender groove, which is followed to the top.

Cat O' Nine Tails   100 feet   E1   5b †   (1.8.89)
A slight pitch, squeezed in between *Peyote* and *Overbored*. Start 15 feet left of *Peyote* beneath a rightward-slanting crack. Move up to the crack and follow it into a niche. Go up and left to a ledge and step left again into the groove of *Overbored*. Continue up this for 15 feet; then step back right into a yellow groove leading to the top.

Overbored   100 feet   Hard Very Severe   5a   (28.9.85)
To the left of *Cat O' Nine Tails* is a slim, black groove. Start beneath stepped ledges to its left. Gain the groove from the ledges, and climb it (peg runner) to unstable ground just below the top. Move left and up to a block belay.

Jezebel   90 feet   E1   5b †   (17.8.93)
A deceptively steep pitch up the blocky groove 20 feet left of *Overbored*. Climb directly up the groove-line to a prominent deep slot. Jam steeply up the slot and exit onto a small ledge above. Continue up a slim groove and a short wall above to finish slightly leftwards. Block belays.

Tindale Route   80 feet   Hard Very Severe   5a   (5.65/10.8.80)
The prominent white groove on the right-hand side of the left-bounding arête of the wall. A varied and enjoyable pitch. Move steeply up into the groove and climb it for 60 feet to where an awkward step right leads onto the arête. Climb this to a block belay.

★Sliver   80 feet   Hard Very Severe   5a   (1.9.78)
The attractive slim groove in the arête left of *Tindale Route*. Start beneath a slabby arête leading to the groove. Go up the arête and climb the groove above in its entirety to a small bay and block belays.

★Black Looks   90 feet   E2   5b   (28.9.85)
To the left of *Sliver* is the large black corner of *Shy Tot*. A shallow groove and crack in its right wall gives an open and surprisingly good climb. Start as for *Sliver*. Traverse left onto the wall and climb the groove and crack past a small bulge to where the wall narrows. Continue up until it is possible to move right to the arête, which leads to the top.

Shy Tot   110 feet   Hard Very Severe   5a   (25.8.78)
The large black corner. A strong natural line with some worthwhile climbing. Start as for *Sliver*. Traverse left across the wall beneath an overhanging nose to reach the corner. Climb the corner, and where the going gets
tough step left into a crack leading to some overhangs. Move back right
into the upper section of the corner and climb it to the top.

Between *Shy Tot* and *Deep Zawn* is a small bay of rock containing two
routes. These can be gained by a slippery low-tide traverse from *Shy Tot*
or by two abseils to small tidal ledges at the foot of the routes. The first
abseil is from twin threads on the edge of the boulder-field 40 feet south of
the top of Deep Zawn to a good crack (*Friend 2* placement) at the top of a
white arête. The second abseil down the north side of the arête gains the
ledges in the bay. Ideally, both routes require a combination of low tide,
calm sea, and the early evening sun.

★★Head-strong   110 feet   E4 6a †   (3.8.87)
Elegant, bold climbing up the strikingly-clean white arête. Start on a
square ledge beneath the arête. Climb the arête on its left-hand side, and
then move right and up for a few feet to gain a crack on its right-hand
side. Follow this for 15 feet to good protection; then move left to regain
the arête and climb it to where the angle eases. Continue boldly up its
left-hand side before easier climbing leads to the top.

★★Arm-strong   110 feet   E4 6a †   (4.8.87)
The left-hand corner of the bay gives an excellent arm-and-leg-pumping
pitch. Start on brown ledges at the foot of the slim right-hand corner of the
bay. Move up and left to climb the right-hand corner (peg runner) to reach
a slim overhang. Pull over this and gain a small ledge at the point where
the two corners merge. Intricate moves up the main corner (peg runner)
lead to easier ground and the top.

Deep Zawn   OS Ref 1324 4574

Pat showed me Deep Zawn a few days before we did Antiworlds by
swimming round from The Devil's Chimney – we went on swimming under
what was to become Egyptian Slabs and failed to make an underpants-
clad solo ascent of the broken spur north of the slabs; we had to be
rescued by Graham Gilbert with a top-rope!   (Bob Moulton)

The zawn is easy to identify lying at the centre of Jenny's Cove 100 yards
to the south of Halfway Wall. Above it stands the most southerly of a series
of crystalline, outcrop 'sentries' named The Cheeses owing to their prominent, stacked appearance. The zawn itself is very narrow with impres-
sively high sides and back walls plunging vertically into the murky depths.
On a dull, damp day it is a sombre place to be, yet on a clear day with the

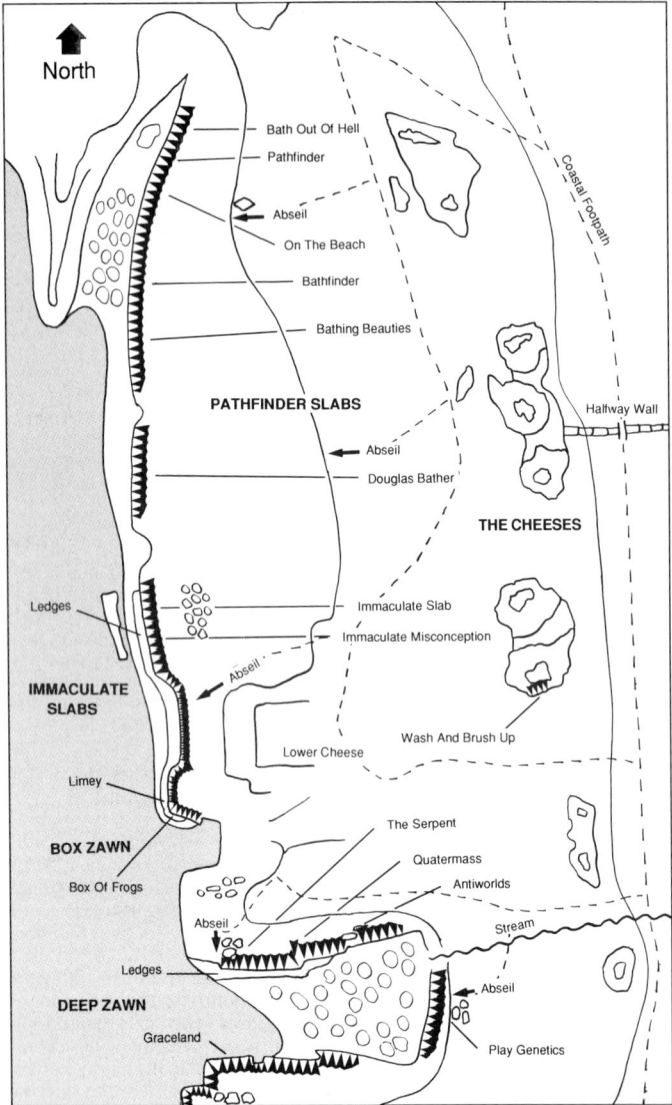

North

Bath Out Of Hell
Pathfinder

Abseil

On The Beach

Bathfinder

Bathing Beauties

PATHFINDER SLABS

Abseil

Douglas Bather

THE CHEESES

Halfway Wall

Coastal Footpath

Ledges

Immaculate Slab

Immaculate Misconception

Abseil

IMMACULATE SLABS

Wash And Brush Up

Lower Cheese

Limey

BOX ZAWN

Box Of Frogs

The Serpent

Quatermass

Antiworlds

Abseil

Stream

Ledges

Abseil

DEEP ZAWN

Graceland

Play Genetics

sun glinting on its walls it takes on a whole new atmosphere, with isolation and great climbs to match.

Typical of its climbing genre from the mid 70s, this impressive zawn continues the scenario from the neighbouring Devil's Chimney Cliff of big, adventurous climbs. Here, Littlejohn made his 'ground-up' attacks on the biggest lines in the zawn, thus tackling the problems head-on. Inevitably, as attitudes changed, a few more modern-style routes have been introduced and all the old aid-points tidied up to give climbs second to none on the island. Any climber seeking adventure and atmosphere with a sense of history will find them here amongst the walls of the zawn.

Approach to the non-tidal routes on The North Wall is relatively quick and straightforward. Scramble down the ridge above the wall to a jumble of boulders at its seaward tip. From here, a 150-foot abseil leads down to a series of ledges, non-tidal except in high seas, that extend into the zawn; most of the routes start from these. For the routes starting from the zawn-bed, namely *Underworld*, *The Stone Tape*, and *Creation*, a short abseil from below the large groove-line of *Antiworlds* is necessary at low tide. Approaches to the remaining routes are described in context.

THE SOUTH WALL
This is perhaps the least attractive of the walls, seeing very little sunshine and hence appearing rather green and uninviting. In its centre lies the prominent groove-line of *Underworld*, while towards its seaward tip a large tapering chimney is the line of *Genesis*. To the right of this lies the wall's finest climb.

★★Gracelands   140 feet   E6   (6.8.87)
An elegant pitch. Make a long abseil to a spike stance at the foot of the chimney from threads above. These are best gained by traversing round from the top of The Devil's Chimney Cliff.
1 100 feet 6b. Step out right onto the wall and climb up to gain a thin crack-system. Follow this to its end (*Friend 2½*); then move up the wall above to an obvious slot on the right with a good finger-jam above. Move up to a sloping ledge and, using a good hold up and left, attain a standing-position upon it. Shuffle right to an open runnel, and climb it and a short crack to exit right to a stance.
2 40 feet 5a. Move back left and climb the large chimney groove, exiting right at the top.

Genesis   130 feet   E1 5b †   (8.78)
The chimney-line in the right-hand side of the south wall provides a prominent landmark but an unpleasant climb. Start by abseiling down the line to the spike belay at its foot. Move up into the chimney and climb it, via an overhang, to gain the crack above. Follow this to easier ground and the top.

★Underworld 200 feet E3   (21.4.73)
The most striking line on the wall is the smooth green groove in its centre.
This is gained by a precarious and acrobatic traverse beneath a line of
overhangs and provides a fine pitch. Once committed, one is quickly cut
off by the tide from any form of retreat save upward movement. Start in
the zawn bed below the start of the traverse-line.
1 20 feet. Climb up to a cave.
2 40 feet 5c. Traverse right beneath the overhangs to reach a good
crack after a very thin section. Move round the nose to a small stance and
nut belays below the smooth groove.
3 90 feet 5c. Climb the groove by excellent bridging to a small stance on
the left arête (old peg belays).
4 50 feet 5a. Continue up the groove above and proceed in the same
line to the top.

THE BACK WALL
Though the most slender of the zawn's faces, this wall provides a network
of highly worthwhile climbs. A small stream emanating from plateau-level
trickles down its left flank but affects none of its climbs directly. Unfortunately, a small damp patch in the lower centre of the face does affect the
climbs, but usually this dries out in the summer months.

The first three climbs, while accessible from the zawn bed via the first pitch
of *The Stone Tape*, are best gained by a 200-foot abseil from summit
boulders to a small constricted ledge in the lower right-hand corner of the
slab. *The Stone Tape* is complete in its own right and should be contemplated only by the original access to amplify its atmosphere.

★A Friction Romance 200 feet E4 †   (11.8.89)
A good route taking the slim corner on the right-hand side of the slab. Dry
conditions, which are not always available, are an essential requirement.
1 140 feet 6a. Follow the faint thin cracks in the black slab to where the
angle eases off. Move up and rightwards to the base of the slim corner.
Climb this with increasing difficulty by technical bridging until large holds
are reached at its top. Continue over a vegetated area of rock to a grassy
ledge and move up past a horizontal white flake to a ledge beneath the
final crack.
2 60 feet 5a. The converging, right-hand crack in the headwall. Block
belay.

★★★Play Genetics 200 feet E3   (22.7.84)
The central line of the slab gives its best route, via a straight thin crack.
Immaculate climbing with trustworthy protection after a bold start. A few
grassy tufts may need removing beforehand but this is quickly done on the
abseil descent.
1 130 feet 5c. Climb the centre of the narrow black slab via faint cracks
through an easy-angled section and over a small overlap as the crack
begins to steepen. Continue directly by beautiful, delicate climbing to
reach a good ledge and a hidden peg belay.

2 70 feet 5a. Step up onto the next ledge; then follow a rightward-trending flake and a pleasant straight crack to the top.

★If I Should Fall from Grace with God 210 feet E5 † (17.10.89)
An atmospheric route, which follows the crackline just right of the arête of the slab with some sections borrowed from *The Stone Tape*. A superbly exposed stance on the arête adds further to the experience. A preplaced belay rope helps avoid a lethal grassy finish.
1 70 feet 6a. Step onto the slab and move left into the crescent-shaped groove almost immediately. Climb this; then make a hard traverse leftwards, just below where the groove turns into a roof, to gain the base of the crack on the left. Follow this to a ledge, where a traverse left gains the arête. Take a stance a few feet higher, level with the base of the crack in the arête.
2 140 feet 5c. Move into the groove on the left and climb it, mainly on its right wall, until it can be crossed leftwards at its top (in common with *The Stone Tape*). Continue through a steeper section above on sidepulls to a large ledge. Step left and climb the crack above until it reaches the arête. Layback into a groove in the arête and make a couple of steep moves up it before pulling back rightwards onto the slab. Belay to the preplaced rope.

★★The Stone Tape 315 feet E3 (17.4.73)
Although this route has since been superseded in part by the network of climbs on the upper slabs, it still remains a magnificent outing and fully deserves attention as a line in its own right. The epitome of zawn climbing and a superb adventure in these modern climbing times. Start at low tide below the foot of the south wall, some 20 feet right of the wet chimney-line that forms the lower part of the junction between the south and back walls of the zawn.
1 90 feet 5b. Climb up to a spike, and then move left and up a shallow groove to a ledge, which is gained at its right-hand end. Climb straight up to a stepped groove, which leads to a large ledge. Continue up the corner to another ledge beneath the big slab in the back of the zawn. The lower half of this pitch will always be damp.
2 65 feet 5c. Climb the thin cracks in the black slab for 30 feet; then make a delicate leftwards traverse to a good foothold at the bottom of the groove and crackline that descends to the lowest point of the slab. Follow the crack to a tiny ledge beneath the overhang.
3 70 feet 5b. Step left and move up to stand on a flake. Climb the groove with difficulty; then move onto the right wall and climb up until the groove can be crossed using an incut flake on its left wall. Belay a few feet above on a small ledge at a crack.
4 90 feet 4c. Vegetated. Continue up the groove to the narrow grassy ledge that crosses the slab. Climb the slab direct to the obvious shallow grooves, which are followed, bearing left where they peter out. More grooves lead to a short final slab, after which 15 feet of grass leads to a huge block belay. NB: this pitch may be difficult to identify since the gardening of the previous route. It may therefore be more appropriate to follow the more inviting line at 5b.

THE NORTH WALL
By way of almost complete contrast, this wall is steeper and more compact, with routes of a finer lineage. Here the climbs take natural features: *Antiworlds* the awesome groove-line in its right half; *Quatermass* the twin cracks in the centre of the face; *Supernova* a searing thin crack in the upper left-hand headwall; and *The Serpent* the snaking crack bounding the edge of the zawn. This is a rock-climber's playground, but none of the routes should be underestimated.

Creation   280 feet   E3   (19.4.73)
The totally overgrown slanting crackline on the right-hand side of the wall requires a good clean before an ascent. Start at low tide on the zawn bed below the crack.
1 120 feet 5b. Follow the crack to a small stance above the large overhang. Peg belays.
2 90 feet 5a. Continue in the same line to a smooth shallow section of crack. Move up and then right to reach excellent holds leading to a stance. Peg belays.
3 70 feet 4b. Continue up the crackline until above a shallow chimney; then make a rising leftwards traverse to escape.

★★★**Antiworlds**   245 feet   E4   (11.9.72/5.8.89)
The original route of the zawn and without question still its finest. A combination of atmosphere, good line, and an exhilarating finale make this outstanding climb one of the best on the island. Unfortunately, the first pitch is rarely dry. Start from an old peg belay at the right-hand end of the ledge-system running below the wall.
1 110 feet 6a. Make a series of tricky moves right to gain a steep thin crack and follow this (technical) to gain a resting-place at the foot of the impressive groove. Climb the thin slanting crack on the right for 15 feet, then the groove itself to where a smooth fin of rock divides it. Climb up past the fin by hard moves until it becomes possible to swing out right to better holds. Continue more easily to a stance.
2 70 feet 5c. Climb the corner above until it starts to bulge, and then make hard moves to gain excellent holds at its top. Swing out left and take a fine, airy belay.
3 65 feet 6a. Move back right and climb the twin thin cracks in the pink-coloured headwall with difficulty past a horizontal slot. An impeccable pitch and a suitable finale.

★★**Quatermass**   200 feet   E2   (16.4.73/10.74/15.8.86)
A very fine route centred around the conspicuous twin cracks in the centre of the wall left of *Antiworlds*. Sustained throughout with good protection and plenty of atmosphere for the grade. Start where the crackline extends down to the ledges at the base of the wall.
1 80 feet 5c. Take a vague leftwards line to gain a scoop, and step left into the crack. Follow this with difficult moves to gain a small incut ledge, and then continue up to an overhang and unsound block. Go straight up for 25 feet until moves right along some small ledges past a dubious flake,

but still standing the test of time, lead to the half-way ledge. Nut belays.
2 40 feet 5a. The twin cracks lead to another ledge.
3 80 feet 5c. Climb the excellent thin crack in the right wall of the stepped corner-system to the top. The original finish took the stepped corner leading off leftwards at 4b. Thread belays lie well back.

★★**Supernova** 200 feet E5   (20.4.73/30.7.84)
The striking thin crack splitting the ochre-flecked headwall in the left-hand side of the face provides the '*London Wall* of Lundy'. Infinitely protectable but with a bold first pitch. Start just to the right of the seaward edge of the wall.
1 60 feet 6a. Climb up to an obvious thin crack and follow it, via a series of scary moves, to a good ledge. Move right and follow a second thin crack rightwards to a commodious ledge. (The original route avoided this latter section by moves leftwards from below the second thin crack to the prominent ledge-system, which was then traversed rightwards for a second pitch to gain the belay ledge below the top pitch.)
2 100 feet 6b. Move up left along the ledge to below the line. A thin move gains the crack proper, where sustained climbing leads to a peg runner at 65 feet. From here there are two alternatives: either step out left onto the wall and move up to a small ledge before regaining the crack; or, for purists only, climb it direct. Sprint quickly up the remainder of the crack to easier corners and the top. Breathtaking.

★**The Serpent** 160 feet E1   (16.4.73)
The top pitch up the obvious snaking crack in the left-hand side of the headwall provides a good pitch and a fine appetizer to the atmosphere of the zawn. Sustained and strenuous rather than technical. Start from some ledges below the arête of the wall.
1 70 feet 4b. Climb the groove just left of the arête for 40 feet; then move right to and up some ledges on the rib to a stance at a pointed block.
2 90 feet 5a. Move up and right to a ledge, and then enter the crack from the right. Follow it with the hardest moves at 35 feet where it narrows. As the crack widens the climbing eases for the top to be gained.
Variation
The Sadistic Snakes Symphony E3 †   (18.9.91)
1a 70 feet 5c. Starting just right of the arête inside the zawn, make difficult and awkward moves up the shallow groove (bold). Move up on some loose ledges, and then go up a corner to the belay ledge.

To the north of Deep Zawn is an area of more open and easy-angled slabs of fine rock. While of a 'go-anywhere' nature, these can provide a pleasant day's meandering from a good sea-level platform which is non-tidal. This is best gained by a direct abseil from one of a number of blocks lining the rim of the cliff. This area of slabs is terminated quite abruptly by the square-cut Box Zawn.

The Egyptian Slabs Area

The crystalline pinnacles known as The Cheeses are a conspicuous feature on this section of coastline and form the rim of the main plateau in the vicinity of Halfway Wall. Below The Cheeses lies an area of slabby cliffs and walls extending northwards from Box Zawn. These gradually increase in size beyond a prominent streaked slab and rotten chimney to a series of larger and more imposing slabs. The slabs are eventually terminated by a huge gully just north of Halfway Wall. The climbing in this area is often on very good rock with an isolated and unusual feel to it.

THE CHEESES   OS Ref 1333 4586 to 1327 4561
There are three main buttresses with a couple of miniature versions above Deep Zawn, including The Cheesemite. The largest and central buttress is 100 feet high. Below the most southerly of the trio lies a similar buttress rising from the top of the sea-level cliffs below: The Egyptian Slabs. It is possible to pass below this buttress via a convenient ledge-system.

Owing to the vegetated nature of the cliffs, the routes are left for the adventurous to rediscover. One route, however, is worthy of more detailed description and is useful for a leisurely day without the complications of tide or abseil approach.

Wash and Brush Up 75 feet E1 5b   (3.8.84)
An unusual route for the area, taking a flake-and-crack-system on the southern face of the south Cheese. Start by scrambling up to a belay on a good ledge below the line. Climb a good crack moving out left and back right to a flake. From the top of this, take the wall above via a thin crack and short flake to a sloping ledge. Move right and finish up a flake to summit belays. Descend via the easy gully.

BOX ZAWN   OS Ref 1325 4577
This small square-cut zawn provides three routes, which are all located near the northerly edge of the zawn. Owing to a large bird population, it may be more suited to ornithologists wearing Pac-a-macs.

Access to the cliff is via the main descent to Immaculate Slabs and then a traverse across easy mid-tidal ledges to the south.

Jack-in-the-Box 130 feet Very Severe   (29.3.75)
The right-hand of the two grooves in the north wall, gained by a traverse from the left, and often climbed past numerous irate seagulls.

★★Box of Frogs 80 feet E4 6a   (25.9.85)
A hidden gem on flawless rock with brilliant sustained climbing throughout its relatively short length. Low tide essential. Climb the groove

in the arête of the zawn, left of *Jack-in-the-Box* to easy ground. Easy climbing remains.

Open the Box   60 feet   E2 5b   (25.9.85)
The arête to the left of *Box of Frogs* gives pleasant moves. This is the right arête of *Limey*. Climb up through a wide crack to a small ledge below the blunt arête. Move out right and follow this to easy ground. Easy climbing remains.

IMMACULATE SLABS   OS Ref 1325 4586
The next series of routes lie on the area of rock directly beneath the lichen-covered tower that forms the lowest of The Cheeses. The slabs are separated from Box Zawn by a narrow strip of wedge-shaped white slab. To the left of this, a steep-walled recess is bounded by a fine, yellow-streaked slab, which the original route of the face, *Immaculate Slab*, finds its way up. This area of cliff is then terminated by a series of tiered overhangs and a large chimney.

Since its inception as a climbing venue during the boom years of the 70s, the number of climbs has steadily increased to include routes throughout the grades. These are always to be found on impeccable rock, usually, but not always, with reliable protection.

The approach is from a recess at the foot of the lowest of The Cheeses by a 130-foot abseil to the large sea-level ledges below the recessed area of rock. An abseil from the boulder-strewn slopes 50 yards to the north allows a more direct approach to the yellow-streaked slab. At the beginning of the non-restricted season this can be a relatively unpleasant approach owing to the amount of seagull refuse in the area.

Limey   110 feet   Hard Very Severe   (25.4.74)
This route climbs the right-hand side of the narrow, white slab forming the boundary of the Immaculate Slabs. Begin by traversing below the foot of the slab to a large ledge just inside Box Zawn, as for *Open the Box*, at low tide.
1 40 feet 5a. Climb the corner just right of the edge of the slab and, where it steepens, swing out left to a small ledge. Continue more easily up to a white ledge and belay.
2 70 feet 4a. Follow the cracks in the slab above to the top, from where scrambling remains.

Live Gold   125 feet   Hard Very Severe   (25.4.74)
Similar in character to *Limey*, taking the left-hand side of the slab. Start on a sloping ledge above sea-level, gained from the left.
1 45 feet 5a. Move up right into a chimney and exit from its top onto the slab. Continue up and leftwards to a good ledge (peg belay).
2 80 feet 4b. The pleasant cracks above lead to a finishing-corner complete with a dangerously loose wedged block. Finish by scrambling up over easy ground.

The large recessed area to the left, passed on the traverse into Box Zawn, provides a myriad of small corners, ledges, and walls, all of good rock. This gives two routes and an easier, but hard to find, escape route (Severe).

Wallybaldi   100 feet   Very Severe 5a †   (13.9.82)
Start just right of a prominent large block, 20 feet left of the edge of the narrow white slab of *Live Gold*. An obvious square-cut chimney leads to an overhang, where a step right gains a layback crack and large ledge above. Climb the corner above this to a second ledge; then follow the next corner (crux) to a good stance and belays.

To the left again, the area of steep grooves and walls continues with a large stepped slab at its foot. Here, a break in the sea-level ledges provides a slab with a silvery, open-book corner above.

Silverado   130 feet   E1 †   (24.9.90)
Exposed towards the top of the first pitch. Start on a good belay ledge to the right of the slab.
1 80 feet 5b. Climb the front face of the slab onto a ledge, and continue up and slightly left via a square-cut corner to the foot of the groove. Climb a series of ledges to its right until some exciting moves gain the top of the groove proper. Move leftwards over blocks for a few feet to reach a good belay ledge.
2 50 feet 4a. Climb a square-cut groove to where the rock becomes poor, and then make a traverse round to the right along a narrow foot-ledge. Continue carefully over loose blocks to the abseil point at the foot of The Cheeses.

The left-hand side of the recess is bounded by the arête of the streaked slab of *Immaculate Slab*, the main feature of the cliff. Just to the right of the arête lies a V-shaped groove.

Fools Gold   110 feet   Very Severe 4c   (25.9.80)
Climb the groove to gain the chimney and ledge. Tackle the overhang above to reach the base of a second groove. Traverse left across the wall to a narrow ledge and finish via some cracks to a flake and nut belay. Scrambling remains.

★The Ride and the View   100 feet   E2 6a   (29.7.84)
Enjoyable climbing up the right-hand edge of the streaked slab after a technical entry. Start below some thin parallel cracks just left of the arête. Climb the cracks using the arête to gain the slab and continue up the right side of this to a system of broken ledges. Pull over a slight bulge to gain a thin crack, a ledge at the top of which provides the belay. Scrambling remains.

★The Gem   100 feet   E2 6a   (16.4.74/26.7.85)
Pleasant slab-climbing but with a hard, technical start. Climb the tiny

IMMACULATE SLABS

B Box Zawn
1 Limey   HVS
2 Live Gold   HVS
3 Wallybaldi   VS

4 Silverado   E1
5 The Ride and the View   E2
6 The Gem   E2
7 Immaculate Misconception   E2
8 Egyptian Reggae   E5
9 Immaculate Slab   HVS
10 Tutankhamun   E2

corner and thin crack 10 feet left of the arête, through a prominent overlap, to reach some thin cracks in the slab above. Follow these to the steepening, and finish via a short crack and flake to a ledge. Scrambling remains.

★★**Immaculate Misconception** 100 feet   E2 5c   (26.7.84)
A superb route directly up the centre of the streaked slab. A difficult technical start is followed by easier but bolder climbing on the slab above. Start 15 feet left of the edge of the slab below thin cracks in the wall, left of the tiny corner taken by *The Gem*. Climb the cracks to get established on the slab proper. Trend slightly leftwards to gain a prominent black streak and follow this up the centre of the slab, taking time to ponder any awkward moves, to a good hold where it steepens. Swing left to finish more easily.

★**Egyptian Reggae** 100 feet   E5 5c †   (26.7.85)
The smoother slab to the left. A bit unprotected to say the least, except for a small wire low down. Take an LSD for the ascent (Lightweight Snorkelling Device). Start 5 feet from the left-hand end of the ledge-system below the wall. Climb straight up the wall and move onto the slab via a delicate mantelshelf manoeuvre. Continue up the slab above via a very faint crack until thin moves high up gain *Immaculate Slab* to finish. The seriousness is proportional to how high you get before chickening out (by moving left into *Immaculate Slab*)!

★★**Immaculate Slab** 100 feet   Hard Very Severe 5a   (15.4.74)
An established classic of the island with well-balanced climbing on perfect rock throughout. It takes the left-hand side of the streaked slabs below an obvious angular retaining wall. Start at the left-hand end of the thin ledge below the wall. At low tide, a pleasant 20-foot pitch is possible up to this point from the boulders below. Climb the wall via a tiny groove leading up and left onto the slab. Trend rightwards up this below the retaining wall to a final steep section gained from a good hold on the right. Thread belays, from where scrambling remains.

★**Tutankhamun** 110 feet   E2   (29.8.87/29.3.89)
The crackline left of the start of *Immaculate Slab* and the short overhanging groove in the headwall above give a good route, once again on superb rock. Start as for *Immaculate Slab*.
1 80 feet 6a. Make a delicate leftwards traverse for 20 feet to the crackline and climb it with difficulty to rejoin *Immaculate Slab*. Follow this for a few feet and take a belay on nuts.
2 30 feet 5b. Move up right to the foot of the flaky groove in the headwall and climb it to an exciting finish.

PATHFINDER SLABS   OS Ref 1325 4592
In this final section, the slabs are far grander in size and lie directly beneath the most northerly of The Cheeses. These slabs provide some excellent climbing with an isolated atmosphere. The routes are generally

well protected, except for *Bathing Beauties*, *Bathfinder*, and *Little Bath*, and receive the sun's rays from early afternoon onwards.

Access to the foot of the slabs for all its routes except *Douglas Bather* is straightforward but requires the correct line to be taken. Take a rope from a large flake below the most northerly of The Cheeses to a large diamond-shaped block on the cliff edge. From here, double 150-foot climbing ropes can be used to gain a convenient half-height ledge with twin peg belays. A second abseil from these leads to the zawn bed at mid to low tide, or a peg belay on the small pedestal atop the common first pitch to *Bathfinder, Roy of the Rovers*, and *On the Beach* at high tide.

Douglas Bather   150 feet   E1 †   (5.8.89)

This route takes the obvious groove, slab, and streaked depression on the right-hand side of the slabs. Start by placing a rope from a large flake 80 feet south of the normal descent-point and taking it to a peg belay just below the top of the slabs. From here, abseil down to a constricted stance in a chimney within sight of *Immaculate Slab*.
1 70 feet 4c. Move left to the groove and climb this to a large ledge and peg belay.
2 80 feet 5a. From the left-hand end of the ledge, climb the crack and slab to some white streaks below the overhang. Move left through this; then step back right to a small stance and peg belay. Exit through vegetation, where the preplaced rope will prove useful.

★Bathing Beauties   230 feet   E4 †   (6.8.93)

A leisurely route meandering up the open slabs to the left. Good climbing but with a bold penultimate pitch. Start 70 feet right of the left-hand end of the slabs, below a slim groove.
1 30 feet 5b. Climb the pleasant groove to a rounded belay ledge.
2 70 feet 5c. Continue up the blunt rib above to a good flake crack, and pull out right onto the slab. Climb up to a prominent overlap and good flake; then pull thinly through to gain a good ledge and peg belay.
3 100 feet 5c. Move up above the ledge to an undercut ledge, and then trend rightwards up the slab to the final overlap. Pull blindly through and follow a thin crack before trending leftwards to a bolt belay.
4 30 feet. Traverse gingerly off to the right.

★★Bathfinder   230 feet   E6 †   (31.7.89)

Thin and sustained, with awkward protection on its most difficult section. A quality route that merits attention as well as a good deal of respect. Start on a greasy boulder 30 feet right of the wide chimney (left of the lower slabs) taken by *Pathfinder*.
1 40 feet 4c. Pull up, and then climb easily rightwards up the black ramp to a pedestal stance. Peg belay.
2 160 feet 6b. Move right and climb the centre of the strip of smooth-looking slab (thin and bold), then the shallow groove on the right to the overlap (peg runner). Step left and heave through (peg runner) to reach the foot of the beckoning thin crack. Intricate climbing up this leads to

easy ground. Step right and pull through a second overlap to follow a
rightward-trending crack to a bolt belay where vegetation encroaches.
3 30 feet. Traverse easily right to finish.

★★**Roy of the Rovers**   250 feet   E5   (1.8.88)
Fine direct face-climbing with short hard sections that are well supplied
with *in-situ* protection. Bolder sections lie in between. Start as for
Bathfinder.
1 40 feet 4c. Climb the black ramp to a peg belay.
2 90 feet 6b. Climb straight up above the belay, keeping left of a faint
rib, via a series of good holds to gain the overlap. Pull up onto the short
wall above (bolt runner); then make hard moves over the second overlap
to gain a scoop (peg runner). A direct line up the white streak in this gains
a long, thin ledge in the centre of the wall. Peg belays, which are also used
as one of the abseil points.
3 120 feet 6b. From the right end of the ledge, climb the slab just left of
an obvious strip of grass to reach another ledge. Climb the steeper wall
above (peg runner), and pull leftwards through the overlap (bolt runner)
onto the fine white headwall. Take a direct line up its centre, passing two
bolt runners and plenty of thin climbing. Finish through the obvious gap at
two pointed blocks.

★★★**On the Beach**   260 feet   E3   (2.8.88)
An excellent and classic route taking a fine line up the slabs to finish via a
prominent diagonal gash in the left-hand side of the white headwall.
Perfect rock and fine climbing with sound protection.
1 40 feet 4c. *Roy of the Rovers* pitch 1.
2 100 feet 6a. Traverse diagonally leftwards across the slab, and then
move up to some white streaks at the foot of a groove (peg runner). Pull
out leftwards across the groove onto the arête and move up this on its
left-hand side (peg runner) to an easier-angled section and some
diagonal slots. Continue direct up the white streak (peg runner) to gain the
long, narrow, half-height ledge.
3 120 feet 5c. From the left-hand end of the ledge, follow a thin crack to
reach a second ledge-system. Continue direct past a small overlap into
the obvious 'funnel' above, and bridge sensationally up it, exiting to reach
the foot of the diagonal crack. Climb this in a fine position to gain the top
between two pointed boulders.

Pathfinder   300 feet   E2   (15.4.74)
This route takes the highest part of the slabs and would be an exceptional
route if thoroughly cleaned. Start below the wide chimney in the left-hand
side of the lower slabs.
1 45 feet. Climb the chimney to a large boulder and flake belay.
2 85 feet 4a. Traverse up to the right for some 30 feet to the foot of a
short rib. Climb the rib, starting on its right side, to a narrow ledge (peg
runner). Move left to a broken groove, which is climbed to a small stance
and peg belay at the point where the groove merges into the slab above.
3 40 feet 4c. Climb up above the stance to gain the left-hand end of a

narrow broken ledge. Traverse right, beneath the obvious white slab, to the spacious ledge at the foot of the large overhung recess (peg belays).
4 80 feet 5a. Move back left to gain the spur left of the recess and climb steeply up to the left onto the prominent white slab (peg runner). Climb the crack in the slab to narrow ledges beneath the final groove (peg belays).
5 50 feet 5a. Climb the cracks in the left wall of the groove to join the groove above a small overhang (peg runner). Follow the groove to the top and belay well back.

Bath out of Hell　280 feet　E3 †　　　　　　　　　　(14.8.93)
The final line of the slabs up the massive gardened streak in its left side. Good climbing interspersed with some easy ground.
1 70 feet. Climb the chimney as for *Pathfinder*, but belay a little higher at the start of a basalt intrusion.
2 90 feet 5b. Move out right and then up to gain a leftward-trending groove-line. Climb this for 15 feet; then pull out right onto the slab. Trend pleasantly leftwards up this and follow an excellent thin crack to a peg belay on the first ledge encountered.
3 120 feet 5c. Step right and trend leftwards onto a rounded ledge. Climb the slab above to where it eases over onto a glacis (peg runner). Move diagonally right to a thin crack (peg runner), which gives sustained, technical climbing for more ledges to be gained. Move diagonally rightwards to pass the final overhang and short wall from the right.

The final route of the cliff takes the small undercut wall sandwiched in at the top of the rotten gully/zawn below Halfway Wall. This is gained by direct abseil down the slab, which also enables any surface debris to by brushed away and an exit to be prepared.

★Little Bath　90 feet　E5 ,6a　　　　　　　　　　　(1.8.89)
Worthwhile. Pull through the lower roof (peg runner) via a flake to reach a small ledge at the foot of the slab. Technical moves up this (peg runner) gain a thin crack leading to a short headwall (peg runner) and the top. Bold climbing.

Beaufort Buttress Area

The northern-most point of Jenny's Cove is formed by a long, grassy headland at the tip of which lies a flat-topped, rocky island. The most obvious feature here is a squat buttress with a slender 120-foot face, Beaufort Buttress. Immediately to its south lies the bitingly-narrow Freak Zawn and at its back the appropriately named Black Hole.

THE PYRAMID　　　　　　　　　　　　　　OS Ref 1311 4597
The large, dirty gully forming the extreme left-hand side of The Egyptian Slabs marks a distinct decrease in the height and form of the coastal cliffs.

They now continue as a series of isolated buttresses and ramparts without easy identification. To the north, the first clear feature is a small triangular headland with a prominent slab forming its southern side. This is The Pyramid and has, on occasions, been used as a landing-point in the unusual event of a strong south-easterly wind; it is also a popular swimming venue.

To the south of The Pyramid lies an isolated brown buttress consisting of numerous grooves and cracks. For the most part, and during normal sea conditions, this buttress has a good ledge-system below it which is relatively unaffected by tides. This said, access to these ledges is a little problematic since the sea cuts off all methods of direct access by forcing a deep channel between it and the mainland. To reach the base of The Pyramid, therefore, a direct 150-foot abseil is necessary from good thread belays at the cliff-top. This leads down a grassy groove, which also provides the half-height belay for the first three routes. The rock here is solid and has a sunny aspect.

★**A Geometric Study**   145 feet   E4 6a †   (5.8.93)
A good route taking the scoop right of the hanging, brown arête in the centre of the cliff. Start below a groove.
1 85 feet 6a. Trend awkwardly rightwards into the groove and follow it for 15 feet. Step left and climb a thin crack into the broad, open scoop. From its top, move out left onto the arête and climb up to the large grassy groove. Nut and abseil rope belay.
2 60 feet. Scramble up on the right, taking care with the exit.

★★**The Pyramid of Success**   140 feet   E6 †   (2.8.88)
The prominent, brown hanging arête in the centre of the cliff provides a daunting proposition. The entry is desperate; the remainder merely sustained! Well protected. Start as for *A Geometric Study*.
1 80 feet 6c. Step left from the initial groove, then left again to a sloping ledge below the arête (peg runner hidden round to the left). Slap up onto the arête proper (bolt runner) and battle up it on its right-hand side (two bolt runners) until better holds lead left into the grassy groove. Nut and abseil-rope belay.
2 60 feet. Scramble up the ridge on the right taking care at the exit.

★**The Pyramid Game**   140 feet   E1 †   (2.8.88)
An enjoyable route taking the stepped crack-system to the left of *The Pyramid of Success*.
1 80 feet 5b. Climb the crack, passing left of the overhang. Move up past two ledges to a finger-crack and, after 10 feet of this, step right. Climb the obvious white groove to a nut and abseil-rope belay.
2 60 feet. Use the ridge on the right for a finish.

★★**Sphinx Crack**   150 feet   E5 6b †   (5.8.93)
Direct, technical, and absorbing. The straight thin crack in the face to the left gives fine climbing. Gain the crack and follow it by sustained moves

past a peg runner and a downward-pointing spike (*Friend 2*) to gain a prominent overlap. Move up left below this and pull over onto the clean white face above. Continue straight up the face to finish direct to the abseil-point.

★★Carnage in Carthage   150 feet   E5   6b †   (5.8.93)

An excellent companion to *Sphinx Crack* via the large beak of rock to the left. Blind and strenuous climbing demanding a positive approach. From ledges, move up and left to a constricted niche (*Friend 3*) in the wide crack above. Pull out right to some undercut rockings, and power through the overhangs (*Rock 7*) into a niche on the lip. Step left and follow a thin crack before moving rightwards onto the arête. Climb this and a groove above; then pull out right and finish direct to the abseil-point.

Luxor Nothing   150 feet   Hard Very Severe   5a †   (5.8.93)

Pleasant climbing. From the foot of *Carnage in Carthage*, move out left and follow a series of small ledges up the wall to the top of a sharp arête and groove. Pull out left into a continuation groove and climb this until moves rightwards lead to blocky ground (belay possible). Finish direct.

★Phoenix in the Groove   165 feet   E2 †   (9.8.93)

Enjoyable. Start as for *Luxor Nothing*.
1 30 feet 4b. Traverse left at a low level to gain a niche in the arête. Step down into a groove, and then climb diagonally leftwards to a pedestal stance (*Friend 3* belay).
2 135 feet 5b. Move up to the groove above and climb it (poor protection) to its conclusion. Move out left to a second groove, which leads in a short distance to easy climbing on the right arête and the top.

The final routes on the buttress are gained via the southern slab of The Pyramid but the state of the tide is of major importance.

★★★A Wild Trip on Jugs   130 feet   E4   (15.10.89)

A stunning little route, which turns out to be much easier than first appearances might suggest. Just worth the grade. An obvious overhanging groove-line capped by roofs faces the base of the slab. Start at a huge rounded boulder in the very bottom of the zawn – extreme low tide is required.
1 60 feet 5c. Enter the groove to the right of the boulder and climb it to a small roof. Traverse left into the bottom of the groove. (*Friend 1* essential for the belay.)
2 70 feet 5b. Climb the groove to the huge jutting shelf below the roof; then hand-traverse the lip leftwards to a jammed block. Move right to another block and continue straight up to finish via a right-facing groove.
Variation

★★Outrageous Voyage on Buckets   E4 †   (8.8.90)

A very good and suitable alternative should the sea-swell prove too great. Start 15 feet left of the arête on a boulder below an alarmingly overhanging wall.

1a 50 feet 6a. Climb straight up (*Friend 1½* and *Rock 7*) to gain a thin horizontal crack. Traverse right along this to a roof; then swing right and up on a pinch-grip and layaway to the belay at the foot of the groove.

PICNIC BAY CLIFF
OS Ref 1314 4603

The coastline beyond the northern section of The Pyramid, and in the northern part of Jenny's Cove, rapidly deteriorates into a series of low-lying and scrappy cliffs. Just beyond The Pyramid, in a hidden bay, lies a short, north-facing wall with four climbs.

Descent to the base of the cliff is by scrambling down its northern side at Difficult standard, starting from above The Pyramid. Other descents are also possible. A direct abseil, or a scramble round from the foot of The Pyramid at very low tide also leads to the foot of the routes.

Time for Tina 60 feet Very Severe 4c (3.8.84)
Start at the right-hand end of the face, 15 feet right of some obvious slanting cracks. Climb the short wall split by a thin crack to a small ledge below a depression in the light-coloured slab. Climb this direct to the top.

Out with the Boys 55 feet Severe 4a (1.9.89)
Ascend the pleasant slanting cracks 15 feet left of *Time for Tina* to the top.

The next two routes start from a small isolated pinnacle in the back of the bay.

Saturday Night 80 feet Severe (21.4.76)
Climb the dark-coloured groove on the right wall.

Sunday Morning 80 feet Very Severe 4c (21.4.76)
A neat little pitch up the clean-cut groove bounding the face on the left-hand side of the cracked slab. Climb up over easy slabs and step up to the foot of the groove. Climb it, or the crack in the slab to the left, and move left to finish.

DIHEDRAL ZAWN
OS Ref 1308 4618

This esoteric little zawn lies 100 yards to the south of Freak Zawn and The Black Hole, and 300 yards north of The Pyramid. The best approach to the cliff-top is via the grassy headland and then a traverse to the south. It is far more arduous walking in from The Pyramid.

The southern, north-facing, wall of the zawn provides the routes, though these are attainable only at low tide and get any sunshine only late in the summer evenings. As a result the rock is sometimes rather damp in less than ideal weather.

The most prominent feature on the south wall is a large corner, giving the name of the zawn, with a rather sombre-looking right wall. Access to the two routes hereabouts is best by direct abseil from large block anchors directly above the corner. Alternatively, it is possible to gain these and the first route described by descending a rib to the south of the zawn and then traversing back round at low tide. Another more adventurous approach is to reverse down easy rock on the zawn's north wall and to traverse back into the zawn. At the narrowest point it will be necessary to jump across a narrow gap onto the south wall – take a snorkel and flippers just in case!

Illusion   105 feet   Severe   (27.8.79)
Start beneath a short crack, 50 feet north of the rib to the south of the zawn and 100 feet right of the large corner. Move up to a large ledge (belay possible); then climb the steep crack above to a lessening in angle. More reasonable climbing leads to the top.

★★**Blood Poison**   90 feet   E4 6a   (1.8.88)
This route takes the black wall right of the corner of *Dihedral*. A fine pitch with steep and technical face-climbing. Solid *in-situ* protection abounds but dry conditions are essential. Start on the lowest ledge beneath the corner, preferably on an outgoing tide for the second's sake. Stride right across a gap to a small ledge and then follow a series of discontinuous thin cracks (three peg runners) into a niche. Exit left from this (peg runner) to gain the foot of the upper wall. Continue a little more boldly up this to a break (peg runner), and finish direct (peg runner). By this time your second may be submerged!

★**Dihedral**   90 feet   E1 5b   (15.4.73)
The big corner-line gives an excellent pitch. Again, well protected but often damp. Take a belay 15 feet left of the corner. Follow a rightward diagonal line to gain the corner proper. Continue on small holds to reach the corner-crack, and climb this to the top.

The north wall of the zawn offers a handful of poor lines over suspect rock. The groove opposite *Dihedral* is **What's the Worst Job You Ever Had** (90 feet E1 5a † 31.7.84), a dirty, poorly-protected, and fractured pitch unworthy of attention.

THE BLACK HOLE   OS Ref 1309 4623
'So named because it swallows stars.'   (Mick Learoyd, 1986)

This is the name given to the narrow, inner confines of the zawn at the foot of the grassy headland. It gives an unusual and sometimes damp, though always exciting environment, smaller than but not dissimilar to Huntsman's Leap in South Pembrokeshire. Access to the foot of the routes, all of which are on the north wall, is by abseil using at least a 165-foot (50m) rope, which should be left in place. Carrying some form of ascender is also advisable should the routes or weather prove inhospitable.

★★★**Milky Way**   160 feet   E3 5c   (8.8.86)
A brilliant, atmospheric pitch, taking the prominent left-to-right diagonal crackline towards the left-hand side of the face. The start is always

greasy. Start on some small ledges exposed only at low tide. Further description seems superfluous save to comment that the crux is low down and the remainder sustained. At the top, belay to the abseil rope.

★★Out Come the Freaks Again   160 feet   E6 6b   (2.8.88)
A direct line on the upper wall between *Milky Way* and *Andromeda*. Scary climbing low down is followed by a thin crux; award yourself an extra technical grade should you be of only average reach. Follow *Andromeda* to the peg runner; it is advisable to belay here, using also the abseil rope. Continue airily up the thin crack (spaced small-wire protection) to a point where the crack closes (peg runner). Make a series of hard moves up (bolt runner) and then a crucifix left to join the crackline of *Milky Way*. Finish up this.

★★Andromeda   160 feet   E5 6a   (9.8.86)
Another very fine route with technically interesting climbing requiring a good selection of small wires and careful ropework. Once again it can be greasy at the start. Take a belay 15 feet above the water, midway between *Milky Way* and the ramp to the right. Climb leftwards up a corner/ramp and over a bulge to a ledge. Traverse right along this (peg runner – belay possible) to reach a thin crack-system. Follow this by sustained climbing to gain a finishing-crack. Belay to the preplaced abseil rope.

FREAK ZAWN   OS Ref 1306 4623
Most of the routes are affected by the tide and, except where stated, gained by abseil. For the north, south-facing, wall it is possible to traverse into the zawn at low tide from the descent to Beaufort Buttress.

THE SOUTH WALL
The first routes start from a low-tide ledge at the mouth of the zawn.

Puffin Simon   45 feet   Severe 4a   (2.9.87)
From the left side of the ledge, climb the crackline to the top.

Towards the right-hand side of the face, a wide chimney marks the line of *Fat Freddy*.

Dealer McDope   70 feet   Very Severe 4c   (3.8.87)
Start on ledges beneath the slabby groove right of the chimney. Climb it past an obvious spike at half height.

Fat Freddy   70 feet   Very Severe 4c   (29.8.85)
Start at a wall 5 feet above a boulder at the mouth of the zawn, exposed only at low tide. Otherwise abseil direct. Climb slightly leftwards towards the chimney and climb it.

Phineas   70 feet   Hard Very Severe 5a   (29.8.85)
Start 10 feet left of *Fat Freddy*. Climb up to the bottom of the left arête of the chimney. Move up this before finishing up a crack slightly leftwards.

Freewheelin' Franklin 80 feet Very Severe 4b (29.8.85)
Climb up to the ledge on *Phineas*; then traverse left to the bottom of a very narrow ramp. Climb it.

Norbert the Nark 90 feet Hard Very Severe 5a (29.8.85)
This route takes the large ramp with the white mark. Abseil to its foot. Climb the ramp, starting in the corner and moving onto the slab at half height.

★★**Space Oddity** 100 feet E5 6a (4.8.87)
An atmospheric pitch deep into the bowels of the zawn and requiring dry conditions. Intimidating. Abseil down the arête of *Norbert the Nark* until it is possible to swing round the corner to a thin ledge with a spike belay 50 feet above sea-level. Climb the ramp on the left to its end and continue via a series of flakes to their end. Step left and make hard moves up into a continuation-crack, which leads to the top.

The routes on the seaward end of the north wall are a little less intimidating owing to their sunnier aspect and a small ledge-system running below the face. This ledge is non-tidal and it can be traversed from left to right to a slabby rib marking the start of:

THE NORTH WALL
Salty Dog 150 feet Very Difficult (26.4.79)
1 80 feet. Climb the left side of the rib until it is possible to step around it and traverse right to a diagonal ramp. Follow this to a good ledge.
2 70 feet. Continue up the easy ramp, via a steep corner, to finish.

Diabetic Dog 140 feet E3 (29.8.85)
1 80 feet. *Salty Dog* pitch 1 or abseil to the belay ledge.
2 60 feet 6a. Good climbing. From the left-hand end of the ledge, gain a thin crack and make technical moves up it and the wall above directly to the top.

Hot Dog 140 feet E1 (3.8.87)
1 80 feet. *Salty Dog* pitch 1 or abseil to the belay ledge.
2 60 feet 5b. Move left off the left-hand end of the ledge and climb the wall to a thin horizontal break. Continue up the wall in the same line to easy ledges and the top.

Dog Day Afternoon 100 feet E1 5a (3.8.87)
A pleasant, open climb. Start by following *Salty Dog* and taking a belay at the start of the ramp, or abseil directly to this point. Now climb direct up the centre of the wall, via a tiny groove, with little protection.

★**Deputy Dawg** 100 feet Very Severe 4c (3.8.87)
Start on some small ledges down and to the left of *Dog Day Afternoon*, again reached from *Salty Dog* or by abseil. Move up and left to reach some rightward-trending cracks, and follow these to easy ledges and the top.

Ship's Cat   150 feet   Very Difficult   (26.7.85)
Start 15 feet left of *Salty Dog* at a black cleft.
1 50 feet. Bridge up the cleft for 15 feet; then follow a crack on the right
to a large ledge.
2 100 feet. Scramble up in the same line aiming for the foot of a steep
crack below a V-shaped notch in the skyline left of a big roof. Gain and
climb the crack.

BEAUFORT BUTTRESS   OS Ref 1304 4629
The slender face at the seaward tip of the grassy headland. This excellent
crag is ideal for climbers operating up to Very Severe standard. Superb
rock, a splendid open aspect, and a straightforward approach make it
well worth a visit.

The best approach is by a grassy slope to the north and then a traverse
back to the south. The routes are described from **left to right.**

The climbs start from the large platform beneath the face, which is
accessible at low to mid tide. **However, the platform is particularly vulnerable in high seas.**

**Streaky   120 feet   Very Severe   (31.8.79)
The grey-streaked corner-line in the left-hand side of the main face. A
fine, sustained upper pitch, giving the best climbing on the cliff.
1 50 feet 4c. Climb a short corner to belay on a terrace below the
grey-streaked upper corner.
2 70 feet 4c. The corner above.

*Hurricane   120 feet   Severe   (25.9.71)
Another very worthwhile proposition. Start below a stepped corner-line
midway between *Streaky* and the central corner-line of *Force Eight*.
1 40 feet. Follow the corner to belay on the terrace below a green corner
on the left-hand side of the face.
2 80 feet. Step back right onto the face and climb directly and steeply to
a small ledge. Continue easily to the top.
Variation
Capstan's Arête   Very Severe   (24.3.85)
2a 60 feet 4b. The left arête of the second pitch gives pleasant climbing.

*Force Eight   120 feet   Severe   (23.5.69)
The excellent central corner-line.
1 45 feet. Climb the corner and continue to a ledge below an overhang.
2 75 feet. Climb twin cracks via an overhang; then move left to a ledge.
Continue up a crack and exit right to finish.

*Stuka   120 feet   Hard Severe   (23.5.69)
Start 5 feet right of *Force Eight*.
1 45 feet. Climb a crack, then a wall to the ledge of *Force Eight*.
2 75 feet 4b. Continue up the corner on the right to the top.

Variation
Admiral's Arête   E1   (24.3.85)
2a   75 feet 5a. The crack and arête to the right of the second pitch. Bold.

Fifty Pumps   120 feet   Very Severe   (31.8.79)
Start 5 feet right of *Stuka*.
1 60 feet. Climb the obvious corner and then a groove to an overhang.
Pass this to the right and trend right to a recess.
2 60 feet 4c. Climb the left-hand crack above the recess to the top. The
right-hand crack can also be climbed but much more strenuously.

Minesweeper   100 feet   Very Severe   (19.8.87)
Start at a groove 15 feet right of *Fifty Pumps*.
1 50 feet. Climb the most southerly corner to a good belay ledge in a
niche, 10 feet right of *Fifty Pumps*.
2 50 feet 4c. Step left and pull into some cracks above. Continue up,
trending rightwards, until broken rock leads to the top.

The following trio of routes lie on the north face of the minor buttress
landward of the main face and passed on the descent scramble. **Cliché
Corner** (35 feet Hard Severe 4a 18.8.87) takes the central corner;
Percy's Paradise (50 feet Hard Severe 4b 18.8.87) follows a leftward-
slanting line 15 feet from the west end; **Naughty but Niche** (50 feet
Hard Severe 4a 18.8.87) utilizes two niches on a line to the right again.

Grand Falls Zawn Area

DOUBLE HEADED ZAWN   OS Ref 1320 4634
This zawn lies at the back of the grassy headland of Beaufort Buttress and
has a large vegetated slab forming its rear wall. To the right of this a series
of large corners degenerate into a cornice of overhanging mud and
boulders. The zawn gives two mediocre routes.

A 280-foot abseil approach is possible by joining ropes together but it is far
more exciting to approach via Grand Falls Zawn at low tide, as described
for that cliff. Once the sea-level boulders below the *American Beauty* slab
are reached, continue south over the boulder-field to pass through one of
two caves leading through the headland into the zawn. This approach
considerably enhances the routes, turning them into something of a day out.

Jumbo's Corner   170 feet   Very Severe †   (5.8.86)
A system of grooves to the right of the main slab in the centre of the zawn.
Start at the first prominent groove 25 feet right of the right edge of the slab.
1 50 feet 4b. Climb the groove and wall above to a small stance (spike
belay).
2 70 feet 4c. Follow the brown dyke; then step left to the foot of a

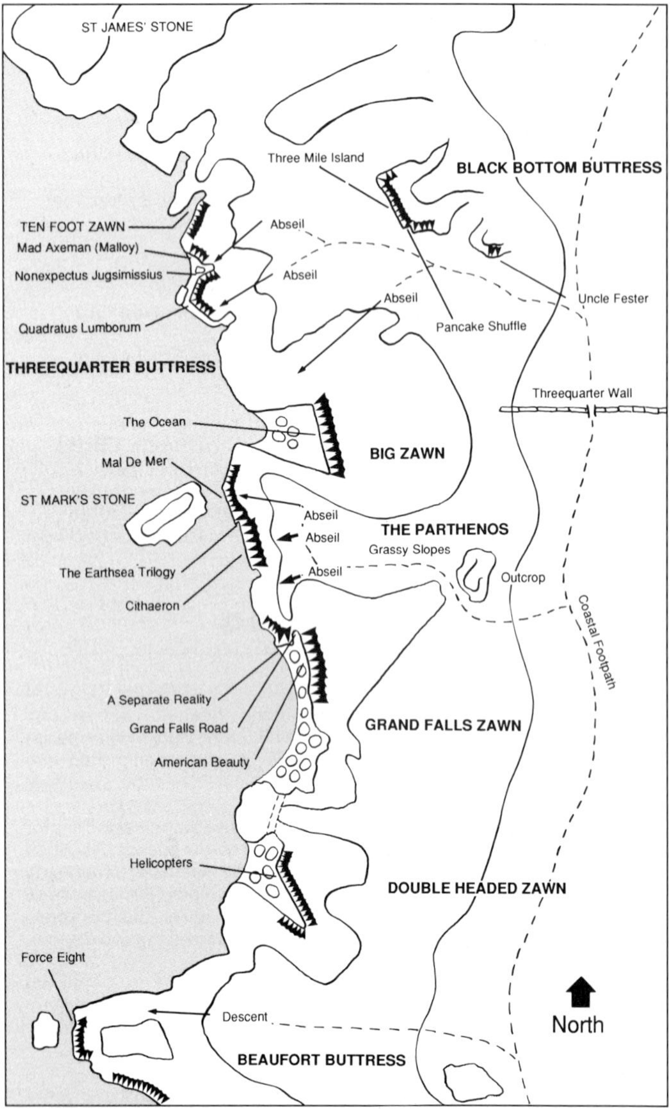

ST JAMES' STONE

Three Mile Island

BLACK BOTTOM BUTTRESS

TEN FOOT ZAWN
Mad Axeman (Malloy)
Nonexpectus Jugsimissius

Abseil

Abseil

Quadratus Lumborum

Abseil

Pancake Shuffle

Uncle Fester

THREEQUARTER BUTTRESS

Threequarter Wall

The Ocean

BIG ZAWN

Mal De Mer

ST MARK'S STONE

THE PARTHENOS

Abseil
Abseil

Grassy Slopes

The Earthsea Trilogy

Abseil

Outcrop

Cithaeron

A Separate Reality

Grand Falls Road

GRAND FALLS ZAWN

American Beauty

Helicopters

DOUBLE HEADED ZAWN

Force Eight

Descent

North

BEAUFORT BUTTRESS

Coastal Footpath

prominent groove. Climb this until it is possible to move 10 feet left to another spike belay.
3 50 feet. Scramble over blocks and grass behind the belay to the top.

Helicopters   350 feet   Very Severe   (6.8.80)
Good upper pitches. Start below the centre of the slab.
1 70 feet. Climb the lower, blank slab to a stance at its apex (nut belay).
2 140 feet 4a. Traverse right across some ledges, and then go up on vegetated rock to the base of a grey-streaked slab (stance possible). Climb the slab and continue via a line of ledges leading left to a peg belay below a small overlap slanting leftwards.
3 50 feet 4a. Follow the overlap and gain the slab above. Climb it and a curving line of cracks to a large flake belay on the left of the slab.
4 90 feet 4b. Move back right onto the slab above and go up to a leftward-slanting crack. Follow this over an overlap, and step right onto a blank slab. Climb straight up this to the summit overhangs and break through these near their left edge. Exit left at the top. Thread belay well back.

GRAND FALLS ZAWN   OS Ref 1320 4641
This is the large bay/zawn to the north, and immediately south of the long fern-covered slopes below a prominent plateau-level outcrop. As one descends this slope, Grand Falls Zawn comes into view and as the spur curves to the south (left facing out) the *American Beauty* slab is obvious. First appearances of this can be quite misleading, for while the slab looks vegetated in places the climbing in between is indeed delightful. The left-hand side of this slab is undercut by a cave, from which the cliff swings seawards and changes appearance. This face is mostly brown in colour, descending in height towards its seaward end. For the most part the routes on the face take diagonal lines to make the most of the available rock.

To reach the zawn, descend the fern-covered slopes and ridge until they degenerate into steeper and less friendly terrain. Scramble carefully down, bravest first and preferably with a fixed rope, until just above sea-level. Now traverse south on one of a number of lines, all about Very Difficult standard, to reach a large pillar leaning against the face. This leaves two possibilities.

If the tide is high, *American Beauty* and its adjacent routes cannot be reached, so a scramble up the groove on the left side of the pillar leads to its top. From here, the first pitches of *Grand Falls Road* and *A Separate Reality* can be omitted (these are the only two routes affected since the other routes on this wall begin before the pillar). To gain the *American Beauty* slab and the first pitches of the aforementioned climbs, arrival within two hours either side of low tide is necessary. From the pillar, continue traversing to the zawn bed and so to the routes.

Alternatively, for lovers of quick and easy access, a magnificent 250-foot abseil down the *American Beauty* slab from blocks at its top can be made, thus avoiding any tidal problems. Jumars are useful to bypass any knots in joined ropes.

The routes in this zawn, all of which have an open aspect, are described **from left to right** in relation to the former descent from the north and the subsequent traverse back into the zawn.

The China Syndrome   330 feet   Hard Very Severe   (31.8.79)
High on the cliff is a large scoop with a brown slab and earthy ledges forming its base. This route climbs up from the left to finish up the left-hand side of the scoop. An exposed top pitch. Start to the left of the pillar below a crack-system.
1 50 feet 4b. Follow the cracks to a belay below some roofs on the left edge of the buttress.
2 150 feet 4b. Continue up the cracks, and move right along a system of ledges to an arête overlooking the inner zawn, right of the large pillar. Various belays are possible before this point is reached.
3 60 feet 4b. After a step down, walk right along earthy ledges into a series of cracks leading up the slab to the top of the scoop. Follow the lower crack, moving into the upper when possible. Belay a little higher.
4 70 feet 5a. Go up the crack for a further 5 feet, and then cross the steep slab on the right into the centre of the face. Climb a groove to a pinnacle; then move back left into a crack. Move left again into a V-groove and exit left at its top. It is also possible to climb the steep crack direct (5b).

Gorgeous Guano   170 feet   Severe   (11.8.79)
A poor and unpopular route taking a direct line from the top of the pillar and crossing *The China Syndrome*. Start below the two grooves to the left of the pillar.
1 75 feet. Climb the left-hand groove to belay on a ledge at the apex of the pillar.
2 95 feet. Continue up the groove on the left; then move right and go up to some earthy ledges. Climb over a large flake on the left, traverse left to a spike (*The China Syndrome* crosses here), and finish up the left edge of the slab.

*A Separate Reality   250 feet   E1   (11.8.79)
This route, in no way comparable to its American namesake, takes a direct line up the cliff to gain the large scoop and an exciting finale. The climbing is enjoyable, slightly broken on the easier ground but very worthwhile. Start on the right-hand side of the pillar below a groove.
1 75 feet 4c. Climb the groove past some chockstones to a belay just below the top of the pillar.
2 85 feet 5a. Move right to a spike before climbing a leaning crack to a groove. Follow this and a line of good holds leading rightwards to the foot of a large brown slab. Move up to a belay in its centre. It is also possible to follow the rightward-leaning crack directly onto the slab.
3 90 feet 5a. Follow a faultline in the slab above and go over an overlap

Zorba the Greek (first ascent) The Parthenos
Climber: Gary Gibson   *Photo:* Hazel Gibson

Araucaria (first ascent) Starship Zawn
Climber: Nick White   *Photo:* John Houlihan

to where the rock begins to steepen. Move diagonally leftwards across the wall until a spectacular swing leads into a groove formed by the right wall of a protruding nose. Swarm merrily up this and belay to some blocks well back. A fine, exposed pitch

★**Grand Falls Road** 460 feet   Hard Very Severe   (30.8.79)
A lengthy expedition line rising left to right across the wall overlooking the small cave to the right. Some good climbing and fine positions, though slightly monotonous towards the top. Start on a series of flat ledges at the foot of the pillar.
1 80 feet 4c. Descend a slab to a line of holds on the right wall leading around the arête and onto a slab. Cross the slab and move up to a belay on a second slab.
2 60 feet 4b. Climb the crack above the belay into a groove on the right, which leads to an overhang. Move right into a second groove, and belay just below the top of the pillar, as for *A Separate Reality*.
3 85 feet 5a. As for *A Separate Reality*. Move right to a spike before climbing a crack and groove to a line of holds leading rightwards and up to a belay in the centre of the brown slab.
4 35 feet. Step back down and walk gingerly right past some detached, hollow flakes to a small ledge. Flake and nut belay high up.
5 150 feet 5a. Move up to and climb a crack rightwards to a bulge. Overcome this rather awkwardly before stepping right to continue via a faint crackline to gain a series of ledges. Follow these to a peg belay 20 feet below the top of the cliff.
6 50 feet 4b. Move right for 10 feet, and climb on widely-spaced holds to a crack. This leads to the top and a belay well back.

The remaining routes are situated on the slab at the back of the zawn and at right-angles to the wall containing *Grand Falls Road*. From the zawn bed a 40-foot pitch of Severe standard leads up the slab 20 feet right of the left-hand groove to a ledge-system. All the routes begin from here. Should the abseil approach be chosen, this first pitch can be omitted.

The left-hand side of the slab is formed by a long, slim corner. A poor and dirty route, **Robbo's Route** (300 feet Very Severe † 12.8.80), takes this corner, and on occasions the slab to its right, before finishing up the vegetated slabs above and to the left.

★**American Shrapnel** 280 feet   E3   (24.7.81)
A good slab-route taking the slab right of the corner direct. The main difficulties are centred around the overlap on pitch 2, which proves a little 'sporting'. Start at the first crack right of the corner.
1 100 feet 4c. Follow the crack slightly leftwards to a small overlap. Pull over this into the continuation crack and follow it until level with a large flat block on the right. Move right to belay on this.
2 120 feet 5c. Move back left to climb the thin crack above the first pitch to a ledge. Continue up the large slab above by the same, now much thinner crack to reach the overlap. Step left and, leaving the protection

behind you, pull through on 'tinies' onto the slab above. Climb this to belay in the corner above.
3 60 feet 4c. *American Beauty* pitch 3.

★★★**American Beauty**   300 feet   E1   (31.3.75)
The slab to the right provides an elegant classic and the most seductive line hereabouts. When combined with the low-tide approach the seriousness is increased and the atmosphere enhanced.
1 90 feet 4c. Climb the next crack right of *American Shrapnel* through the overlap to the ledge with the large flat block.
2 150 feet 5a. Sustained. Move left and climb the thin crack to the ledge, as for *American Shrapnel*. Move back right and climb up to gain some holds just left of a tongue of grass. Continue up the cracks (small-wire protection) until the overlap is reached. Traverse right to its narrowest point and pull through on surprisingly good holds. Cross the slab above diagonally leftwards to a belay in the corner.
3 60 feet 4c. Climb the corner, exit left, and finish up easy slabs.

Toucher   230 feet   Hard Very Severe   (10.8.80)
The first of a trio of routes to the right of *American Beauty* and interfering with that route at certain points; hence the name.
1 80 feet 4c. Climb the indefinite crack 15 feet right of *American Beauty* until a faultline leads up and right to an obvious V-groove. Climb this and the crack above to the large flat block.
2 100 feet 4c. Climb the two staggered corners on the right to a short slab leading to a ledge. Continue straight up the slab to the overhang and pull through it, as for *American Beauty*, onto the slab above. Step left, and then go up to belay below a steep crack.
3 50 feet 5a. The crack is steep and serious for its grade. It may prove more prudent to traverse left and finish up the corner of *American Beauty*.

Paydirt   260 feet   Very Severe †   (7.8.80)
The less appealing slab to the right. Start just right of *Toucher*.
1 100 feet 4b. Climb diagonally rightwards into a groove, which leads to a bulge. Surmount this and continue up a crack to a nut belay.
2 70 feet 4b. Trend easily leftwards to a ledge and climb the slab above to a second ledge. Move up and right to a grassy belay ledge.
3 90 feet 4b. Climb up above the belay to an overhang and go through it via a square-shaped groove. Take the indefinite crack above past a bulge to a vertical crack. Traverse left and finish up a V-groove, exiting left to easy scrambling.

The Bristol Flyer   250 feet   Hard Very Severe †   (8.8.81)
The final route on the slab up its rightmost side. Overgrown. Start at the right-hand end of the ledges.
1 50 feet. Climb diagonally rightwards to a nut belay below a line of overhangs.
2 130 feet 5a. Continue by following a line beneath the overhangs to a

GRAND FALLS ZAWN

1 American Beauty	E1
2 Grand Falls Road	HVS
3 A Separate Reality	E1
4 The China Syndrome	HVS
5 Gorgeous Guano	S

corner. Climb the slab just left of this for 60 feet to gain a sentry-box. Belay here.

3 70 feet 4b. Climb diagonally left to a crackline and follow it to the top and easy scrambling.

THE PARTHENOS   OS Ref 1317 4649

One of the show-pieces of the island, this lies immediately north of the fragile descent-slope to Grand Falls Zawn, and is adjacent to a small offshore island, St Mark's Stone. It presents one large concave face with a very impressive hanging corner high in its left flank. It is bounded to the north by a smaller, hidden wall. The main mass of the cliff offers superb, steep, and intimidating climbing, though usually with good protection and all non-tidal.

To gain the routes on the main face, approach as for Grand Falls Zawn by descending the fern-covered slope and the unstable ridge (fixed rope advised) before traversing north, 30 feet above tide level, to the start of the climbs. Alternatively, abseil directly down the right-hand side of the face from good thread belays 30 feet back from the cliff edge; 165-foot (50m) rope suffices.

On the right-hand side of the main face a dyke runs the full height of a subsidiary wall.

Start 80 feet Severe   (28.3.67)
Start midway between the dyke and the descent ridge. Move onto a slab and climb it by a crack to gain a small niche just right of a sentry-box. Continue directly through the niche to finish up a shallow corner.

Dyke 120 feet Very Severe 4c   (28.3.67)
Climb the dyke – surprise, surprise! There is an overhang at 80 feet and an awkward finish. Pleasant.

On the right-hand side of the overhanging face is a slabby ramp, hidden from view, below which is a slim brown ledge-system. All of the remaining routes on the main face start from this ledge.

300 Spartans 150 feet Very Severe 4b   (26.7.85)
This route makes the best of the easy-angled rock right of the ramp-line. Start from the right-hand end of the ledge. Trend rightwards up the streaked slab to its edge, and then go up and over a slight steepening into a dirty V-groove. Climb this and move left to a spike at the top of the ramp (belay possible). Scramble carefully to the top via the obvious line.

⋆Zephuros 150 feet Very Severe 4c   (26.7.85)
The slabby ramp-line gives pleasant climbing, particularly low down. From the ledge, climb the easy-angled slabs to reach the base of the ramp. Follow this past a break until it begins to degenerate at a spike (belay possible). Scramble carefully up the obvious groove-line to the top.

★★Zorba the Greek 150 feet E5 6b (3.8.87/9.92)

An excellent and highly enjoyable route making the most of the upper walls left of *Zephuros*. A tough crux is followed by technically easier climbing. Quite bold. From 60 feet up *Zephuros*, at a point where some overlaps appear on the left, step left above the first small overlap and pull through the main overhang (crux) onto the upper wall. Follow a thin crack to its end; then move up to stand on a small black ledge. Move right for 8 feet to gain a scoop and climb it, slightly rightwards, to finish direct via a short steep wall.

★★Cithaeron 140 feet E4 6a (27.7.84)

A tremendous pitch weaving a line up the right-hand side of the large concave face. Tenacious route-finding is combined with sustained, though nowhere-over-technical climbing. A strong will to succeed is required – high in its grade. Start below a beckoning flake above the left-hand end of the ledge-system. Climb the slab to reach the flake and follow it with increasing difficulty to its end. Pull through the bulge and move up into a scoop guarded by a black fang of rock. Pass this to the right into a second scoop and exit steeply leftwards to a black block (peg runner). Pull round the bulge above to gain the well-defined and superbly-positioned final groove.

★★Ex-Cathedra 150 feet E6 (4.8.89)

A wild, wild route taking a rightward-slanting crack up the centre of the overhanging face. Steep, sustained climbing but so well protected it proves to be one of the safest pitches on the island.
1 30 feet 5b. From the left-hand end of the ledge-system, traverse left, rising slightly, to reach a crack at some white ledges.
2 120 feet 6a. Climb up to the first roof; then move up and rightwards into the crackline. Follow this – exciting – past two peg runners to finish up a layback flake on the left-hand side of the final niche.

★★Too Precious 150 feet E6 (2.8.87)

Another superb crack-climb taking the roofed cracks above the start of *Ex-Cathedra*. Although well protected and low in the grade the pitch still proves strenuous and no less intimidating.
1 30 feet 5b. *Ex-Cathedra* pitch 1.
2 120 feet 6b. Climb up to the first roof where the crack appears and go through this and the next roof above by a series of sustained moves. Continue direct to the final roof and pass this, once again by difficult moves, to reach easier ground and the top. Peg and spike belay.

★★The Earthsea Trilogy (Part 2: The Groove) 160 feet E6 † (6.8.89)

The awesome hanging groove in the left-hand side of the face. Manful wrestling is combined with some exhilarating, albeit claustrophobic climbing.
1 50 feet 5b. Follow *Ex-Cathedra* for a short way to some cracks; then move down for 5 feet before continuing the traverse leftwards across a

slab to its edge. Bridge up the chasm to gain a second slab and a peg and nut belay.

2 110 feet 6b. Climb a leftward-leaning flake-line and then a slab to reach a thin crack leading to the start of the groove proper. Jam the crack and struggle up into the first groove (peg runner at its top). Continue up the groove past a further peg and thread runner to join *Too Precious* below its final roof. Go over this and up easier ground to the top.

★Hidden Treasures   150 feet   E3 6a   (7.8.89)
A line up the slabs overlooking the left-hand side of the face. Interesting climbing. Thirty feet below the cracks of *Too Precious* is a slabby orange rib at sea-level. Gain this by abseil (a peg belay and low tide required). Follow the flake-system above and leftwards to reach some large black spikes at the base of a short corner. Tackle the overhang up and right via a black flake and continue on more flakes, always on the edge of the slab, rightwards to a short black slab. Cross this rightwards in a good position to finish up a short white groove. Thread belay *in situ* back and to the left.

The final three routes lie on the small, hidden wall bounding the main face to the north. Access is a little awkward and although a sea-level traverse from *Cithaeron* may well be possible it has yet to be proven as a valid means of approach!

The top of the wall is identifiable by a small pillar of rock 40 feet down a steep slope below the main grassy slopes above the cliff. Locate this and arrange an abseil rope to its top from thread belays well back. Another abseil of 150 feet from the top of the pillar then leads directly down to a stance in the corner at the foot of an obvious ramp. This is alongside a large pinnacle/flake on the left wall.

★The Same Old Story   130 feet   E3 5c   (2.8.87)
Intricate climbing connecting a series of ramps and grooves up the right-hand side of the wall. A good route though not in the class of its neighbour. Climb the slab for 40 feet until an undercut on the wall allows a swing left to be made onto some face holds. Using good holds at the back of the ramp, move up for a few feet and then pull up onto the next ramp. A sustained series of bridging moves follow to reach good holds and the slim pillar above. Climb this to gain the abseil rope and belay to it.

★★★Mal de Mer   130 feet   E4 6a   (3.8.87)
A classic route combining superb rock with brilliant climbing and striking features, all enhanced by the isolated atmosphere and approach. Dry conditions are essential. From the belay at the foot of the ramp, bridge out left and pull up onto the pinnacle/flake. Move left; then climb the inviting layback flake above to gain a rest on a sloping ledge. Continue up and slightly right via good holds on the leaning headwall to a good ledge near the top, which is just right of a thin crack. Swing left and pull up and over onto the top of the pillar. Move right to belay to the abseil rope.

THE PARTHENOS

1 Zephuros   VS
2 Zorba the Greek   E5
3 Cithaeron   E4

4 Ex-Cathedra   E6
5 Too Precious   E6
6 The Earthsea Trilogy   E6
7 Hidden Treasures   E3
8 The Same Old Story   E3
9 Mal de Mer   E4

Part Man Part Henos   120 feet   Hard Very Severe †   (19.8.93)
Approach as for *Mal de Mer* and traverse left around the arête to the
right-hand end of some ledges. Alternatively, an abseil is possible to the
same point from ledges close to the entrance of Big Zawn: joined ropes
required.
1 80 feet 5a. Climb easily into a niche and continue leftwards into a
groove. Move up for a few feet and pull out left into a second groove. This
leads rightwards to a good ledge and belay.
2 40 feet. Scramble up over rock and steep ground to belay on the abseil
rope.

Threequarter Wall Area

Directly below Threequarter Wall is a huge, open zawn – Big Zawn, its
southern spur formed by The Parthenos. To the north of Big Zawn are an
interesting collection of small cliffs and buttresses, both at sea-level and
at plateau-level, before the promontory of St James' Stone is reached.
This in turn has a small bay and a rock island to its north. In the south-east
corner of the bay is a long brown wall – Starship Zawn – with The Devil's
Slide to the north.

BIG ZAWN   OS Ref 1320 4653
The huge zawn contains just one route, which takes the centre of the
immense vegetated slab that almost reaches the western end of
Threequarter Wall. Approach is by abseil down the north side of the zawn
from a flat boulder on the grassy slopes below a steep plateau-level
buttress situated just north of Threequarter Wall (Black Bottom Buttress). A
300-foot abseil down steep grassy slopes leads to a small confined
boulder-beach, accessible only at low to mid tide.

∗∗The Ocean   420 feet   E1   (13.8.86)
An expedition of great character and one of the longest routes on the
island. It follows the obvious cleaned streak up the centre of the huge slab.
Take a packed lunch! Start in the right-hand corner of the zawn where the
slab meets the sidewall in a black corner.
1 70 feet 4c. Straightforward climbing up the corner leads to a good
flake-line on the left. Follow this for 10 feet, move left into a trough, and
then move left again into a broken groove. Climb it to good holds; then
step left and take an airy stance on the arête (peg belay on the right).
2 100 feet 5a. Step right past a large perched block, and climb the arête
and slab above to good holds beneath the overlap. Pull through this and
move up and right to a nut and peg belay.
3 130 feet 4c. A serious pitch. Move left from the belay and climb the
cleaned streak in the slab to a large grassy ledge on the left. Peg belay at
a downward-pointing 'fang' of rock.
4 120 feet 5b. Step right to a thin crack and follow it over a small

overlap. Climb diagonally rightwards until beneath a larger overlap (peg runner over to the right). Pull through and continue up the crack to a third overlap. Go rightwards over this onto the final slab and follow the crackline, now much thinner, to a tricky move and good holds leading to the top. This excellent pitch can be climbed independently by abseiling to the stance at the top of pitch 3. No tick, however!

BLACK BOTTOM BUTTRESS   OS Ref 1316 4660

The buttress lies just below plateau-level, immediately north of Threequarter Wall. The cliff has a friendly, outcrop atmosphere and the rock is excellent on all the routes.

A small subsidiary buttress on the grass slopes above Black Bottom Buttress yields **Uncle Fester** (65 feet Very Severe 5a 2.4.85), a worthwhile pitch up the rightward-trending flake-system, gained from the crack in the slab below.

The first route on the main crag is also its poorest. **Finale** (80 feet Very Severe 4b 27.9.80) climbs the wide, vertical crackline in the right wall of the buttress.

Pancake Shuffle   100 feet   E1   5b   (28.8.77)
A good climb up the right-hand side of the buttress. The highlight is an exciting hand-traverse below the big roof. Start beneath the overhang on the right-hand side of the buttress. Climb boldly up the steep slab to a corner just right of the overhang. Hand-traverse wildly left past the 'pancake' and swing up into the twin cracks above. If your ropework passes the test, continue up the cracks to an awkward finish where they disappear. Alternatively, an uncomfortable stance can be taken at the base of the cracks.

*The Bottom Inspectors   90 feet   E4   6a †   (9.8.89)
A direct and technical approach to the twin cracks of *Pancake Shuffle*. Start at a crack in the black-streaked wall. Climb the crack and move right into a much thinner crack, which leads with increasing difficulty to the overhang. Pull steeply through this on the left to join and finish up *Pancake Shuffle*.

**Three Mile Island   120 feet   E4   6a   (31.3.85)
A very good pitch up the front face of the buttress. Bold in its upper half. Start at a crack in the left edge of the buttress. Climb the crack and step right at a hanging flake. Step right again to the base of a thin crack (peg runner). Increasingly difficult climbing where the crack disappears gains the sanctuary of a horizontal break. Stand up in it and continue direct over a small overlap to finish via a faint scoop.

Funky Chicken   90 feet   Hard Very Severe   5a   (28.8.77)
Start as for *Three Mile Island* and climb the crack to the hanging flake. Move up; then step right into a vegetated groove. Climb this and the prickly crack above to the top.

⋆Conga Corner   100 feet   Hard Very Severe   5a   (28.8.77)
A good sustained pitch up the leftward-slanting crackline in the left-hand
side of the buttress. Start as for *Three Mile Island*. Climb the initial crack
but move left at the hanging flake into the crack proper. Follow it and the
continuation chimney above to a bristly finish up a lichen-covered ramp.

North of Black Bottom Buttress is a large grassy gully. High up on its
south-facing wall is **Norma Shearer** (80 feet E1 5a † 12.8.88). Climb
directly up a clean, dark streak with a detour to the right at 25 feet.
Continue up a vegetated crack to the summit.

THREEQUARTER BUTTRESS   OS Ref 1313 4659
A pleasantly situated cliff rising from sea-level, directly below the grassy
slope west of Black Bottom Buttress. Descend the easy slope north of Big
Zawn, passing beneath Black Bottom Buttress, to the top of two spurs.
Threequarter Buttress lies directly below the southern spur, while *The
Gold Run* and surrounding climbs are on the southern side of the northern
spur. Useful landmarks are twin open gullies of steep grass separated by
a narrow rib to the south and a distinctive narrow zawn to the north.

Scramble down the southern flank of the buttress and descend Moderate
standard rock past a narrow ledge leading across the face of the buttress
to a platform above high-tide level.

Talcum   70 feet   Very Difficult   (24.9.71)
A slight climb up the right-hand side of the buttress. Start on the platform
beneath a cracked slab.
1 40 feet. Climb the thin crack a few feet right of the arête for 25 feet,
and follow the obvious line up and right into another crack, which leads to
the narrow ledge.
2 30 feet. The twin cracks above provide the finish.

⋆Quadratus Lumborum   150 feet   Severe   (24.9.71)
Delightful climbing in a fine position up the centre of the buttress.
Justifiably popular. Start as for *Talcum*.
1 40 feet. Climb the thin crack just right of the arête, and at 25 feet make
a tricky move left to reach the arête. Follow this to a stance on the narrow
ledge.
2 70 feet. Take the obvious traverse-line across the left wall of the
buttress, descending at first before gradually ascending to below a steep
wall. Climb the wall by a zigzag line to a good ledge and belay.
3 40 feet. Climb the wall behind the belay.

⋆Ligamentum Flavum   140 feet   Severe   (2.4.85)
A direct version of *Quadratus Lumborum*. Equally enjoyable.
1 40 feet. *Quadratus Lumborum* pitch 1.
2 100 feet. Step round the arête and follow the obvious twin slanting
cracks leading back onto the arête after 70 feet. Continue easily up the
arête to finish.

The next routes are situated on the south side of the northern spur of rock. Approach down a short grassy slope to ledges at the top of the spur, which overlooks a large recessed slab, *The Gold Run*. A short abseil down slabby rock leads to the large boulder-choke beneath the slab. No tidal restrictions.

★★Nonexpectis Jugsimisius   125 feet   Very Severe 4c   (25.9.85)
A superb pitch up the hidden crack in the left arête of the buttress. Pleasantly exposed and on excellent rock. Start below the recessed slab, on the upper of two large jammed boulders. Step awkwardly down until it is possible to swing blindly right round the arête to reach excellent holds at the base of the crack. Follow the crack to a ledge at half height and finish up the thinner, continuation crack.

Trogus-Lo-Dyticus   100 feet   Very Severe 4b †   (5.9.86)
The big chimney/blowhole right of the recessed slab. A headtorch could prove useful! Squeeze into the chimney from the boulder-choke and clamber up to a standing position on the third chockstone. Continue up to a ledge on the impending wall and emerge through the skylight to the top.

★★The Gold Run   130 feet   E3 5c   (26.9.85)
The large recessed slab. A high-quality pitch with an air of seriousness for both members of the party. Start from the large boulder beneath the slab. Climb the slab to reach a thin crack and follow it into and up a shallow groove. Make a thin traverse left to regain the crack beneath a tiny overlap, pull over, and trend leftwards beneath the capping overhangs (peg runner). Traverse diagonally left along the faultline to reach good belay ledges.

The routes on the slabby, south-facing wall opposite and to the north of *Quadratus Lumborum* start from black ledges below the wall. These are exposed two hours either side of low tide. The approach is by abseil down the slabby grey rib at the eastern end of the wall. Alternatively, the ledges can be reached by a short leftwards descent from the boulders below *The Gold Run*.

Ribsnorter   75 feet   Very Difficult   (25.9.85)
At the right-hand end of the black ledges is a chimney. This route climbs the obvious slabby rib to the right of the chimney, starting on its left and finishing on the right.

★Hotspot   80 feet   E2 5b   (25.9.85)
The wall and shallow grooves just left of the chimney. Woeful protection. Climb the wall direct to reach the first groove. Delicate moves up this lead to a small ledge beneath a second groove. Move up for better holds above and finish direct over an awkward bulge.

★Mad Axeman (Malloy)   80 feet   E1 5b   (28.3.85)
The thin, rightward-slanting crack above the left-hand end of the ledges.

Start 15 feet left of *Hotspot* at a crack. Climb the crack to a ledge on the right below the pencil-thin crack. Ascend this (micro-wires) until a difficult move across the wall on the left brings better holds into reach. Finish up the groove above.

Lobsterisimus Bummerkissimus   75 feet   Hard Severe 4a
(28.3.85)

Climb the slabby groove just left of *Mad Axeman* to an overlap on the right. Pull over onto the slab above and take the slim groove rightwards to finish.

La Isla Bonita   75 feet   Severe   (11.8.86)

The obvious slabby groove at the far left-hand end of the ledges. Finish direct over a tiny bulge.

True Blue   65 feet   Very Difficult   (2.8.92)

The slabby arête to the left of *La Isla Bonita*.

TEN FOOT ZAWN   OS Ref 1310 4662

This is the small narrow zawn to the north of Threequarter Buttress. Two routes have been recorded on the slabby south wall, the approach to which is incorporated into the first route. Alternatively, it is possible to abseil down the seaward tip of the south wall to small sea-level ledges at the mouth of the zawn.

The Bastard's Name Was Bristow   90 feet   Severe   (11.8.86)

An interesting excursion. Descend as for *Ribsnorter* to the sea-level ledges. Whilst pondering the name, traverse round the northern tip of Threequarter Buttress along the easy ledges into the zawn. A prominent leftward-slanting flake crack is now climbed with a move back right to finish.

★Free Rain   90 feet   E3 5c   (11.8.89)

The vague, leftward-slanting crack in the south wall. Protection is reasonable but perseverance is required to find it. Start from sea-level ledges near the mouth of the zawn gained by abseil, or from *The Bastard's Name Was Bristow*. Climb easy cracks until it is possible to move left above an overlap for 10 feet to the start of the crack. Follow it leftwards, crossing a white streak, to gain a small ledge. Finish more easily up a short groove.

St James' Stone Area

Immediately north of Ten Foot Zawn is a rocky spur descending all the way down to sea-level. On its seaward side is a slabby, west-facing wall rising from the sea with a prominent chimney/crack above – *The Onedin*

Line. The top of the spur can be located from plateau-level adjacent to St James' Stone. Scramble down the spur to a point some 60 feet above the sea. A short abseil down the seaward face leads to small ledges just above sea-level. Low to mid tide required.

The Onedin Line   180 feet   Hard Very Severe   (9.8.92)
Varied climbing in a wonderfully isolated position.
1 90 feet 5a. Follow some thin cracks to a small overlap, pull over, and continue more easily to a spacious ledge. Trend easily leftwards up a diagonal rake to a stance beneath the prominent lichenous chimney/crack.
2 90 feet 4c. Climb the chimney/crack and move left along a horizontal break at its top. A short wide crack provides a steep finish.

ST JAMES' STONE   OS Ref 1304 4675
This is the large rocky headland at the tip of the promontory running out from the mainland south of The Devil's Slide. There are two stones, an Inner and an Outer, which are reached by scrambling over the narrow neck of land connecting the Inner Stone to the mainland. The nature of the rock is such that the climber can wander at will over the many obvious lines at Difficult to Severe standard. It is quite an interesting scramble over the Inner Stone to the Outer Stone and down to the sea, set in magnificent coastal surroundings.

A number of lines offering sterner resistance have been recorded. The next two routes are situated on the seaward face of the Outer Stone.

Kathleen Turner   75 feet   Hard Very Severe 5a †   (3.8.91)
Start beneath a large, undercut slab just left of a prominent, open groove. Climb over the right edge of the slab and continue up a crack above to an overlap. Layback round this and finish up the groove above.

Lerina   85 feet   E1 5b †   (20.8.93)
A good pitch on excellent rock. Start below a groove, 30 feet left of *Kathleen Turner*. Climb the groove, and step right at its top onto a short slab. Follow this to a flared crack and climb the crack through an overlap onto a slab above. Proceed boldly up it to the summit of the Outer Stone.

The prominent leftward-slanting chimney/groove on the north face of the Inner Stone is **James** (90 feet Very Severe 4b † 8.8.92)

On the north face of the Inner Stone is a short orange wall with a large platform below and a narrow black zawn to the east. Approach the wall by abseil from good block belays above to the platform. This is sea-washed in high seas.

Harry the Hake   75 feet   Hard Severe   4a †   (21.8.90)
From the right-hand edge of the platform, climb a flake and the slabby groove above. Block belay well back.

Herbert the Turbot   75 feet   E1 5a †   (21.8.90)
The wall and slab just left of *Harry the Hake* offers little in the way of
protection. Block belay well back.

Neptune Rising   80 feet   E2 5c   (20.8.90)
The best route hereabouts. Start from the left-hand end of the platform.
Climb a thin crack and continue up the shallow groove above. Tackle the
final wall on its left-hand side. Block belay well back.

NARROW ZAWN   OS Ref 1312 4675

The small black zawn immediately north-east of St James' Stone. The
approach to its only route to date is by abseil down the south wall of the
zawn from good block belays on the promontory running out to St James'
Stone. The floor of the zawn is accessible only one hour either side of low
tide. Leaving the abseil rope in place may be a good idea, as escape
otherwise is possible only by a long swim.

Crack Climbing for Beginners   140 feet   E1   (4.8.89)
Despite its name, the prominent crack splitting the south wall of the zawn
requires some proficiency in the art. The rock is rather crumbly towards
the top.
1 90 feet 5a. Climb the crack, thin and often damp at first, over a small
overhang to where it begins to widen and the angle eases. Belay a little
higher below a steep groove.
2 60 feet 5b. Bridge up the groove above and exit awkwardly right to a
ledge. Scramble back to good block belays on the promontory.

STARSHIP ZAWN   OS Ref 1316 4678

To the east of St James' Stone is a very impressive brown undercut wall,
which is best viewed from the grassy slopes to the north. The wall consists
of a series of spectacular bottomless grooves, which, with one exception,
await future pioneers. At the seaward end of the wall are three, more
pronounced, leftward-facing grooves.

The most convenient approach for *Starship Trooper* is to make a 180-foot
abseil from good spike belays on the ridge above to small ledges at its
base. For the other routes in the zawn, descend the narrow ridge on the
northern side to sea-level, and cross the large boulders in the narrow inlet
to reach the start of the routes. Low tide and a calm sea are essential.

An escape route from the zawn is possible from the ledges at the foot of
Starship Trooper by following cracks up the arête to the right of that route:
Klingon (100 feet Very Difficult).

★Starship Trooper   100 feet   E2 5b   (8.8.79)
The right-hand and most prominent of the three grooves. A good bridging
exercise, low in its grade. Climb the groove direct past two decaying peg
runners.

★**Mars Bar**   100 feet   Hard Very Severe   5b   (22.8.80)
The central groove gives a worthwhile pitch. Climb the stepped groove to
a small ledge at 70 feet (stance possible). The steep crack above leads to
good holds at its top. Exit carefully over steep grass and belay well back.

★**Moondance**   110 feet   E1   5b   (4.8.89)
Enjoyable climbing up the thin cracks in the narrow face left of *Mars Bar*.
Start as for *Mars Bar* but move left and climb a thin rightward-slanting
crack. Transfer left into a thinner crack and go up this before moving left
again to an easier finishing groove. Exit carefully left at the top and belay
well back.

★**Space Bandit**   130 feet   E2   (2 pts aid) †   (22.8.80)
The left-hand groove bristles with overhangs. A fine, powerful line crying
out for a free ascent. Unfortunately, the start is nearly always wet.
1 90 feet 5c. Climb the groove to the first overhang, swing left, and
move up into the corner above. Follow a horizontal break left to some thin
vertical cracks and climb these to a second overhang. Overcome this
using two nuts for aid and make a difficult move to reach the corner
above. Peg and nut belay.
2 40 feet 5b. From the belay, swing out right onto the arête and climb
the groove above to the top. Belay on the right.

★★**Araucaria**   150 feet   E6   (1 pt aid) †   (6.9.91)
An outrageous proposition requiring all-out commitment from both
members of the party to reach a tantalizing, flawless groove in the upper
wall. Start well above sea-level atop a large boulder perched on the slab
at the landward end of the zawn. A long stick and a long neck seem
necessary.
1 80 feet 6a. Stick clip the *in-situ* nut in the break above, and jumar or
hand-over-hand up to it. Without dwelling too long on the situation,
hand-traverse right along the crack formed by an apparently detached,
suspended beam of rock. Swing up and right into the hanging groove
above and climb it for 20 feet to a good ledge and *Friend* belay.
2 70 feet 6c. The continuation groove gives fine, technical climbing (two
peg runners) to a problematic finish. Good belays can be found directly
above, and 60 feet back from the edge.

The Devil's Slide Area

Three hundred yards north of Threequarter Wall is The Devil's Slide, an
unmistakable feature and the focus of attention hereabouts. Tucked away
to its north is a steep, orange-and-black-streaked wall, not surprisingly
known as The Back of the Slide. To *its* north is a large, grooved cliff –
Fluted Face – which has a smaller buttress north again – Benson's Buttress.

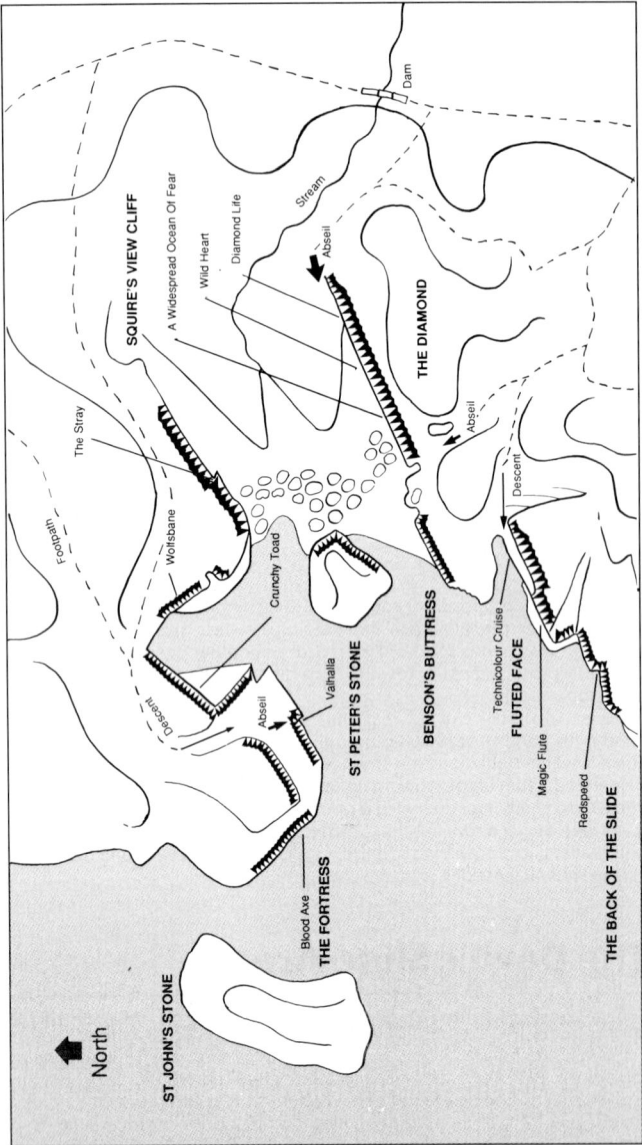

North

SQUIRE'S VIEW CLIFF

A Widespread Ocean Of Fear
Wild Heart
Diamond Life

Stream

Dam

Abseil

THE DIAMOND

Abseil

The Stray

Footpath

Wolfsbane

Crunchy Toad

Descent

Vahalla

Abseil

Descent

Technicolour Cruise

FLUTED FACE

Descent

Magic Flute

Redspeed

ST PETER'S STONE

BENSON'S BUTTRESS

THE BACK OF THE SLIDE

Blood Axe

THE FORTRESS

ST JOHN'S STONE

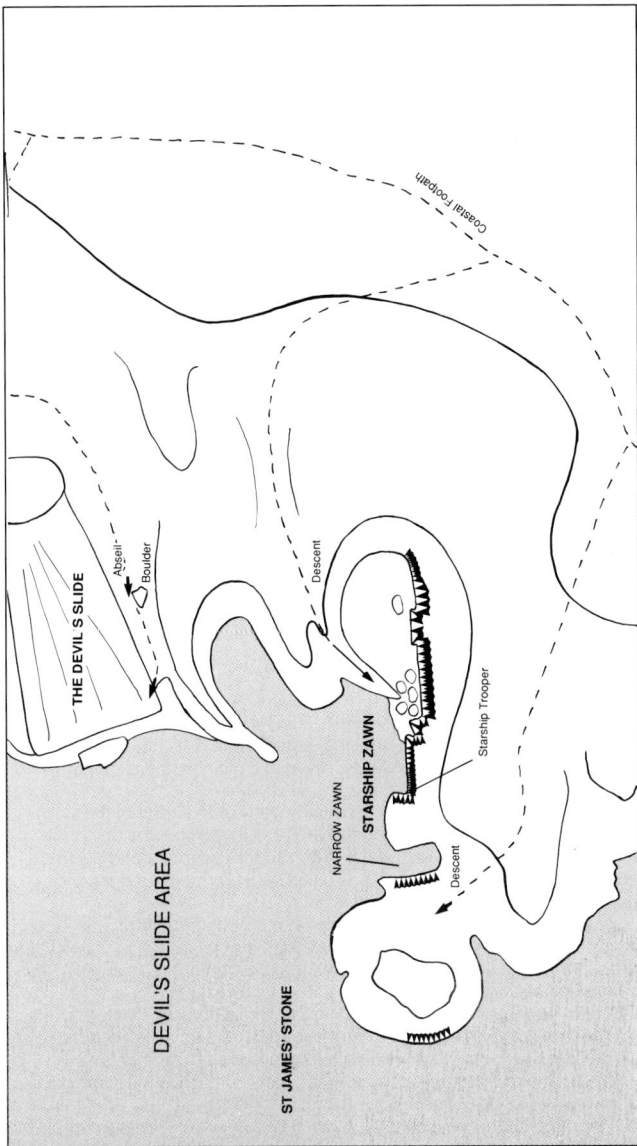

DEVIL'S SLIDE AREA

THE DEVIL'S SLIDE

Abseil
Boulder

Descent

NARROW ZAWN

STARSHIP ZAWN

Starship Trooper

Descent

Coastal Footpath

ST JAMES' STONE

THE DEVIL'S SLIDE APPROACH CLIFF   OS Ref 1314 4688

This is the collective name given to the series of short grooves and ribs immediately south of the slender rib used as a descent to The Devil's Slide, and opposite St James' Stone. The rock is unfortunately very broken and consequently climbable anywhere at up to Severe standard. Combining one of the grooves or ribs with the prominent smooth groove in the lichen-covered rock on the right gives an enjoyable, if contrived route:

Gollum (100 feet Very Difficult).

THE DEVIL'S SLIDE   OS Ref 1314 4688

One day there might even be a route straight up the middle – if anyone has a plentiful supply of bolts!   (Mike Banks in *Mountain* 8 1970)

The island's famous climbing landmark, a magnificent sweep of orange-and-black-streaked granite rising majestically out of the Atlantic Ocean. All the routes on 'The Slide' are first class and the ascent of at least one of them should be obligatory to the first-time visitor.

The slab is supported at its foot by a convenient large platform, which is sea-washed at high tide and can be particularly exposed in stormy seas. To approach the platform, descend the broad grassy gully immediately south of the Slide. Where the gully ends, move left (facing out) and scramble down a narrow rib of rock to the south of The Slide at Moderate standard. A short traverse to the north then gains the platform. Alternatively, a 165-foot abseil from a large block at the foot of the grassy gully to the platform below is becoming increasingly popular. At high tide the climbs can be started from a horizontal faultline which crosses the slab 25 feet above the platform.

★★★**The Devil's Slide**   400 feet   Hard Severe   (6.61)

The classic climb of Lundy. The route follows a line just in from the right edge of the slab, gradually increasing in angle and difficulty before the final, delicate, airy traverse. A fitting finale to a memorable climb. Start on the large platform.

1 60 feet. Taking a line 20 feet in from the right-hand edge of the slab, climb easily to a belay in a horizontal break.

2 100 feet. Continue in the same line at a slightly harder standard to a poor nut belay in the half-way break. Alternatively, traverse right and belay on the large block in the gully.

3 130 feet 4a. Keeping left of the right-hand bounding rib of The Slide, aim for the obvious white scoop. Delicate moves up this, or more easily up the rib to the right, lead to some small ledges. Good nut-placements can be found a little higher.

4 80 feet 4a. Continue up the right edge of the slab until the steepening in angle prevents further upward progress. Tiptoe daintily left along the obvious line, just below the headwall, to a large recess and belay.

5 30 feet. Finish easily over cracked blocks on the left to the summit.

Variations

4a 70 feet. The traverse on pitch 4 can be avoided by sneaking off The

Slide to the right. Easier, vastly inferior, and often tackled by goats!
The Direct Finish   Hard Very Severe   (4.71)
4b 70 feet 4c. Instead of traversing left, climb straight up to a bulging
groove/crackline and follow it to the top. A more logical finish, but much
harder than the rest of the climb.
Devil's Downfall   E1   (4.71/26.3.85)
4c 70 feet 5b. The groove and evil off-width crack in the headwall left of
The Direct Finish and above the finish of *Satan's Slip*.

⋆⋆**Fear of Faust**   180 feet   E1 5a   (26.7.84)
A high-calibre slab pitch squeezed in between *The Devil's Slide* and
Satan's Slip. The climbing is technically straightforward but sustained and
very bold. Start from the half-way break at a small spike.
1 150 feet 5a. Step off the spike and follow a faint crack to a tiny
overlap. Go over on its right to a larger overlap and pull through it past a
peculiar hole to a third overlap. Take this on the left and continue,
trending diagonally left, into the corner of *Albion*. Follow it to a belay or,
better, continue up and across to the traverse of *The Devil's Slide*.
2 30 feet. Finish easily leftwards over the large blocks.

A slight route has been squeezed in between the crux pitches of *Fear of
Faust* and *Satan's Slip*. **Muffin the Puffin Meets Dykinbad the
Tongueflayler** (130 feet E1 5a † 26.8.88): blinkers essential!

⋆⋆⋆**Satan's Slip**   330 feet   E1   (29.3.70)
The magnificent central direttissima of the slab, one of the finest slab
climbs of its grade in the South-West. Modern small-wire protection has
helped reduce the route's seriousness but, although low in its grade, it
should not be underestimated. Start beneath the centre of The Slide.
1 150 feet. Climb easily up the middle of the slab to the half-way break.
Belay on the right.
2 150 feet 5a. A lonely lead. Move back into the centre of the slab and
climb it just right of some black streaks, aiming for a small overlap at 100
feet. Continue over this to where the black streaks meet the corner of
Albion and follow it for 15 feet to a flake belay in the large recess.
3 30 feet. Finish easily leftwards over the large blocks. For those with a
'devil may care' attitude, *Devil's Downfall* provides a suitably contrasting
finale.

⋆⋆⋆**Albion**   350 feet   Very Severe   (15.4.63)
The black-streaked corner bounding the left-hand edge of the slab. A
terrific main pitch, perhaps the best of its grade on the island. Start below
the left edge of The Slide.
1 120 feet. Climb easily up the left-hand side of the slab to a small stance
on its left-bounding rib.
2 80 feet. Move back right and climb directly up the slab to a small
stance with flake belays beneath the steep retaining wall.
3 120 feet 4c. Sustained. Climb the curving corner (peg runner), which
eventually eases to a belay in the large recess.

4 30 feet. Finish easily up to the left as for *The Devil's Slide*.

Three routes follow lines up the impressive retaining wall bounding the corner of *Albion*. They can be approached by one of the lower pitches on The Slide or, more quickly, by traversing the break crossing the slab at half height.

The Opium Den   120 feet   E1   5b   (4.4.85)
A slight, but exciting excursion across the steep wall. Good positions. Start beneath pitch 3 of *Albion*. Follow the corner of *Albion* to where the black streaks end. Step awkwardly left to gain a leftward-leaning ramp and climb it delicately to some vertical corners. These provide a steep, difficult finish.

Ticket to Ride   100 feet   E5   †   (23.6.89)
Powerful climbing up the intermittent crackline above the start of *Albion* pitch 3. Well positioned, with the crux at the top.
1 80 feet   6b. Follow *Albion* for a few feet before launching up the wall on the left. Climb straight up a crack for 15 feet, where an extending move left gains a line of sidepulls (peg runner). Reach back right and move up to another peg runner below a small groove. Move up and left into the groove and reach a 'thank God' ledge just above. A steep, blocky corner leads to a good ledge and block belays.
2 20 feet. One short wall remains before the top.

★Shark   150 feet   Hard Very Severe   (8.7.71)
An exciting pitch up the elegant fin of rock overlooking the upper reaches of The Slide. Some fine climbing with increasingly airy (or hairy?) situations. Start at a stance on the left edge of The Slide, level with the half-way break.
1 90 feet   5a. Climb the groove in the steep arête (peg runner) and continue up a small slab on the left to a small overhang. Turn it on the right to gain a deep crack, which leads to a fine stance atop a large flat-topped block.
2 60 feet. Climb up over the large stepped blocks above to the top.

The next four routes are centred around the lichenous rib that bounds the left-hand side of The Slide. From the foot of The Slide, an easy ascending traverse to the north leads to some blocky ledges, well above high water.

Devil Dodger   225 feet   Very Severe   †   (29.8.70)
A poor, vegetated route starting up the broken rib which bounds The Slide to its left. Start 15 feet left of the foot of The Slide.
1 90 feet. Climb up over stepped ledges to reach the left-hand edge of the slab and follow it to a belay.
2 110 feet   4a. Climb the broken rib until it steepens and then move left into the gully. Continue up this, moving diagonally left where it steepens, to belay on the prominent flakes on the arête. A poorly-protected and very lichenous pitch.

3 25 feet. *Devil's Spine* pitch 4.

Devil's Spine 215 feet   Very Severe   (15.4.63)
The prominent slabby rib 50 feet left of The Slide. Pleasant and sustained but gradually disappearing beneath the lichen. Start from spacious ledges beneath the rib, as far north as it is possible to scramble.
1 80 feet 4b. Climb up to the left; then move steeply back right and take the rounded rib above to a nut belay on a small ledge.
2 40 feet 4a. Climb the centre of the lichenous depression above to a ledge and block belay where the rib becomes an arête.
3 70 feet 4a. Go up the arête and, where it steepens, climb its left-hand side, before moving back right to a notch on the arête. Continue past a step in the arête to a second notch and flake belay.
4 25 feet.   Traverse right for a few feet and then climb a short groove back onto the arête (block belay). Scrambling remains.

Devil's Honeymoon 210 feet   Very Severe   (20.9.76)
A good, clean first pitch but rather featureless above. Start as for *Devil's Spine*.
1 65 feet 4c. Move left and climb the leftward-trending groove to an overlap. Go directly over via a steep crack to gain a small stance and nut belay.
2 60 feet 4b. Traverse left for a few feet; then climb diagonally left to a corner, which leads to a good stance adjacent to *Devil's Spine*.
3 85 feet 4a. Follow *Devil's Spine* to finish.

Dexter 80 feet   Very Severe 4c   (29.3.70)
Of little individual merit but a useful means of gaining access to The Back of the Slide and Fluted Face from The Devil's Slide. Start as for *Devil's Spine*; low to mid tide and a calm sea are required. Move left onto the slabby face and descend a crack to the left for 15 feet. Continue along the obvious traverse to the left, dropping down below a bulge to gain the large area of ledges beneath the orange-and-black-streaked wall.

THE BACK OF THE SLIDE   OS Ref 1314 4688
The name given to the steep, orange-and-black-streaked wall just north of The Devil's Slide. A notable feature is the clean hanging groove of *Redspeed*, while to the left the prominent leftward-trending chimney/groove of *Seventh Seal* divides the wall from Fluted Face. Beneath the wall is a large area of slabby ledges, sea-washed at high tide.

There are a number of approaches. The traverse of *Dexter* provides low-to-mid-tide access from the base of The Slide. The ledges can also be reached by abseil from the terrace on Fluted Face (see Fluted Face approach), and a short, easy traverse back to the south. An increasingly popular approach is to traverse the half-way break across The Slide, from where a careful descending traverse around the arête leads to a good spike above the groove of *Redspeed*. A 130-foot abseil from this gains the ledges beneath the face. This approach allows a number of climbs on the face to be undertaken.

Godspeed   80 feet   E1 5b †   (20.8.90)
An alternative approach to the crack of *Devil's Honeymoon*. Start from the
northern end of the traverse of *Dexter*. Pull onto the slab above, and climb
diagonally right above the bulge of *Dexter* to reach a flake. This and the
slab above lead to a junction with *Devil's Honeymoon* at the steep crack,
which is followed to the small stance. *Shark* provides a suitable finish.

★★★Redspeed   130 feet   E2 5c   (3.8.78)
A brilliant pitch up the slim hanging groove in the upper wall. Although it
is high in its grade, the rock and protection are excellent. Start directly
beneath the groove. Pull steeply up to gain the obvious leftward-slanting
crack in the black-streaked wall and climb it almost to its end, from where
a short traverse right gains the foot of a small leftward-slanting ramp.
Climb the ramp until it is possible to make a hard step left into the groove.
This leads to the convenient spike belay on the arête. Finish up *Devil's
Spine* or, more appropriately, traverse right to *Shark*.
Variations
The route originally reached the crux ramp by a line of rightward-curving
flakes. This is to the left of the described start and the same grade. A
harder alternative gains the main groove direct by pulling through the
overhangs below at E3 6a.

★Elan   120 feet   E3 6a †   (10.8.92)
Sustained, technical climbing through the overhangs just left of *Redspeed*.
Start beneath the rightward-curving flakes. Gain the flakes and follow
them to where a thin crack splits the overhangs to the left. A strenuous
sequence up the crack leads to a larger overhang. Pull through via a good
crack and continue more easily up the vegetated crack and groove above
to the good spike belay on the arête.

★Lightspeed   120 feet   E2 5c   (13.6.88)
An exciting pitch weaving through the overhangs left of *Redspeed*. Start
beneath a smooth brown groove running up to the left-hand end of the
overhangs. Climb directly into the groove and follow it (small-wire
protection) to the overhang. Make a wild undercling right and layback
round the end of the roof into a crack, which leads to the huge flake belay
on *Seventh Seal*. Finish up *Seventh Seal*, or take the diagonal crack
running rightwards to the spike belay of *Redspeed*.

Antonius Block   120 feet   E1 5c †   (7.8.92)
The slim groove left of *Lightspeed*. Start at the base of the open chimney of
Seventh Seal. Gain the groove from the chimney and climb it; move
diagonally rightwards at its top to a steep crack. Climb this and finish
diagonally rightwards to the spike belay of *Lightspeed*.

Seventh Seal   185 feet   Hard Very Severe   (23.8.71)
Steep, varied climbing up the open chimney/groove at the left-hand end
of the face. The upper pitches are very vegetated. Start below the open
chimney.

1 45 feet 4c. Climb the chimney, gradually steepening, with an awkward move to gain a good hold. Stance and peg belay just above.

2 30 feet 4a. Traverse easily right beneath a large flake and gain its top by a crack. Belay down and right of the flake.

3 60 feet 4c. Step right into a steep crack and climb it until a ledge on the right can be gained. Move leftwards more easily, and follow a series of flakes up the rib to a stance.

4 50 feet. Climb the rib above the stance, and move right onto the rib of *Devil's Spine*. This leads via a short crack on the right to a block belay. Scrambling remains.

FLUTED FACE   OS Ref 1314 4692

To the north of The Back of the Slide is a large face, which is separated from it by the large slanting chimney/groove that *Seventh Seal* starts up. The face is divided into two halves by a narrow terrace: the upper half of the face is characterized by a series of white, partly lichen-covered flutings; the lower half consists of a perfect sheet of orange granite rising from a narrow sea-channel.

The pitches on the upper face generally follow sustained, slabby groove-lines, which owing to a lack of traffic are becoming increasingly over-grown. The lower face gives some exquisite steep slab-climbing in a dramatic position. Apart from *Magnificat* and *Friends in High Places*, the pitches here can be swapped at random to provide a variety of combinations, the most appropriate being *Tempest/Performance* and *Performance/Magic Flute*.

The most interesting approach to the face is by means of *Dexter* (see The Devil's Slide), and continuing the traverse north along slabby ledges to their left-bounding arête. Though somewhat time-consuming, this is a fine excursion amidst spectacular rock scenery. A more direct approach can be made down the large grassy gully immediately north of the summit of The Slide. From the gully's end, an awkward, exposed step leads onto the terrace crossing the face. A 75-foot abseil from the right-hand end of the terrace reaches the northern section of the slabby ledges. Sea-washed at high tide, these ledges can also be affected by a heavy sea swell.

The first two climbs begin just south of the abseil and to the left of the steep chimney/groove of *Seventh Seal*.

Magnificat 200 feet E2   (9.5.71)

An excellent first pitch precedes some bold, precarious climbing up the slender rib forming the right-hand edge of Fluted Face. Unfortunately, the top pitch is becoming increasingly overgrown. Start beneath a prominent stepped groove.

1 80 feet 5b. Climb up to the groove and make a difficult move to gain its foot. Once you are established, more amenable climbing leads to an overhang. Turn this to its left, and continue up either of the grooves above to a stance.

2 50 feet 4a. Move up into the crack above the stance, and then stride left onto the arête. Climb this via a crack to a pinnacle stance.
3 70 feet 5c. Climb the rib above with increasing difficulty to a stance and spike belay. A serious pitch, not unlike climbing up the outside of a toilet brush!

★Friends in High Places   280 feet   E3   (20.8.81)
A brutal initial pitch leads to sustained, open climbing up the cleaned headwall to the right of *Fluted Face*. Start beneath the overhang-capped groove left of *Magnificat*.
1 80 feet 5c. Climb the groove to the overhang and pull strenuously leftwards into a second groove. Follow this diagonally rightwards to a small stance.
2 50 feet 4a. Continue rightwards into the vegetated gully. Step right onto the central wall; then climb up and right to a small ledge below a downward-pointing flake. Peg and nut belay.
3 150 feet 5b. Step left from the belay and climb a series of flakes and cracks, trending slightly left, to reach an easier flaky section. Climb up to the final crack, step right onto the wall, and finish directly up this to a spike belay.

The next five climbs begin from a small stance in a groove in the left-hand bounding arête of the slabby ledges.

Sandpiper   190 feet   Hard Very Severe   (17.4.73)
The main pitch climbs the heavily overgrown right-hand groove in the upper face, immediately left of the slender rib of *Magnificat*.
1 70 feet 4a. Follow the arête to an overhang, and move left onto the slab. Climb steeply up on good holds before moving easily back right into a groove, which leads to the terrace.
2 120 feet 5a. Trowel at the ready! From the right-hand end of the terrace, follow steep twin cracks, and move slightly right into the right-hand groove. Climb this to a flake and nut belay on the easy rib above. Scramble to the top.

★Magic Flute   200 feet   Hard Very Severe   (17.4.73)
An enjoyable climb; the easiest on *Fluted Face* and the least affected by vegetation. The main pitch takes the central and deepest groove in the upper wall.
1 70 feet 4a. Climb easily up the arête to the overhang and move left to continue steeply on good holds. Go over the bulge above and follow rounded cracks to the terrace. Spike belay beneath a short square-cut crack.
2 130 feet 5a. Climb the crack for 10 feet; then move right on rounded flakes to the foot of the central groove-line. Climb this, exiting right at its top to a belay on the easy rib. Scrambling remains.

★**Performance** 230 feet Hard Very Severe (10.5.71)
The left-hand groove provides a fine sustained main pitch, the best on the
upper face. A large selection of nuts is useful.
1 90 feet 4b. Climb easily up the arête to just below the overhang, and
traverse left for 15 feet to a thin crack. Climb this to the terrace. Spike
belay below a square-cut crack.
2 140 feet 5b. Climb the crack for 10 feet and then the continuation
cracks above to a small ledge below the long groove. Follow the crack on
the left, and where it peters out move back right into the main groove.
Continue directly up until the angle relents and traverse right to a stance
on an easy rib. Scrambling remains.

★**Tempest** 240 feet E2 (20.4.73)
An excellent first pitch is followed by scruffy but precarious climbing on
the second. Pitch 1 gets the star!
1 100 feet 5b. As for *Performance*, climb easily to a thin crack. Step
down and traverse left for a further 10 feet to reach another, thinner crack,
and climb it in a fine position to the terrace.
2 140 feet 5c. From the left-hand end of the terrace, climb twin cracks
and their narrow continuation groove until it is possible to move left to a
small spike. Move left again and climb a shallow groove onto a large
hollow flake (poor peg runner). Traverse carefully right for 10 feet to a
thin vegetated crack and climb it, moving delicately right after 10 feet onto
a small ledge. Step back into the crack and continue to a ledge. Belay on
the next ledge above. Scrambling remains.

★**Surf City** 110 feet E2 5c (25.7.85)
Delightful climbing up the thin crackline to the left of the first pitch of
Tempest. Climb diagonally left to reach a prominent grey sloping ledge.
Traverse left beneath the crack of *Tempest* and move up into a thinner
crackline, which is climbed to the overlap. Traverse 5 feet left, pull
through via a faint crack, and so reach the terrace.

The next route climbs the smooth face to the left of *Surf City*. Start from a
small sloping ledge below the grey sloping ledge on *Surf City*. This is
gained by a 75-foot abseil from twin flakes midway along the terrace. The
abseil rope is used to belay.

★★**Technicolour Cruise** 100 feet E5 6a (25.7.85/6.89)
A superb, bold face climb up the left-hand side of the face. The line suffers
some seepage but remains climbable. From the sloping ledge, move up
and follow a leftward traverse-line beneath the thin cracks of *Tempest*
and *Surf City* to the base of two small, vertical overlaps. Climb to the left
of these and continue up and slightly right via an indistinct crack to a
junction with *Surf City* at the overlap. Traverse 5 feet left, pull through via
a faint crack, and so reach the terrace.

Basejumper 125 feet E1 5b (14.8.86)
An enjoyable eliminate, taking a diagonal right-to-left line across the

THE DEVIL'S SLIDE AREA

1 The Devil's Slide — HS
2 Devil's Spine — VS
3 Dexter — VS
4 Godspeed — E1
5 Redspeed — E2
6 Elan — E3
7 Lightspeed — E2
8 Seventh Seal — HVS
9 Magnificat — E2
10 Friends in High
  Places — E3
11 Magic Flute — HVS
12 Sandpiper — HVS
13 Performance — HVS
14 Tempest — E2
15 Surf City — E2
16 Technicolour Cruise — E5
17 Shark — HVS

lower face. Start at the base of *Magic Flute*. Follow *Magic Flute* for 40 feet – easily up the arête to the overhang; then climb diagonally left, crossing the cracks of *Performance* and *Tempest*. Continue along a thin diagonal break beneath the overlap of *Surf City* to a junction with the big corner bounding the left-hand side of the face which is followed to the terrace.

BENSON'S BUTTRESS
OS Ref 1314 4695

A small, accessible buttress situated just north of Fluted Face and directly opposite the large, square, high-tide island of St Peter's Stone. Descend the grassy gully north of The Devil's Slide (as for Fluted Face); where it ends, make a descending traverse right (facing out) to a large flake 30 feet back from the cliff-top. A 100-foot abseil from the flake leads to slabby ledges below, accessible at all states of the tide. The buttress has three prominent inverted V-grooves in its upper half.

Slave Labour   80 feet   E1 5c   (5.8.91)
Start beneath the central V-groove. Climb easily to a short brown wall guarding access to the groove, from where technical moves lead into the groove. Pull steeply through the overlap above and finish carefully up the leftward-slanting cracks in the slab.

Skullduggery   80 feet   Hard Very Severe 5b   (6.8.91)
The left-hand V-groove. Climb a slabby wall to where it steepens, pull into the groove, and exit awkwardly. Finish up the cleaned crack in the headwall above.

Squires View Zawn

To the north of The Devil's Slide is a large zawn or cove. On its southern side, and dominating it, is a magnificent sheet of perfectly formed granite – The Diamond. Seaward of The Diamond is the rather indistinct Forgotten Pinnacle. Its claim to pinnacle status is somewhat specious since only its top 15-foot section is detached from the mainland. On the north side of the zawn is a large brown cliff, Squires View Cliff, which in turn has a small overhang-capped slab to its north, Crunchy Toed Zawn, and a steep, grooved cliff to the west, The Fortress.

At its head, the zawn splits into three shallow valleys. On the north side of the most northerly of these valleys is a dome-shaped, lichenous buttress facing south. This is split by three chimney-lines, each giving a scrappy 80-foot route of Very Difficult standard.

The dammed stream immediately north of The Devil's Slide flows down the southerly of the three valleys and leads down a steep grassy slope to the head of the zawn. The safest descent is by abseil down the basalt dyke that slants up from below and forms the lower left-hand side of The

Diamond. There are good block belays at the top of the dyke. Although a 165-foot (50m) rope does not quite reach the foot of the dyke, the bottom section is an easy scramble to the zawn bed. The abseil descent, though demanding care, is recommended in preference to more immediately obvious descents.

FORGOTTEN PINNACLE   OS Ref 1314 4695
The base of the pinnacle can be reached at low to mid tide from the jumbled blocks in the zawn bed. An alternative, high-tide approach can be made by traversing north from the foot of Benson's Buttress.

Forget It   100 feet   Very Severe   4b   †   (17.8.93)
An unpleasant pitch up the leftward-leaning corner in the right-hand side of the pinnacle. Start from the zawn bed beneath the corner. Climb easily up to a blocky ledge at the foot of the corner (belay possible). The corner leads past two ledges to a loose chimney; finish up this and belay on a large spike well back from the edge.

Echo   100 feet   Very Severe   4c   (13.4.74)
The prominent leftward-slanting cracks in the seaward face of the pinnacle. Start from the boulder bed. Go up easy broken rock to the base of the cracks (belay possible). Climb these, avoiding a few loose blocks, to the top. Cross easily over to the mainland and a large spike belay.

Forgotten Pinnacle   120 feet   Hard Severe   (30.3.67)
An interesting outing up the slabby groove in the left-hand side of the pinnacle. Start on the boulder-bed below the line.
1 40 feet. Climb easily to ledges at the foot of the groove.
2 80 feet 4b. Climb the groove to where it ends at a shoulder. Either step left to easy ground or, better, step right into a crack and follow it to the summit. Cross easily to the mainland.

Forget-me-not   120 feet   Very Severe   (29.8.70)
A greasy, repulsive climb of some character up the right-hand bounding corner of The Diamond where it adjoins Forgotten Pinnacle. Sea-cliff esoterica!
1 35 feet. Follow the corner past an interesting assortment of jammed driftwood and fisherman's buoys to a flake stance on the right.
2 85 feet 4b. Continue up the corner, now a narrow chimney, to a recess. Climb broken rock to the summit of the pinnacle and cross easily over to the mainland.

ST PETER'S STONE   OS Ref 1312 4698
The large, square island in the middle of Squires View Zawn. Some pleasant climbing with spectacular views of the surrounding cliffs make it well worth a visit. The boulders in the sea-channel separating the island from the mainland can be crossed at low tide only.

★The Great Diamond Robbery   70 feet   Very Severe   4c   (1.8.85)
A great little route on perfect rock. Climb the central crackline in the
black, diamond-shaped slab on the landward face of the island. Descend
the next route.

St Peter's Stone   60 feet   Very Difficult   (22.8.71)
Climb the wide leftward-slanting crack and its continuation corner just left
of the diamond-shaped slab. The descent is either by abseil or by reversal
of the route.

Free Brown Rat   60 feet   Severe   (1.8.85)
Fifty feet left of *St Peter's Stone* is a narrow ledge running beneath the cliff.
Climb an obvious slabby groove near the left-hand end of the ledge and
finish up the juggy slab to its left.

Vernon Martin's Home Brew   65 feet   Very Severe   4c   (1.8.85)
The groove at the extreme left-hand end of the ledge. Climb the groove to
a small overhang, which is bypassed on the left to a tight finish via a small
chimney.

THE DIAMOND   OS Ref 1317 4700

The showpiece of the island: a magnificent sweep of perfectly formed
granite rising over 300 feet from the bottom of Squires View Zawn. The
subject of many feasibility studies in the past, The Diamond has now
reached maturity and boasts some of the finest high-standard face-
climbing in the country.

Appearing as a majestic, turreted wedge of high-angled slab driven into
the heart of the zawn, the face is tilted on its left-hand side and supported
by a large basalt dyke running almost the full height of the zawn. Two
diagonal breaks slice across the face. *Coast to Coast* follows the upper
break, effectively dividing the face into two: the confined lower face is
clean and orange-tinged with few discernible features; the upper half,
now free of its green lichen-curtain, presents a more open aspect with a
series of large overlaps and thin cracklines. A prominent feature is a
shallow white flake-line just right of centre, the line of the classic *A
Widespread Ocean of Fear*. The orange-streaked slab to its right is
climbed by *Smear or Disappear* and *Smear? No Fear*. To the left of *A
Widespread Ocean of Fear*, an arching line of overlaps is the substance
of *Chase the Ace*, with the larger overlap of *Wild Heart* above and to its
left. Left again are the long, thin, bottomless cracklines of *Ace of
Diamonds* and *Diamond Life*.

The descent is described at the beginning of this section and access is
unrestricted by any tidal considerations. Facing north-west, The Diamond
receives any available sunlight in late afternoon and early evening.

★★★Smear or Disappear   300 feet   E5   (27.7.81/30.7.89)
An apt name, especially since the demise of the bolt runner! Exceptionally

bold and sustained climbing directly up the right-hand side of the face. Unfortunately (or perhaps fortunately), the first pitch is often damp. Start at the lowest point of the face.

1 130 feet 5c. Climb a shallow, stepped groove, and then step up right and onto the slab to gain a thin diagonal crack. Intricate moves up the slab above via some thin cracks lead to a diagonal break. Continue up a faint line of weakness to a heart-stopping move to the second break and a small foot-ledge just above. Peg belay up to the left and good wires up and right.

2 90 feet 6a. Move up a tiny groove on the left and climb diagonally left to an arched overlap (junction with *A Widespread Ocean of Fear* and peg runner). Pull through and climb to a larger overlap, which is turned to its left to gain the third and largest overlap. Pull over to a crackline and follow this to a niche and good nut belay.

3 80 feet 4c. Swing out right and follow a line of large rugosities to a rib, which leads easily to the top.

★★★Smear? No Fear   310 feet   E5   (24.7.84/30.7.89)

The orange-streaked slab just left of *Smear or Disappear*. An immaculate pitch, sustained and with marginal protection, it proves demanding on both the toes and the mind. Start at the stepped groove at the foot of the face.

1 140 feet 6a. Follow the groove to its end, and climb a thin crackline leftwards over a bulge and onto the slab. Go directly up the slab, passing a quartzy section after 15 feet. Move boldly into some streaks (climbable when wet) and tiny grooves, which lead to a break and a small overlap. Continue straight up to the sanctuary of the second break. Move up and rightwards to a thin break (peg runner); then climb down a shallow groove to a small foot-ledge (peg belay and wires up and right).

2 90 feet 6a. *Smear or Disappear* pitch 2.

3 80 feet 4c. *Smear or Disappear* pitch 3.

★★Blood, Sweat and Smears   310 feet   E6 †   (8.8.93)

Characteristic of the climbing on the face, this route provides a stringent test of nerve and edging ability. Start 10 feet left of *Smear? No Fear*.

1 140 feet 6a. Follow a faint crack and groove-line trending leftwards by unprotected climbing to a downward-pointing fang of rock. Serious moves lead rightwards to a thin diagonal crack. Move up and right to a prominent scar; then climb slightly rightwards up a faint crack, often wet, to a break (peg runner). Stand in the break, and then trend boldly rightwards up a green slab to arrive at the left-hand side of the foot-ledge belay of *Smear or Disappear*.

2 90 feet 6a. *Smear or Disappear* pitch 2.

3 80 feet 4c. *Smear or Disappear* pitch 3.

★★★A Widespread Ocean of Fear   310 feet   E5   (22.7.81)

One of the classic hard routes of the South-West. A superbly intricate face-climb following The Diamond's strongest natural line, the compelling white flake. Protection is adequate but spaced. Start at the foot of the basalt dyke.

1 100 feet 5c. Climb up the dyke for 20 feet until just above a flat-topped block. Scary: stride right onto the black wall, and climb rightwards onto the slab at a large orange scar. Move up to a thin break and a good wire-placement above. Take a line of leftward-trending holds to an uncomfortable stance in the lower diagonal break. Good small *Friend* and wire-placements.

2 130 feet 6a. Move up to the overlap and pass it on its right to gain the diagonal break (*Friend 3* runner). Technical moves where the flake vanishes lead to an arched overlap (peg runner). Pull through and move up to a larger overlap. Climb this on its left and continue over the third and largest overlap to a thin crackline, which leads to a niche and nut belay. Alternatively, take an uncomfortable belay 20 feet below on good nuts.

3 80 feet 4c. As for *Smear or Disappear*, swing out right and follow a line of large rugosities to a rib which leads easily to the top.

✴✴★★Chase the Ace 270 feet E6 (30.7.87/30.7.89)
Brilliant technical climbing, tracing a tenuous line up the shallow, arching groove left of *A Widespread Ocean of Fear*. Start 100 feet down the dyke and 15 feet below the thread belay on *Watching the Ocean*. Abseil-rope belay.

1 60 feet 6a. Pull out right onto the edge of the slab, where bold, difficult moves right lead to the base of a vague crack. Climb this for 10 feet and move up to a slim groove leading to the diagonal break. Traverse left to a peg and *Friend 2½* belay.

2 130 feet 6b. The slim groove above is climbed on its right wall to the break (peg runner). Stand up and move diagonally right beneath the overlap by a sustained and serious sequence of moves to a junction with *A Widespread Ocean of Fear* below the large overlap. Pull over and climb the thin crackline above to a niche and nut belay.

3 80 feet 4c. *A Widespread Ocean of Fear* pitch 3.

✴✴★★Watching the Ocean 250 feet E6 (25.7.85/4.5.89)
Uncompromising in line and quality. The magnificent central line of The Diamond. A very sustained lead requiring strong calves and a lot of small wires. Start at an *in-situ* thread belay 90 feet down the dyke. The abseil rope serves as a useful back-up.

1 40 feet 6a. Step out right onto the face and make committing moves right to reach a flake. Sprint up this to a belay in the diagonal break (two pegs and a selection of *Friends*).

2 130 feet 6a. Climb the stepped groove above the belay to a standing-position in the next diagonal break. Move right above the overlap and follow twin hairline cracks boldly up the slab to a good slot. Continue up the thin leftward-slanting crack above to the large overlap. Bear rightwards beneath this and exit right to a large niche. Large *Friend* and nut belays.

3 80 feet 4c. *A Widespread Ocean of Fear* pitch 3.

★★Waves of Romance 165 feet E6 6a (10.8.89)
A subtle, direct line to the left of *Watching the Ocean*. Eliminate in nature, but the options for escape are the routes either side! A 165-foot (50m)

rope is essential. Alternatively, preplace a rope down the finishing groove of *Wild Heart*. Start at a peg belay just above the belay of *Watching the Ocean*. Move out diagonally right along an obvious thin hand-ledge to some small flakes, and continue up a much larger flake to the diagonal break. A small white groove above leads to the next break (good wire runners), from where committing moves gain the thin seam/crack above (poor peg runner). Follow the seam boldly to the large overlap; pull directly over and continue diagonally rightwards to the finishing groove of *Wild Heart*.

★★★**Wild Heart**   165 feet   E5   (30.7.85)
A magnificent, audacious face climb. The long, arching flake and overlap in the left-hand side of the face lead to a hard, well-positioned crux. With a 165-foot (50m) rope and a preplaced belay rope down the finishing groove it is possible to climb the route in one long pitch. Start from a small ledge 70 feet down the dyke, at a good thread belay through a sheet of rock. Abseil-rope back-up.
1 30 feet 5c. Move awkwardly out right onto the face to a good hold and climb a short flake to the diagonal break. Peg and *Friend* belay.
2 135 feet 6a. Step left and climb a series of flakes to the next diagonal break (peg runner). Move up and left to good small-wire placements, and stride confidently right to the base of the long flake. Climb this (peg runner) until below the large overlap (peg runner above and to the right). Pull through the overlap on its left-hand side and move back right above it to good holds and the long, easy finishing groove. Good flake belay at its top.

★★**Ace of Diamonds**   140 feet   E5 6a   (29.7.85)
The long, thin right-hand crack in the left-hand side of the face. At the lower limit of the grade and an excellent introduction to The Diamond's bolder face climbs. Start as for *Wild Heart* at the prominent thread through a sheet of rock. Go up the dyke to a peg runner at 20 feet. Step out onto the face and move up and right to a small ledge and a diagonal break. Continue to the second break (peg runner); then bear rightwards to the start of a thin crack (small wires). Run it out up the faint crack, heading for the dubious security of a poor peg runner. Continue up the crack and an easy finishing groove. Good spike belays.

★★**Diamond Life**   130 feet   E4 6a   (29.7.85)
The compelling central crackline gives the most popular pitch on the face. A confident approach is rewarded by a fine, runner-sinking crack. Start as for *Wild Heart*, at the prominent thread belay. Move up the dyke to a peg runner at 20 feet. Step out onto the face and go up and right to a small ledge and a diagonal break. Continue up to the second break (peg runner) and climb the faint crack above for 15 feet. Attain a standing-position on a thin ledge above and to the left; then stretch back right to regain the crack (crux, easier for the tall). Sprint up this to a spike belay at its top.

The Devil's Slide
Climber: Howard Darwin

Photo: Tom Valentine

Satan's Slip The Devil's Slide
Climbers: Simon Walley and Josie Welsh   *Photo:* Gary Gibson

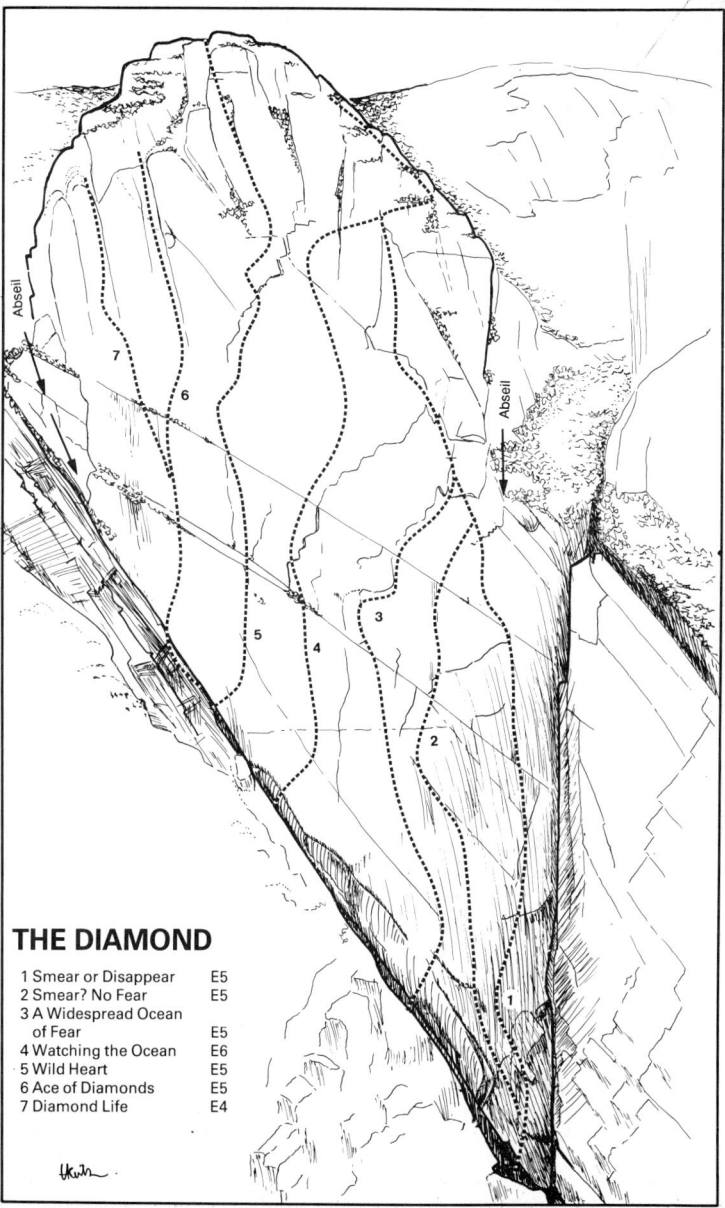

THE DIAMOND

1 Smear or Disappear		E5
2 Smear? No Fear		E5
3 A Widespread Ocean of Fear		E5
4 Watching the Ocean		E6
5 Wild Heart		E5
6 Ace of Diamonds		E5
7 Diamond Life		E4

Abseil

Abseil

The Last Rubber   100 feet   E3 6a   (10.8.90)
The thin crack in the very left edge of the face. Well protected but
escapable at half height. Start as for *Diamond Life*, at the prominent
thread belay. Follow *Diamond Life* to a grassy ledge 15 feet up the face,
step left, and climb a thin crackline to the second diagonal break. Move
up to the thin crack above and climb it to the top.

The Diamond has two right-to-left girdles, each beginning from the base
of the broad grass gully that bounds the right-hand side of the face.
Locate the top of the gully and descend it by abseil from a good rock-
spike near its top.

★★★**Coast to Coast**   140 feet   E4 6a   (31.7.85)
The upper diagonal break gives a brilliant pitch crossing the vast 'ocean'
of granite. Sustained but with good protection. Take a lot of small wires
and a steady second. Start from a good stance 100 feet down the gully
and level with the right-hand end of the break. Good spike and abseil-
rope belay. Step onto the slab and proceed along the break with little
deviation up or down, the interest being maintained right to the very end.
Belay on large blocks well back.

★★**Motion in the Ocean**   120 feet   E5 6a †   (19.10.89)
A high-level girdle of the face. An excellent and varied pitch proving
exciting for both leader and second. Start 70 feet down the gully at a
stance level with a roof in the right-hand side of the face. Traverse left
beneath the roof to a junction with *A Widespread Ocean of Fear* at its
second overlap. Pull through this and go up to and over the third overlap.
An intricate leftward-rising line just above the overlap leads to a short
traverse left into the large groove of *Watching the Ocean*. Move down the
groove and traverse left beneath the large overlap to a junction with *Wild
Heart* at a downward-pointing spike (peg runner above). Follow the rising
flake crack to the left (sustained and technical) to the final groove of *Ace
of Diamonds*. Finish up this.

THE DIAMOND – GRADED LIST

E6	Motion in the Ocean
Chase the Ace	A Widespread Ocean of Fear
Blood, Sweat and Smears	Ace of Diamonds
Watching the Ocean	**E4**
Waves of Romance	Coast to Coast
E5	Diamond Life
Smear or Disappear	**E3**
Wild Heart	The Last Rubber
Smear? No Fear	

SQUIRES VIEW CLIFF   OS Ref 1317 4702
Opposite The Diamond and on the north side of the zawn is a large,
brown, undercut cliff. The routes here generally follow strong natural
groove-lines, most prominent being the clean-cut groove in the upper

right-hand side of the wall – *The Stray*. The rock has a coarse, gritty texture and is not always beyond suspicion, particularly near the top. Belays at the top of the cliff can be awkward to arrange; there is a good block just to the left of the top of *The Stray* which can be used for the majority of the routes. Alternatively, good nut belays can be found 150 feet back from the cliff-top (spare rope required).

The abseil approach is described at the beginning of this section. This is followed by a short traverse north over large boulders and round a slabby rib at Very Difficult standard to the base of the cliff, which is accessible three hours either side of low water.

Breakaway   150 feet   Hard Very Severe †   (5.9.73)
The big undercut groove in the right-hand side of the cliff. Start to the left of the groove at the foot of a rightward-slanting rake.
1 60 feet 5b. Follow the rake, easily at first (peg runner), to the foot of the big groove. Make a difficult move into the groove and follow it to below an overhang on the left (nut and spike belay).
2 50 feet 5a. Climb the corner on the right and then follow the slab, trending right, to a ledge and poor belay. It may be wiser to continue.
3 40 feet. Step left and shake your way up the crumbling dyke to the top. Block belay.

Digitalis   150 feet   Hard Very Severe   (19.4.73)
Some good climbing based on the right arête of the groove of *The Stray*. Start as for *Breakaway*.
1 60 feet 5b. *Breakaway* pitch 1.
2 35 feet 5a. Climb up and left onto the arête using the crack below the overhang. Follow a groove past a rocking stone to a constricted stance with nut and flake belays just right of the groove of *The Stray*. It may be better to continue.
3 55 feet 4b. Climb the cracks in the left side of the arête to a crumbly finish. Block belay.

The Stray   150 feet   Hard Very Severe   (31.3.72)
A compelling line with some good climbing. Unfortunately, the rock quality deteriorates towards the top, the final groove being particularly crunchy. Start beneath a short steep crack 25 feet left of the big groove of *Breakaway*.
1 40 feet 4b. Climb the crack, and step right to a ledge below the rightward-leaning corner which forms the left edge of a slab.
2 110 feet 4c. Go up the corner to the foot of the main groove; climb this and exit carefully to the left. Block belay.

Bloody Ages   125 feet   Very Severe †   (6.9.73)
A poor route taking a direct and unstable line up the left-hand side of the cliff. Start as for *The Stray*.
1 50 feet 4b. Climb the steep crack, and continue up a short groove over doubtful rock to a peg belay below the large slab.

SQUIRES
VIEW CLIFF

1 Breakaway   HVS
2 The Stray   HVS
3 Good Vibrations   E1
4 Sheep's Eyes in Aspic   E1
5 Shark's Head Soup   HVS

2 75 feet 4c. Climb the corner above to a small grassy ledge below a steep section. Move up and right into a wide crack and follow it carefully to a leftwards exit at the top.

Good Vibrations   170 feet   E1   (17.4.73)
A good, well-positioned route taking a diagonal line up the steep slab to the left of *The Stray*. Start below and to the left of the slab, beneath a smaller, rightward-slanting slab.
1 60 feet 4a. Move up to the slab and follow it rightwards to the peg belay of *Bloody Ages* beneath the larger slab.
2 110 feet 5a. Climb the corner above for 20 feet, until level with a small overlap on the right. Make a rising traverse rightwards across the slab to reach a good crack, 10 feet above the big overhang. Climb the crack to the arête and finish up this in a fine position. Block belay.
Variation
Certainly Squire   E2   (14.8.91)
2a 100 feet 5b. From the peg belay, move immediately right to the arête and climb it until level with the overhang on the right. Traverse right just above the lip of the overhang until a step up leads to a junction with *Good Vibrations*. Follow this to the top.

Sheep's Eyes in Aspic   120 feet   E1 5b †   (22.8.93)
To the left of *Good Vibrations* are two prominent sentry-box-shaped grooves. This interesting and varied route climbs the right-hand groove. Start beneath the groove, 15 feet left of *Good Vibrations*. Move steeply up to the groove on good holds and climb it, stepping left at its top into a thin crack. Continue up this and the shallow groove above to a leftwards exit. Thread and peg belay.

Shark's Head Soup   120 feet   Hard Very Severe 5a †   (10.8.92)
The left-hand sentry-box-shaped groove. Worthwhile. Climb steeply up to the foot of the groove and ascend it direct to a large spike. Step right and take the shallow groove, as for *Sheep's Eyes in Aspic*, to the top. Thread and peg belay.

CRUNCHY TOED ZAWN   OS Ref 1311 4704
North of Squires View Cliff and east of The Fortress is a small, overhang-capped zawn. The smooth east wall of the zawn is climbed by the formidable *Wolfsbane*, while the huge hanging slab in the back of the zawn is crossed by *Crunchy Toed*. The west wall of the zawn is split by a hidden crackline, *Bite Size*, with the prominent *Carol Anne Butler Corner* to its left.

The first three climbs require a preplaced belay rope from good nut belays 140 feet back from the cliff-top. From this, a 120-foot abseil down the east wall of the zawn leads to slabby ledges at its foot. These are accessible at low to mid tide. Alternatively, a sea-level traverse from Squires View Zawn is possible two hours either side of low tide at Very Difficult standard: an interesting expedition amidst superb rock scenery.

Marine Boy   120 feet   Very Difficult †   (23.7.85)
Combined with the sea-level traverse, this gives an adventurous outing for
the grade. At the right-hand side of the wall is a large stepped-face. Pick
the easiest line up the face to an unstable finish.

Soft Mick   120 feet   Severe †   (23.7.85)
This route climbs the long stepped corner-line to the left of *Marine Boy*.
Gain the corner from easy rock steps to the right, and squirm up its
chimney to easier ground on the right.

***Wolfsbane**   120 feet   E7 6c   (25.8.90)
Highly improbable climbing up the superlative orange wall just right of
the large overhang-capped slab. Protection is reasonable but well
spaced. Start on the slab beneath the wall below a grey, V-shaped scoop.
Gain the scoop and a large spike at its top, step up and left to a good
hold, and climb boldly leftwards to a peg runner. Continue direct to a
bulge (peg runner); then step up and left to gain a finger-crack and climb
it to the capping roof. Pull boldly over at its left-hand end and storm the
headwall via a sinuous crackline (three peg runners). *Friend* belay just
below the top, or, more wisely, belay to a preplaced rope.

The next three routes are all approached by abseil down the west wall of
the zawn. Low to mid tide is required. Convenient belays can be found on
the descent to The Fortress.

Crunchy Toed   150 feet   E1 5a †   (22.9.82)
A very impressive line crossing the large, hanging black slab in the back
of the zawn. This is not as steep as it looks but the climbing is bold and the
rock not beyond suspicion. A preplaced belay rope to the edge of the cliff
is necessary. Start at a short overhanging corner below and to the left of
the slab. Climb the corner and slab above until level with the black slab.
Traverse right into its centre and climb up to the roof. Move right and
struggle over at the obvious break, from where steep climbing leads to a
loose finish.

Bite Size   100 feet   E5 6a   (2.8.87)
The striking crackline in the west wall of the zawn. A powerful and
worrying pitch with some very crumbly rock. Start below the crack from
ledges well above sea-level. Go up and across a ramp to reach the foot of
the crack and climb it, with escalating difficulty and mounting trepidation,
to the overhang. Pull round the overhang and follow the continuation
crack and small groove to the top.

*★Carol Ann Butler Corner**   90 feet   E1 5b   (5.8.86)
The large corner in the western arête of the zawn gives a tough but honest
pitch. Abseil directly down the corner to a small ledge at its foot (low tide
required). Climb the corner, sustained but well protected, direct to an exit
left just below its top.

THE FORTRESS
OS Ref 1309 4703

The steep, south-facing cliff on the northern spur of Squires View Zawn. The spur runs out to form a steep turreted nose overlooking the large rock island of St John's Stone. The composition of the south face is one of many vertical crack-and-groove-lines, divided by a wide boulder-strewn terrace at half height. The terrace rises on the eastern side of the cliff as a grassy ramp to the col known as Squires View. Strong lines, good rock, and a sunny aspect will reward a visit.

Approach by scrambling down the grassy ramp to the terrace, the initial few feet being steep and demanding care (fixed rope preferable). The terrace can be approached also by scrambling round the northern end of the cliff. The pitches above the terrace are unaffected by the sea, although parties have been known to get thoroughly soaked when a big sea is running!

★Slender Boris 70 feet E1 5c   (25.9.85)
The clean, shallow groove at the right-hand end of the terrace gives a neat technical pitch. Climb the groove, sustained but with good protection, over a small overhang to easier climbing above. Belay well back.

Jane Eugene 70 feet Very Severe 4c †   (25.9.85)
The twin cracks and scruffy groove just left of *Slender Boris*.

★Worlds Apart 100 feet Hard Very Severe 5b   (6.4.85)
A good, sustained pitch, perhaps the best on the cliff. Start beneath the clean, black-streaked groove 10 feet left of *Jane Eugene*. Climb the groove direct, starting up a short wide crack. Well protected.

Hel 90 feet Hard Very Severe 5a   (27.8.71)
Lurking beneath the vegetation to the left of *Worlds Apart* lies another groove-line. This is rumoured to be 10 feet right of the top pitch of *Valhalla* and is climbed direct with a difficult section at half height. Pure hell!

The next four climbs begin from sea-level ledges beneath the lower wall. An abseil from the half-way terrace, beneath the top pitch of *Valhalla*, leads to ledges at the foot of a large corner, the first pitch of *Valhalla*. Low to mid tide required, although the top pitches are always available.

★Valhalla 140 feet Very Severe   (26.8.71)
An interesting main pitch, varied and sustained, it takes the long groove right of the prominent line of overhangs. Start at the foot of the corner in the centre of the lower wall.
1 40 feet. Climb the corner to the terrace.
2 100 feet 4c. A short steep wall leads to the groove, which is followed directly to the top.
Direct Start Very Severe   (9.81)
1a 50 feet 4b. Climb the first crack to the left of the initial corner to the terrace.

Ceaseless Tide   150 feet   E2   (30.3.85/25.7.85)
The large bottomless chimney/groove just left of the second pitch of
Valhalla. Start beneath the second crack to the left of that route's initial
corner.
1 50 feet 5a. Climb the thin crack directly to the terrace.
2 100 feet 5c. A short steep wall guards entry to the groove above.
Climb this from the right with difficulty and continue more easily up the
groove. At 50 feet, a thin crack on the right wall allows a traverse right to
be made to an easy crack with a small overhang to finish.

Stormy Waters   160 feet   E4 †   (31.3.85/25.7.85)
A sustained exercise in bridging and 'back-and-footing' up the shallow,
bottomless groove left of *Ceaseless Tide*. Start at dead low tide on ledges
beneath the fourth crack left of *Valhalla*.
1 60 feet 5a. Follow the crack direct to the terrace.
2 100 feet 5c. A bold, bulging wall gives a difficult entry into the groove
(ancient peg runner). Climb the groove to its top with little respite.

Prospero   165 feet   Hard Very Severe   (21.4.73)
The long groove at the left-hand end of the terrace and just left of *Stormy
Waters*. Some interesting and sustained climbing. Start at dead low tide
beneath the fifth crack left of *Valhalla*.
1 65 feet 5a. Climb the crack steeply to the terrace, and belay beneath
the deep groove left of the undercut section of the wall.
2 100 feet 5a. Follow the groove, and move left 30 feet below the top
where the vegetation takes over.

The next two climbs lie on the seaward nose of the buttress. Both start from
a ledge 25 feet above the sea and are approached by scrambling down
from the half-way terrace via the blunt western rib of the buttress. This is
just right (facing out) of a narrow gully.

Siegfried   135 feet   Very Severe   (23.8.71)
A slight, vegetated climb following the right-hand edge of the nose of the
buttress.
1 60 feet. From the ledge, move right and cross the narrow gully to gain
a rounded rib, which is followed to a stance at the narrowest point of the
half-way terrace.
2 75 feet 4b. Climb the flat-topped pinnacle immediately above the
stance. Move right to the base of a steep crack; then traverse right for 10
feet until good holds lead steeply to an exposed rib and a belay ledge.
Scrambling leads to the top.

Blood Axe   150 feet   E1   (23.8.71/30.3.85)
Steep, open, but rather bristly climbing up the actual nose of the buttress.
Start as for *Siegfried*.
1 70 feet 4a. A descending leftward traverse on good flakes leads to a
steep crack rising from the sea. Climb this, passing a small bulge, to the
half-way terrace.

THE FORTRESS

1 Bite Size	E5
2 Carol Ann Butler Corner	E1
3 Slender Boris	E1
4 Jane Eugene	VS

5 Worlds Apart	HVS
6 Valhalla	VS
7 Ceaseless Tide	E2
8 Stormy Waters	E4
9 Prospero	HVS

2 80 feet 5b. Above is a steep leftward-trending groove, 15 feet right of the edge of the face. Climb the groove and step awkwardly left to a peculiar projection of rock. Move up and left again onto a small knob of rock, from where a few difficult moves lead to the top. Scramble off right to the summit.

Torrey Canyon Bay

To the north of the headland containing The Fortress is a large open bay, with the large rock island of St John's Stone at its southern end. The partly lichen-covered Christos Bitas Buttress occupies the southern half of the bay, with a large open gully to its north. The northern side of the bay consists of an impressive line of sea cliffs some 250 yards long and between 100 and 200 feet high; they are broken by a number of small sea-channels at their base. The most southerly and largest of these cliffs is Torrey Canyon Cliff. Running north-west, the cliffs gradually lose height before terminating in a small zawn with a huge capping overhang, visible from as far south as Jenny's Cove. Seal Slab forms the eastern side of the zawn and Wonderlands Wall the back.

CHRISTOS BITAS BUTTRESS   OS Ref 1307 4712
The prominent crest of the buttress runs down from the top of the cliff, first as a narrow ridge and then as a steep arête dividing the cliff. To the south are two groove-lines slanting from right to left. To the north, the face is split by the prominent zigzag crackline of *Pelmets of Delirium*, which is just above a small triangular pillar.

Descents to the routes hereabouts can be particularly trying. The large gully to the north of the cliff can be descended, though the first 40 feet are steep and potentially lethal and a fixed rope is strongly advised. A safer alternative is the abseil approach described under Torrey Canyon Cliff. A short boulder-hop south leads to the foot of the buttress. Non-tidal.

The first two climbs are located on a smaller, slabby buttress to the south. A preplaced belay rope would be sensible, as would a low to mid tide.

The Ancient Mariner   130 feet   E1 †   (14.8.91)
A bold but pleasant climb up the right-hand side of the slab.
1 100 feet 5a. Take a direct line over cleaned rock to a small ledge and peg belay just below the top of the slab.
2 30 feet. Step right (peg runner) and climb a short slab to easy ground. Scrambling remains.

Moss Side   130 feet   Severe   (8.81)
The long slabby groove in the left-hand side of the buttress.
1 100 feet. Climb the groove to its top and step right to a small ledge (peg belay).

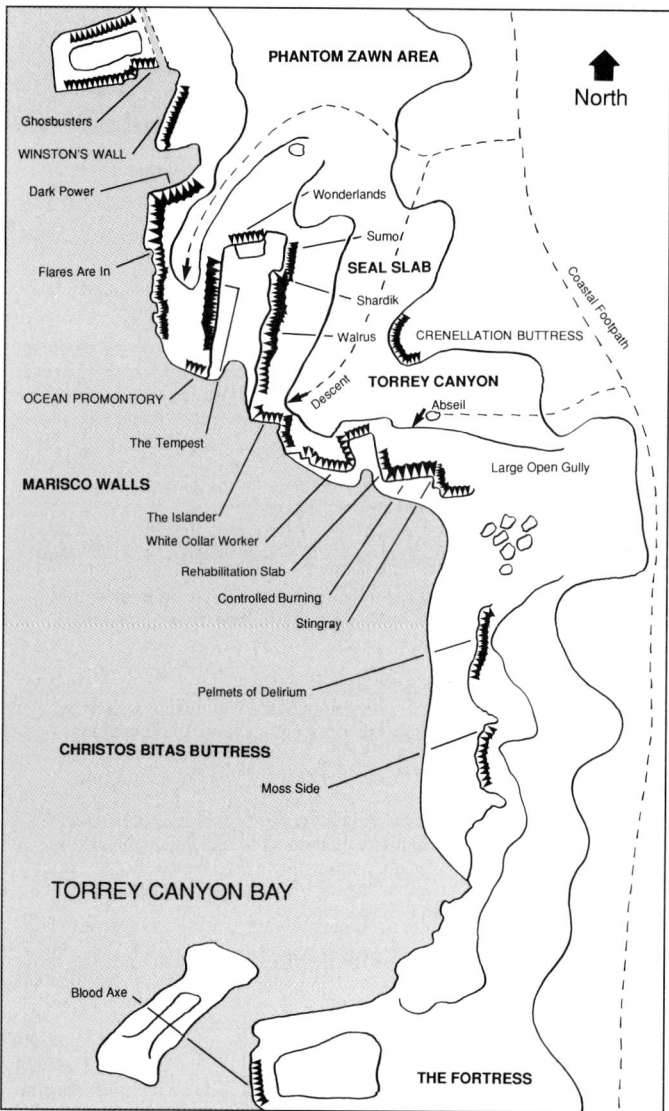

PHANTOM ZAWN AREA

North

Ghosbusters

WINSTON'S WALL

Dark Power

Flares Are In

OCEAN PROMONTORY

MARISCO WALLS

The Tempest

The Islander

White Collar Worker

Rehabilitation Slab

Controlled Burning

Stingray

Pelmets of Delirium

CHRISTOS BITAS BUTTRESS

Moss Side

TORREY CANYON BAY

Blood Axe

THE FORTRESS

Wonderlands

Sumo

SEAL SLAB

Shardik

Walrus

CRENELLATION BUTTRESS

Coastal Footpath

Descent

TORREY CANYON

Abseil

Large Open Gully

2 30 feet. Step right (peg runner) and climb a short slab to easy ground. Scrambling remains.

Stuffin' the Puffin   170 feet   Hard Very Severe   (7.8.86)
A direct line up the southern side of the main buttress. Start beneath the right-hand groove-line.
1 90 feet 5b. Climb the groove, pleasantly at first, to a ledge. Difficult moves over the bulge above lead into another groove. Climb this to a belay amidst some large blocks.
2 80 feet. Climb carefully leftwards over loose rock to the top.

Reprise   190 feet   Hard Very Severe   (26.4.79)
The right-to-left slanting groove left of *Stuffin' the Puffin* gives an interesting first pitch on good rock. Start as for *Stuffin' the Puffin*.
1 80 feet 5a. Climb the groove to the ledge and continue up the slanting groove on the left to a smaller ledge. Take a nut belay just left of the arête.
2 110 feet 4b. Climb steep, vegetated cracks on the very crest of the buttress to a ledge. Easier climbing in the same line leads to the top.

Demian   190 feet   Very Severe   (28.8.79)
The slanting groove below and left of *Reprise*. A good initial pitch but poor and scrappy above. Start below the groove.
1 80 feet 4c. Climb the groove to an overhang and step left onto a steep slab. The narrow continuation ramp leads with difficulty to a small ledge and nut belay.
2 110 feet 4b. Traverse diagonally right to the stance on *Reprise* and continue right along a ramp. Move up and left; then traverse right to a crack and flakes, which lead to the top.

★Pelmets of Delirium   160 feet   E1   (25.8.82)
The fine zigzag crackline in the north side of the cliff. Steep, satisfying, and well protected. Start below the triangular pillar at the foot of the buttress.
1 30 feet 4a. Take a direct line up the centre of the pillar via some cracks to a belay at its top.
2 90 feet 5b. The wall above is split by a series of diagonal breaks. Climb direct to the second of these via a good crack. Step right into the third break and follow it with increasing difficulty to the base of the zigzag crack. Climb this and step left at its end to a belay on the arête.
3 40 feet. Scramble carefully to the top.

Tommy Butler's Pigeon Coop Route 100 feet   Very Severe   4b †
                    (7.8.86)
Like the pigeon coop, filthy! The system of grooves and cracks in the north face of the buttress and 30 feet left of *Pelmets of Delirium*.

TORREY CANYON CLIFF   OS Ref 1304 4716
This steep cliff is the most easterly of the line of cliffs on the northern side of the bay. It is distinguished by its golden walls and impressive crack-

and-groove-lines. The rock in places is rather crumbly, particularly in the cracks. Nevertheless it sports some extremely worthwhile climbing.

In the centre of the cliff is a prominent brown wall, which is bounded on its left-hand side by the big corner of *Norseman*. At the right and southern end of the cliff is the large, clean-cut corner of *Stingray*, and to its left, occupying centre-stage, the striking crackline of *Controlled Burning*. In the right wall of *Stingray* a loose pod bears the remnants of **Conger** (1974) and the once elegant **Rachel** (1980).

The large open gully to the south of the cliff gives a rather perilous approach, the initial 40 feet being steep and loose where a fixed rope is strongly recommended. A quicker and far safer approach is to descend the grassy diagonal rake across the top of the crag over broken ground to a convenient large finger of rock situated at the top of *Rehabilitation Slab*. A 120-foot abseil from this leads to large ledges just above sea-level, which can then be traversed in both directions. The routes to the south of *Rehabilitation Slab* are non-tidal; the routes to the north require low to mid tide for a narrow sea-channel to be crossed.

Screams of Tight Daughters 110 feet E2 † (9.92)
The rockfall to the right of *Stingray* has left a wide pea-pod-shaped groove and a lot of loose rock!
1 80 feet 5b. Dangerously loose. Move up to the pod and climb it to a large ledge and block belay.
2 30 feet 4b. *Stingray* pitch 2.

Stingray 120 feet E1 (31.3.67)
The big corner-line has lost little of its early reputation; the difficulties are sustained and the rock leaves a lot to be desired.
1 90 feet 5a. Climb the corner direct past a small ledge on the left wall to a belay on the large ledge above.
2 30 feet 4b. Carefully climb the continuation corner, moving right near its top to finish.

★★★Controlled Burning 135 feet E3 5c (26.7.81)
The striking roofed crack in the left wall of *Stingray* gives one of the purest crack climbs this side of the Atlantic. A magnificent test of jamming technique and energy conservation, though the rock within the crack is a little gritty in places. Start at the foot of the large diagonal flake. Climb the flake until it is possible to step left into the crack proper. Power up this over two roofs to the crux moves: standing in the break at the crack's end. Finish slightly right via a small groove.

Half Man, Half Biscuit 130 feet E5 6b (1 pt aid) † (7.8.86)
Savage climbing up the thin crackline in the wall left of Controlled Burning. Climb the crack (rest-point used on first ascent), crumbly in

places, to a junction with *Cornflake Crack* at 80 feet and finish up this. A very sustained and painful effort.

Cornflake Crack   130 feet   Hard Very Severe 4c   (31.3.67)
The huge leaning flake-crack in the left edge of the wall. Poor protection and doubtful rock make it a proposition not to be undertaken before breakfast. Move easily up to the base of the crack and climb it and its narrow continuation chimney to the top.

★Rehabilitation Slab   130 feet   Very Difficult   (30.3.67)
The west-facing slab to the left of *Cornflake Crack* forms the right wall of a large gully with a small sea-channel below. The slab can be climbed by a number of pleasant lines, the most popular being the crackline in its right-hand side.

The small sea-channel west of *Rehabilitation Slab* can be crossed at low to mid tide. Alternatively, an abseil directly down the corner of *Norseman* from a good spike leads to large sloping ledges below the line.

★★Wall of Attrition   150 feet   E6   (29.7.88)
Steep, dramatic wall-climbing in a fine position. Start beneath the left-hand corner of the large brown wall in the centre of the cliff.
1 30 feet. Climb easily over some large rock steps to a small sloping ledge and belay beneath the brown wall.
2 120 feet 6b. From the right-hand end of the ledge, move up into the left-hand of two cracklines and follow it to a diagonal break at 40 feet. Step up and left, quite close to the corner, and make difficult moves to gain a good flake in the vague crack above. Continue more easily to a good break before embarking on the final crux wall. Climb it initially direct and then back left to a shallow finishing groove. Block belays well back.

★Norseman   140 feet   Very Severe   (30.3.67)
A climb of traditional style with great character up the big right-angled corner. Start on the large sloping shelves below the left arête of the corner.
1 110 feet 4b. Climb up over stepped rock to the sloping ledge beneath the main corner. Climb this past a bulging section to a large ledge on the left.
2 30 feet. Follow the wide continuation crack to the top.

★White Collar Worker   140 feet   E2   (8.81)
A good, varied route up the wall left of *Norseman*. Start beneath the right-hand of two leftward-slanting cracks.
1 100 feet 5c. Climb the crack with difficulty to a resting-position at 30 feet. Step right and take the obvious traverse-line rightwards to a line of flakes and cracks. Climb these to a large sloping ledge and belay.
2 40 feet 4c. Climb the slabby arête behind the stance to a spike belay at the top.

Blue Collar Blues   140 feet   Hard Very Severe 5a   (8.81)
The left-hand slanting crack, finishing up the face to its right. Climb the
slanting crack, almost a groove, to easier ground. Step right and traverse
across the face to a large, thin flake. Step onto this and finish leftwards,
taking care with some loose blocks near the top.

The next four climbs all start from a large sloping platform 20 feet left of
Blue Collar Blues. This can be gained by a leftward traverse from the base
of that route at Very Severe standard. Alternatively, abseil to the platform
from good block belays directly above. This is sea-washed at high tide.

The Great Unwashed   120 feet   Very Severe 4c †   (16.9.88)
Start beneath a recessed groove in the arête in the right-hand end of the
platform. Move up to the groove and climb it to a bulge. A swing right
gains some cracks in the arête; follow these to a rightward-trending
groove and finish direct (some brittle rock). Scramble to a large block
belay well back.

Portia   120   Hard Very Severe 4c   (8.81)
The big corner at the right-hand end of the platform and 10 feet left of *The
Great Unwashed*. A good line, marred by poor rock in its upper half. Start
at the foot of the corner. Climb the slabby lower section and then its
steeper continuation to a loose finish. Large block belay well back.

Thumbnacker Crack   100 feet   Very Severe 4b †   (24.9.83)
In the left wall of *Portia* is a wide leftward-slanting crack. Climb this to
where easier climbing on good holds leads to a large ledge. Pick a
careful route over unstable ground to the top.

⋆**Mono Man**   80 feet   E4 †   (19.8.93)
A short high-quality pitch on good rock up the centre of the steep wall to
the left of *Portia*. Start beneath a series of straight thin cracks.
1 60 feet 6a. Start up the left-hand crack before transferring to the
right-hand crack and so to the first of three diagonal breaks. Continue
straight up the wall, past a peg runner in the final break, to a good ledge.
2 20 feet. Climb easily leftwards to a good block belay.

Finally, a titbit for the connoisseur of the micro-route. **Like it or Limpet**
(25 feet E3 6a 18.8.90) climbs a short, shallow runnel in the south wall of a
hidden gully just below plateau-level. This is just north of the grassy
diagonal descent-rake to Torrey Canyon Cliff.

MARISCO WALLS   OS Ref 1298 4717
Although the routes are short, good rock and straightforward access
make the area well worth a visit. There are two walls at right-angles to
each other, facing west and south respectively. The west-facing wall has a
large platform beneath it, while the south-facing wall is undercut and
slants up to the right.

The approach lies down the southern spur of Seal Slab. This leads at Moderate standard to sea-level ledges, exposed at low to mid tide. A short traverse left (facing out) leads to ledges beneath the walls. The walls can also be reached by an awkward traverse from the base of Torrey Canyon Cliff at Very Severe standard.

Marisco Striptease   75 feet   Hard Very Severe   5a   (6.8.92)
Varied and entertaining. Start from the large platform at the foot of a short groove in the west-facing wall, just right of a straight thin crack. Climb the groove and the crack above to a small overhang. Pull strenuously through on the right and follow a slabby groove to the top. Block belay.

★Taxiarchis   70 feet   E4   6a †   (7.8.92)
Deceptively sustained and fingery. The straight thin crack in the left-hand side of the west-facing wall. Start in a recess beneath the crack. Pull into the crack and climb it on small sharp holds to a good ledge. The easier continuation crack leads to a good block belay at the top.

Sidewinder   90 feet   Hard Very Severe   4c †   (10.9.88)
The corner-system at the junction of the two walls. Start from a small cave-like recess. Climb the initial corner, and move right to another corner which leads to a strenuous finish. Scramble up the gully on the right and belay on a spike 60 feet higher.

In the south-facing wall is a wedge-shaped buttress split by a vertical crackline: *The Islander*.

Friday I'm in Love   80 feet   E3   5c †   (15.8.93)
A sustained and strenuous route climbing the undercut crack and large groove just right of *The Islander*. Start on the slab beneath the undercut crack. Bridge across to the base of the crack and make a fierce pull into it. Climb the crack until it is possible to step right to a large ledge beneath the upper groove. Continue up this to its top. Scrambling remains.

★The Islander   80 feet   E2   5c   (6.8.92)
The vertical crack splitting the wedge-shaped buttress. A fine, well-protected pitch. Start beneath the crack at low to mid tide. After an undercut start, climb the crack and its easier continuation groove to the top. Scrambling remains.

Harrison Crusoe   70 feet   E3   6a   (15.8.93)
Fierce, technical climbing up the leftward-slanting groove just left of *The Islander*. From 6 feet up *The Islander*, traverse left beneath a small overlap to the base of a thin crack. Difficult moves lead into and up the groove. An awkward exit left leads to a nut belay a little higher. Easy rock to the top.
Variation   E3   6a †   (18.8.93)
From the base of the crux groove, pull right over a small overlap and climb the thin crack just left of *The Islander* to where the angle eases.

Gimbal   60 feet   Very Severe   4b   †   (18.8.93)
The deep chimney just left of *Harrison Crusoe*. Climb the chimney on its slabby left wall to an overhang. Exit left into a groove; then go up and right to a block belay.

Gyre (50 feet Very Severe 4b † 18.8.93) is a slight climb up the blocky groove and small overhang to the left of *Gimbal*.

CRENELLATION BUTTRESS   OS Ref 1301 4721
On the slopes above the western end of Torrey Canyon Cliff are a number of small lichen-covered buttresses. At nearly 100 feet high, Crenellation Buttress is the largest and most westerly of these. Situated directly above Seal Slab, it is recognizable by a battlement-shaped summit.

Crenellation Groove   80 feet   Hard Severe   4a   (28.9.66)
Undistinguished climbing up the open, heavily vegetated groove in the nose of the buttress. Start just right of the toe of the buttress. Move up and left to reach the base of the groove and climb it, touching rock occasionally, to finish leftwards up the tower.

Felice   75 feet   Very Severe   4c   (24.8.90)
Clean and friendly. The rightward-slanting flake in the face left of *Crenellation Groove*. Start beneath the flake. Climb slightly rightwards and mantelshelf onto a small ledge. Move up the scoop above and continue up the flake to good finishing holds where it fades. **The Direct Finish** (Hard Very Severe 5a 1.8.91) steps left just below the top of the flake and climbs directly up the face to huge finishing holds. A bolder but better conclusion.

SEAL SLAB   OS Ref 1295 4718
This is the large, west-facing slab directly below Crenellation Buttress and forms the eastern side of the overhang-capped zawn. The broken, right-hand side of the slab is climbable just about anywhere up to Severe standard. However, the two climbs described both give enjoyable climbing in impressive surroundings and are very worthwhile. The two climbs on the left-hand side of the slab are a totally different proposition, each taking a powerful, committing line.

The approach to the foot of the slab lies down its southern spur. Descend the broad, grass gully to the south of Seal Slab's summit, passing beneath Crenellation Buttress. Bear right (facing out) down Moderate standard rock to the large, tidal ledges that run along the base of the slab. Alternatively, locate the summit of the slab and make a 160-foot abseil down its centre to the tidal ledges.

★**Seal Slab**   170 feet   Difficult   (28.9.66)
Exhilarating climbing on large holds. Start beneath the right-hand edge of the slab. Climb leftwards over excellent juggy rock into the centre of the slab and continue more or less direct to the top. Numerous variations and belays are possible along the way.

★★Walrus   180 feet   Severe   (6.67)
Impeccable climbing on excellent rock. Start below a groove-line near the
left-hand end of the ledges which run beneath the slab. Climb the groove
and move out right onto the main slab. Trend diagonally left up a thin
crack and step onto a nose above an overhang. Continue over grey,
crystalline rock and then on lichen-covered rock to the top. Belays are
plentiful and best taken as and when required.

★★Shardik   150 feet   E5 6a †   (10.8.89)
The elegant, hour-glass-shaped slab in the left-hand side of the slab.
Stylish, intricate, and bold, with the crux at the very top. Start at the
extreme left-hand end of the ledges just above sea-level. Trend leftwards
to the bald-looking slab, which is just left of the prominent big groove.
Climb the centre of the slab, following the curve of the groove, to the base
of a thin crack which splits the steep headwall. Climb the crack to a peg
runner at its end and finish direct. Peg and nut belay 10 feet back from the
edge.

Sumo   160 feet   E3 5b   (7.8.91)
The huge hidden groove in the left-hand corner of the slab. A sobering
pitch of great character, reminiscent of *Walsh's Groove* on Cloggy.
Unfortunately, the deteriorating quality of the rock as height is gained
culminates in a frightening finish over crumbling rock and loose earth. A
preplaced rope on this section is strongly advised. Start at the extreme
left-hand end of the ledges. Move up and left to a recessed slab and climb
it to its end. Step right and climb steeper rock to the base of the groove
(peg runner up and right). Make a difficult entry into the groove, often wet,
and 'wrestle' up it to just below its top. Move left across the slab and finish
up the disintegrating slope.

WONDERLANDS WALL   OS Ref 1294 4721
The brown, south-facing wall at the back of the overhang-capped zawn is
split centrally by a leftward-slanting dyke and is supported at its base by a
small slabby buttress. *Badlands* climbs the wall right of the dyke and
Wonderlands the wall to its left.

The approach is by abseil from a curiously-shaped block high on the
grass slope above the wall. A spare rope is needed to reach the top of the
non-tidal slabby buttress beneath the wall. The slope above the cliff-top is
loose and devoid of any good belays, and so a well-placed abseil rope
also serves as the finishing belay. At low tide it is possible to traverse in
from the tidal ledges below Seal Slab.

★Dreamlands   125 feet   E4 5c †   (14.8.91)
A serious route up the right-hand edge of the right-hand wall, protection
on the crux being notable by its absence. Start at a good spike belay on
the buttress beneath the right-hand wall. Step down and right to gain a
small brown groove and climb it to the beginning of a rightward-slanting
ramp. Go up this to an undercut flake, from where bold climbing above

TORREY CANYON BAY

1 Controlled Burning	E3	
2 Cornflake Crack	HVS	

3 Wall of Attrition	E6
4 Norseman	VS
5 White Collar Worker	E2
6 Blue Collar Blues	HVS
7 Portia	HVS

8 Thumbnacker Crack	VS
9 Mono Man	E4
10 The Islander	E2
11 Friction Impossible	E4
12 Death and Weirdness	E1

leads to the sanctuary of a large leftward-leaning groove. Follow this to the top and belay to the abseil rope.

★Badlands   120 feet   E3 5c   (8.8.91)
The central line of the right-hand wall. A fine sustained pitch on generally good holds and with adequate protection. Start as for *Dreamlands*. Step up and traverse right to the beginning of the rightward-slanting ramp of *Dreamlands*. Climb directly up via a series of breaks to reach a vertical crackline and follow this with difficulty to better holds. Finish direct via a small rightward-leaning groove. Belay to the abseil rope.

★Wonderlands   100 feet   E2 5c   (3.8.88)
Enjoyable, well-protected climbing up the discontinuous crackline in the left-hand wall. Start on a ledge atop the buttress beneath the wall. Climb the gritty crack on the left edge of the wall for 15 feet; then traverse right into the centre of the wall. Follow the crackline direct, gradually easing in difficulty, before a move right gains good holds and a loose finishing crack. Belay to the abseil rope.

Direct Start   E4 6a †   (6.8.92)
The obvious direct start, joining the original route at the end of its traverse. A bold, fingery and sustained piece of wall climbing with just sufficient micro-wire protection.

The west wall of the zawn is severely undercut with a narrow sea-channel beneath. The best approach to the only route to date is by abseil directly down the wall from good block belays on the rock-promontory above. Low to mid tide required.

★★The Tempest   100 feet   E6 6b †   (19.10.89)
An awesome proposition: the leftward-slanting crack in the overhanging wall. The start is intimidating and rarely dry, though climbable when wet. Start directly beneath the huge roof, on a large boulder in the back of the sea-channel. Traverse left on good flakes to a small corner. Enter this and bridge up it to a ramp on the left. From the top of the ramp, climb steeply up and left, with a difficult move (peg runner) to good flakes and a large rounded jug. Pull onto the slabby wall above and power up the crack directly to the top.
Note: on the first ascent the stainless steel peg was tied-off and the tape later removed; this can be replaced when the abseil approach is used.

Phantom Zawn Area

The collective name given to the group of small buttresses and zawns at the north-western extremity of Torrey Canyon Bay. The rock promontory to the west of the overhang-capped zawn and opposite Seal Slab is Ocean Promontory and marks the southern limit of the Phantom Zawn Area.

At the seaward tip of Ocean Promontory is a clean hanging arête, *Friction Impossible*. Running north along the west, seaward, side of the promontory is a long, golden-coloured wall split by the prominent flared chimney of *Flares Are In*. To the north a deep, narrow zawn cuts into the cliff. This is Phantom Zawn, conspicuous by the two large caves in its depths. North of Phantom Zawn and rising vertically from the sea is a crack-seamed wall, Winston's Wall, with a deep inaccessible through-cave at its northern end. Opposite Winston's Wall is a clean, south-facing wall supported by a small rock platform, Ghostbusters Wall. To its north is a small steep-sided zawn, Short Story Zawn.

The Phantom Zawn Area has its own distinct atmosphere, quite apart from some of the more 'popular' areas. Here is to be found a wealth of short, quality climbs on generally excellent rock and of relatively easy access.

The area is a popular meeting-place for the island's resident seal population, their antics providing a suitable distraction for any bored belayer. The seal's curious melancholic wailing can often be heard echoing around the zawn and gives the area its name.

OCEAN PROMONTORY   OS Ref 1292 4720
The first routes described lie on the southern, or seaward tip of the promontory. Scramble down to the top of the promontory and a small rock platform 70 feet above the sea. An abseil from large blocks reaches the non-tidal ledges below. Alternatively, climb down the short awkward corner on the west side of the promontory to the ledges below at Very Difficult standard.

A poor route, **Alice** (230 feet Severe 5.68), starts up the corner of the descent route before following a long and meandering traverse-line across the face to the left.

★**Friction Impossible**   70 feet   E4 6b   (6.8.88)
The elegant, hanging arête opposite Seal Slab. A short but extremely frustrating problem. Start on ledges below and left of the arête. Place a small wire runner in the crack above and begin a highly technical traverse right, just above the cutaway, to the arête. Follow this to the top in a fine position.

Island Life   60 feet   E3 6a †   (14.9.92)
Short and sharp. Start up a thin crack 15 feet left of *Friction Impossible*, and then take a diagonal crackline rightwards across the wall to a horizontal break. Step right; then go up and back left to a flake crack leading to a short crack and the top.

Death and Weirdness in the Surfing Zone   45 feet   E1 5c
                                                                (16.8.90)
Short and surreal. Start as for *Island Life* but continue direct up the thin, stubborn crack to the top.

Apparition   60 feet   E1 5b   †   (14.9.92)
To the left of the descent corner is a short, steep wall in a small, recessed
bay. Climb the right-hand groove in the wall and step right to a crack in
the arête which leads to the top.

Bed Bugs Bite My Bollocks   90 feet   Very Severe 4b †   (3.8.88)
Start from sea-level ledges below and left of *Apparition* and the descent
corner. Low tide required. Climb over slabby rock to the base of a steep
corner-crack and follow this, moving left at its top, to a small ledge. The
thin flake above provides a tricky finish.

The following climbs are situated on the west-facing wall of the promon-
tory and are centred around the huge flake chimney of *Flares Are In*.
Descent is by abseil from one of the large blocks directly above the wall.
No tidal restrictions.

★**Atlantic Grey**   80 feet   E2 5c   (6.8.87)
An enjoyable and well-protected pitch up the attractive thin crack just
right of the flake chimney. Start from a small ledge just inside the chimney
and well above sea-level. Gain the crack from the left and climb it, on
sharp holds and with little respite, to the top.

Flares Are In   100 feet   Hard Very Severe 4c   (31.7.88)
Unlikely to become fashionable! The huge chimney/flake gives a unique
pitch even by Lundy standards; recommended for a wet day. From the
belay on *Atlantic Grey*, 'back-and-foot' up into the bowels of the cliff.
Avoiding the temptation of a direct finish, continue up and left to an exit
just below the cliff-top. A short crack completes the route.

★★**On a Wing and a Prayer**   70 feet   E6 6b   †   (27.7.88)
A spectacular and dangerous undertaking up the flying arête to the left of
Flares Are In. Friends 1 and 3½ are particularly useful. Start on a
pedestal below the overhanging right wall of the arête. Technical moves
past a small sloping shelf lead to a good flake on the arête, where a
committing swing left gains a good horizontal break on the slab. Hand-
traverse right to the arête and layback a short crack before moving back
left onto the slab. Climb boldly up the centre of this to twin flakes and a
scoop, move left to a break, and press on up to where a difficult step right
leads to a final thin move. An alternative finish climbs more of the arête at
the same grade. From the scoop, follow flakes rightwards to the break,
where a difficult mantelshelf and a quick shuffle right lead to the arête and
good finishing holds. Equally frightening!

To the left of *On a Wing and a Prayer* is an attractive orange slab. Three
routes start from the slabby ledges at its base; this is 30 feet above
sea-level and gained by abseil.

Cunning Devil   70 feet   E1 5b   (27.7.88)
The right-hand line of the slab via the obvious crack-system. Climb easily

rightwards to the base of a flared crack, where a sly manoeuvre right gains another crack. Difficult moves right again lead to the right-hand crack. Step onto the slab and continue quickly to the top.

★Something in the Shadows 75 feet E5 5c (27.7.88)
Your worst nightmare! The central line of the slab is devoid of any useful protection. Climb easy flakes to where they form a small curious hole. Step up and right into a vague scoop in the centre of the slab. Now 'switch off' and climb direct in a gripping runout to a large ledge at the top.

★Things That Go Bump in the Night 75 feet E3 5b (27.7.88)
More mind games. The left-hand line of the slab is technically easier but equally scary. Follow *Something in the Shadows* to the small hole. Climb the flake above to its end; then step up and left to a blind crack (*Rock 2* sideways). Move up to a thin break and gain the obvious scoop above. Follow it boldly to a tricky exit onto the large ledge.

PHANTOM ZAWN OS Ref 1291 4723
The next two climbs start from a small ledge on the southern arête of the zawn, exposed only at low tide. The ledge is gained by a diagonal abseil from good block belays at the top of the golden-coloured slab to its south.

Hyperspace Bypass 130 feet Very Severe (3.8.84)
Pleasant climbing up the face just right of Phantom Zawn. So called because it avoids the 'hyperspace' of *Dark Power*. Start on the small tidal ledge.
1 40 feet 4c. Climb twin cracks on the left for 20 feet; then follow a rightward-slanting break to a belay at its end.
2 90 feet 4a. Traverse horizontally left for 20 feet until beneath the evil-looking chimney-crack. Climb this to the top with unexpected ease.

★★★Dark Power 150 feet E2 (2.8.78)
The finest climb in the area. An improbable diagonal line across the impending south wall of the zawn, gives access to the right-hand of twin cracks. Steep and satisfying, with mounting exposure and good protection when most needed. Start from the small tidal ledge.
1 80 feet 5b. Climb the twin cracks on the left to a small overhang and turn it on the left to reach a cracked groove. Follow this to its end and exit left to a niche and good nut belays.
2 70 feet 5b. Pull out of the niche on its left-hand side and move up to the higher line of grey flakes. Place protection in the crack above, and then traverse the flakes leftwards to gain the crack after 15 feet. Climb this strenuously to a belay in a recess. Scramble off to the left.
Variations
1a 50 feet 4c. The niche belay at the end of pitch 1 can be gained by a horizontal traverse left from the ledges to the south and some 40 feet above sea-level.
2a 70 feet 5c. The lower line of grey flakes can be hand-traversed to gain the crack at a slightly lower level (a wild E3).

An Audience of Seals   70 feet   Severe †   (6.8.88)
Who's watching who? A pleasant little pitch, just inside Phantom Zawn.
Start from ledges revealed at low tide beneath the north wall of the zawn.
Climb the most seaward crackline.

WINSTON'S WALL   OS Ref 1291 4724
The crack-seamed wall to the north of Phantom Zawn drops cleanly into
the sea. All the routes start from hanging belays as close to the sea as one
dares! Needless to say a calm sea and outgoing tide are desirable. Abseil
in from the broken ledges above the wall.

Squatter and the Ant   70 feet   E2 5c †   (2.8.84)
Interesting crack-climbing up the right-hand side of the wall. Take a
hanging belay below *Winston's Bogey*, the obvious groove with a stepped
ledge. Move out right to good holds in a rightward-slanting break. Climb
the wall above to reach a good crack and follow it direct to the top.

Wooooooo!   70 feet   E2 5c †   (6.8.88)
The thinner, discontinuous crackline just left of *Squatter and the Ant*. From
the same belay, climb direct to the start of the crackline and ghost up it to
the top.

Winston's Bogey   70 feet   Very Severe 4c   (2.8.84)
The stepped crack-and-groove-line in the centre of the wall gives an
enjoyable pitch. Start at a hanging belay beneath the groove with the
stepped ledge. Climb the groove and step left to a crack. Follow this to
where it runs out; move left and climb more cracks to a large slanting
break. Move right along this and continue up another crack to the top.
Direct Finish   Hard Very Severe 5b   (6.8.88)
The obvious direct continuation is equally fine.

★**Nous Sommes du Soleil**   75 feet   E2 5c   (3.8.88)
A stylish pitch up the thin crackline in the black wall to the left of *Winston's
Bogey*. Take a hanging belay just right of the base of the crack. Step left to
the crack and climb it to a small ledge. The troublesome continuation
crack leads directly to the top.

GHOSTBUSTERS WALL   OS Ref 1289 4724
At the northern extremity of the Phantom Zawn Area is a small rocky
headland. This is immediately south of a small zawn and roughly 120
yards south of Arch Zawn. Ghostbusters Wall is the clean, south-facing
wall on the southern side of the headland and at right-angles to Winston's
Wall.

Approach the wall by a brief scramble down the seaward tip of the small
rocky headland to sea-level ledges. A short traverse left (facing out) gains
the large platform at the foot of the wall. This is accessible three hours
either side of low tide.

The routes are described as they are approached, **from left to right.**

Signed and Sealed   40 feet   Very Severe 4c †   (6.8.92)
At the left-hand end of the wall is a flake crack, prominent only near the top of the buttress. Climb the easy lower crack to the more interesting upper section.

Achilles' Seal   60 feet   E2 5c   (3.8.88)
In the centre of the wall are two thin cracklines. Climb the indistinct, left-hand crack to a small overhang. Awkward moves over its left-hand side lead to stubborn, rounded cracks leading to the top.

★**Ghostbusters**   70 feet   E2 5c   (31.7.88)
The more prominent, right-hand crackline slants to the right. This gives tough, sustained climbing with excellent protection.

★**Seal of Approval**   80 feet   E4 6a †   (3.8.88)
To the right of *Ghostbusters* is a dramatic, leaning arête. This exciting route gives sustained climbing up the wall to its left. Start beneath the arête at low to mid tide. Climb the wall via some small horizontal breaks to a flake. Use an undercut up and left to reach a thin crackline and follow it, finishing slightly right via a short, leaning groove.

Right again is a narrow, recessed wall, overlooking the sea-channel separating Ghostbusters Wall from Winston's Wall. This is reached by a short traverse beneath Ghostbusters Wall at low tide.

★★**The Howling**   80 feet   E3 5c   (31.7.88)
A brilliant little pitch with a big feel to it. Sustained and exposed climbing at the upper limit of its grade. Start below the crack in the centre of the wall. Climb the crack to a small overhang. Traverse right beneath the overhang to a thinner crack and move right again to the arête. Climb this, with plenty of fresh air, to the top.
Variation
★**Banshee**   80 feet   E4 6a †   (3.8.88)
A direct and harder version of *The Howling.* Follow *The Howling* to the small overhang, where a difficult sequence up and left leads into a short, shallow groove. Climb this, sustained, to the top.

SHORT STORY ZAWN   OS Ref 1288 4728
On the north side of the Ghostbusters headland, and approximately 100 yards south of Arch Zawn is a small, steep-sided zawn. Bounding its northern side is a broken, rocky promontory, giving an uncomplicated descent to the climbs on the northern side of the zawn. At low to mid tide, the floor of the zawn can be crossed, enabling the climbs on its southern side to be reached. Alternatively, a 70-foot abseil down the south wall of the zawn from good block belays at its top leads to small ledges at its base. These are exposed two hours either side of low water.

The most prominent feature of the south wall is the leftward-slanting fault of *Short Story* in its centre. The first routes lie on the black wall to its right.

Basement   60 feet   Very Difficult   †   (6.8.91)
A straightforward route up the stepped slab just right of a prominent leftward-slanting groove.

Mezzanine   70 feet   Very Severe   5a   (14.8.86)
The shallow, leftward-slanting groove near the entrance to the zawn. Gain the groove by a low-tide traverse from *Short Story* or direct by abseil, and climb it to a difficult exit at the top.

★A Pack of Lies   70 feet   E2   5c   (14.8.86)
The compelling thin crack in the black wall gives a good but deceptively difficult pitch. Start from the large ledge beneath *Short Story*. Follow the rightward-trending ramp to a small ledge at the base of the crack. Climb this on improving holds, and exit right onto a slab at the top.

★Clinging to the Wreckage   70 feet   E4   6a   †   (31.7.88)
Sustained and fingery wall-climbing to the left of *A Pack of Lies*. Adequately protected with a large selection of small wires. Start from the large ledge beneath *Short Story*. Follow some faint cracks up and slightly left and with mounting difficulty reach a small overlap. Step left and finish direct.

Short Story   95 feet   Severe   (20.7.69)
The leftward-slanting faultline. A pleasant slab leads to a rather crumbly finish. Start from the large ledge at the foot of a narrow leftward-slanting slab.
1 70 feet. Climb up to a large crack in the slab and follow it to a good stance on the left on a large ledge.
2 25 feet. Move awkwardly right across a basalt dyke to reach a small ledge. From its left-hand end, finish carefully on suspect holds.
Direct Finish   Hard Very Severe   †   (4.8.87)
2a 30 feet   4c. Follow the natural continuation of the faultline to the top over some particularly unpleasant rock.

Ripping Yarn   85 feet   E2   †   (6.8.88)
Neat, technical climbing up the short wall left of and beneath *Short Story*. Start as for *Short Story*.
1 60 feet   6a. Move out left onto the obvious stepped ramp-line and follow it to a narrow ledge. From the left-hand end of the ledge, climb on small pockets directly up the technical wall, past a break, to a stance on a large ledge.
2 25 feet. *Short Story* pitch 2.

★Jug of Punch   120 feet   Very Severe   4b   (9.9.74)
The impressive, steep slab in the back of the zawn. An enjoyable and highly improbable pitch at the grade. Start beside a large boulder,

PHANTOM ZAWN AREA

1 Walrus		S
2 Felice		VS
3 Bed Bugs Bite My Bollocks		VS
4 Atlantic Grey		E2
5 Flares Are In		HVS
6 On a Wing and a Prayer		E6
6a Variation		E6
7 Cunning Devil		E1
8 Something in the Shadows		E5
9 Things That Go Bump		E3
10 Hyperspace Bypass		VS
11 Dark Power		E2
12 An Audience of Seals		S
13 Squatter and the Ant		E2
14 Winston's Bogey		VS
15 Nous Sommes du Soleil		E2
16 Seal of Approval		E4
17 Ghostbusters		E2
18 Achilles' Seal		E2
19 Signed and Sealed		VS
20 Serpentine		E1

A Seal Slab
B Wonderlands Wall
C Phantom Zawn
D Winston's Wall
E Short Story Zawn

beneath a blunt rib leading up onto the slab. Climb the rib for 20 feet and move awkwardly up onto the slab. Follow good holds rightwards to an exposed ledge and continue steeply back left below the large overhang. Climb the groove above until an obvious hand-traverse left can be made to a good ledge and the top.

Moonfleet   100 feet   Very Severe 4c   (13.10.89)
Worthwhile climbing up the blunt rib to the left of *Jug of Punch*. Start as for that route but take the rib direct to rejoin *Jug of Punch* at the large overhang.

Tall Story   90 feet   E2 5c   (6.9.80)
The steep, off-width crack in the back wall of the zawn and left of *Jug of Punch*. The difficulties are concentrated into the first, awkward, 25 feet...honest!

In One Bound   80 feet   E2 5c †   (6.8.91)
In the north-east corner of the zawn is the steep, rightward-slanting crack of *Big Shiner*. Climb the crack to a small ledge at 30 feet. Traverse right above the lip of an overhang until a long stride right across the void leads onto the wall left of *Tall Story*. Continue directly up the wall to the top.

Big Shiner   80 feet   Very Severe 4b   (25.9.70)
The obvious steep crack slanting to the right. A difficult lower section eases towards the top.

Shaggy Dog Story   45 feet   E2 5c †   (7.8.91)
A short but interesting problem up the wall 30 feet left of *Big Shiner*. Start beneath a small overlap at the base of the wall. Move up to the overlap and pull through it at the obvious weakness. Finish up the wall and short crack above.

Above the northern point of Short Story Zawn and just below plateau-level, is a small, slabby outcrop with a clean, winding streak up its centre. **Serpentine** (25 feet E1 5a 23.8.90) snakes its way up the streak, with an unprotected crux just below the top.

Arch Zawn to North Light

The coastline to the north of Phantom Zawn Area consists of a number of deep, incut zawns and coves, the most important of which is Arch Zawn. Further north the cliffs lose height before they rise again within the deep recess of Heron Zawn. Beyond is a large cove with a boulder-strewn floor, Cyclops Zawn, which has to its north a series of small zawns with a number of broken, plateau-level buttresses above; the largest of these is Rock Pool Buttress.

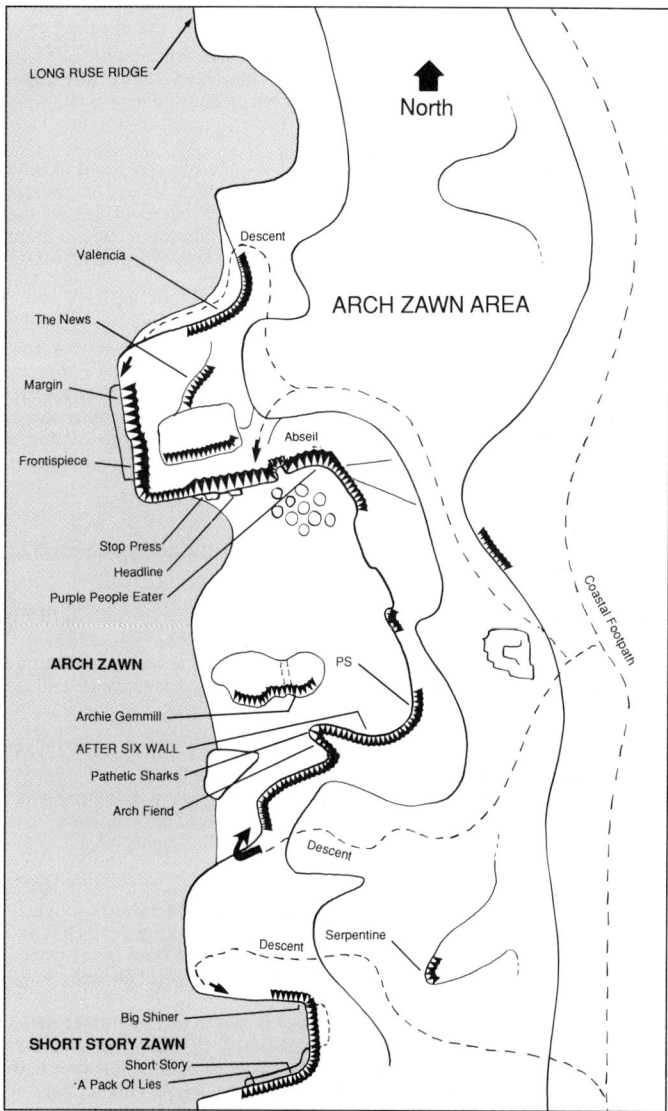

LONG RUSE RIDGE

North

ARCH ZAWN AREA

Descent

Valencia

The News

Margin

Frontispiece

Abseil

Stop Press
Headline
Purple People Eater

ARCH ZAWN

PS

Archie Gemmill
AFTER SIX WALL
Pathetic Sharks
Arch Fiend

Descent

Coastal Footpath

Descent

Serpentine

Descent

Big Shiner

SHORT STORY ZAWN

Short Story
A Pack Of Lies

ARCH ZAWN   OS Ref 1293 4738
Not truly a zawn, this is the large open cove 100 yards north of Short
Story Zawn and some 500 yards north of The Devil's Slide. The zawn
takes its name from the large, though inconspicuous natural arch in the
rock island in the middle of the zawn.

The climbing on the south side of the zawn is generally steep and of easy
access. Unfortunately, the cliffs see little sunlight and tend to remain
damp until late in the day. The best climbing in the zawn lies on the
impressive, golden-coloured headland on the northern side, where
excellent rock and dramatic situations make for some of the finest routes
in the area. Certainly well worth the walk.

On first acquaintance the zawn can be difficult to locate and a useful
landmark at plateau-level is the prominent Gannet's Rock on the east
coast. Arch Zawn lies down the broad, shallow, grassy gully directly
opposite. There is also a prominent perched block situated near the top
of the north side of the gully. Follow easy-angled grassy slopes round
the southern spur of the zawn and continue down Moderate standard
rock to a narrow sea-channel, which is exposed at low to mid tide. Cross
this to the large boulders on the floor of the zawn. At high tide, a higher
though more awkward approach is possible.

The first three climbs are situated on a small, west-facing wall south of
and opposite the rock island.

The Flue   80 feet   Severe   (6.10.73)
Pungent! The prominent guano-streaked chimney in the right-hand side
of the wall. Climb the chimney and exit left at its top. Move up to a large
ledge on the right (belay possible); take the continuation chimney and
then the wall on its left to the top.

Denver Scoines   80 feet   Hard Very Severe 5a †   (1.8.89)
An eliminate line but pleasant nonetheless. Start just left of *The Flue*.
Climb directly up a short black wall to a slab, and follow its left arête to
the base of twin cracks. The right-hand crack leads to good spike
belays.

★**Arch Fiend**   80 feet   Hard Very Severe 5b   (6.10.73)
Fine climbing with one hard move. The right-hand of two short grooves
in the arête left of *The Flue*. Climb the groove and step right at its top to
a large ledge. The stubborn corner above leads to the base of the twin
cracks. Follow the left-hand crack to good spike belays at its top.

The rock island in the centre of the zawn is in fact two buttresses, tenuously joined at the top to form a large natural arch. A number of climbs
which offer some good climbing and an excellent view of the surrounding cliffs have been recorded on the south face of the island. Descent
from the top is via the shelving slabs on the western side of the seaward

buttress at Difficult standard. This is followed by a short traverse right, round the base of the arch, and so back to the start. **From left to right:**

The Arch 60 feet Very Difficult (18.4.73)
A pleasant pitch climbing the narrow slab to the left of the prominent groove on the seaward buttress.

Escapist 60 feet Severe (3.85)
Climb the short groove just right of *The Arch* to a bulge, pull over, and finish up the cracked wall above.

The Archers 60 feet Very Difficult (2.8.87)
Climb the arête to the right of *Escapist* via a short crack.

★**Archie Gemmill** 70 feet E2 5c (4.8.87)
A high-quality pitch centred on the hanging corner above the arch. Start on the landward buttress. Place a sling on a spike on the right arête, step down, and traverse left to the base of a slim groove. Delicate moves up the groove bring the corner into reach; layback steeply to the top.

Geoffrey Archer's Whorle 70 feet E1 5b † (2.8.87)
The wall and rib just right of *Archie Gemmill*. Climb the arête to the large spike, move slightly right, and continue up steeper rock to a small ledge. Follow the rib on the right to an easy finish.

Arch Enemy 70 feet Hard Very Severe 5a † (2.8.87)
Interesting climbing up the steep, cracked wall 15 feet right of *Geoffrey Archer's Whorle*. Climb direct to a rightward-slanting crack and move up via a small ledge to the base of a prominent crack. Jam up this to the top.

THE AFTER SIX WALL
Back on the mainland, the steep, brown north-facing wall opposite the arch catches any available sunshine only in the early summer evenings. In the right-hand side of the wall is a stepped, broken corner. Two steep, thin cracklines split the short, overhanging tower to its right.

★**Pathetic Sharks** 70 feet E4 6b † (1.8.89)
Short but with a nasty bite! Start directly beneath the right-hand crackline. Climb easily up to a large ledge just left of the foot of the crack (belay possible). Step awkwardly right into the crack and climb it by some tenacious finger-jamming to a slab and a welcome resting-place. Finish up the easy corner-crack. Good block belay.

★**Bastard Wet Crack** 70 feet E4 6a † (8.8.91)
The left-hand crackline, technically easier but equally sustained. Well protected but rarely dry! Climb easily to the base of the crack where a difficult sequence past a peg runner brings better holds to reach within the crack. Finger-jam frantically to where the angle relents and finish carefully up the large blocky corner above.

For the climbs on the left-hand section of the wall, a preplaced belay rope is necessary. This can be arranged from a prominent split block, 40 feet back from the cliff-top. At the foot of the wall is a small, ill-defined pinnacle.

Rigging in the Frigging Arête   110 feet   E4 †   (9.8.91)
Start beneath the chimney in the front face of the pinnacle.
1   50 feet   5a.   Climb the chimney and the layback crack above to a belay atop the pinnacle.
2   60 feet   6a.   After a worrying start, the cracks in the left-hand side of the arête are climbed to the top.

★**Woman in Chains**   120 feet   E5 6a †   (8.8.91)
An unrelenting pitch up the crackline in the centre of the wall. Start in the corner on the left-hand side of the pinnacle. Climb the corner to the right-hand end of a large detached flake. The corner above leads into a steep, stubborn crackline. Climb this to the top.

★**Smoke on the Water**   120 feet   E5 6b †   (7.8.91)
Forceful climbing up the steepest part of the wall leads to a prominent finishing-groove. Start at the base of the wall to the left of the pinnacle. Climb rightwards up flakes to reach the large detached flake (peg runner on the left). Move up and right of the peg to a good hold and stride left to reach a crack (peg runner). Move left again to a flake, from where hard climbing through the bulges above leads into the groove. Climb this to the top.

P.S.   200 feet   Very Severe   (8.81)
In the southern corner of the zawn and slanting up beneath The After Six Wall, is a long black slab. An interesting route, marred by some loose rock on the first pitch and a grassy finish. Start below the centre of the slab.
1   100 feet   4a.   Climb directly up the middle of the slab to steep grass and a nut belay.
2   100 feet   4c.   Step down and right to the bottom of the upper slab and climb it direct via the central crackline.

Footnote   200 feet   Hard Severe †   (18.4.73)
A poor route up the subsidiary rib to the left of *P.S.* The second pitch is particularly loose. Start beneath the rib.
1   100 feet.   Climb the rib direct to a small pinnacle, and traverse left along a faultline to a small stance in a corner.
2   100 feet.   Follow a ramp up to the left, where a traverse left for 15 feet along a grassy horizontal break leads to a groove. Climb this carefully to the top and belay well back.

Way Out   200 feet   Very Severe †   (27.3.75)
Not recommended, even as an escape route – it would probably be safer to swim! It climbs the distinctive black gully in the north corner of the zawn, finishing up the broken slabs above.
1   100 feet.   Ascend the gully direct on disintegrating rock and either move

A Widespread Ocean of Fear The Diamond
Climbers: Andy Popp and John Codling

Photo: Gary Gibson

Controlled Burning Torrey Canyon Cliff
Climber: John Lyth

Photo: Pete Milner

left onto the large slab at a slim groove to a poor nut belay, or continue to a large spike on the right.

2 100 feet. From the stance at the base of the slab, climb either of two broken cracklines, and finish over loose, broken ground.

The most obvious feature in the right-hand section of the north side of the zawn is a large, pinkish slab. The base of this is sea-washed at high tide.

★Letters to the Editor 150 feet E3 † (2.8.87)
A delicate first pitch up the centre of the slab precedes a brutal jamming-crack in the leaning headwall. Start as for *Way Out.*
1 110 feet 5b. Follow *Way Out* for 20 feet until it is possible to bridge across to a small groove below the main slab. Climb the groove to an awkward exit onto the slab and move up and left to its centre. Easier climbing leads to a belay at a small ledge below the headwall.
2 40 feet 5c. Move up to the crack that splits the headwall and climb it with conviction to a difficult exit. Scramble well back to a good belay.

Purple People Eater 150 feet E1 5a (19.4.73)
Colourful and frightening. The big, stepped corner bounding the left-hand side of the slab. Protection is sparse and the rock crumbly in places. Start to the left of the corner below a crack leading to an overhang. Climb the crack and traverse right beneath the overhang, past a downward-pointing fang of rock, to join the main corner. Go up this to another overhang and step right into the upper corner, which is taken to a steep finish.

Rainbow 120 feet Very Severe 4c (21.4.73)
A pleasant climb picking the easiest line up the overlapping slabs to the left of *Purple People Eater*. Start on top of a huge boulder. Step onto the slab and move up to and over the overhang with difficulty. Go rightwards across slabs to a wide crack on the right. Climb the corner to the left of the slab for 20 feet until a traverse left along a line of large flakes leads to steep moves and a small ledge (optional belay). Finish up the easy slabs above.

Late City Extra 120 feet E2 5c (19.9.84)
A direct line up the overlapping slab and prominent black V-groove to the left of *Rainbow*. Start on top of the huge boulder. Follow *Rainbow* over the overhang and then traverse diagonally left to the base of the V-groove. Climb this precariously to a small ledge above. Continue up a slab to a steep layback crack and climb it to a small ledge (optional belay). Finish up the easy slabs above.

Blizzard 140 feet Very Severe 4c (28.3.75)
Enjoyable and pleasantly exposed. To the left of *Late City Extra* are two ribs; the light grey right-hand rib is conical in shape and leads to a chimney. Start in the chimney just left of the right-hand rib. Climb the chimney for a few feet and move right onto the rib. Move up a little; then

descend rightwards onto the slab, almost ʊ. the lip of the large overhang. Continue rightwards on good holds, passing a suspect flake, to a ledge and a junction with *Rainbow* (optional belay). Finish up the easy slabs above.

Papa Joe   110 feet   Hard Severe   4a   (20.4.73)
The corner, crack, and slab between *Blizzard* and the main buttress give a pleasant route when dry. Start beneath the crack at low tide. Climb up past a good chockstone until it is possible to move right onto the slab. Climb straight up on good holds, crossing the top of a chimney, to the apex of the slab. Finish up easy ledges to a good thread belay.

The south face of the headland forming the northern side of Arch Zawn bristles with overhangs and gives some of the finest climbs in the area. The approach to the base of the cliff is accessible only at low tide and not at all during neap-tides or when there is a big swell. Careful timing is therefore necessary if one is to avoid belaying and treading water simultaneously!

The quickest approach is to abseil down the gully just left (facing out) of the headland from a large, prominent block at its top. Alternatively, the descent to the routes on the southern side of the zawn can be used and the boulders on the zawn floor crossed at low to mid tide. During neap-tides, the starting-belays can be gained by an exciting direct abseil from half-way down the broken ramp-line that splits the face.

★★Pawsher   170 feet   E4   (25.7.83)
A pushy thin crack leads to a delightfully exposed upper section. Start on the large boulders beneath the right-hand arête of the buttress and to the left of *Papa Joe*.
1 70 feet 6b. Move up and left into the steep, thin crack just left of the arête. Climb forcefully up this to the *Headline* stance, a small ledge alongside a huge flake.
2 50 feet 5a. Traverse horizontally left along the lip of the overhangs to reach a belay on the broken ramp-line.
3 50 feet. Finish easily up the ramp-line.

★★★Headline   150 feet   E1   (19.4.73)
Sensational, well-protected climbing on perfect rock. It finds the most amenable line through the impressive rock architecture of the right-hand side of the wall. Start from the left-hand of two large pointed blocks leaning against the base of the wall.
1 75 feet 5b. Awkward initial moves up a thin crack lead to a small bulge. Climb this strenuously before reaching good holds on the right. Traverse right to a break in the overhangs above, pull through, and traverse right again for 15 feet to a superbly exposed stance alongside a large flake.
2 75 feet 4c. Climb the flake and groove above the right-hand side of the stance to an overhang. Step up and left into a V-chimney and follow the wide crack to the top.

★★**Stop Press** 150 feet E2 (21.4.73)
A superbly intricate climb, flirting with the barrier of overhangs in the centre of the face before turning them to their left. Start as for *Headline* on the left-hand block.
1 80 feet 5c. Step down to good holds and climb up to a traverse-line leading left into a large niche. Quit this via a diagonal crack, which leads to a block at the right-hand side of a hanging slab beneath the overhangs. Step left and climb the overhanging arête to a smooth slab. Cross the slab low down, difficult, to a crack below a small overhang. Pull through on good holds to belay in a convenient recess on the ramp.
2 70 feet 5a. Climb the rightward-leaning crack and groove above the stance direct to the top of the headland.

★★**Today** 150 feet E4 † (7.8.87)
A powerful, superdirect on *Stop Press* climbing the straight, rightward-leaning crack to its left. Start from a small ledge at the foot the crack, gained by abseil from the ramp or by a leftward traverse from the start of *Stop Press*. Low tide and a calm sea are essential.
1 80 feet 6a. Climb the crack, which is both strenuous and technical, to a junction with *Stop Press* at the small overhang. Pull over and belay in the recess on the ramp.
2 70 feet 5a. *Stop Press* pitch 2.

The seaward, western, face of the headland gives a series of fine climbs on excellent rock. Scramble down to the north of the headland, initially on grassy slopes and then over broken rock, to large ledges well above sea-level. Traverse south, crossing a small inlet at low tide, to a large wave-washed platform at the foot of the face. At high tide, there is a higher, more exposed alternative avoiding the inlet.

★**Frontispiece** 150 feet Very Difficult (18.4.73)
Enjoyable and pleasantly exposed. The groove and slab in the right-hand side of the face leads to an easy finish up the ramp which crosses the south face of the headland. Start from the right-hand end of the platform.
1 75 feet. Climb the groove and then the slab to a belay at the foot of the broken ramp-line.
2 75 feet. Continue up the ramp to the top. Numerous variations are possible along the way.

★**Bulletin** 100 feet E1 5b (18.8.80)
An energetic encounter with the band of overhangs in the centre of the face. Fine climbing. Start from the platform beneath a shallow groove. Climb the groove to the first overhang and pull through to the left to gain a sandwiched slab. Move right across this for 5 feet and pull over the second overhang at a hollow block. Climb the groove and bristly rib above to the top. Belay well back.

★**Margin** 100 feet Very Severe 4c (20.4.73)
Steep and spectacular climbing for the grade. It takes the overhang in the

left-hand edge of the face. Good holds and protection. Start from the left-hand side of the platform. Climb the slab to an overhang and step left into a groove, which leads to a much larger overhang. Swing over this using a good handhold on the right, and climb the crack above to the top. Belay well back.

In the north face of the headland, just left of *Margin* and at a slightly higher level, are a series of slanting cracklines.

★The Weather   70 feet   Hard Very Severe   5b   (22.8.86)
Tough jamming up the right-hand crackline. Start beneath the crack at a pillar in the lower wall. Go up the pillar and the bulge above to gain the crack. Climb it, and step left at its top to a tricky finish.

★The News   70 feet   Hard Very Severe   5b   (21.8.86)
The central and most continuous crackline. Steep moves up to and over a difficult bulge lead into the crack. Climb it.

The Time   50 feet   Very Severe   4c   (22.8.86)
Climb discontinuous cracks in the wall just left of *The News* and continue up to a small crescent-shaped undercling. Step right; then move up and left to finish.

To the north of *The Time*, the cliff rapidly loses height. A number of short problem pitches have been climbed here on good rock and with no access problems. **London Fields** (30 feet E1 5c † 14.9.92) climbs the thin crack and overlap in the wall to the left of *The Time*. **Finisterre** (30 feet Severe 11.8.91) climbs the short jamming crack left again. To the left are three prominent deep grooves. **Sole** (35 feet Very Severe 5a 11.8.91) takes the right-hand groove finishing up a flake crack. **Lundy** (35 feet Very Severe 5a 11.8.91) follows the central groove after a difficult start. **Fastnet** (35 feet Very Severe 5a 11.8.91) climbs the left-hand groove, which overhangs at the start. **Valencia** (40 feet Very Severe 5a 11.8.91) is the best route hereabouts, climbing the slim buttress left of *Fastnet*: from the toe of the buttress, move up and rightwards to gain a small bottomless groove and climb it direct. Finally **Smith Knoll Automatic** (35 feet Very Severe 5a 11.8.91) takes the face just left of *Valencia*, finishing up a leftward-slanting groove.

Just north of the descent route is a small bay displaying the remnants of a rockfall: this is all that remains of **Tenex, Stubborn Candle**, and **The Thick Plotter**.

Opposite the descent route is a clean 70-foot slab providing some short pitches; the upper left-to-right slanting crack goes at Difficult standard, with harder variations up the right edge and a thin line directly up the centre.

LONG RUSE RIDGE   O.S. Ref. 1290 4750
North of Arch Zawn and at the southern end of the large bay to the south
of North Light are a number of ridges. *Long Ruse Ridge* is the longest of
these, extending nearly all the way from sea-level to plateau-level.

The foot of the ridge is reached by scrambling down its northern side to a
small platform at sea-level. An alternative approach from the south is also
possible, starting from the top of Arch Zawn.

Long Ruse Ridge   200 feet   Very Difficult   (28.4.69)
Although not in the same class as its Cornish counterparts, the ridge is
worthwhile for its isolated position and relative lack of seriousness. Start
from the platform at the foot of the ridge beneath an open chimney, just
left of a short steep wall.
1 50 feet. Climb up the large rock steps to the left of the chimney to a
square ledge and optional belay. Continue up the steep groove above, or
steep broken rock on the right, to a grassy col.
2 80 feet. Scramble up to the left and climb the broken left-hand section
of the wall above to another grassy col (optional belay). Move down and
right to a leftward-slanting crack in the slab above.
3 70 feet. Continue up the broken chimney to the top.
Variations
There are numerous variations on the ridge and, by combining these,
individual routes of up to Severe standard can be climbed. The most
substantial variations are at the bottom, where both the open chimney
right of the normal start and the stepped corner right again give
worthwhile pitches. A good direct finish is also possible up the grey dyke
above the small slab.

HERON ZAWN   OS Ref 1300 4765
Situated 150 yards to the north of *Long Ruse Ridge*, this steep, narrow
zawn is the largest of a series of zawns to the south of the North Light. The
impressive back wall dominates the zawn, providing a steep, smooth face
with little line of resistance. Two routes take lines up either side of the wall,
but the central line remains a challenge for future generations. In complete contrast, the sombre, south wall of the zawn is very broken and
always damp, and it remains popular only with the gulls. The climbing on
the north side of the zawn is concentrated around the slabby wall at its
centre, itself capped by a short but much steeper wall. This is bounded to
its right by the big corner of *Pedes Incandescens*. Towards its seaward
end the wall takes on a golden and much friendlier appearance.

The approach is down the broad, grassy gully 50 yards north of the zawn,
passing beneath a steep buttress high above sea-level, Grapefruit Buttress. A straightforward scramble down the northern spur leads to slabby
ledges at sea-level. A short traverse south then reaches the large boulders
on the zawn bed; these are exposed two hours either side of low tide. An
alternative, high-tide approach can be made by abseiling down the north
wall of the zawn from a huge spike at the base of Grapefruit Buttress.

Two routes breach the back wall. A 165-foot (50m) rope is essential and the prudent will secure a preplaced belay rope at the top of their chosen route. The boulders at the foot of the wall lie well above sea-level.

★★★Demons of Hilti   170 feet   E6 6b †   (31.7.88)
A real monster of a pitch, forcing a powerful line up the right-hand side of the huge wall. Initially on doubtful rock but improving as height is gained to an excellent upper section. The route, however, remains possessed! Start just right of centre on a pile of large blocks. Move up on crumbly rock and climb a large rightward-trending flake crack. A shallow groove signals the start of the hostilities and leads past two peg runners to a good ledge (peg runner above). Continue in the same line (peg runner) to another ledge (peg runner and optional belay). Move right to the end of the ledge and pull up the wall (bolt runner) stepping left to a good 'edge'. Continue up into a shallow groove, and from its top (bolt runner) move right and take the wall above to a square ledge on the arête (bolt runner). Overcome a short awkward wall and follow a cleaned streak of rock to easy ground. Even with 165-foot (50m) ropes the second may be climbing by this time.

Bosch Street Kids   160 feet   E5 6a †   (5.8.88)
The mighty crackline in the left-hand side of the wall gives a committing and very demanding lead. The rock also requires respect, particularly in the lower section. Start from boulders where the back wall meets the north wall of the zawn. Move up through increasingly steep rock to a small corner and climb this past a precarious jammed block. Difficult, sustained climbing, moving first right and then back left, leads up the crackline into the prominent upper groove. Ascend this to a steep grassy finish and belay well back. Five peg runners help show the way.

Pedes Incandescens   140 feet   Hard Very Severe 5a   (11.8.81)
The large corner formed by the junction of back and north walls. Climb the initial slabby corner, and move left to continue on dubious holds up the impending wall rightwards back into the upper corner. Climb the corner steeply over a bulge to a flake and follow this to an awkward finish.

The climbs on the north wall begin from a platform formed by huge blocks beneath the slabby, capped wall.

Slab and Groove   90 feet   Very Difficult   (9.75)
Start below the initial corner of *Pedes Incandescens*. Climb the corner to the second horizontal break on the slab above. Traverse the break leftwards to easy ground below a groove, which is taken to the top. Block belay.

Channel Wrack   90 feet   Very Severe   (9.8.79)
A mediocre climb. There remains some loose rock on the upper pitch. Start at a block to the left of *Slab and Groove*.
1 50 feet   4b.   Move up to the first horizontal break and continue directly

to the second break. Climb a thin crack above; then traverse left to a belay below an overhanging groove.

2 40 feet 4c. Climb the crack to the right of the groove to a steep finish.

Salty Slip   80 feet   Very Severe 4c †   (9.75)
A more direct approach to the upper groove of *Slab and Groove*. Start as for *Channel Wrack*. Move up to the first horizontal break and traverse left for 15 feet. Go diagonally left and up to a second break beneath the groove of *Slab and Groove*, and climb this to the top.

Rusty Silk   80 feet   E3 6a   (29.8.79/30.7.89)
A short, well-protected problem. Start at a slightly lower level, beneath the left-hand side of the slab. Go up the slab to a horizontal break, which leads to a good spike. Climb the overhanging wall above by the obvious weakness to a ledge a little higher. Move right into the groove of *Slab and Groove* and climb it for 10 feet before stepping left to finish up a crack.

Standing on a Beach   70 feet   E1 5b   (7.8.86)
A neat little pitch up the leftward-leaning, shallow groove at the seaward end of the wall, some 40 feet left of *Rusty Silk*. Move up and rightwards into the groove, and climb it to a small overlap. Pull over and climb leftwards to the top.

Boris Day   60 feet   Hard Very Severe 5b   (7.8.86)
The thin, leftward-slanting crack in the slab just left of *Standing on a Beach*. Climb the crack and step right just before its end into the centre of the slab. Proceed delicately and directly past a small overlap to the top.

GRAPEFRUIT BUTTRESS   OS Ref 1304 4766

The steep, north-facing buttress just below plateau-level passed under on the descent to Heron Zawn. This is just south of the large boulder-strewn cove of Cyclops Zawn. The buttress features some fine, powerful climbing on excellent rock, with the added bonus of no tidal restrictions. The most prominent feature is a large central corner capped by an overhang.

The climbs are described as approached, **from left to right.**

★**Serious Lobster Juggling**   80 feet   E4 6a †   (2.8.89)
Elegant, forceful climbing up the cleaned left-hand arête of the buttress. Start beneath a rightward-leaning flake just left of the central corner. Move up to the flake and climb it until it is possible to gain the hanging flake in the arête to the right. Gain a standing-position on its top and launch up the blind flake above (peg runner). Step left just below the top and finish direct via a short crack.

★**Pomplemousse**   80 feet   E1 5b   (31.8.79)
Tough, strenuous climbing up the large central corner. An acquired taste. Climb the corner on good jams until a series of hard moves allows a curious 'pancake' of rock on the right wall to be gained. Move up to the

overhang and, using holds on the left, pull through with difficulty to reach the top.

★Ain't No Wienie Roast   85 feet   E4 6a †   (22.8.90)

A high-quality pitch based on the right arête of *Pomplemousse*. Start beneath a short corner. Climb the corner to a bulge, pull awkwardly through, and move up to a horizontal break (peg runner). Utilizing a small diagonal vein of rock, make difficult, technical moves diagonally right to reach a good flake on the arête. Step up to the bulge and finish via the flake above.

Mussel Up   85 feet   E3 5c   (11.8.89)

Steep, sustained climbing up the overhanging crackline in the right-hand side of the buttress. Start just right of *Ain't No Wienie Roast* beneath a slabby wall. Climb the wall until it is possible to step left to a ledge occupied by a large flake. Move up to the crackline and climb it on insecure jams, stepping right just below its top. Finish up the scruffy continuation crack.

HIDDEN SLAB AREA   OS Ref 1300 4770

Below Grapefruit Buttress and north of Heron Zawn is a small slab at sea-level: Hidden Slab. Opposite the slab and immediately north of Heron Zawn is a small square tower-like buttress of excellent rock known as Hidden Tower.

HIDDEN TOWER

This is approached by a short traverse north from the northern spur of Heron Zawn. **Late in the Day** (35 feet Very Severe 5a 4.8.92) climbs twin cracks leading to a pod near the right arête of the tower, whilst **Head!** (35 feet Hard Very Severe 5b 24.8.93) climbs the thin crackline just left again. **Mr T** (40 feet Very Severe 5b † 4.8.92) is a short, hard, but well-protected pitch up the left-hand corner of the recess to the left of the tower.

HIDDEN SLAB

The slab gives a number of short pleasant pitches on good rock. Approach down the grassy slope 100 feet north of Heron Zawn and just south of the large boulder cove containing Cyclops Zawn to the top of the slab. From here, a short scramble down to the north leads to sea-level ledges. The central crackline gives a worthwhile 60-foot pitch of Difficult standard with harder variations possible. The wall on the north side of the descent gives two 50-foot climbs of Difficult standard.

CYCLOPS ZAWN   OS Ref 1305 4773

Not truly a zawn, this is the large cove with a boulder-strewn floor 500 yards south of the North Light and 50 yards north of Heron Zawn. It takes its name from the distinctive buttress that rises from its back and which has a large 'eye' near its summit, visible only from certain angles. To its north a clean, south-facing slab slants up from the boulder-strewn floor with the prominent crack of *Chopper Squad* in its left-hand side. Flanking the slab is a large, black, west-facing wall overlooking the northern side of the zawn, which is climbed by *Out of the Blue*.

There are two possible approaches: either scramble down the grassy slopes just north of the zawn and then down easy rock steps to the boulder floor – straightforward and with no tidal restrictions; or, slightly more demanding, descend the grassy rib beneath the south-facing slab. The latter is convenient for the first two routes described.

Reverberations   160 feet   Hard Very Severe   (4.9.86)
A curious diagonal line across the south-facing slab. Start on the grassy rib immediately above an overlap 30 feet above the obvious crack of *Chopper Squad*.
1 70 feet 5a. Traverse left above the overlap to just below a small corner. Climb this and continue up the rib and groove above, before climbing diagonally right to a belay on a foot-ledge. Good nuts in the overlap above.
2 90 feet 4b. Step right to a foothold and go over the overlap. Take a diagonal line, keeping just below the vegetation, to the top right-hand corner of the slab. Belay well back.

Beach and Surf Check   90 feet   E3 6a †   (2.8.89)
Thin, technical climbing up the blue slab left of *Reverberations*. Start at a thin crack on the grassy rib just below *Reverberations* and above and to the right of *Chopper Squad*. Climb the crack to where it disappears (poor peg runner). Crimp up the slab to an overlap and pull directly through to a junction with *Reverberations*. Climb more easily and directly to the top. Block belay well back.

Chopper Squad   120 feet   Severe   (6.8.80)
The prominent, vegetated crack in the south-facing slab. Climb the crack until just above the first overlap. Traverse horizontally right before continuing diagonally right to a second overlap. Climb this on good holds to an earthy slope and the top.

The next two climbs begin from large boulders beneath the black, west-facing wall.

Out of the Blue   190 feet   Hard Very Severe   (8.79)
Near the right-hand edge of the large black wall is a system of grooves and corners. An interesting line but the rock is suspect in a few places. Start just right of a basalt dyke.
1 90 feet 4c. Climb into a bay from the right and traverse left across the dyke into a slabby groove leading to a pinnacle high up. Continue up the groove and then slabs on the left to a peg and block belay.
2 50 feet 5a. Take the obvious traverse-line right past two peg runners and continue around the arête into a corner. Climb this to a ledge and belay.

3 50 feet. Finish easily up the slabs to the left and scramble to large thread belays above.

Blues in Sea   170 feet   Hard Very Severe †   (9.8.81)
A direct and rather serious continuation to *Out of the Blue*. Start as for that route.
1 90 feet   4c.   *Out of the Blue* pitch 1.
2 80 feet   5a.   Climb the crack and wall above to a jamming crack which leads to the top of a pinnacle. Move up and left onto some precarious jammed blocks and finish awkwardly to the right. Scramble to safe ground and good thread belays.

CORMORANT ZAWN   OS Ref 1307 4785
A small, narrow zawn 100 yards north of Cyclops Zawn and 300 yards south of the North Light. A useful landmark is a prominent, triangular block on the slopes above the zawn. It is also directly below Rock Pool Buttress, a large broken buttress at plateau-level. Its two routes to date lie on the south wall of the zawn, which at this point is a narrow water-filled inlet leading into a sea-cave. The climbs take the left and right-hand cracklines respectively.

Approach by scrambling down the southern spur of the zawn to some large blocks. A short abseil down the zawn's seaward face leads to small sea-level ledges exposed from low to mid tide.

The Great White   100 feet   E2 5b †   (5.8.89)
The right-hand crack slants to the right. Start on ledges at a slightly higher level. Climb directly to the crack and follow it to a good ledge below a large overhang at 60 feet. Ascend a short corner above the left-hand end of the ledge to reach the prominent ramp. Climb this to the top, taking care with the loose rock.

The Buoy Prophet   100 feet   E2 5b †   (4.8.89)
The left-hand crack and steep slab above give an enjoyable but poorly-protected pitch. Step left from the belay into a groove and climb it with increasing difficulty to a small ledge below the slab. Trend left at first and then climb up the centre of the slab, following a faint crackline, to gain and finish up the obvious ramp.

ROCK POOL BUTTRESS   OS Ref 1317 4787
About 300 yards south of the North Light are a group of small buttresses just below plateau-level. Rock Pool Buttress is the largest of these. Its position is due west of the point where the track begins to lose height, and it can be recognized in most climatic conditions by a small rock pool on its flat summit.

Transition   120 feet   Severe   (26.9.69)
A scruffy line up the left flank of the buttress. Vegetated. Start just left of a triangular recess in the centre of the crag, beneath a subsidiary buttress.

1 40 feet. The broken groove to the left of the recess leads to a large ledge with a good belay.
2 80 feet. Follow a grassy crackline up the slabs to the left to a ledge on the north flank of the buttress (belay possible). Continue up wide, rounded cracks to the summit.

★**Fish out of Water**   80 feet   E3 5c   (4.8.89)
Savage climbing up the prominent roofed crack in the south wall of the buttress north of Rock Pool Buttress. Wonderfully obscure. Start beneath a short left-facing corner some way up the gully. Move up to the corner and climb it to the roof. Cross this on good jams and flounder over into a short corner. Continue up the rightward-trending line beneath the overhangs to a slabby finish.

STORM ZAWN   OS Ref 1311 4792
This remote, steep-walled zawn is the most northerly on this section of coast. Its location is just north of Cormorant Zawn and immediately south of a large sea-channel. At the back of the zawn a deep cave disappears into the bowels of the island and can provide some fascinating exploring after stormy weather. The zawn's solitary route to date ascends the narrow wall to the right of the cave.

The approach is by abseil from large blocks at the top of the northern spur of the zawn. The boulder-beach below is exposed for two hours either side of low tide.

Herbert Bronski's Back   140 feet   E2 5b †   (27.8.93)
A big, adventurous pitch up the narrow wall at the back of the zawn, finishing up the exposed upper arête overlooking the cave. A preplaced belay rope to the top of the route safeguards the exit. Start beneath a straight, deep crack in the right-hand side of the narrow wall. Climb the crack on excellent jams and trend leftwards after 30 feet towards the arête to reach a guano-streaked ledge and some large flakes. Ascend direct (peg runner on the left) to a small ledge (peg runner). Continue boldly up the arête on hollow but positive holds (peg runner) to reach a cleaned ledge and the preplaced belay rope. Scramble up steep grass to the top.

North Light Area   OS Ref 1306 4797

The final cliffs on the west coast are situated at the northern end of the large bay to the south of the North Light. There are three buttresses which, although short, are of generally excellent rock and are easily accessible. The cliffs face south-west and are separated from each other by narrow sea-channels and a series of basalt dykes that run the full height of the cliff.

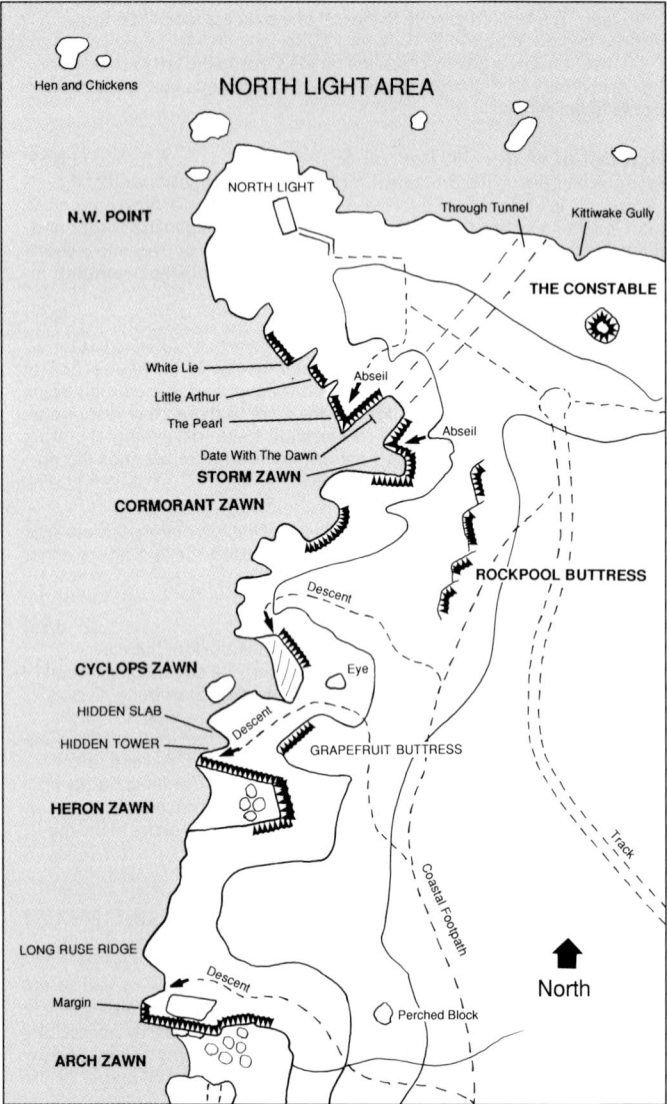

Hen and Chickens

NORTH LIGHT AREA

NORTH LIGHT

N.W. POINT

Through Tunnel

Kittiwake Gully

THE CONSTABLE

White Lie

Little Arthur

The Pearl

Abseil

Date With The Dawn

STORM ZAWN

Abseil

CORMORANT ZAWN

ROCKPOOL BUTTRESS

Descent

CYCLOPS ZAWN

Eye

HIDDEN SLAB

HIDDEN TOWER

Descent

GRAPEFRUIT BUTTRESS

HERON ZAWN

LONG RUSE RIDGE

Descent

Coastal Footpath

Track

North

Margin

Perched Block

ARCH ZAWN

Descend the first set of steps to the lighthouse and then walk down the grassy slope to the south to some large blocks at the top of the buttresses. A 90-foot abseil down the seaward face of Right-Hand Buttress reaches a large platform at its foot. This is non-tidal, although low to mid tide is required to cross to Central Buttress.

Bounding Right-Hand Buttress is a large, steep-walled sea-channel. This cuts dramatically through North West Point to emerge on the north coast below the North Light. The first route in this area takes a line up the east wall of the channel and is gained by a 150-foot abseil down the rocky spur overlooking Storm Zawn.

★**Mary Patricia Rosalea**   170 feet   Hard Very Severe †   (26.8.93)
A well-positioned climb taking a diagonal line up the white, lower wall to gain a prominent, pod-shaped groove in the wall above. Start by traversing north along the wall of the sea-channel to a recessed ledge just above high water.
1 80 feet 4c. Traverse left on good holds and follow a gradually rising line to join an arête. Climb this to a belay on the basalt dyke beneath the pod-shaped groove.
2 90 feet 5a. A gritstoner's delight! Move up to the groove, and jam and layback up it to a small ledge. Climb the leftward-leaning groove above to the top. Good block belays.

The next four routes venture onto the west wall of the sea-channel and all start from a large non-tidal platform beneath Right-Hand Buttress, overlooking the channel.

Date with the Dawn   160 feet   E1   (13.8.81)
A secluded route with good situations, marred only by some very poor rock on the top pitch. Start on the large platform.
1 80 feet 4c. Step down slightly and traverse right to a basalt dyke. Cross this and follow an ascending traverse-line into the stepped corner on the right. Climb the cracked right wall of the corner to belay on the first of a series of white ledges.
2 80 feet 5a. Move up to the right-hand of two groove-lines and climb it to an overhang. Step left and follow a loose, wide crack to easy ground. Scramble first right and then left to the top.

★**A Night Out with Doris**   170 feet   E2   (29.8.85)
An exciting and strenuous excursion onto the steep wall to the left of the top pitch of *Date with the Dawn*.
1 80 feet 4c. *Date with the Dawn* pitch 1.
2 90 feet 5b. Climb the left-hand groove for a few feet, and then follow the obvious hand-traverse leftwards into the centre of the wall. Pull round onto a slab and move up to the base of a small chimney. Stride left and go over a bulge on good hidden holds, and continue directly to the top. Block belays.

★The Abyss   100 feet   E3 6a †   (27.8.93)
The elegant, undercut groove above the traverse of *Date with the Dawn*. A very technical crux with good protection. Step down and traverse right as for *Date with the Dawn* across the basalt dyke until below a steep right-facing groove. Move up to the groove and climb its right wall to the second of two horizontal breaks. Step right and make a difficult pull over the overhang into the undercut groove (peg runner). Climb the slabby right wall of the groove to the base of a small chimney. Step left and pull over an overhang to reach the easier upper wall. Climb this to good block belays at the top.

★Song to the Siren   90 feet   E3 5c †   (26.8.93)
Powerful climbing up the steep crack in the left-hand side of the wall. Strenuous but with good protection. Climb *The Abyss* to the second horizontal break and step left into the top of the right-facing groove. Swing confidently round the overhang above to gain the base of the crack, and climb it quickly and directly to the top.

RIGHT-HAND BUTTRESS
The seaward face of Right-Hand Buttress has a large tidal rock pool at its foot.

Northern Lights   75 feet   E3 5c †   (27.8.93)
The short but deceptively difficult crack in the right arête of the buttress. Start on the platform beneath the crack. Climb up to the base of the crack and make committing moves up it to a good ledge. The straight thin crack above provides the finish.

Promenade   80 feet   Hard Very Severe 5a †   (5.8.82)
The slim ramp crossing the wall to the left of *Northern Lights*. No stroll at the grade. Start at the first groove to the left of *Northern Lights*. Climb up to gain the rightward-trending ramp and tiptoe along it before stepping up to the good ledge. Climb the thin slanting crack above to the top.

An unsatisfactory climb, **Sea Front** (80 feet Very Severe 4c 12.8.81), starts up the small groove just left of *Promenade* and finishes up the straight thin crack of *Northern Lights*.

★The Pearl   75 feet   Hard Very Severe 5b   (5.8.82)
A little gem. The discontinuous corner-system in the centre of the buttress, directly above the large rock pool. Move up to a slim corner just right of a chimney and climb it. A step left across the top of the chimney gains a small ledge in the corner. Go up the corner and surmount the overhang above to reach a good ledge. Finish up the continuation corner in the wall to the right.

Struggler's Sidestep   70 feet   Very Severe 4c †   (9.8.81)
Start as for *The Pearl* but struggle up the short chimney and the corner above to the overhang of that route. Traverse left beneath the overhang until a step up gains a short bottomless groove. Follow this to the top.

NORTH LIGHT AREA

1 Date with the Dawn	E1	
2 A Night Out with Doris	E2	
3 The Abyss	E3	
4 Song to the Siren	E3	
5 Northern Lights	E3	
6 Promenade	HVS	
7 The Full Monty	HVS	
8 Stuff at the Top	E2	
9 White Lie	VS	

All the Business   60 feet   Hard Very Severe   5a   (12.8.81)
A good pitch up the slim corner in the left-hand edge of the buttress and just right of a large basalt dyke.

CENTRAL BUTTRESS
The Full Monty   70 feet   Hard Very Severe   5a   (12.8.81)
Good Value. Climb the corner in the right-hand edge of the buttress, just left of the large basalt dyke. Continue over some large blocks to finish.

Stuff at the Top   70 feet   E2   6a †   (26.8.93)
A rightward-trending ramp crosses the centre of the buttress. Reach the left-hand end of the ramp by a technical move over a small overlap and follow it more easily to a flake finish.

Dave the Knock   70 feet   Very Severe   4c †   (26.8.93)
Climb a series of slim corners in the arête immediately left of *Stuff at the Top* and just right of a larger, left-facing corner. Continue up the easiest line above to the top.

Little Arthur   70 feet   Very Severe   4c   (21.8.93)
An enjoyable pitch up the prominent left-facing corner. Step left at the bulge and follow an easier continuation corner to some good ledges. Climb over large blocks to the top.

Waiting for the Sun   70 feet   Hard Severe   4b   (5.8.87)
In the left-hand side of the buttress are two slanting cracks in a slab above a rock step. Climb the right-hand crack and move right beneath a small overlap. Continue along a line of rightward-trending flakes to a ledge. Scramble over blocky rock to finish.

Rock Obster   70 feet   Very Severe   4b   (24.8.93)
Traverse left to the left-hand crack and climb it to a good ledge. Continue over blocky rock to the top.

LEFT-HAND BUTTRESS
The buttress is approached by scrambling down the easy ledges to its west. It contains just one route, **White Lie** (60 feet Very Severe 4b 30.7.89). A pleasant pitch up the clean, right-hand arête of the buttress.

Situated at North West Point is the North Light lighthouse. The cliffs here are short and broken and there is little of interest to the climber. Just offshore are the Hen and Chickens: these treacherous rocks with their foaming tidal race have been the graveyard for many a shipwrecked mariner. Hours can be spent here watching the seals at play off Seal's Rock, and the more diligent observer may see dolphins or perhaps a basking shark. Of course, a trip to the North End would be incomplete without an ascent of:

The Constable

I have viewed rock specialities all over the five continents, but The Constable looks among the most difficult, and I understand has never been climbed.
(*The Tempestuous Isle*, 1950 by Colonel P T Etherington and Vernon Barlow)

Rising proudly from the steep grassy slopes at the north end of the island, this granite monolith stands sentinel-like over the ocean stretching away to South Wales and beyond. Local legend has it that The Constable was a Cornish giant who came to Lundy to rid it of snakes and other reptiles. His task complete, he was then turned into the monolith. Some reward!

The Constable is situated 300 yards south-east of the North Light and directly below the northern end of the main track. Reaching 80 feet on its northern face, it can muster barely half that on the more broken southerly face. Descent from the narrow summit ridge is by abseil from large spike belays, from which it may be desirable to leave a long sling in place. The climbs are described **from the south in an anti-clockwise direction.** The south face is split by three cracklines.

Thug   50 feet   E1 5b   (18.8.80)
The left-hand crack is aptly named and would not look out of place at Ramshaw Rocks! Move easily up to the base of the crack and climb it strenuously until a wider crack on the right can be gained. Grovel up this to a tricky finishing-groove.

Eveninawl   45 feet   Very Severe 4c   (6.7.71)
The central crackline. Ascend the corner just right of *Thug* and exit with difficulty to the right. Move up, then traverse left, and go awkwardly up into the finishing-groove of *Thug*.

The Original Route   40 feet   Hard Severe 4b   (6.61)
One of the earliest routes on the island. Start at a large detached block above and right of *Eveninawl*. Move up and right into the steep right-hand crack and climb it to a point 6 feet left of the summit.

The east face begins at a lower level and is split by a clean jamming-crack in its lower half.

★The Chief Constable   65 feet   E4 6a †   (4.8.89)
An attractive line. The delightful crack leads to a bold and precarious finish. Jam up the crack to a horizontal break and good *Friend* placements. Crux moves up the thin flake above lead into a deceptively difficult finishing-groove.

The Constable.

Jude the Obscure 70 feet   Hard Very Severe 5a   (20.4.79)
Even more obscure since recent direct additions. Worthwhile nevertheless.
Start as for *The Chief Constable*. Climb the jamming-crack and step right
to gain the arête at a small flake. Stand on the flake; then traverse right to
a deep crackline on the north face, which leads to the top.

★**Serious Climbs Squad** 70 feet   E2 5c   (4.8.89)
The elegant north-east arête of The Constable. Poorly protected. Climb
the arête on its right-hand side with a particularly thin stretch to good
holds and a small ledge. Step right into the deep crackline of *Jude the
Obscure* and climb it to the top.

Naked Gun 80 feet   E2 5b   (18.8.90)
This successfully avoids the challenge of The Constable's north face! Start
at the foot of a crack in its centre. Climb the crack to an overlap. Go over,
and traverse right along a line of rightward-leaning flakes to a small
ledge above. Continue in the same line to a junction with the much larger
flake of *The Summons*. Traverse left past an ancient peg runner to gain a
stubborn finishing-crack.

★**Caught in the Act** 75 feet   E1 5b   (18.8.90)
An arresting little pitch and the best way up the north-west arête. Start at
the foot of a clean, brown-streaked groove. Ascend the groove with a nice
balance of delicate and strenuous climbing to a small sloping ledge on
the arête. Move up to the flake crack of *The Summons* and climb it to the
top.

The Summons 70 feet   Hard Very Severe 5b   (6.7.71)
The bristly flake crack high on the north-west arête. Start on the jumble of
bocks below the arête. Climb easily over broken rock on the right to gain
a standing-position on a small sloping ledge to the left. Difficult moves up
and left lead to good holds at the base the flake. A brisk layback brings
the top within reach.

The East Coast

The climbing on the east coast of Lundy is in total contrast to that on the
west coast. A small collection of old quarries and isolated buttresses
protrude from the bracken and rhododendron-clad slopes, presenting an
altogether more tranquil aspect. There are some pleasant climbs here that
are worth seeking out, particularly in the lower grades. These require little
commitment and have no great access problems. The coast can also
provide a welcome haven when the fierce westerly winds are blowing in
from the Atlantic.

The climbs are described from the south and **left to right.**

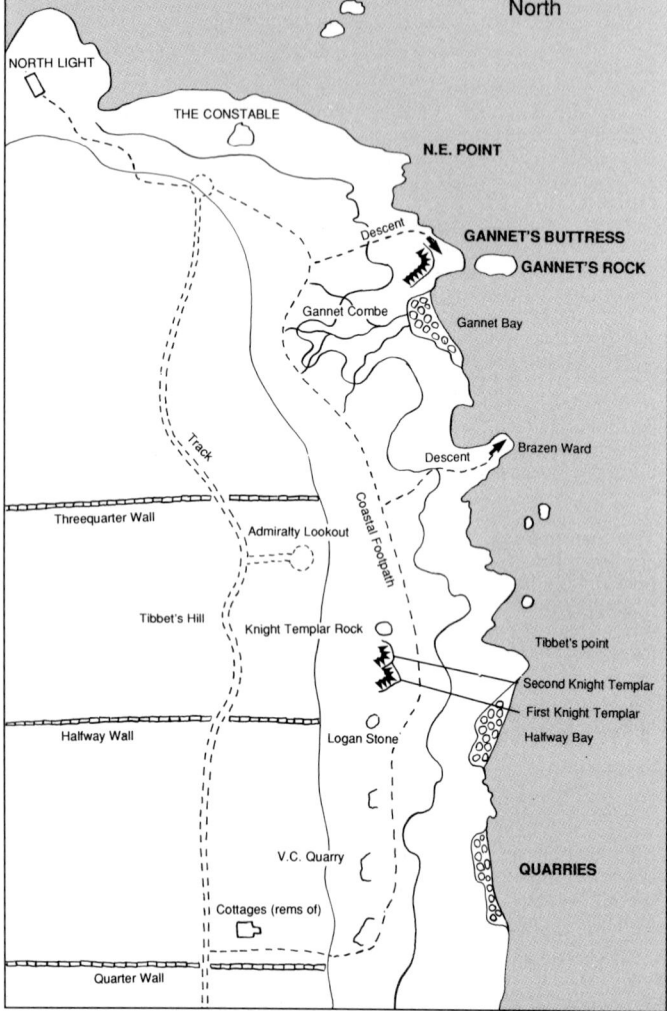

EAST COAST

N.W. POINT

NORTH LIGHT

THE CONSTABLE

N.E. POINT

North

Descent

GANNET'S BUTTRESS

GANNET'S ROCK

Gannet Combe

Gannet Bay

Track

Descent

Brazen Ward

Threequarter Wall

Admiralty Lookout

Tibbet's Hill

Knight Templar Rock

Coastal Footpath

Tibbet's point

Second Knight Templar

First Knight Templar

Halfway Wall

Logan Stone

Halfway Bay

V.C. Quarry

QUARRIES

Cottages (rems of)

Quarter Wall

THE QUARRIES

The quarries were at their productive peak at the turn of the century. They provided employment for over 140 workmen and boasted their own tramway and jetty. They now provide a number of short pitches in generally dismal, though sheltered surroundings. From the eastern end of Quarter Wall a track leads down to a good path that contours along the east coast.

There are three quarries. The first encountered (OS Ref 1376 4503) is distinguished by an old goldfish pond at its foot. There is a straightforward aid pitch and a number of short problem pitches. Further north is VC Quarry (OS Ref 1386 4537), which provides a number of short, broken pitches. The final and largest quarry (OS Ref 1382 4559) is situated just north of VC Quarry. **St Swithin's XIII** (60 feet A2 9.6.66) pegged its way up the impending south wall above the remains of a dry-stone wall. More substantial is **St Loosifer** (70 feet E2 5b 10.8.79) which climbs the deceptively difficult ramp in the back wall of the quarry; three peg runners may be in place. The north wall of the quarry has a few isolated problems.

THE HALFWAY BUTTRESSES & KNIGHT TEMPLAR ROCK

The Halfway Buttresses are a collection of small jumbled outcrops grouped around the eastern end of Halfway Wall. Further north can be seen two much larger, broken buttresses – First and Second Knight Templar respectively. The Knight Templar Rock itself is approximately 100 yards north of Second Knight Templar.

The approaches to all these buttresses can be particularly tedious in the summer and early autumn, when the dense bracken makes progress very trying. It is advisable to stay on the paths as much as possible, venturing into the bracken only when necessary.

THE HALFWAY BUTTRESSES   OS Ref 1382 4590
Directly below Halfway Wall is The Logan Stone. This large block is perched on top of a narrow granite pedestal but no longer rocks. It does, however, give one route, **Logan** (50 feet Very Difficult 7.65), up the slender seaward face of the pedestal with variation pitches to either side.

Below the Logan Stone and directly in line with Halfway Wall is another, larger buttress. **Rubus** (75 feet Hard Severe 7.81) traverses diagonally left across the slab at the foot of the buttress, continuing over blocks and up a vegetated corner to the top. **No Shots** (50 feet Hard Very Severe 5a 7.81) climbs the steep crack in the landward side of the buttress to a ledge, before moving right and up to finish.

A few yards north of these two buttresses are three smaller buttresses. The leftmost and southerly buttress is very vegetated and broken, giving two scrappy climbs of Difficult standard up its slabby, seaward face. The central buttress is lower down the hillside and gives one reasonable climb. **Hard Labour** (50 feet Very Severe 4c 27.3.67) climbs a crack in the left edge of the front of the buttress to an overhang, finishing up the continuation chimney. The foot of the right-hand buttress is separated from the summit of the central buttress by a small col. It has one short and unpleasant route of Very Difficult standard. There is one further buttress, higher up and to the right. This is small and of little interest to the climber.

FIRST KNIGHT TEMPLAR   OS Ref 1389 4603
The routes take lines up either side of the vegetated central section of the buttress. The white rib on the left-hand side of the cliff is climbed by *Bored* and *Twelve Bore*, whilst *Bideford Ridge* makes the most of the broken rib bounding the right-hand side.

Bored   80 feet   E1 5a †   (20.8.90)
Bold and direct. The smooth, white rib. Climb directly to and up the rib on its right-hand side until just above an overlap. Step left and follow the slab and arête to a ledge and the top.

Twelve Bore   85 feet   Very Severe   4b   (14.5.69)
Start as for *Bored*, beneath the clean, white rib. Climb the rib for 30 feet to just above the overlap. Move diagonally right and climb the wide, vegetated crackline 6 feet right of the arête to the top.

Permanent Nerve Damage   90 feet   E1 5b   (25.3.89)
A good clean pitch up the smooth, overlapping slabs to the right of *Twelve Bore*. Start at a clean rib below the slabs, 20 feet right of *Twelve Bore*. Climb the rib to a small overlap and move up and rightwards to a second overlap. Step left and go over this at its narrowest point to a smooth slab. Climb directly up the slab, past a thin horizontal break, to reach some good flakes below a larger overlap. Move left until good holds lead up to a final bulge and white slab to finish. Spike belay above.

Bideford Ridge   110 feet   Very Difficult   (4.63)
A pleasant, though escapable climb up the broken, right-hand rib of the buttress. Start at a step in the arête about 40 feet up, and below the first steep section.
1 30 feet. The block above is split by two cracks. Climb the left-hand crack to a large ledge.
2 50 feet. Climb easily up the broken slab to the left of the arête for 10 feet. Traverse right onto the arête above a steep section and follow it to a ledge.
3 30 feet. Move up to the left onto a flake and continue up the short crack above to the top.

SECOND KNIGHT TEMPLAR   OS Ref 1392 4607
The cliff is split by a large platform just above half height; this is more distinct to the right and more vegetated to the left. Below the ledge, in the centre of the cliff, is a pinkish wall which is broken and vegetated. To its right is a steeper, cleaner area of rock with the groove of *Scafoid* in its centre. The first climb can be found on the left, southerly, wall of the

southern descent gully: **Blood Crystal** (40 feet E1 5c † 6.4.87) climbs the prominent right-to-left-slanting crack.

Scafoid   150 feet   Very Severe   (20.3.72)

The clean groove in the centre of the wall. Start below and to its right.

1 80 feet 4c. Move up to the groove and climb it (poor protection) to an overhang. Step out right and move up into a niche. Continue up the cracks above to a good belay ledge.

2 70 feet. Follow the juggy grooves above to the top.

Variations

Left Hand Finish   Hard Very Severe 5a   (1.9.92)

At the step right on pitch 1, instead climb diagonally left between two overhangs to finish up a wide crack.

Foot Off   Very Severe   (4.72)

1a 80 feet 4c. Follow pitch 1 to the overhang; then traverse left to a large sloping ledge (belay possible). Climb the deep groove on the right to the belay ledge.

Sepulchre   Very Severe   (3.9.88)

1b 80 feet 4c. Start 10 feet left of pitch 1 at a rock pinnacle. Ascend the wall trending left until beneath a large overlapping slab. Pull onto this and climb its left edge to a junction with *Foot Off* at the large sloping ledge.

★**Flake Route**   130 feet   Very Difficult   (1964)

Short, clean pitches interspersed with good belay ledges. A good route, perhaps the best of the easier-grade routes on this coast. Start at the bottom right-hand corner of the smooth wall, below a prominent jutting block.

1 20 feet. Climb easily over blocks to a belay ledge below a large flake just right of the prominent block.

2 40 feet. Traverse steeply up to the left for 10 feet to below the overhang formed by the base of the large flake. Surmount this on large holds and proceed up the crack to the left of the flake to a belay at its top.

3 20 feet. Move up to the ledge above and climb a short, steep groove to the large platform.

4 50 feet. Continue up the groove in the large block above to the top.

KNIGHT TEMPLAR ROCK   OS Ref 1387 4616

Viewed from the south, the rock presents an uncanny profile of a helmeted face gazing defiantly out to sea. The central section of the southern side of the rock is capped by overhangs. A poor route, **Heatwave** (70 feet Very Difficult), climbs the broken corner-line to the left of these, with a tougher, Very Severe finish available through the overhangs to the right.

Fat Freddy's Cat   95 feet   Hard Very Severe   (16.9.82)

A worthwhile route with an exciting finish through the right-hand side of the big overhangs. Start at a rib, 5 feet left of a short V-groove capped by a small overhang.

1 65 feet 5a. Climb the rib past a bulge into a rightward-slanting groove, which leads in turn to an overhang. Step left and pull over another bulge into a groove. Climb this for 10 feet to where an obvious traverse leads right to a stance below the large overhangs.
2 30 feet 5a. Move up to the overhangs and climb the right-hand of two cracks to a good hold. Pull out onto the exposed rib and follow it to the top.

Crusader   90 feet   Very Severe   (13.4.63)
An interesting route with an intimidating first pitch. Start below the second groove to the right of *Fat Freddy's Cat*.
1 60 feet 4c. Climb the groove to a slab and flake (belay possible). Move up to the right of a narrow, overhanging chimney and take a stance below the overhangs.
2 30 feet. Traverse right across the slab to a nose of rock and continue up an easy corner to finish.
Direct Finish   Very Severe   (1967)
2a 25 feet 4c. A short, steep problem up the wide, shallow chimney to the right of the overhangs. Finish up the crack above.

A poor climb, **Sir Gareth** (90 feet Severe 14.5.69), takes a line up broken vegetated rock from the foot of *Crusader* to the top of *Saladin*.

Big Ed   90 feet   Very Severe   (22.10.78)
The rib to the right of *Crusader* and 10 feet left of *Saladin*. Start below a small overhang.
1 60 feet 4b. Turn the overhang on its right-hand side and make an awkward step left onto the rib. Follow this over a bulge at 40 feet to a ledge on the front of the buttress.
2 30 feet. *Crusader* pitch 2.

Saladin   90 feet   Very Severe   (26.3.67)
A good initial pitch, sustained and deceptively steep. Start below a steep crack in the front of the buttress.
1 70 feet 4c. Climb the crack for 30 feet; then follow the obvious line up to the right until almost on the arête. Continue up to a large ledge on the left and a belay.
2 20 feet. The easy corner of *Crusader* is climbed to the top. Alternatively, climb the broken wall on the right.

The tapering chimney to the right of *Saladin* is reached from the vegetated slab below: this is **Split Infinitives** (90 feet Severe 8.8.85). In the north face of the buttress are two distinctive corners: **Fag Ash** (70 feet Difficult 5.68) climbs the left-hand corner, very close to front of the buttress; **White Horse** (70 feet Very Difficult 9.68) climbs the right-hand corner with a chimney in its upper section. The short corner to the right of *White Horse* is taken by **Can I Have a Mars Bar Please?** (70 feet Very Severe 4c † 26.3.87), which then moves right to climb a bottomless groove. At a higher level is a grassy ramp, just left of some bulging overhangs.

The Jolly Rodger (30 feet Very Severe 5a † 6.6.90) takes a strenuous line up a wall, crack, and triangular block 25 feet left of the ramp. **Sir Patrick Splends** (30 feet E2 5b † 2.8.86) starts just right of the ramp and climbs a small corner, a crack, and the wall above, finishing direct.

GANNET'S ROCK AREA

Approximately 700 yards north of Threequarter Wall is a shallow, secluded valley which runs all the way down to the sea: Gannet's Combe. Gannet's Rock is the large rock island at the northern end of the combe and Gannet's Buttress the large, white buttress overlooking the island. Sadly, the gannets have long gone.

GANNET'S BUTTRESS   OS Ref 1365 4756

The approach lies down a steep path on the north side of the buttress which leads in turn to a long, sloping ledge crossing the buttress at half height. A short scramble down easy rock then gains the tidal ledges at its foot. The rock below the ledge is steep but very broken and consequently it is possible to climb anywhere without too much difficulty. However, **Gannet's Traverse**, a 200-foot Moderate, takes an interesting diagonal line across this area. Start from the foot of the descent and keep below the half-way ledge to finish up the left side of the buttress where the angle relents.

On the south face is a large, black wall above the half-way ledge. This can be reached by walking along the ledge or by scrambling down from the west side of the buttress. In the left-hand side of the wall is an inverted U-shaped overhang at 25 feet, giving a short climb, **Gannex** (40 feet Very Severe). **Tytler's Cop Out** (50 feet Very Severe 5a † 6.10.87) climbs a thin crack 10 feet left of *Gannex* before traversing into that climb to finish. Also starting from the ledge is:

The Squirmer   90 feet   Very Severe †   (27.3.67)
Start below a jammed block in a break, 25 feet left of a right-angled corner.
1 50 feet. Climb up to a niche above the block and move right along a sloping crack before stepping up to a higher crack. Move right to a grass ledge and continue up the crack above.
2 40 feet. Traverse left to a shallow cave and climb the chimney above to a slab. Stride left across this to a finishing-chimney.

★Stormbound   80 feet   E3 6a   (11.8.89)
Steep climbing up the impressive wall some 40 feet right of *The Squirmer* and left of the top pitch of *Gannet Front*. Start above the half-way ledge below a prominent small roof. Pull over the roof to reach a scoop with an overlap above and climb this and the short groove above to a thin crack. Follow the crack with difficulty to reach a short, shallow, wide crack at the

left-hand end of a thin, long roof (peg runner above). Foot-traverse the ledge above the roof for 10 feet to a good hidden hold; then pull over the bulge and finish easily rightwards.

★**Gannet Front**   210 feet   Hard Very Severe   (6.71/4.74)
A good climb following the crest of the buttress with a difficult, well-positioned crux. Start at sea-level at the foot of the descent route.
1 90 feet. Take a line up easy rock, to the left of a blunt arête, to a belay at the foot of a groove.
2 25 feet 4c. Climb the groove and belay on the half-way ledge below a large pinnacle.
3 95 feet 5b. Ascend the pinnacle and a short, shallow groove before moving left and up to below a bulging arête. Cross the arête by moving below a bulge to reach good holds on the impending wall above. Difficult moves up the steep wall lead to the easier finishing slabs.

★**Gale Force**   90 feet   E2 5c   (11.8.89)
The fine jamming-crack just left of the pinnacle of *Gannet Front*. Start on the half-way ledge beneath the crack. Climb the crack to a large ledge on *Gannet Front*. Move up to the bulge on the right and pull up and right to reach a good hidden layaway. Swing boldly over to get established above the bulge, and then climb easily rightwards to belay in a large 'nest'. A short scramble remains, followed by a nice little jump!

Arrowhead   200 feet   Very Severe   (9.7.66)
The main pitch climbs the large overhung chimney in the north-eastern nose of the buttress. Start as for *Gannet Front*.
1 90 feet. *Gannet Front* pitch 1.
2 50 feet 4a. Go diagonally left to the half-way ledge, and walk back right along it to climb broken rock to the pinnacle of *Gannet Front*. Move right again to belay in a niche.
3 60 feet 4b. Using the overhanging block above the belay, pull steeply up into the chimney and climb it and its continuation to the top.

On the descent to *Gannet Front*, a steep north-facing wall is passed; here lurks: **The Gannet That Was Still Hungry** (65 feet E1 5b † 15.8.90) which climbs a series of black-streaked grooves in the centre of the wall.

GANNET'S ROCK   OS Ref 1370 4758
The sea-level boulders that lead out to the Rock can be crossed only at low tide, and are reached by a brief scramble from the foot of Gannet's Buttress. The summit can be gained by traversing easily round to the south face and then taking a zigzag line, with some Difficult standard climbing, to the easy-angled seaward ridge. The ridge can also be reached by taking a line across the north face, starting up the first 30 feet of *Gannet's Rock Crack* at Very Difficult standard.

Gannet's Rock Crack   100 feet   Hard Severe   (7.65)
The ascent of the prominent crack in the landward face gives an

interesting excursion. Start from a grass ledge with a prominent boulder, some 50 feet above the boulders between the Rock and the mainland.

1 50 feet. Climb a broken groove on the left to a ledge that leads round onto the north face. Continue up and then back right to a belay ledge below the crack in the landward face.

2 50 feet. Ascend the crack directly to the summit. The descent lies down the seaward ridge and then by a traverse back across the south face. An exciting tyrolean traverse back to the mainland is also possible.

First Ascents

1961 June	**Gannet Front** J Logan, R Shaw (AL)
	Previously referred to as The Original Route. The described finish was climbed by R S Macnair and N Allen in April 1974. The original finish went off to the right but it is not known exactly where.
1961 June	**The Original Route** (The Constable) J Logan, R Shaw
1961 June	**The Devil's Slide** K M Lawder, J Logan
	The largest granite slab in Britain and a major breakthrough. The Direct Finish was climbed by P H Biven in April 1971 though there are rumours that a Bill E Goat climbed it first!
1961 June	**The Ordinary Route** (Needle Rock) K M Lawder, E C Pyatt
1961 June	**Devil's Chimney** R Shaw, J Logan (AL)
	Pitch 2 as described was climbed by R J Tancred and R S Macnair in August 1969.
1962 Aug	**Flying Buttress** P H Biven, C Fishwick, A Goodwin
1963 Easter	**Bideford Ridge** P H Biven, C Fishwick (AL)
1963 April 13	**Crusader** P H Biven, C Fishwick (AL)
	The Direct Finish was climbed by G Clarke, J B Cooper in 1967 as a finish to Saladin.
1963 April 15	**Devil's Spine** V N Stevenson, P H Biven, C Fishwick, A Goodwin
	Pitch 3 was originally climbed by a diversion into the gully on the right. Pitch 3 as described was first climbed by R D Moulton, P Cannings, G J Gilbert on 18 April 1973.
1963 April 15	**Albion** P H Biven, V N Stevenson (AL), C Fishwick
	The Direct Finish was added by P H Biven in April 1971 with two pegs for aid and climbed free as Devil's Downfall by M Edwards, R Cooper at Easter 1985.
1963 April	**Capuccino, Alouette, Thread** P H Biven and party
1964 Summer	**Flake Route** M Steele, C Dyson
1964 Oct	**Horseman's Route** J F McBratney, P Gwilliam
	The Variation Start was soloed by G Gibson in July 1983. Riding High was climbed by G Robinson, N Preston and K Smith in September 1982.
1965 May 2	**Battery Rib** B Martindale, T Wright (AL)
1965 May 5	**Puffins' Parade** B Martindale, J F McBratney (AL)
1965 May 5	**Diamond Solitaire** J F McBratney, B Martindale (AL)
	The original ascent used some aid in wet conditions but went free to the same team the following day in much drier weather.
1965 May	**The Obverse Route** A Swan, B Martindale
1965 May	**Tindale Route** (2 pts aid) B Martindale, T Wright, J F McBratney
	The route had to wait fifteen years for a second and free ascent by G Gibson and D Beetlestone in August 1980.
1965 July	**Gannet's Rock Crack** R Tyler, H Tyler
1965 July	**Logan** R S D Smith, P N Cooke
1966 June 3	**Ember Wall** R B Quine, D W Limbert
1966 June 9	**St Swithin's XXIII** M T Mills, W N Tolfree
1966 July 9	**Arrowhead** P Wenham, R S D Smith (AL)
1966	*Rock Climbing in Devonshire* by **R D Moulton**

1966 Sept 28	**Seal Slab** I M Peters, K M Lawder, M G White
1966 Sept 28	**Crenellation Groove** I M Peters, K M Lawder
1967 March 26	**Saladin** G Clarke, J B Cooper
1967 March 27	**The Squirmer** G Clarke, J B Cooper
1967 March 27	**Hard Labour** D W Brown, P Bingham, J Gill
1967 March 28	**Dyke** M J Luetchford, J Barraclough
1967 March 28	**Start** J Barraclough, M J Luetchford
1967 March 28	**Banana Crack** P Bingham, J Gill
1967 March 29	**Integrity** D W Brown, P Bingham, J Gill, J A Gaskill
1967 March 29	**Mellow Yellow** P Bingham, J Gill
1967 March 30	**Banana Split** G Clarke, J B Cooper
1967 March 30	**Solitaire View** P Bingham, J Gill
1967 March 30	**Rehabilitation Slab** J B Cooper (solo)
	Originally known as Rehabilitation Wall.
1967 March 30	**Norseman** M J Luetchford, J Barraclough
1967 March 30	**Forgotten Pinnacle** J Barraclough, M J Luetchford
1967 March 31	**Stingray** J Barraclough, M J Luetchford
	Remained the island's hardest route for some time.
1967 March 31	**Cornflake Crack** G Clarke, M J Luetchfor
1967 June	**Walrus** S Dawson, D Rogers (AL)
1968 May 28	**Alice** K Vickery, D Vickery
1968 May	**Fag Ash** W N Tolfree, K Vickery
1968 Sept	**White Horse** R J Ebdon, H A M Warren
1969 April 28	**Long Ruse Ridge** K M Lawder, I M Peters (AL) M E B Banks
	The variations were climbed by S Westmacott and M Westmacott in September 1975 as Long Ruse Ridge Direct and by I Richards and P Rogers in August 1979 as a climb called Goat.
1969 April 30	**Rubus** M E B Banks, I M Peters
1969 May 14	**Twelve Bore** G Raymont, S Miller
1969 May 14	**Sir Gareth** W N Tolfree, M T Mills
1969 May 23	**Force Eight** W N Tolfree, G Raymont
1969 May 23	**Stuka** G Raymont, W N Tolfree
1969 July 20	**Short Story** S Miller, K Vickery
	The Direct Finish was added by S Cardy and P Harrison on 5 August 1987.
1969 Aug	**Punchbowl Arête** R D Moulton, J L Moulton
1969 Sept 26	**Transition** M E B Banks, K M Lawder, J Douglas
1969 Sept 30	**Cable Way** I M Peters, M E B Banks (AL)
	Variation 1 by N Elliot, T Gifford; Variation 2 by D Craig. Both on 29 October 1981.

1970   *Lundy Rock Climbs: First Edition* by **R D Moulton**

1970 March 29	**Satan's Slip** L P Fatti, D G Ward
	The first route on the island to utilize a bolt runner. Removed by I F Duckworth in August 1980. A swift blow with a karabiner was all that was needed to remove a very rusty piece of metal.
1970 March 29	**Dexter** T J Kerrich, L P Fatti
	Climbed in reverse as a route finishing up Devil's Spine. Climbed as described and used as an approach to Fluted Face by R D Moulton and T D Thompson on 8 May 1971.
1970 March 31	**Focal Face** T J Kerrich, L P Fatti (AL)
1970 Aug 1	**The Bow** (1 pt aid) L P Fatti, T J Kerrich
1970 Aug 29	**Devil Dodger** R D Moulton, R B Stone (AL)
1970 Aug 29	**Forget-Me-Not** J Hammond, R D Moulton

1970 Aug 29	**The Kiln** I F Howell, P H Biven (AL)
1970 Aug 29	**Ulysses Factor** P H Biven, I F Howell (AL)
1970 Aug 30	**Cable and Wireless** P H Biven, I F Howell (AL)
1970 Sept 25	**Big Shiner** W F Wright, V N Bentinck
1971 April 8	**Lucifer** P H Biven, A Alvarez
1971 April 8	**Pony and Trap** P H Biven, B M Biven, A Alvarez
1971 May 7	**Ramrod** P R Littlejohn, M C Chambers

Littlejohn's first route on the island, which unfortunately has fallen down!

1971 May 8	**Albacore** P R Littlejohn, M C Chambers
1971 May 9	**Magnificat** F E R Cannings, K J Wilson
1971 May 9	**Juggernaut** P R Littlejohn, M C Chambers
1971 May 10	**Performance** F E R Cannings, K J Wilson

Frenzied cleaning activities even involved the use of the toilet brush from Old Light West. Pitch 1 was climbed as a route called Sinister by L P Fatti and T J Kerrich on 29 March 1970.

1971 July 6	**The Summons** K Darbyshire, P H Biven
1971 July 6	**Eveninawl** J Cleare, K Darbyshire, P H Biven
1971 July 8	**Shark** K Darbyshire, P H Biven
1971 Aug 22	**St Peter's Stone** F E R Cannings (solo)

Climbed on the day of Cannings's fall and subsequent helicopter rescue.

| 1971 Aug 23 | **Blood Axe** (1 pt aid) O Eliasson, P H Biven, J Cleare |

Free-climbed 30 March 1985 by P Harrison and S Boydon.

1971 Aug 23	**Siegfried** P H Biven, A Chadwick
1971 Aug 23	**Seventh Seal** K J Wilson, P W Thexton
1971 Aug 25	**Sundance** R D Moulton, K J Wilson
1971 Aug 26	**Valhalla** P W Thexton, C J Henwood

The Variation Start was added by B Smith and P Amphlett in September 1981.

| 1971 Aug 27 | **Hel** (1 pt aid) P W Thexton, C J Henwood |

First free ascent unknown.

1971 Sept 24	**Quadratus Lumborum** C J Lawrance, J Brown, S D Perry, A D Caswell
1971 Sept 24	**Talcum** G W H Smith, I Marriott
1971 Sept 25	**Hurricane** C J Lawrance, J Brown, A D Caswell, I Marriot
1972 March 17	**Shamrock** T D Thompson, R D Moulton (AL), P B de Mengel

The fall of a large flake, completely altered the nature of the top pitch, which took the upper section of the large corner. The present second pitch was climbed as part of a route called Ringroad by K Darbyshire and S B Jones in October 1974. The top pitch was the original finish to Evictor.

1972 March 19	**Alpine Ridge, Occidental Groove** R D Moulton, T D Thompson (AL)
1972 March 19	**Garden Rake** T D Thompson, R D Moulton (AL)
1972 March 19	**Zig Zag Zig** S D Roberts, W F Wright (AL)

This was on Second Buttress North, which has fallen down.

| 1972 March 20 | **Scafoid** (1 pt aid) P B de Mengel, K Roche |

First free ascent unknown. Variations: Foot Off was climbed by G Rigby and N Stuart in April 1972 and Sepulchre by S Rogers, M Hime on 3 September 1988. The Left-Hand Finish was climbed by M and S Wilson on 1 September 1992.

| 1972 March 29 | **Time Bomb** (2 pts aid) P R Littlejohn, C A G Morton |

Climbed free by P R Littlejohn, C King, F E R Cannings in August 1977.

| 1972 March 31 | **The Black Hand** K Darbyshire, I F Duckworth, A McFarlane |

1972 March 31   **The Stray**   P R Littlejohn, C A G Morton
1972 April 1   **Evictor**   P R Littlejohn, K Darbyshire
The original finish has now been used for Shamrock. *The present finish was climbed as part of a route named* Ringroad *by K Darbyshire and S B Jones in October 1974. The Direct Finish was climbed by M Ward and G Gibson on 24 July 1985.*
1972 April 2   **The Minstrel**   C A G Morton, P R Littlejohn (AL)
On Second Buttress North, which has fallen down.
1972 April 2   **Scrabble**   I F Duckworth, A McFarlane
The variation was climbed by C Morton and J Warburton in August 1984.
1972 April 2   **Destiny**   P R Littlejohn, C A G Morton
1972 April 3   **Cow Pie**   K Darbyshire, C A G Morton
1972 April 3   **Rampart** (1 pt aid)   P R Littlejohn, A McFarlane, I F Duckworth
Climbed free by D Beetlestone and G Gibson on 11 August 1980.
1972 May 30   **Centaur** (1 pt aid)   C J Lawrance, A D Caswell
Cleaned and climbed free by P R Littlejohn in September 1972.
1972 Sept 6   **Formula One**   P R Littlejohn, R D Moulton, G J Gilbert
1972 Sept 7   **Motorman** (1 pt aid)   G J Gilbert, R D Moulton
Free-climbed and superseded by Meninirons, *G Gibson and D Beetlestone on 19 July 1982.*
1972 Sept 9   **Road Runner** (1 pt aid)   G J Gilbert, P R Littlejohn, R D Moulton
Free-climbed by S Cardy and M Bartley in August 1989.
1972 Sept 10   **Overlord**   G J Gilbert, R D Moulton, P R Littlejohn
Gilbert had a boat to catch and the route was a race against time. Littlejohn completed the gardening of the upper pitch as Gilbert completed the traverse. The two met half-way across when Gilbert had a short fall as a large block came out and Littlejohn swung round from the slab to see what was happening. This nearly gave Moulton a heart attack owing to the nature of his belays.
1972 Sspt 10   **Wodwo**   P R Littlejohn, R D Moulton
1972 Sept 11   **Antiworlds** (4 pts aid)   P R Littlejohn, R D Moulton
Using a tension traverse on the first pitch and three points of aid on the top pitch. Despite the aid, this was one of the most important leads of Lundy's early years and a forceful piece of climbing from Littlejohn. The top pitch was done as something of an afterthought the following day. The first day the pair finished more or less up what was to become Quatermass. *The aid had been slowly whittled down until a completely free ascent was made on August 5 1989 by M Carr and B Molyneux.*
1973 April 15   **Dihedral**   P R Littlejohn, C A G Morton
1973 April 15   **Flashback** (2 pts aid)   F E R Cannings, J W A Kingston (AL)
Climbed free and the Variation Start added by climbers from the University of Kent MC in August 1982.
1973 April 16   **Quatermass** (some aid)   K Darbyshire, H Clarke
Subsequently climbed with one aid-point by P R Littlejohn in April 1973 and finally free by R Evans in October 1974. The Variation Finish was climbed by P Harrison and S Wilkie on 15 August 1986.
1973 April 16   **The Serpent**   P R Littlejohn, C A G Morton (AL)
1973 April 16   **Beamsplitter**   J W A Kingston, F E R Cannings (AL)
1973 April 16   **Jetset** (2 pts aid)   F E R Cannings, J W A Kingston
The two aid-points were required to clean loose rock and vegetation during the on-sight lead. Free-climbed in August 1977 by P R Littlejohn and C King.
1973 April 17   **The Stone Tape** (4 pts aid)   P R Littlejohn, K Darbyshire

The tension traverse and three pegs for aid were eliminated by R Harrison in the exceptionally dry summer of 1976.

1973 April 17   **The Reluctant Teamaker** (4 pts aid) I F Duckworth, A McFarlane (AL)
Climbed free by the line described by S Boydon and P Harrison on 2 August 1988.

1973 April 17   **Bender** (2 pts aid) F E R Cannings, J W A Kingston
Two rest-points were used to clean loose blocks from the crack. Free-climbed by P R Littlejohn, C King in August 1977.

1973 April 17   **Quandary** F E R Cannings, J W A Kingston (AL), P Cannings
1973 April 17   **Sandpiper** G J Gilbert, R D Moulton
1973 April 17   **Good Vibrations** G J Gilbert, R D Moulton
The variation was climbed by S Findlay and M Hopkins on 14 August 1991.

1973 April 17   **Magic Flute** R D Moulton, G J Gilbert
1973 April 18   **Frontispiece** F E R Cannings, J W A Kingston (AL), P Cannings
1973 April 18   **The Arch** J W A Kingston and F E R Cannings (both solo)
1973 April 18   **The Fifth Appendage** A McFarlane, I F Duckworth (AL)
1973 April 18   **Navigator** P R Littlejohn, C A G Morton
1973 April 18   **Footnote** F E R Cannings, J W A Kingston (AL)
1973 April 19   **Digitalis** G J Gilbert, R D Moulton
1973 April 19   **Purple People Eater** J W A Kingston, F E R Cannings
1973 April 19   **Headline** F E R Cannings, J W A Kingston (AL)
Originally named 'The Classic of the South West'.

1973 April 19   **Sambo** K Darbyshire, H Clarke
Variation: P R Littlejohn, K Darbyshire on 12 April 1974.

1973 April 19   **Chair Ladder** K Darbyshire, H Clarke
1973 April 19   **Creation** P R Littlejohn, C A G Morton (AL)
1973 April 20   **Supernova** (3 pts aid) P R Littlejohn, C A G Morton
A peg for aid on the first pitch and two on the third. G Gibson climbed the third pitch with one rest-point in 1983. S Boydon and P Harrison free-climbed the first pitch and used a wire for aid on the top pitch on 30 July 1984. They returned the following day for a free ascent of the top pitch. The first pitch as described was first climbed by A Perkins on 16 August 1986.

1973 April 20   **Tempest** (Fluted Face) G J Gilbert, R D Moulton (AL)
1973 April 20   **Papa Joe** F E R Cannings, J W A Kingston, P Cannings
1973 April 20   **Margin** F E R Cannings, J Kingtson
1973 April 21   **Prospero** G J Gilbert, R D Moulton
1973 April 21   **Stop Press** (1 pt aid) F E R Cannings, J W A Kingston (AL)
The first free ascent remains a bone of contention.

1973 April 21   **Rainbow** J W A Kingston, F E R Cannings
1973 April 21   **Underworld** P R Littlejohn, K Darbyshire (AL)
1973 July 7   **Atlantic Reject** P H Biven, C P Gibson, J D Fowler
1973 July 7   **Celtic Shield** J D Fowler, C P Gibson, P H Biven
1973 July 7   **Pacific Portal** C P Gibson, P H Biven, J D Fowler
1973 July 7   **Quay Hole Corner** J D Fowler, P H Biven, C P Gibson
1973 July 21   **Hunky Dory** J Lister, M Putnam
1973 July 23   **Moby Dick** J Lister, M Putnam
1973 Sept 5   **Breakaway** P W Thexton, P Whitear
1973 Sept 6   **Bloody Ages** P Whitear, P W Thexton
1973 Sept 7   **Flak, Tracer** P W Thexton, P Whitear
1973 Sept 25   **Vallum** R J F Brown, C J Lawrance (AL)
Alternative finish: A J Parker, G Thomas on 23 April 1975; now incorporated into Under the Bridge.

1973 Oct 4	**The Green Light**	P W Thexton, R Owen, R G Cooper
1973 Oct 5	**The Vice** (2 pts aid)	P W Thexton, R G Cooper

Climbed free by a variation start on 2 August 1992 by S Cardy, P Harrison, and M Bartley.

1973 Oct 6	**Arch Fiend, The Flue**	P W Thexton, R G Cooper
1974 March 20	**Irish Roulette**	C P Gibson, N Stein
1974 March 22	**The Exorcist** (Flying Buttress Area)	C P Gibson, N Stein
1974 March 25	**Strider**	C P Gibson, N Stein, R Dorkins, S Braim
1974 April 12	**Peyote** (2 pts aid)	A McFarlane, D Hardy

One peg was eliminated by A Hudson in July 1984. The other had fallen out! The route was climbed free by C Hardy and C Dent on 20 August 1986.

1974 April 13	**Echo**	J de Montjoye, J Brennen, T Walker, D Irons
1974 April 13	**Diablo**	P R Littlejohn, K Darbyshire (AL)
1974 April 13	**Wolfman Jack** (4 pts aid)	P W Thexton, K J Wilson

Reduced to two points in April 1974 by P W Thexton and to one by P R Littlejohn in August 1977. Climbed entirely free by R Edwards in August 1979.

1974 April 14	**Blue Jaunt**	P R Littlejohn, K Darbyshire
1974 April 14	**Stalingrad**	P R Littlejohn, K J Wilson

Littlejohn kicked a hold off the slab, which gave Wilson the excuse to use the rope as a handhold when his turn came. He did this in such a manner that the witnesses nearly missed it!

1974 April 14	**Round the Horn**	K Darbyshire (solo)
1974 April 15	**Immaculate Slab**	P W Thexton, K J Wilson

A route name that started a fashion in West Penwith, and then got completely out of control.

1974 April 15	**Pathfinder** (1 pt aid)	P W Thexton, R D Moulton

Free-climbed a few days later by P W Thexton.

1974 April 16	**The Promised Land** (1 pt aid)	P R Littlejohn, K Darbyshire

Inspired route-finding from Littlejohn. Various people have claimed the first free ascent.

1974 April 16	**Wild Country** (2 pts aid)	P R Littlejohn, K Darbyshire

The first route to venture onto a very impressive wall.

1974 April 16	**The Gem**	P W Thexton, R D Moulton

The described direct start was soloed by G Gibson in August 1985 and the original start incorporated into Immaculate Misconception.

1974 April 17	**Hob's Lane**	K Darbyshire, P R Littlejohn
1974 April 17	**The Mexican Connection** (3 pts aid)	A McFarlane, K J Wilson (AL)
1974 April 18	**Spacewalk**	P R Littlejohn, K Darbyshire (AL), P W Thexton

Another race against time; at one point the leader (Littlejohn) and the third man (Thexton) were both climbing extreme rock simultaneously, the second man (Darbyshire) being enmeshed in a nightmare of belaying.

1974	*Lundy Rock Climbs: Second Edition* by **R D Moulton**

1974 April 25	**Live Gold, Limey**	P W Thexton, N Groves
1974 April 26	**Conger**	P W Thexton, N Groves

Fell down in the storms of 1991.

1974 Sept 19	**Jug of Punch**	R Hughes, D McGowan
1974 Oct	**Montagu Python**	K Darbyshire, S B Jones
1974 Oct 16	**The Good Ship Lollipop, Hooka, Sunblest**	C Phillips, M Barnicott (AL)

1974 Oct 16	**The Queen's Gambit** R Evans, M Sharp, P W Thexton	
1975 March 27	**Way Out** L R Holliwell, E Brook	
1975 March 28	**Blizzard** L R Holliwell, E Brook	
	Climbed during an extremely rare Lundy snowstorm.	
1975 March 29	**Jack-in-the-Box** M Putnam, J Lister	
1975 March 31	**Messin' with the Kid** P R Littlejohn, D C Garner	
1975 March 31	**American Beauty** P R Littlejohn, D C Garner	
	The line had originally been cleaned by P W Thexton on one of his infamous excursions onto vegetated ground.	
1975 April 3	**Verdict** P R Littlejohn, D C Garner	
1975 April 3	**Apsara** N J Allen, R D Moulton	
1975 July	**Umbgozi** (2 pts aid) R Baillie, J Cunningham	
	The aid-points were eliminated by A Strapcans and F E R Cannings on 19 April 1976 during the first ascent of Mirage Oasis.	
1975 Sept	**Slab and Groove** S Read	
1975 Sept	**Salty Slip** S Read	
	Climbed as a variation start to Slab and Groove but named from an ascent by B Goodwin and J Vose in 1979.	
1976 April 18	**Eclipse** F E R Cannings, A Strapcans (AL), S K Berry	
	Climbed by a right-hand start, now part of Beam Up. The described start was climbed by F E R Cannings in August 1977.	
1976 April 18	**Winkle Picker** A Strapcans, F E R Cannings, S K Berry	
1976 April 19	**Mirage Oasis** A Strapcans, F E R Cannings (AL)	
1976 April 21	**Saturday Night, Sunday Morning** S K Berry, P Cannings	
1976 April 23	**Labyrinth** F E R Cannings, A Strapcans (AL)	
1976 April 24	**The Exorcist** A Strapcans, F E R Cannings (AL)	
	The line was originally attempted on-sight from the floor of the Limekiln!	
1976 April 26	**Biggles** A Strapcans, F E R Cannings both (solo)	
1976 Aug 30	**Sexcrime** A Strapcans, F E R Cannings (AL)	
	Direct Start: J Lister, A Renshaw 19 April 1981.	
1976 Aug 31	**Bleed for Speed** A Strapcans, F E R Cannings	
1976 Sept 3	**Pinstripe** C K Wand-Tetley, W Hoy, B Scott	
1976 Sept 20	**Devil's Honeymoon** D Langmead, R McElligott	
1977 April 8	**Muffin the Mule** F E R Cannings, A Strapcans	
1977 April 9	**Gulf Stream** F E R Cannings, A Strapcans	
1977 April 10	**Fusion** F E R Cannings, A Strapcans	
1977 April 11	**Hot Rod** C K Wand-Tetley, J G Phillips	
1977 April 11	**Scorched Earth** A Strapcans, F E R Cannings	
1977 April 11	**Lemon Pie** D Tempest, M Newton	
1977 April 14	**The Great Divide** (5 pts aid) F E R Cannings, A Strapcans	
	Using aid to gain the thread. Two other aid-points were used while cleaning out the crack in an on-sight lead. These were eliminated by P R Littlejohn and C King in August 1977.	
1977 July	**Escape Route** S Lees, P Horth (AL), R Wainer, M Wilbourn	
1977 Aug 4	**Flashing into the Dark** T Jones, R J Hughes	
1977 Aug 22	**Astral Traveller** P R Littlejohn, C King, F E R Cannings	
1977 Aug 23	**Beam Up** P R Littlejohn, F E R Cannings	
1977 Aug 26	**Captain Cat** F E R Cannings, P R Littlejohn (AL)	
1977 Aug 27	**Golden Gate** (3 pts aid) P R Littlejohn, F E R Cannings	
	Using aid to gain the thread.	
1977 Aug 27	**The Minatour** C King, C K Wand-Tetley	
1977 Aug 28	**Olympica** P R Littlejohn, C King	
	A fitting conclusion to Littlejohn's development of the island. He was not to return for twelve years; a powerful parting shot.	

1977 Aug 28	**Conga Corner** R J Berry, C K Wand-Tetley
1977 Aug 28	**Funky Chicken** C K Wand-Tetley, R J Berry
1977 Aug 28	**Pancake Shuffle** R J Berry, C K Wand-Tetley (AL)
1978 Aug 2	**Dark Power** R J Hughes, L McGinley
	Variation: S Cardy and P Harrison on 6 August 1988.
1978 Aug 3	**Redspeed** R J Hughes, L McGinley
	Originally climbed by the variation start. The start as described was first climbed by P Harrison and M Bartley on 14 August 1991.
1978 Aug 25	**Shy Tot** A Phizacklea, R Knight
1978 Aug	**Genesis** K Wilkinson, G Hounsome
1978 Aug	**American Graffiti Finish** K Wilkinson, G Hounsome
1978 Sept 1	**Sliver** B R E Wilkinson, A Gallagher
1978 Oct 5	**The Lantern Man** R Dean, K Lyle (AL)
1978 Oct 9	**Lady in White** K Lyle, R Dean (AL)
1978 Oct 22	**Big Ed** P G James, E J Kamp
1978 Oct 24	**Diamond Crack** P G James, T W McDonald
1979 April 20	**Jude the Obscure** B R E Wilkinson, A Gallagher
1979 April 26	**Reprise, Salty Dog** B R E Wilkinson, A Gallagher
1979 Aug 8	**Starship Trooper, Solomon Grundy** M Hunt, M Elms, V Ho
1979 Aug 9	**Channel Wrack** B Goodwin, J Vose
1979 Aug 10	**St Loosifer** M Hunt, V Ho
1979 Aug 10	**Out of the Blue** B Goodwin, J Vose
1979 Aug 11	**A Separate Reality** D Carr, A Cowcill
1979 Aug 11	**Gorgeous Guano** M Cox, B Goodwin, J Vose, P Thompson
1979 Aug 27	**Illusion** A Gallagher, C Nicholson
1979 Aug 28	**Demian** B R E Wilkinson, S R Bondi
1979 Aug 29	**Incantations** A Stewart, P Liptrot (AL)
1979 Aug 29	**Rusty Silk** (Some aid) C Nicholson, A Gallagher
	The first free ascent was by S Cardy and M Bartley on 30 July 1989.
1979 Aug 30	**Grand Falls Road** R Edwards, S Salmon
	One of Edwards's surprisingly few contributions on the island.
1979 Aug 31	**Pomplemousse** C Nicholson, B R E Wilkinson
1979 Aug 31	**The China Syndrome** R Edwards, S Salmon
1979 Aug 31	**Streaky** S A Lewis, A Stewart
	Pitch 1: R Guest and G Robinson 15 September 1979.
1979 Aug 31	**Fifty Pumps** P Scraton, A Stewart (AL)
1979 Sept 1	**White Riot** R P Hastings, M Winstanley
1979 Sept 17	**Spanner** F A S Robinson, F Lunnan

1980   *Lundy Rock Climbs: Third Edition* by **R D Moulton**

1980 Aug 6	**Chopper Squad** J Waddell, M Glaister, R D Moulton, B R E Wilkinson
1980 Aug 6	**Helicopters** R D Moulton, B R E Wilkinson
1980 Aug 7	**Paydirt** B Goodwin, J Vose (AL), J Atkinson
1980 Aug 9	**Roller Coaster** S Keeling, R Lewsley (AL)
1980 Aug 10	**Toucher** B Goodwin, A Cowcill (AL)
1980 Aug 11	**Holiday in Cambodia** G Gibson, D Beetlestone
1980 Aug 12	**Robbo's Route** D Roberts, J Vose (AL), B Goodwin
1980 Aug 13	**Ice** G Gibson, A Kassyk
	The top pitch was added two days later by G Gibson.
1980 Aug 16	**Venus Flytrap** S Keeling, G Gibson, D Beetlestone
	The route was at one point named Massey Ferguson the Hay Baler *owing to the copious amount of lichen removed. The Direct Start was added by B Woodley and A Morley on 27 July 1986.*

1980 Aug 18	**Thug** A Gallagher, C Nicholson	
1980 Aug 18	**Bulletin** C Nicholson, A Gallagher	
1980 Aug 22	**Rachel** K Marsden, F Thompson, M Brown	

Has since fallen down.

1980 Aug 22	**Space Bandit** (2 pts aid) C Nicholson, A Gallagher
1980 Aug 22	**Mars Bar** C Nicholson, A Gallagher (AL)

A belay was taken at the small ledge.

1980 Sept 6	**Tall Story** P W Thexton, H Lancashire
1980 Sept 20	**Spare Rib, Brisket** M Meysner, R Egelstaff
1980 Sept 20	**Jumpers** R Egelstaff, M Meysner, D Banner
1980 Sept 25	**Fools Gold** P Greenhow, R W Lanchbury
1980 Sept 27	**Finale** R W Lanchbury, C Jewell
1981 July 19	**Meninirons** G Gibson, D Beetlestone
1981 July 19	**Second Coming** G Gibson, D Beetlestone

Variation: M Chapman, D Thomas 3 August 1988.

1981 July 20	**Accidental Crack** G Gibson (solo)
1981 July 20	**Silent Storm** G Gibson, D Beetlestone
1981 July 22	**A Widespread Ocean of Fear** G Gibson, D Beetlestone (VL)

*The first pitch had previously been climbed by P W Thexton and
H Lancashire in 1980 but 'rain stopped play'. Nine peg runners were
placed by Thexton prior to his attempt. The one that remains is a
remnant from this: most of the rest were removed before the
complete first ascent of this major line.*

1981 July 23	**Shotgun Rider** D Beetlestone, G Gibson
1981 July 24	**American Shrapnel** G Gibson, D Beetlestone

*The first pitch had previously been climbed by A Hubbard and
B Goodwin in mistake for American Beauty.*

1981 July 25	**Doctor Fever** G Gibson, D Beetlestone (AL)

*The first 15 feet of the route had been climbed as a variation start to
Venus Flytrap by R Harrison and D Swinden on 6 September 1980.*

1981 July 26	**Controlled Burning** G Gibson, D Beetlestone, M Brown

*A plum line which succumbed only after much effort and badly
scarred hands. The large flake had been climbed in its entirity as a
route called Desperado by I Hibbert and R Middleton in September
1980.*

1981 July 26	**Slip Tide** G Gibson, M J Brown
1981 July 27	**Smear or Disappear** G Gibson, D Beetlestone

*With a bolt runner and belay. These were removed and the route led
without by G Gibson, R Thomas and M Ward on 30 July 1989*

1981 July	**No Shots** P Kay
1981 Aug 8	**The Bristol Flyer** D Roberts, J Vose (AL)
1981 Aug 9	**Blues in Sea, Struggler's Sidestep** B Goodwin, O Smith
1981 Aug 11	**Pedes Incandescens** B Goodwin, J Vose
1981 Aug 11	**Wall Street Shuffle** R Fifield, J Warburton
1981 Aug 12	**The Full Monty** J Warburton, B Goodwin, R Fifield
1981 Aug 12	**All the Business** J Warburton, R Fifield
1981 Aug 12	**Sea Front** B Goodwin, J Warburton, R Fifield
1981 Aug 13	**Date with the Dawn** B Goodwin, R Fifield
1981 Aug 20	**Friends in High Places** P W Thexton, G Cooper
1981 Aug 30	**The Brick Wall** R Brookes, P Caley
1981 Aug	**P.S., Portia, Moss Side, Blue Collar Blues, White Collar Worker** K Marsden, F Thompson
1981 Sept 30	**Duffin the Dog** C Dale, S Cox
1981 Oct 11	**Loose Living** R Crocket, M Learoyd, J Bryan
1981 Oct 15	**Duelin Mk 1** K Dalton, S J Hall

1982 Aug 3	**Duracell** N Faulkner, C Heard
1982 Aug 5	**The Pearl, Promenade** A Hubbard, B Goodwin
1982 Aug 21	**McVitie Man** S Boydon, P Harrison
1982 Aug 25	**Pelmets of Delirium** S Harry, G Sharpe, M Proust
1982 Aug	**Soho Sue** D Gluck, A Fairbairn
1982 Sept 13	**Wallybaldi** K Smith, M Wright, G Robinson
1982 Sept 13	**Wimp's Wall** D Drake, T Walker
1982 Sept 16	**Fat Freddy's Cat** G Robinson, K Smith, M Wright
1982 Sept 22	**Crunchy Toed** S Lewis, R Brookes
1982 Oct 10	**Black and Blue** M Priestman, A Kassyk
	The first venture onto the main Black Crag.
1983 July 25	**Pawsher** G Gibson, J Walker
	The first attempt ended in near disaster when the tide was misjudged and the second man was left negotiating an incoming, rather than outgoing, tide.
1983 July 26	**Treasure Island** G Gibson, A Hudson
1983 July 26	**Pieces of Eight** G Gibson (solo)
1983 Sept 24	**Thumbnacker Crack** M Jones, P Roberts, P Haynes
1984 July 21	**Matt Black** G Gibson, M Ward, A Hudson, S Whalley
1984 July 22	**The Indy 500** G Gibson, A Hudson, S Whalley, J Welsh, M Ward
	Old brushing techniques revealed this route. The first ascensionist emerged like a coal-face worker!
1984 July 22	**Play Genetics** G Gibson, S Whalley (AL)
	Climbed from the top of the first pitch of The Stone Tape. *One of the old peg runners on* The Stone Tape *disappeared into oblivion at only the slightest hint of being clipped.*
1984 July 23	**Ocean Rain** A Hudson, M Ward
1984 July 23	**Leprechauner** M Ward, A Hudson
	Most of the corner had been climbed before, first as the upper part of Shamrock *and later via the left wall by B Parker in 1977.*
1984 July 23	**Under the Bridge** G Gibson, S Whalley
1984 July 23	**Double Diamond** S Whalley, G Gibson
	Mostly climbed before but certainly warrants a separate description.
1984 July 24	**Smear? No Fear** G Gibson, S Whalley, M Ward, A Hudson
	With a bolt runner and belay. These were removed and the route climbed without on 30 July 1989 by G Gibson, M Ward, R Thomas.
1984 July 24	**The Italian Job** G Gibson, M Ward, S Whalley
1984 July 25	**Tame Zone** S Whalley, G Gibson, A Hudson
1984 July 25	**Wile E. Coyote** G Gibson, S Whalley, A Hudson, M Ward
1984 July 26	**The Cullinan** G Gibson, S Whalley, M Ward
	With a bolt runner. Climbed by a different line to bypass the bolt which was then removed, by P R Littlejohn and N White on 6 May 1989 as Flying the Colours. *The original line was climbed without the bolt by P Cobb in August 1989.*
1984 July 26	**Immaculate Misconception** G Gibson, M Ward
1984 July 26	**Fear of Faust** S Whalley, A Hudson
1984 July 27	**Oxtail Soup** G Gibson, J Welsh, M Ward
1984 July 27	**Cithaeron** G Gibson, M Ward
1984 July 28	**Peanut Power** S Boydon, P Harrison
1984 July 29	**The Ride and the View** D Kerr, S Wilkie
1984 July 31	**What's the Worst Job You Ever Had?** A Perkins, M Wilson
1984 July 31	**Kyalami Caper** P Harrison, S Boydon
1984 Aug 1	**Eye of the Needle** S Boydon, P Harrison
1984 Aug 2	**Winston's Bogey** M Wilson, A Perkins

	The Direct Finish was climbed by S Cardy, D Naul, M Bartley on 6 August 1988.
1984 Aug 2	**Squatter and the Ant** A Perkins, M Wilson
1984 Aug 3	**Hyperspace Bypass** M Wilson, M Raven
1984 Aug 3	**Wash and Brush Up** D Kerr, M Snell, P Harrison
1984 Aug 3	**Time for Tina** G Bennett, C Gilbert
1984 Aug 17	**I Scream** S Nadin (unseconded)
1984 Aug	**Rampant Finish** M Ryan, A Gleadell
1984 Sept 19	**Late City Extra** S Brown, N D Griffiths
1985 March 23	**Gorillas Don't Care** M Edwards, B Cooper
1985 March 24	**Admiral's Arête** R Edwards, B Humphreys
1985 March 24	**Capstan Arête** R Edwards, B Cooper
1985 March 28	**Lobsterisimus Bummerkissimus, Mad Axeman (Malloy)** M Wilson, S Wilson
1985 March 28	**Viscount** M Edwards, B Humphreys
1985 March 30	**Ceaseless Tide** P Harrison, S Boydon
	Pitch 1 was added by the same team on 25 July 1985.
1985 March 31	**Stormy Waters** S Boydon, P Harrison
	Pitch 1 by the same team on 25 July 1985.
1985 March 31	**Three Mile Island** D Kerr (unseconded)
1985 March	**Escapist** M Edwards, (solo)
1985 April 2	**Ligamentum Flavum** D Kerr, S Homfray
1985 April 2	**Uncle Fester** D Kerr (unseconded)
1985 April 4	**The Opium Den** P Harrison, S Boydon
1985 April 6	**Worlds Apart** D Kerr (unseconded)

1985	*Lundy Rock Climbs: Fourth Edition* by **G Gibson**
1985 July 22	**Matt Blanc** G Gibson, H Gibson, M Ward
	With a bolt runner. Climbed without on 31 July 1993 by G Gibson (solo) after top-rope practice.
1985 July 22	**Buried Gold** S Boydon, P Harrison
1985 July 23	**Hidden Treasures** S Boydon, P Harrison
	The removal of a car-sized block proved as gripping as climbing the route
1985 July 23	**Soft Mick, Marine Boy** G Gibson (solo)
1985 July 23	**Harbinger** M Ward, G Gibson, A Lovatt
1985 July 23	**Moooooo** G Gibson, M Ward
1985 July 23	**Mammoth-Sandwich Island** G Gibson (unseconded)
	The variation, Forgotten Sun, was climbed by D Smith and J Hall on 26 June 1990.
1985 July 24	**Second Summer** S Whalley, A Hargreaves
1985 July 24	**Tomorrow** G Gibson (unseconded)
1985 July 24	**Russian Giant** G Gibson (solo) in two stages
1985 July 25	**All Hands Lost** P Harrison, S Boydon
1985 July 25	**Surf City** S Boydon, P Harrison
1985 July 25	**Technicolour Cruise** S Boydon, P Harrison
	With a bolt runner. Eliminated by S Boydon and A Bunning in June 1989
1985 July 25	**Watching the Ocean** G Gibson, M Ward
	With three bolt runners. The route was climbed without clipping the bolts by P R Littlejohn and N White on May 4 1989. Climbed without the bolts in place by G and H Gibson on 1 August 1989.
1985 July 26	**Zephuros** M Ward, A Lovatt, G Gibson
1985 July 26	**300 Spartans** G Gibson, A Lovatt, M Ward

1985 July 26	**The Gem Direct, Egyptian Reggae** G Gibson (solo)
1985 July 26	**Ship's Cat** I Allen, M Entwistle (AL)
1985 July 29	**Diamond Life, Ace of Diamonds** S Boydon, P Harrison
1985 July 30	**Wild Heart** P Harrison, S Boydon (AL), S Cardy
1985 July 31	**Coast to Coast** P Harrison, S Wilkie, S Boydon, S Cardy
1985 Aug 1	**The Great Diamond Robbery** P Harrison, S Wilkie
1985 Aug 1	**Vernon Martin's Home Brew, Free Brown Rat** S Wilkie, P Harrison
1985 Aug 1	**Sunset Wall** S Cardy, P Harrison
1985 Aug 1	**Promises** D Kerr, C Gilbert
1985 Aug 8	**Split Infinitives** S Willis, A R Jardes
1985 Aug 25	**Don Cossack** N Holliday, M Snell
1985 Aug 29	**Diabetic Dog, Fat Freddy, Freewheelin' Franklin, Norbert the Nark, Phineas** T Sawbridge, N Holliday
1985 Aug 30	**Man Overboard** C Hindley, T Sawbridge, M Snell
1985 Sept 22	**Naughty but Nice** D, Kerr, C Gilbert
1985 Sept 22	**Charles Mattless** G Gibson, H Gibson. *With a bolt runner; soloed immediately after. The bolt was removed after a bolt-free ascent by P R Littlejohn and N White in May 1989.*
1985 Sept 22	**Too Salsify** G Gibson (unseconded)
1985 Sept 23	**Udderwise, Fished Fingers** G Gibson (unseconded)
1985 Sept 23	**Sunset Rip-Off** G Gibson (solo)
1985 Sept 25	**Hotspot, Ribsnorter** D Kerr (solo)
1985 Sept 25	**Nonexpectis Jugsimisius, Slender Boris** D Kerr, C Gilbert
1985 Sept 25	**Jane Eugene** C Gilbert, D Kerr
1985 Sept 25	**Grizzled Skipper, The Midnight Hour, Box of Frogs, Death-Watch Beetle-Drive** G Gibson (unseconded)
1985 Sept 25	**Open the Box** G Gibson (solo) *Completed perhaps the busiest day of development on Lundy.*
1985 Sept 26	**The Gold Run** D Kerr, C Gilbert
1985 Sept 26	**Brinkman's Ship** G Gibson (unseconded) *A free ascent of the old aid route Vibration (A2), first climbed by M B Hamilton and S P Braim on 11 July 1973.*
1985 Sept 26	**Crampant** G Gibson (unseconded) *The crack was originally climbed as Rampant Finish by M Ryan and A Gleadell in August 1984, joining Rampart to finish.*
1985 Sept 27	**Alpine Disaster** G Gibson (solo) *Some of this has been incorporated into Alpless.*
1985 Sept 28	**Boris Karloff** G Gibson (unseconded)
1985 Sept 28	**Black Looks** G Gibson, H Gibson
1985 Sept 28	**Overbored** G Gibson (solo)
1986 July 27	**Doctor's Orders** G Gibson, M Ward
1986 July 29	**My Life in My Hands** G Gibson, M Ward *With two bolt runners. Led without these on 5 August 1989 by G Gibson (unseconded).*
1986 July 30	**The Dar-Zim Axis** B Woodley, A Morley
1986 July 31	**Livin' Outa Tins** B Woodley, A Morley
1986 July 31	**San Francisco** J Codling, J Lockett
1986 July 31	**Pastiche** M Ward, G Gibson
1986 July 31	**Mayan Skies** G Gibson, M Ward (AL) *With four bolt runners and a two-bolt belay. Bolts removed and the route led in one pitch by G Gibson on 5 August 1989 – perhaps the most serious lead on the island?*
1986 July 31	**Emergency Ward Ten** G Gibson, M Ward

With two bolt runners. Bolts removed and the route led without by G Gibson (unseconded) on 5 August 1989.

1986 Aug 2	**The Golden Handshake** M Ward, A Popp, G Gibson
1986 Aug 2	**Look Daggers** M Ward, G Gibson
1986 Aug 2	**Atlantic Mocean** G Gibson, M Ward

With a bolt runner. Bolt removed and soloed with a direct start by G Gibson on 1 August 1989.

1986 Aug 2	**Sir Patrick Splends** B Woodley, I Day
1986 Aug 4	**Wishful Thinking** D Kerr, C Gilbert
1986 Aug 5	**Pretender** D Kerr, C Gilbert
1986 Aug 5	**Carol Ann Butler Corner** S Wilkie, P Harrison
1986 Aug 5	**Jumbo's Corner** S Howse, P Parry (AL)
1986 Aug 7	**Stuffin' the Puffin** P Harrison, S Wilkie
1986 Aug 7	**Boris Day, Standing on a Beach** S Cardy, S Roberts
1986 Aug 7	**Half Man, Half Biscuit** (1 rest-point) S Boydon, J Moulding
1986 Aug 7	**Tommy Butler's Pigeon Coop Route** S Wilkie, P Harrison
1986 Aug 8	**Milky Way** L Foulkes, M Learoyd, R Thomas
1986 Aug 9	**Andromeda** M Learoyd, L Foulkes
1986 Aug 11	**Poltergeist** P Harrison, S Wilkie (AL)
1986 Aug 11	**The Bastard's Name Was Bristow, La Isla Bonita** D Kerr (solo)
1986 Aug 12	**Bertie's Route** S Wilkie, S Boydon (AL)
1986 Aug 13	**The Ocean** D Kerr, C Gilbert, S Wilkie (VL)

At nine days, the longest gardening session on the island. There are plenty more to choose from!

1986 Aug 14	**Mezzanine, A Pack of Lies** D Kerr, C Gilbert
1986 Aug 14	**Basejumper** P Harrison, S Wilkie
1986 Aug 16	**Marianne** S Wilkie, P Harrison
1986 Aug 21	**The News** R Lewis, T Valentine
1986 Aug 22	**The Time** R Lewis, J Darwin
1986 Aug 22	**The Weather** T Valentine, R Lewis
1986 Sept 4	**Reverberations** B Goodwin, P Duffy, J Lord
1986 Sept 5	**Trogus-Lo-Dyticus** J Juszczyk, D Kerr
1987 March 26	**Can I Have a Mars Bar Please?** A Williams, A Pennell
1987 April 5	**Beef Curtains** E Cameron (solo)
1987 April 5	**The Crinkly End** R Andrews, E Cameron, P Aisher
1987 April 5	**Shattered Experience** P Aisher, P Taylor
1987 April 6	**Blood Crystal** E Cameron (unseconded)
1987 April 8	**Built to Destroy** E Cameron, P Aisher
1987 June	**Oshun Coming Big** K O'Brien, C Dale
1987 July 26	**Intensive Care** G Gibson (unseconded)

With three bolt runners. The first two were removed and the route led on 5 August 1989 by G Gibson (unseconded).

1987 July 27	**Nigel Mansell, Le Mans** G Gibson (unseconded)
1987 July 30	**Chase the Ace** G Gibson, H Gibson

With two bolt runners. These were removed and the route climbed without by G Gibson, M Ward, R Thomas on 30 July 1989.

1987 July 31	**Mexico Speaks** G Gibson (unseconded)

With four bolt runners. One bolt removed and the route climbed without by G Gibson on 2 August 1993.

1987 July	**First Blood** L Goldstraw, J Crees, B Crees
1987 Aug 1	**Who Can Wait?, Alpless** G Gibson, M Ward (VL)

With a common bolt runner. Climbed without by G Gibson on 1 August 1993. The hanger was not removed.

1987 Aug 2	**Letters to the Editor** S Cardy, P Harrison (AL)

1987 Aug 2	**The Archers** P Harrison, D Naul
1987 Aug 2	**Geoffrey Archer's Whorle** S Cardy, M Snell
	Topical at the time!
1987 Aug 2	**Arch Enemy** M Snell, S Cardy
1987 Aug 2	**Bite Size** D Thomas, D Pegg
1987 Aug 2	**The Same Old Story** M Ward, G Gibson
1987 Aug 2	**Too Precious** G Gibson, M Ward
1987 Aug 3	**Fissure Fergus** S Wilkie, A Brabazon
1987 Aug 3	**Head-Strong, Zorba the Greek** G Gibson, M Ward
	With a bolt runner on Zorba the Greek. This was removed and the route led without by N White in September 1991.
1987 Aug 3	**Dealer McDope, Deputy Dawg** P Harrison, S Cardy
1987 Aug 3	**Dog Day Afternoon, Hot Dog** S Cardy, P Harrison
1987 Aug 3	**Mal de Mer** M Ward, G Gibson
1987 Aug 4	**Archie Gemmill** S Cardy, P Harrison
1987 Aug 4	**Space Oddity** D Pegg, D Thomas
1987 Aug 4	**Arm-Strong** G Gibson, M Ward
1987 Aug 4	**Invincible** G Gibson, H Gibson, M Ward
1987 Aug 4	**Sea of Tranquility** M Ward, G Gibson
1987 Aug 5	**Vincent Price** G Gibson, M Ward (AL)
	Finishing up Evictor Direct. Reclimbed fter a rockfall and the top pitch added by G Gibson (unseconded) on 31 July 1993.
1987 Aug 5	**Waiting for the Sun** M Dale, R Wilson
1987 Aug 6	**Atlantic Grey** P Harrison, S Cardy
1987 Aug 6	**Graceland** D Pegg, D Thomas
1987 Aug 6	**The Colour of Life** G Gibson, M Ward
1987 Aug 7	**The Antichrist** M Carr, M Lasota
	The pegs were home made!
1987 Aug 7	**Today** P Harrison, S Cardy
1987 Aug 12	**Voyage of the Acolyte** D Pegg, D Thomas
	'Thomas was heard to sell his soul as he pulled off a hold and penduled out into the stratosphere.'
1987 Aug 14	**Dirty Lundies** D Thomas, D Pegg
1987 Aug 14	**The Thick Plotter** R Lewis, H Darwin
1987 Aug 14	**Tenex** H Darwin, R Lewis
1987 Aug 14	**Stubborn Candle** H Darwin (solo) after top-roping
	Three routes that have fallen down.
1987 Aug 18	**Cliché Corner, Percy's Paradise** A Evans, J Evans
1987 Aug 18	**Naughty but Niche** J Evans, A Evans
1987 Aug 19	**Minesweeper** A Evans, J Evans
1987 Aug 29	**Tutankhamun** (1 pt aid) N Steen, G Wollven
	First free ascent by N Steen in April 1988.
1987 Sept 2	**Night Moves** S Rogers, A Macaskill
1987 Sept 2	**Puffin Simon, Puffin L** J Juszczyk, S Grove
1987 Sept 2	**Flintstone** S Rogers, A Macaskill
1987 Oct 6	**Tytler's Cop Out** D Tytler, D Atkinson
1988 April 6	**Quickdraw HB** A Dance, P Balcombe
1988 April 8	**Flash Dance** A Dance, P Balcombe
1988 April 8	**Flight of the Valkyrie, Gollum's Revenge** P Balcombe, A Dance
1988 June 12	**Lightspeed** D Carroll, M Seavers
1988 July 26	**The Lesser Spotted Finish** D Thomas, J Gandy
1988 July 27	**Things that Go Bump in the Night, Something in the Shadows** D Thomas, J Gandy
1988 July 27	**Cunning Devil** J Gandy, D Thomas

1988 July 27	**On a Wing and a Prayer** D Thomas, N White
	The alternative finish was soloed by D Thomas on the same day
	after top-rope practice.
1988 July 29	**Wall of Attrition** D Thomas, N White
1988 July 30	**The Day It Rained Forever** (1 rest-point) D Thomas, N White
1988 July 31	**Flares Are In, The Howling** P Harrison, D Naul
	The Banshee Finish was climbed by P Harrison and S Boydon on
	3 August 1988.
1988 July 31	**Ghostbusters** M Snell, M Bartley, P Harrison
1988 July 31	**Clinging to the Wreckage** S Cardy, S Boydon
1988 July 31	**The Demons of Hilti** G Gibson, M Ward
	Leader and second were both climbing simultaneously at one point
	for the former to reach the belay.
1988 Aug 1	**Blood Poison** M Ward, G Gibson
1988 Aug 1	**Roy of the Rovers** G Gibson, H Gibson, M Ward, R Thomas
1988 Aug 1	**Ark of the Covenant** D Thomas, M Chapman
	Originally named Lionheart and referred to as such by Pat Littlejohn
	in South West Climbs.
1988 Aug 2	**The Beguiled** S Boydon, P Harrison, S Cardy
1988 Aug 2	**The Satan Bug** (1 pt aid) S Boydon, P Harrison, S Cardy
	The first free ascent is awaited with interest!
1988 Aug 2	**On the Beach** R Thomas, G Gibson
1988 Aug 2	**The Pyramid of Success, Out Come the Freaks Again**
	G Gibson, M Ward
1988 Aug 2	**The Pyramid Game** G Gibson, M Ward, H Gibson
1988 Aug 3	**Achilles' Seal** M Bartley, D Naul
1988 Aug 3	**Seal of Approval** S Boydon, P Harrison, S Cardy
1988 Aug 3	**Nous Sommes du Soleil** M Bartley, P Harrison
1988 Aug 3	**Bed Bugs Bite My Bollocks** P Harrison, D Naul
1988 Aug 3	**Wonderlands** H Darwin, T Valentine
	The Direct Start was climbed by M Bartley, P Harrison, S Cardy on
	6 August 1992.
1988 Aug 4	**That Semi-Detached Feeling** G Gibson, R Thomas
	With a bolt runner. Removed and the route led without by G Gibson
	(unseconded) on 1 August 1993.
1988 Aug 4	**Terrace Warfare** G Gibson, R Thomas
1988 Aug 5	**The Bosch Street Kids** S Boydon, S Cardy
1988 Aug 5	**Saffron** G Gibson, M Ward (AL), H Gibson, R Thomas
1988 Aug 5	**Asafoetida** G Gibson, M Ward (AL), H Gibson
1988 Aug 6	**Hey Gringo!** G Gibson, H Gibson
1988 Aug 6	**Supercharged** P Harrison, S Cardy
1988 Aug 6	**Friction Impossible** S Boydon, P Harrison
1988 Aug 6	**An Audience of Seals** S Cardy, M Bartley
1988 Aug 6	**Woooooo!** S Cardy, M Bartley
1988 Aug 6	**Ripping Yarn** H Darwin, T Valentine
1988 Aug 12	**Norma Shearer** H Darwin (solo)
1988 Aug 16	**Half Man, Half Hob Nob** D Jones, G Padgett
1988 Aug 25	**The Demons Within, The Stone Gollum** J Chapman,
	M Carr
1988 Aug 25	**The Lost Banshee** M Carr, J Chapman
1988 Aug 26	**Muffin the Puffin Meets Dykinbad the Toungeflayler**
	P Williams, A Grondowski
1988 Sept 3	**Sepulchre** S Rogers, M Hime
1988 Sept 10	**Sidewinder** N Atkin, T Clarke
1988 Sept 16	**The Great Unwashed** M Jones, M Murray

1989 March 25	**Permanent Nerve Damage** R Strube, N Harrison
1989 May 5	**The Price of Admission** P R Littlejohn, N White.

'The image I'll always remember is Pat trying desperately to retrieve a wayward set of RPs while still trying to maintain some sort of contact with the crux groove on the first pitch. I thought he was having an epileptic fit!'

1989 June 18	**Ever Ready** S Boydon, A Bunning
1989 June 20	**The Shade Seekers** S Boydon, A Bunning

Finishing up McVitie Man. The described finish was climbed by H Darwin and T Valentine in August 1989.

1989 June 21	**Powerplus, The Wacky Races** S Boydon, A Bunning
1989 June 23	**Ticket to Ride** S Boydon (unseconded)
1989 July 30	**The Grail Trail** D Thomas, S Berry, T Gallagher
1989 July 30	**White Lie** P Harrison, M Snell
1989 July 31	**Bathfinder** G Gibson, M Ward, R Thomas
1989 July 31	**Little Bath** G Gibson, R Thomas
1989 Aug 1	**Denver Scoines, The Pathetic Sharks** P Harrison, S Cardy
1989 Aug 1	**The Last Crusade** D Thomas, N White
1989 Aug 1	**Cat O' Nine Tails** S Cardy, P Harrison
1989 Aug 2	**Serious Lobster Juggling** P Harrison, S Cardy, M Snell, M Bartley
1989 Aug 2	**Beach and Surf Check** S Cardy, P Harrison, M Snell
1989 Aug 3	**Dweebland** M Ward, R Thomas, G Gibson
1989 Aug 3	**Silver Smile** G Gibson, M Ward
1989 Aug 4	**Serious Climbs Squad** S Cardy, M Snell
1989 Aug 4	**Moondance** P Harrison, M Bartley
1989 Aug 4	**The Buoy Prophet** S Cardy, M Snell
1989 Aug 4	**Crack Climbing for Beginners** M Bartley, P Harrison
1989 Aug 4	**Ex-Cathedra** D Thomas, N White
1989 Aug 4	**The Chief Constable** P Harrison, S Cardy, M Snell, M Bartley

After top-roping.

1989 Aug 4	**Fish out of Water** M Snell, S Cardy
1989 Aug 5	**The Great White** S Cardy, M Snell
1989 Aug 5	**Douglas Bather** R Thomas, M Ward
1989 Aug 6	**The Earthsea Trilogy Part Two: The Groove** N White, D Thomas

Parts One and Three lie on the North and South Devon coasts respectively.

1989 Aug 6	**The Quest** D Thomas, N White
1989 Aug 7	**Hidden Treasures** (The Parthenos) D Thomas, N White
1989 Aug 8	**Steve Bull** P Harrison, S Cardy, M Bartley
1989 Aug 9	**The Bottom Inspectors** S Cardy, M Bartley, P Harrison
1989 Aug 10	**Waves of Romance** D Thomas, N White
1989 Aug 10	**Shardik** N White, D Thomas
1989 Aug 11	**Free Rain** H Darwin, T Valentine
1989 Aug 11	**A Friction Romance** P Cobb, B Molyneux (AL)
1989 Aug 11	**Mussel Up** P Harrison, S Cardy, M Bartley
1989 Aug 11	**Stormbound, Gale Force** N White (solo)
1989 Aug 13	**Digby** J Chapman, P Cobb
1989 Aug 19	**Takes the Biscuit** P Cobb, J Chapman
1989 Aug 26	**Black Beard** D Corben, B Chambers
1989 Aug	**The Flying Dutchman** N White, D Thomas

Climbed after a series of attempts spread out over the first two weeks of August. The route awaits a one-pitch, one-day ascent.

1989 Sept 1	**Out with the Boys** G Sutton, G Bennett

1989 Oct 13	**Moonfleet** S Thomas, W Gladwin, N Callaghan
1989 Oct 14	**Atlas** M Carr, P Cobb.
	Straightened out the earlier Wimp's Wall.
1989 Oct 15	**A Wild Trip on Jugs** M Carr, P Cobb
	Climbed during the widest tidal range. Outrageous Voyage on
	Buckets *was climbed by J Mathias and S Findlay on 8 August 1990.*
1989 Oct 17	**If I Should Fall from Grace with God** P Cobb, M Carr
1989 Oct 19	**Motion in the Ocean** P Cobb, M Carr
1989 Oct 19	**The Tempest** M Carr, P Cobb
	A drilled bolt-hole was mysteriously discovered.
1990 June 4	**Kamikaze Canary** M Watson, D Laddell
1990 June 5	**Dubious Tactics** I Woodrow, D Hanks
	After top-roping.
1990 June 6	**The Jolly Roger** I Woodrow, B Tindall, P Bamford
1990 Aug 9	**Sea of Dreams** S Findlay, J Mathias
1990 Aug 10	**The Last Rubber** M Corbett, S Findlay, J Mathias
1990 Aug 15	**The Gannet That Was Still Hungry** S Cardy, M Snell
1990 Aug 16	**Death and Weirdness in the Surfing Zone** S Cardy,
	M Snell
	After top-roping.
1990 Aug 18	**Caught in the Act** M Snell, P Harrison
1990 Aug 18	**Naked Gun** P Harrison, M Snell
1990 Aug 18	**Like It or Limpet** S Cardy, M Bartley
1990 Aug 20	**Neptune Rising** M Bartley, S Cardy
1990 Aug 20	**Godspeed** S Cardy, M Bartley
1990 Aug 20	**Bored** P Harrison, M Snell
1990 Aug 21	**Herbert the Turbot** S Cardy, M Bartley
1990 Aug 21	**Harry the Hake** M Bartley, S Cardy
1990 Aug 22	**Ain't No Wienie Roast** M Bartley, P Harrison, S Cardy
	After top-roping.
1990 Aug 23	**Serpentine** N White, H Redmond, P Bull
1990 Aug 23	**The Johnny Weed** R Whitwell, K Flemming
1990 Aug 24	**Felice** H Hooper, M Redmond
	The Direct Finish was climbed by P Harrison, M Snell, T Sawbridge
	on 1 August 1991.
1990 Aug 25	**Wolfsbane** N White, P Bull
1990 Sept 24	**Silverado** C Mellor, D Crampton
1990 Sept 25	**Uncontrolled Gurning** C Waddy, I Wilson
1991 Aug 3	**Kathleen Turner** T Sawbridge, M Snell
1991 Aug 5	**Slave Labour** P Harrison, S Cardy
1991 Aug 6	**In One Bound** T Sawbridge, M Snell
1991 Aug 6	**Skullduggery** S Cardy, P Harrison
1991 Aug 6	**Basement** T Sawbridge (solo)
1991 Aug 7	**Smoke on the Water** D Lyon, N Clacher
1991 Aug 7	**Shaggy Dog Story** S Cardy, M Bartley, P Harrison
1991 Aug 7	**Sumo** P Harrison, M Bartley, S Cardy
1991 Aug 8	**Woman in Chains** D Lyon, N Clacher
1991 Aug 8	**Badlands** S Cardy, P Harrison, M Bartley, M Snell
1991 Aug 8	**Bastard Wet Crack** P Harrison, S Cardy
1991 Aug 9	**Rigging in the Frigging Arête** D Lyon, N Clacher
1991 Aug 11	**Sole** S Cardy, M Snell
1991 Aug 11	**Lundy** S Cardy, P Harrison
1991 Aug 11	**Fastnet** S Cardy (solo)
1991 Aug 11	**Valencia** M Bartley, P Harrison, A Piercy, S Cardy, G Taylor
1991 Aug 11	**Smith Knoll Automatic** S Cardy, P Harrison, M Snell,

	M Bartley, G Taylor
1991 Aug 11	**Finisterre** P Harrison (solo)
1991 Aug 14	**Dreamlands** M Bartley, P Harrison
1991 Aug 14	**The Ancient Mariner** S Cardy, M Snell
1991 Sept 3	**The Dog's Bollocks** N White, N Foster
1991 Sept 6	**Araucaria** (1 pt aid) N White, N Foster
	The first of the St James' Stone big grooves to be breached.
1992 Aug 2	**Mad Cow Disease** S Cardy, P Harrison
1992 Aug 2	**True Blue** M Wilson, S Wilson
1992 Aug 3	**Salvaged** S Cardy, P Harrison, M Bartley
1992 Aug 4	**Late in the Day, Mr T** M Wilson, S Wilson
1992 Aug 6	**The Islander, Marisco Striptease** P Harrison, S Cardy
1992 Aug 6	**Signed and Sealed** M Wilson, S Wilson
1992 Aug 7	**Taxiarchis** P Harrison, S Cardy
1992 Aug 7	**Antonius Block** P Harrison, M Bartley
1992 Aug 8	**James** P Harrison (solo)
1992 Aug 9	**The Onedin Line** M Bartley, P Harrison
1992 Aug 10	**Shark's Head Soup** S Cardy, M Bartley, P Harrison
1992 Aug 10	**Elan** M Bartley, P Harrison, S Cardy
1992 Sept 13	**Step We Gaily** P Dewhurst, D Mason
1992 Sept 14	**Cosmic Concord, Gusset Sniffer** P Dewhurst, D Worrel
1992 Sept 14	**Screams of Tight Daughters** P Clavey, A Walker.
	Reascends the remnants of a rockfall in the Rachel/Conger *area.*
1992 Sept 14	**Island Life** B Molyneux, P Cobb
1992 Sept 14	**Apparition** P Cobb, B Molyneux
1992 Sept 14	**London Fields** B Jackson, S Coop
1993 Aug 1	**Splitting the Mighty Atom** G Gibson (unseconded)
1993 Aug 1	**An American Werewolf on Lundy** G Gibson (unseconded)
	The upper section had been climbed with a bolt runner as a route
	called Jack 'O' Bite by G Gibson on 25 September 1985.
1993 Aug 2	**Metamorphosis, Chameleon Kiss** G Gibson (unseconded)
1993 Aug 3	**The Hanmer House of Horror, Right Between the**
	Eyes, Innocent Moves G Gibson (unseconded)
1993 Aug 5	**Sphinx Crack, A Geometric Study, Carnage in**
	Carthage G Gibson (unseconded)
1993 Aug 5	**Luxor Nothing** G Gibson, (solo)
1993 Aug 6	**Bathing Beauties** G Gibson, M Wilson
	Named after two nude swimmers who sought solace on The
	Pyramid.
1993 Aug 8	**Blood, Sweat and Smears** G Gibson, R Thomas
1993 Aug 9	**Phoenix in the Groove** G Gibson, H Gibson, R Thomas
1993 Aug 12	**Specific Nocean** G Gibson, R Thomas
1993 Aug 13	**Chitzen Itza** G Gibson (unseconded)
1993 Aug 14	**Bath out of Hell** R Thomas, G Gibson, H Gibson
1993 Aug 15	**Harrison Crusoe** P Harrison, N Harrison
	The variation finish was climbed by M Snell and T Sawbridge on
	18 August 1993.
1993 Aug 15	**Friday I'm in Love** N Harrison, P Harrison
1993 Aug 17	**Jezebel** P Harrison, N Harrison
1993 Aug 18	**Psylocybin** P Harrison, N Harrison, S Cardy
1993 Aug 18	**Gimbal** M Snell, T Sawbridge
1993 Aug 18	**Gyre** T Sawbridge, M Snell
1993 Aug 19	**Mono Man** P Harrison, N Harrison, S Cardy
1993 Aug 20	**Lerina** M Snell, T Sawbridge
1993 Aug 21	**Little Arthur** N Harrison, P Harrison

1993 Aug 22	**Sheep's Eyes in Aspic**	S Cardy, M Snell, P Harrison
1993 Aug 24	**Rock Obster**	N Harrison, P Harrison
1993 Aug 24	**Head!**	P Harrison, N Harrison
1993 Aug 26	**Song to the Siren**	P Harrison, N Harrison, S Cardy
1993 Aug 26	**Stuff at the Top**	N Harrison, P Harrison, S Cardy
1993 Aug 26	**Mary Patrica Rosalea**	P Harrison, S Cardy (AL), N Harrison
1993 Aug 26	**Dave the Knock**	N Harrison, P Harrison
1993 Aug 27	**The Abyss**	P Harrison, S Cardy
1993 Aug 27	**Herbert Bronski's Back**	S Cardy, P Harrison
1993 Aug 27	**Northern Lights**	M Snell, N Harrison
1993 Sept	**Goodnight Dallas**	D Crampton (solo)

Index

Rescue: Cliff Accidents

Lundy has a recognized Auxiliary Coastguard Station and holds a full range of rescue equipment. Most members of staff train regularly in cliff rescue, first-aid, and marine rescue situations.

The Coastguard liaise and exercise with the RAF Search and Rescue base at Chivenor in North Devon. Visitors can be assured of a quick response no matter what type of incident arises. A first-aid room is available with a static oxygen supply.

In the event of a climbing accident, do not attempt to move the casualty yourself unless you have proper medical training or this is essential. The incident should be reported at the Tavern, Main Office, or shop. Out of hours, any member of staff should be alerted. Give the exact location of the accident but avoid using climbers' names for cliffs, which are not all common usage on the island. Use the grid references provided.

The Climbers' Club

The publisher of this guidebook is the Climber's Club, which was founded in 1898 from origins in Snowdonia. The Club is now one of the foremost mountaineering clubs in Great Britain. Its objects are to encourage mountaineering and rock-climbing, and to promote the general interest of mountaineers and the mountain environment.

It is a truly national club with widespread membership and currently owns huts in Cornwall, Pembrokeshire, Derbyshire, and Snowdonia. Besides managing six huts, the Climbers' Club produces an annual Journal and runs a full programme of climbing meets, dinners, and social events. Club members may also use the huts of other clubs through reciprocal arrangements. The club publishes climbing guidebooks (currently 15 in number) to cover the South East, the South West, Pembrokeshire, and Mid Wales and North Wales regions. The club is a founder-member of, and is affiliated to, the British Mountaineering Council; it makes annual contributions to the BMC's Access Fund.

Membership fluctuates around 900 and at present there are no limits on growth. Members of two years' standing may propose a competent candidate for membership and, provided adequate support is obtained from other members, the Committee may elect him or her to full membership; there is no probationary period.

New Climbs

Lundy Island 2003

Arrived on Saturday 6th Sept. on the
MS Oldenburg. with Andy Platelle,
Alison, Trish, Alan, & Tony.

2nd afternoon we all climbed the
Devil's Slide — Hard Severe, 400ft.

1st Afternoon we climbed
Cable Way V. Diff. 110ft. (Montagu Buttress)

Monday 8th :

     Hurricane (Capstan Arete Variation)
       VS 4b 120ft

+ 2nd pitch of Force Eight Severe 120ft.

Tuesday 9th Needle Rock — ? HVD|Severe.
The Ordinary Route 65ft. Supposedly
a Diff. Tracey started to lead, but sensibly
climbed down after the 1st move put you on
very steep rock with a drop of 80ft.

Wed 10th

— See over —

Wed. 10ᵗₕ.   Tracey's first lead!

Battery Rib   95ft V. Diff.

A very exciting traverse and descent at
Diff. standard to get to the bottom of the
route, above pounding seas in a narrow
channel. Tony led 1st pitch, then
Tracey volunteered to lead the 2nd.
All her gear good and well placed.

Champagne left at home though.

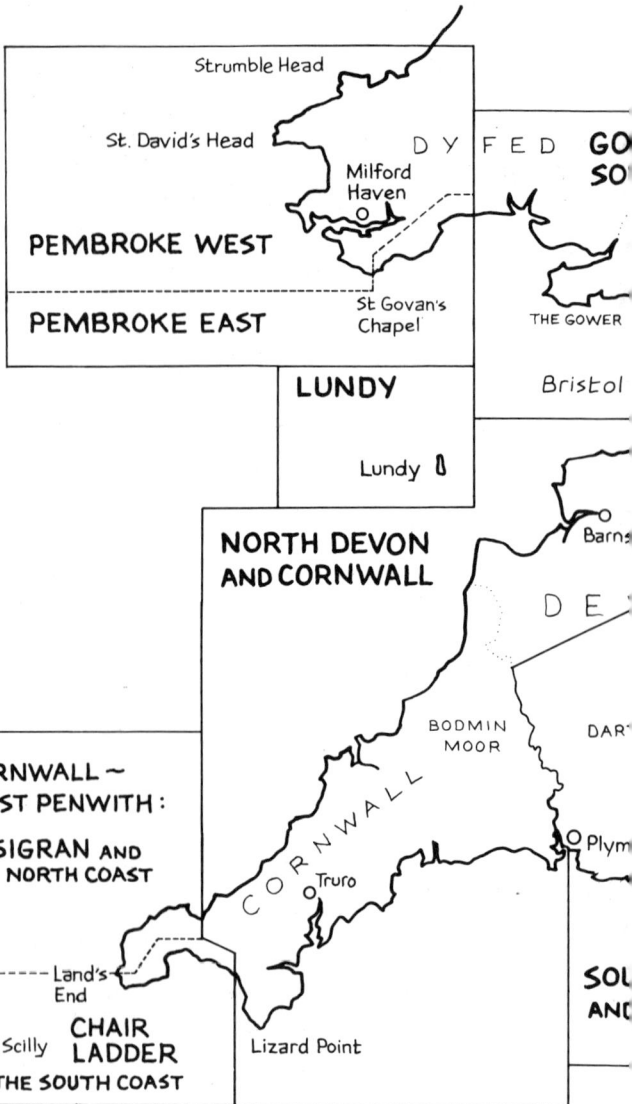

Strumble Head

St. David's Head

D Y F E D

GO
SO

Milford
Haven

PEMBROKE WEST

THE GOWER

PEMBROKE EAST

St Govan's
Chapel

LUNDY

Bristol

Lundy

NORTH DEVON
AND CORNWALL

Barns

D E

BODMIN
MOOR

DAR

CORNWALL ~
WEST PENWITH :

BOSIGRAN AND
THE NORTH COAST

C
O
R
N
W
A
L
L

Plym

Truro

Land's
End

Isles of Scilly

CHAIR
LADDER

AND THE SOUTH COAST

Lizard Point

SOL
AND